HV   Eisenberg, Dennis,
6248   1929-
.L25
E57   Meyer Lansky

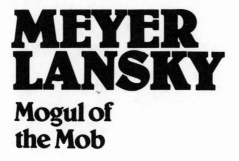

MEYER LANSKY
Mogul of the Mob

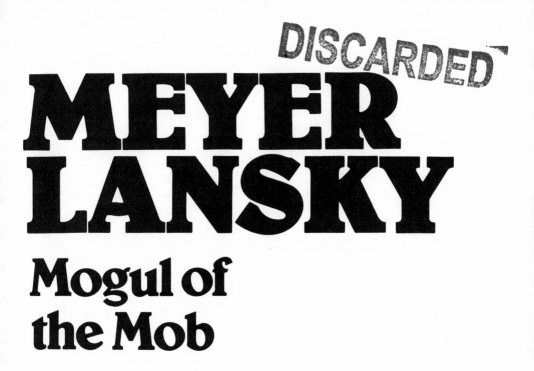

MEYER LANSKY

Mogul of the Mob

Dennis Eisenberg
Uri Dan
Eli Landau

**PADDINGTON
PRESS LTD**

NEW YORK & LONDON

Library of Congress Cataloging in Publication Data

Eisenberg, Dennis, 1929-
    Meyer Lansky: mogul of the mob.
    Includes index.
    1. Lansky, Meyer, 1902-   2. Crime and
criminals—United States—Biography. 3. Mafia.
I. Dan, Uri, joint author. II. Landau, Eli,
1939-   joint author.
HV6248.L25E57   364.1′092′4[B]   79-15979

ISBN 0 448 22206 x (U.S. and Canada only)
ISBN 0 7092 0151 6

Printed and bound in the United States
Designed by Sandra Shafee

In the United States
PADDINGTON PRESS
Distributed by
GROSSET & DUNLAP

In the United Kingdom
PADDINGTON PRESS

In Canada
Distributed by
RANDOM HOUSE OF CANADA LTD.

In Southern Africa
Distributed by
ERNEST STANTON (PUBLISHERS) (PTY.) LTD.

In Australia and New Zealand
Distributed by
A.H. & A.W. REED

Contents

Illustrations following pages 39, 241, and 281.

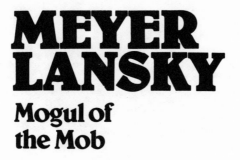

MEYER LANSKY

Mogul of the Mob

Introduction

When I first met Meyer Lansky, it did not occur to me that eight years later I would be writing this introduction to our book about his life. From that initial handshake in Tel Aviv there grew a friendship between us which culminated in the decision by Dennis Eisenberg, Eli Landau, and me to write this book.

During the past eight years Dennis, Eli, and I traveled many thousands of miles in America, Europe, and the Middle East. We met hundreds of people who confided hitherto unknown aspects of Lansky's past to us. We found ourselves attending clandestine meetings with informants who swore us to secrecy. We were given documents that had been tucked away in "top security" files of government offices. In remote corners of the globe we found people who knew him, for his influence and reputation are astonishingly widespread.

It all started innocently enough when Meyer asked me to help trace the graves of his grandparents. It was a strange request from a man I had read about as the most powerful criminal figure in the United States. It was 1971, and Lansky was then in exile in Tel Aviv, seeking asylum and hoping to become a citizen of Israel. He felt that the FBI was determined to put him behind bars in the United States, and so he sought permanent refuge in my country.

He was seventy years old and had the reputation of being the most important criminal figure in the world, recognized as the only survivor of the highest echelons of the American underworld that had reigned supreme for almost half a century. I was a thirty-five-

year-old sabra, the military and special affairs editor of Israel's
largest newspaper. Even before I met him, I was opposed to the
position of the Israeli authorities who wanted to send him back to
the United States. He had not been convicted of any crime that I
knew of. He was not considered a traitor to his country. If he was
such a monster, why had the American authorities not convicted
him? On principle I defended his right as a Jew to come and live in
the land of his ancestors. To this very day, seven years after his
return to the United States, he has still not been convicted of any
crime.

From those first meetings in Israel right up to the last of our
many get-togethers in the Embers Restaurant in Miami, only a few
months ago, our conversations were intense. Sometimes we would
talk continuously for four or five hours at a stretch. We came to
share a friendship based on a kind of mutual respect. Again and
again Meyer told me that I was the only newspaperman he had ever
spoken freely to in his life. When he was in Israel we saw each other
regularly. After he was virtually forced to return to America, I made
sure to meet with him every time I was in the United States on other
journalistic assignments. His confidence in me grew gradually as the
years went by. It was almost as if he unconsciously saw me as the
representative of a new and different generation of Jews. We had to
be told what he considered the truth. We had to understand his
point of view. In his eyes we Israelis had been molded by blood,
violence, and a struggle for survival and power in the sands of the
Middle East. Meyer perceived his background on New York's
Lower East Side as similar, though in a different setting. He felt a
kinship with me that transcended generations, cultures, and conti-
nents. I listened to him with an open and unprejudiced mind. He
fascinated me—Meyer Lansky has that type of personality. He
impressed me as the sort of man who would have succeeded in any
walk of life he had chosen. Eli Landau, Dennis Eisenberg, and I
decided to spend every moment we could searching for the facts
about this most intriguing and mysterious of men. As the years
passed it became almost an obsession to get to the truth about him.

After each of my meetings with Meyer I would immediately
dictate our conversations, as verbatim as possible, into a tape
recorder. These were then transcribed and extra copies were kept in
a special vault in London.

We were determined from the outset to be as objective as
possible. We therefore kept our project a secret from the scores of

underworld figures, bankers, businessmen, politicians, and law enforcement authorities we interviewed. Dennis, Eli, and I often operated independently and minimized the number of times we worked as a team, apart from our too frequent all-night sessions. Eli Landau's contacts with intelligence and law enforcement agents all over the world made ordinarily secret data and information constantly available. Eli, Dennis, and I, over a period of five years, managed to assemble more than six thousand pages of documents. This material originated from more than fifteen different agencies in at least six countries. We crisscrossed the United States several times checking and rechecking whenever possible. Every page was copied and duplicates were deposited for security in our vault in London.

Each interview led to further contacts. The documents unearthed gave rise to more and more sources and information. Promises of confidentiality were sometimes mandatory and they have been kept when made.

An unexpected break was the willingness of Joseph Stacher, a long-time intimate of Lansky, Luciano, Siegel, and Costello, to talk with us in Israel at length and in detail after Meyer had returned to the United States. He was so proud of Meyer that he felt we should know the truth about his old friend's exploits. Stacher met us frequently and disclosed all he would or could, and then, within a month of our last conversation, he died. The only condition he had stipulated during our private meetings was that the material he gave us should not be revealed during his lifetime.

During the past thirty-six months our pace of discoveries accelerated. Dennis Eisenberg assumed the difficult task of creating a structure out of the vast assortment of material and information we had accumulated. Priorities had to be established and, most important, contradictory evidence—especially Lansky's side of the story versus the recollections and testimony of others—had to be presented in a way that came as close to what really happened as we could determine. Eli and I continued our interviews and investigations right up to the last minute, and Dennis continued to write.

The three of us agreed early on that we would not attempt to sit in judgment but only tell the story as accurately as we came to know it. We realized that this was more than the life story of Meyer Lansky; it was also the story of organized crime in America, and particularly the story of the Jewish presence in both the Mafia and the underworld.

I confided in the son of an Israeli friend, telling him about this project. His shock and amazement at discovering that there were and had been substantial numbers of Jewish gangsters made me realize that this book might well break the back of the myth that organized crime in America is the sole province of people of Italian origin. I told my friend's son that our heritage and the historical circumstances of our people may have been partly responsible for a disproportionate number of Jewish doctors, lawyers, scientists, educators, and businessmen, but that it would be naïve not to realize that these same conditions and historical circumstances could also breed gangsters.

Meyer Lansky knows me well enough to understand that we had to tell this story as we saw it.

—Uri Dan
1979

1 The Holy Land

The golden dome of the Mosque of Omar glowed in the midday sun. Not a breath of wind stirred the heat of the spring day on the steep slope of the Mount of Olives. The honey-colored walls of Jerusalem lay below, and the noise of traffic drifted up among the tombstones of the ancient Jewish cemetery on the hillside.

In May 1971, on this hillside sacred to Jews, Arabs, and Christians alike, a small, elderly American stood motionless before two flat gravestones. His eyes were hidden behind big sunglasses and he wore no tie. But his white shirt was crisply laundered and his blue blazer was clearly expensive; it fitted him like a glove. He wore gray trousers and handmade shoes. Deeply tanned, he had a full head of black hair beginning to turn gray.

Nearby, tethered to a wooden stake, an emaciated donkey was searching patiently for odd blades of grass struggling up out of the barren ground. Its owner, an Arab boy, sat on a tombstone and gazed unconcernedly into the far distance, taking no notice of the little group that had stopped close to him.

For several minutes the elderly man stood quietly before the twin graves slumbering peacefully amid the rocks and stones of the Mount of Olives.

"So here is where they are."

His voice was soft, but it had the tone of someone who brooked no questioning of his authority.

Not waiting for a reply, the man bowed his head and recited Kaddish, the Hebrew prayer of remembrance for the dead. Then followed the prayer Eyl Moley Rachamim—God Full of Compassion—and the sound of his voice echoed gently among the gravestones.

Silently watching the scene was a younger man who in his cream-colored Volvo had driven the American up the winding road to Jerusalem from Tel Aviv. They had parked close to the Intercontinental Hotel, near the top of the Mount, and, passing the Crusaders' Church of the Ascension, walked down some steps to the cemetery. The second man, an Israeli journalist, stood aside as the American paid his respects to the memory of his grandparents. Also standing nearby was a rabbi, the keeper of the cemetery. He was very old and poor. He wore a dirty black coat and a yarmulke was on his head. A superb beard streaked with gray reached almost to his stomach.

The newspaperman had met his companion for the first time that morning, when a messenger came into his office to announce, "Uri. You have a visitor. He insists on seeing you right away."

Uri Dan stopped in the middle of an article about his trip to the Suez Canal, at that time the front line between Israel and Egypt.

"I'm Meyer Lansky," the visitor said quietly. "Perhaps you've heard of me. I've come to ask you to do me a favor. I've been trying for many years to trace the graves of my grandparents in Jerusalem, and I would be very grateful if you could take me there and help me find exactly where they're buried."

The journalist stared at him. This mild-looking man was Meyer Lansky, whom he had read about as being the head of the American Mafia, the mastermind for Lucky Luciano and Al Capone. All over the world Meyer Lansky was known as the man who built the vast gambling empires of Las Vegas, Cuba, and the Bahamas; who had been one of America's major bootleggers during the Roaring Twenties. He was feared everywhere as the head of Murder Incorporated, and for thirty years had been called the most powerful gangster of the century, perhaps of all time.

Uri Dan knew, of course, that Meyer Lansky had left the United States a few months before and was living quietly in Tel Aviv, petitioning for asylum. After all these years the authorities in America were determined to bring him to trial. But here was the legend himself walking into his office and asking for help in finding his grandparents' graves.

"My first impression of Meyer Lansky was a shock," Uri Dan remembers. "He looked like a kindly old man with a strong Jewish face, maybe somebody's beloved grandfather himself. Whatever his reputation, I felt that here was a man asking for my help. I agreed to take him to Jerusalem out of compassion—not because of that surprising note in his voice that made his request sound like an order. But as a journalist I also felt that here was a rare opportunity to talk with a man I knew had never given an interview to anybody."

The old man explained that he had tried to get information about his grandparents' burial place for more than twenty years. But the Mount of Olives was in the eastern half of Jerusalem and hence had been under the control of King Hussein of Jordan. It had been impossible for Jews or Israelis to obtain information or visit the area, and they had not even been allowed to pray at such holy places as the Wailing Wall.

But all that had changed in 1967, when the Jordanian army was defeated in the Six-Day War and Hussein's legionnaires were driven back eastward across the Jordan River. Jerusalem had been reunited as a unified city. The national burial society, the Chevra Kadisha, and other groups had set about restoring the ancient sites. Old graves were lovingly restored and carefully recorded in tomes kept in the Chevra Kadisha offices in Jerusalem.

Wondering why Lansky had chosen him, Uri Dan decided to bide his time. He left his office with the visitor and the two men set out for Jerusalem. They spoke very little during the hour's drive.

Uri Dan could not keep his mind off the newspaper headlines about Lansky's arrival in Israel. The papers had revived all the old stories about him—as a boy in the slums of New York he had bossed a street gang of ruthless young toughs; he had run protection rackets and been a strikebreaker in union wars. Perhaps the worst stories were that he had ordered the death of Bugsy Siegel, his closest boyhood friend, and that he was a kingpin in the international narcotics traffic.

When they reached Jerusalem, Uri Dan took Lansky to the office of the Chevra Kadisha, on Pines Street. There they asked the registrar to help them trace the graves of Meyer Lansky's grandparents, born in Grodno, Poland. The old couple had traveled to Palestine at the turn of the century to spend their last days in the Promised Land. A young man in charge of such matters delved into an enormous book containing the names of thousands of Jews who had been buried in Judaism's most holy and venerated cemetery, just across the valley from where Solomon's Temple stood.

With a little difficulty the requested graves were identified:

Benjamin Suchowljansky, son of Mendel Suchowljansky, had died September 10, 1910, and was buried in plot number 15, column B, grave number 80. His wife, Basha, daughter of Rabbi Matityahu, had died shortly afterward, on October 10, 1910, two days after the Day of Atonement, Yom Kippur, and had been buried beside her husband. Fellow townsfolk from Grodno had paid seventeen and a half gold napoleons for the two plots, ten napoleons for Benjamin's grave and seven and a half for Basha's.

Dan and Lansky had given this information to the old rabbi who looked after the site, and he had immediately taken the two visitors to the spot where they were now standing.

Without ceremony the rabbi knelt on the stony ground and with his coat sleeve wiped away the dust of years to expose the names etched into the simple white stones.

The American mourner took a step or two away from the graveside and lifted his sunglasses onto his forehead. With a white handkerchief he wiped the tears from his face. His eyes were red but his voice firm and under control as he summoned the rabbi to his side.

"I want you to replace these old cracked stones with the finest marble you can find in Israel. If necessary I will have slabs specially cut and dispatched from Italy. I want the best. The very best."

Both the black-robed rabbi and the young man demurred, resisting Lansky's plan to turn the simple grave into an elaborate shrine.

They would not want it, the American was told. "Your grandparents were probably simple people, they wouldn't have wanted anything fancy," Dan protested. "This is the traditional Jerusalem stone, and it would be sacrilege for you to put imported marble here. For them it was enough that they were buried here. Just leave them in peace."

This time Meyer Lansky changed his mind. "O.K.," he said. "I agree. And I want to thank you, rabbi," he said to the guardian of the cemetery.

Then, shaking hands with the old man, he said, "I want you to keep the stones clean. I want fresh flowers placed on the graves once a week. A check will reach you regularly for expenses and for your trouble."

A rolled-up bill slid from Meyer Lansky's hand into the rabbi's palm. So delicately was the tip handed over that Dan did not notice the incident until the rabbi took an astonished, unashamed glance at the hundred-dollar bill.

"I will see to the matter personally," he said. "When I have your address I will send photographs from time to time, to demonstrate how well these graves are going to be looked after from now on."

Lansky did not want to leave the Mount of Olives. The sight of his grandparents' graves seemed to roll back the years.

"I've never in my life spoken to any newspaperman or author. Some of them invent interviews, and they all tell lies about me. Not even ten Meyer Lanskys could have done half the things I'm supposed to have done. But friends of mine have told me you can be trusted, and I want to tell you something about my life. It's time people heard my side of the story—the true story."

His companion listened with interest as Lansky began to speak about his early days as a little boy in the Polish town of Grodno.

"I used to attend cheder, Hebrew school, like all the boys—if for no other reason than that my grandfather wanted me to, and I loved my grandfather above all. He spent hours telling me stories about the lives of our ancestors. His eyes used to light up with joy as he spoke about the golden dream of his life—to one day go to the Holy Land. He wanted to die in Jerusalem. The fervor in his voice when he used to pray 'L'shono habo'o biY'rusholayim'—Next year in Jerusalem—is something I've remembered all my life. Even now I sometimes wake up in the middle of the night feeling the warmth of his personality surrounding me. That's how strong my grandfather's memory is."

When the two men finally left the Mount of Olives and walked slowly back up to the car, Lansky insisted on being driven back into Jerusalem, to go to the Wailing Wall. Knowing his passenger's public image, Dan was hesitant about taking the Mafia chieftain to Judaism's most holy site. Passing through the little-used Lion Gates and the Arab quarter of the Old City, he parked near the wall, the vast edifice of uneven granite which once surrounded King Solomon's mighty temple, and urged Lansky to look at it from the car.

"I want to pray there," said Lansky.

"Then I must be frank," said the journalist. "People consider you a gangster. If you're photographed praying there among the devout Jews who throng to the wall every day, you'll do us immense harm. It would be considered a sacrilegious act, for as you must know, the Western Wall is really an open-air synagogue, and the very symbol of Jewish consciousness. You can see how its stones have been worn smooth by the tears and caresses of many millions of our people throughout the ages. I'm not passing judgment on you—that's not a task for me anyway—but I know what the reaction will be if you're seen down there. You will cause a scandal."

Lansky was firm. "Every Jew has the right to pray," he said. "Every Jew will one day face his Maker. I'm going down there to pray, and I want you to come with me."

The authority in his voice was such that Dan went with him down into the vast square before the Western Wall. As the men approached the holy place they saw a table piled high with paper yarmulkes and each put on one of the traditional Jewish skullcaps.

When they reached the wall they joined the throng of religious Jews praying before it. There were Jews from all over the world. Many swayed in the traditional way as they offered up their prayers; others simply stood and prayed quietly to themselves. Lansky stood silently before the Wailing Wall for a full ten minutes. Now and again his forehead touched the stones.

Then he took a piece of paper out of his pocket, rolled it up, and slipped it into a crevice to join thousands of others which had been placed there. It is the custom of pious Jews to write prayers or to offer up thanks for divine intervention in their personal affairs on pieces of paper which they roll up and put into crevices in the wall. Later, Uri Dan returned to the spot to discover what message Meyer Lansky had left there. It was: "Please God, may I be buried next to my grandfather Benjamin on the Mount of Olives."

When the two men walked away from the wall, they replaced their yarmulkes on the table and strolled for several hundred yards around the ancient cobbled walls of the Old City.

Meyer Lansky did not say a word until they were seated in an Arab restaurant just off David Street. The two men were to stop and talk there for many hours during the following months, as trust and friendship grew between them.

On their first visit, while they sipped the sweet black Turkish coffee, the American said, "I want to thank you for bringing me here today. You've done me one of the great favors of my life. I will never forget it."

2 The Promised Land

A hot summer's day in 1979. New York's legendary Lower East Side. Dingy, dirty, memory-filled streets like Delancey, Ludlow, Orchard, Essex, with their crowded tenement buildings. The area is tiny, astonishingly compact, this crucible into which poured the poor, determined Jews of eastern Europe. In their thousands, tens of thousands, and finally hundreds of thousands they came surging into these streets at the turn of the century.

With these downtown Jews came their pain, their expectations, their soaring ambitions, their centuries of persecution. America was the land of the free, the land of opportunity, where there was no cruel czar, no crazed cleric calling up the peasants to slaughter the "Christ killers."

You close your eyes and even though it is 1979 you can still sense the atmosphere: the fierce struggles for survival, the failures and successes of the thousands of people who passed in and out of Delancey Street, Essex Street, Ludlow Street, Hester Street, Orchard Street. And whether they know it or not, the Lower East Side is a central inheritance of most American Jews today, whether they live as devout believers or have drifted away from their religious heritage.

The legend of the Lower East Side is at its most sentimental in the smooth and glossy Hollywood musicals that celebrate the rise to fame and fortune of Fanny Brice, George Gershwin, Irving Berlin, Sophie Tucker, Al Jolson. We know about the Jewish momma, Jewish jokes, the delicatessen store; and about the rich and successful Jews who escaped the Lower East Side for smart uptown apartments, for luxurious homes in Florida and California. For them the crucible of the Lower East Side bubbled up success and fame and fortune.

But for many the reality was failure, poverty, and an early death from hunger or disease. There are to this very day about a quarter of a million poor Jews in New York City. And on the Lower East Side, with its littered, decaying streets, where the only signs of modernity are parking meters and a Kentucky Fried Chicken shop, something like eighteen thousand Jews struggle to make a living.

Such statistics, however, are the dry bones of a social worker's report. The reality is flesh and blood in the form of a seventy-eight-year-old peddler who wears dark blue sunglasses and a suit that is shiny from years of wear. He stands behind a sidewalk table littered with an assortment of cheap razor blades, cut-price scissors, bottles of doubtful eau de Cologne, after-shave lotion, and plastic trinkets which he hawks in a hoarse voice to the passing parade, mainly Puerto Ricans and blacks who now live in the peeling tenement buildings draped with their black and green iron fire escapes. Half-naked children speaking a variety of languages play on the fire escapes and scamper in the street, ignoring the screams of mothers or older children. Washing hangs on lines from heavily barred windows.

"How much are the scissors?" a black teenager asks the peddler.

"Three dollars," says the old man.

"I want one for nothing," says the boy. "I want it to cut up human flesh. Your flesh."

The old man curses him. The teenager walks away. "I will cook your flesh alive, Jew man."

The peddler turns to the three visiting authors. "Like savages."

"Look." He points to his left eye behind the heavy sunglasses. "I had to have seventeen stitches there last year when one of them hit me with a bottle. He ran away and didn't even take anything. That's why I have to wear these glasses. My eyes water all the time now, and they're so weak I have trouble seeing. The blacks buy from me maybe once a year. All they want is drugs. They're crazy—meshuggeners. Who needs them?

"In the old days I used to have a respectable profession," he said. "I was a tailor. Life was hard but nobody hit you. It is all changed now. All changed."

The shops and buildings are part of his past. All around are the store signs still telling their own Jewish story: Moshe's Bakery, Ben's Cheese Shop, Bagels and Bialys, Russian Health Bread, Purim Ladies' Wear, Fiedler's Bargains, Fleisher's Clothes, Nathan Rosen Shoes, Altman's Ladies Wear, the derelict building proclaiming "Hebrew Publishing Company."

The old man pointed out an overgrown lot in nearby Madison Street, filled with garbage and broken bottles. "There used to be a synagogue here, a very nice one, but the blacks or the Puerto Ricans burned it down. They are crazy here. Who wants to burn down a synagogue? What harm did it do anybody?"

Outside Weitzman's Kosher Delicatessen Restaurant at 102 Delancey, a group of black youths are keeping an eye open for passing police cars as they set up their three-card trick game. The victims are other black passers-by.

"The delicatessen used to be owned by brothers, Benny, Max, and Joe," said the old man. "It's been here for more than fifty years that I can remember. Very nice food. But it's been sold now. It's not the same."

The old peddler took us on a tour of the area. "Jews used to live all along Second Avenue right up to Fourteenth Street," he said. "There were Jewish shops and restaurants and places where you could drink coffee and also a Yiddish theater. The Puerto Ricans and others live in this area now, and I don't think many Jews can be found on Second Avenue. But right here on Houston and Allen streets, in what we call Peretz Square, it still reminds me of the old days."

The old man showed us the Jewish bakeries and delicatessen shops which still serve an all-Jewish cuisine. "It's funny," he said. "Spanish-speaking people and Negroes come here, and what I can't understand is that a lot of Israelis have come here from Tel Aviv and started shops. They say life is much easier here than in Israel.

"Right here on Essex Street and Delancey and Grand Street and Hester—this was the heart of the Lower East Side when I was a boy."

The peddler was roughly the same age as Meyer Lansky. On a hunch the authors asked him in Yiddish, "You remember the old days so well—did you happen to know Meyer Lansky?"

"Of course I knew him," he said. "Didn't everybody know Meyer and his friends like Bugsy Siegel and Jakie Stacher?

"Right in front there, where you see the savages cheating everybody with their cards, Meyer Lansky used to shoot craps.

'Schiessen craps'—shooting craps, we called it. Yes, I remember him well. Most people would, but he was just my age. He was a little skinny runt but the bravest boy in the neighborhood. He would gamble and fight with the others even though they were twice his size. Even some of the Jewish mothers used to tell their children not to go near him. He fought the cops, the Irish, the Italians, until they learned to respect him. He was frightened of nothing and nobody. But when we grew up I never made him suits. I used to sew the cheap stuff. Meyer walked around with five-hundred-dollar silk suits on his back, which was a lot of money in those days. Believe me, a lot of money.

"I know they call him a gangster now. I read in the newspapers like he is a monster. Meyer Lansky a murderer, a gangster, a hoodlum? So what if he was a gambler or selling whiskey? I never heard of him killing anybody. He never walked around with a gun or a knife. He was always polite, particularly to older people. That's how I knew him. Maybe he did get involved in other things, I don't know. You never know if you can believe the things you read in the papers. He was a gentleman, though, I can tell you that for sure. A gambler maybe, a seller of booze maybe, but Meyer never hit an old man in the face with a bottle."

Just as one old man stood looking nostalgically at the ruins of a synagogue on the Lower East Side of New York in 1979, so another elderly survivor of the Lower East Side had reminisced about the past in 1971, nearly six thousand miles away. Meyer Lansky drove with Uri Dan on a number of occasions to Jerusalem to inspect his grandparents' grave and talk about his life.

"Not even my friends have heard the full story," he said on their second trip to Jerusalem. "But now that I look back I would like the truth to be known. It all goes back to my grandfather, whose bones are lying here at my feet.

"I will begin at the beginning, Mr. Dan," said the soft voice. "I was born in Grodno, which was then part of Poland. My fondest memories were of my grandfather Benjamin, whom I loved very much. He was not a poor Jew but quite wealthy and lived in a very nice wooden house. Later on he had a stone house which was even grander. My father and mother and we three children lived with them. Of course there were very many poor Jews in the ghettos of eastern Europe. I know what I'm talking about because I saw them.

But I was lucky. Grandfather Benjamin was a successful businessman.

"That's not surprising, because Grodno was a major center of Jewish life. My grandfather told me that Jews had lived there for over eight hundred years. Benjamin was very religious and always went to synagogue. He used to take me by the hand to lessons at the cheder, where I learned the Jewish prayers, the Hebrew alphabet, and the first chapters of the Bible.

"He used to tell me the story of the Jews and how they had been invited to Grodno in the fourteenth century to join a very few who had lived there for nobody knows how many years. At that time the town was under the control of Lithuania, and the Lithuanians felt that the Jews could help them bring commerce to the community with their skills as traders and craftsmen.

"The Jews were allowed to settle in one part of the town, between the castle and the market place. The Jewish shops were strung out along the twisted cobbled road I knew so well, and the houses where we all lived were concentrated in that area. We had a fine synagogue there, because the Jews had prospered in Grodno. They were a dynamic community. Our community was a real Jewish town, with its own little hospital and its cemetery behind the synagogue.

"Many people had already emigrated by the time I was born, at the turn of the century. Some Jews went to America, some to Palestine, and others to places all over the world, like England and South Africa and Australia, because of the anti-Jewish pogroms. Even so, many Jews remained there until the Second World War. Then the Nazis completed the task which eight centuries of anti-Semitism had not achieved—they wiped out every single remaining Jew in the gas ovens of the concentration camps."

Uri Dan knew much of the broad outline of the history of the Jews; his own parents had also been immigrants to the Holy Land. But Meyer Lansky was not a man to be interrupted, as Dan had discovered, so he listened patiently as the story of the American's life unfolded.

"The Street of the Jews, the Koshere Yatkes, was narrow and twisting. In winter it and the little alleys around it were covered in deep snow. In the spring they were a sea of mud. The Jewish traders imported the goods needed by the local peasants and farmers and traded in wheat, honey, iron tools, and farming equipment. They brought merchandise like furs, paper, pepper, salt, and rice from far away. I used to wander from shop to shop fascinated by the sight and smell of all these strange goods. And Grodno was also a very important center of Jewish learning. The wise men of the Torah of Grodno were known for miles around for their piety and knowledge. The community produced many famous rabbis, whom my grandfather told me about. There was great joy on the day when the stone synagogue we called the Grosse Shul was finally completed.

"For a long time the Jews were tolerated in Grodno under the protection of the local rulers, because they did bring prosperity. Yet as my grandfather told me—and I saw the evidence with my own eyes—the Jews of Grodno lived under the shadow of uncertainty and fear. They never knew when the mood of their masters would change, or when there would be different masters. The city was on the Polish-Russian frontier and it changed ownership several times. The good times of the Jews frequently became the bad times, as my grandfather called them, when anti-Semitic riots and pogroms devastated the community.

"For instance, in the seventeenth century the Russians were in command and they wanted to expel all the Jews. For a start the priests demanded that the Jews brick up all their windows that faced churches. They didn't want a dirty Jew to cast his eyes on a church. And my grandfather told me about the time when they tried to make the Jews stop speaking Hebrew. The Jews resisted that, but the priests also kidnaped a number of Jewish children.

"Each time the Jews would band together and raise the ransom money to pay the priests and get the boy or girl released. Some of the Russians adopted the priests' habit and began to kidnap Jewish children too. It was an extra income, you might say. Again and again the Jewish community had to dig deep into their pockets to buy back a kidnaped child.

"Even as a little boy I joined in the special prayer we used to say for one of our rabbis who became a martyr. I never knew why until my grandfather told me the story one night. I remember it was a winter's evening and I had nightmares that night and for months afterward. Grandfather told me about the rabbi going for a walk in the fields and coming across the body of a Christian girl who had been raped and then killed with a stone. It was just the rabbi's bad luck that he was the first one to come across the body. He ran for help, and the priests who came to see the body decided that he must have been the girl's murderer. They said he had done it because he wanted to use her blood for making the unleavened bread, the matzos, which the Jews use at the Passover.

"They took the rabbi away and kept him in prison for two years, torturing him. Then they kept him in a basement underneath their church. Finally they decided that he was no more use to them, and they killed him by cutting up his body into four pieces. They did it while he was still alive. Then, in a big ceremony witnessed by the whole Christian community of the town, they hanged each of the four quarters on the walls of Grodno. You can find that in the history books, Uri.

"The Jews were finally given permission to take down the mutilated pieces and they buried the rabbi's remains in our cemetery. If the cemetery still exists you can see a special corner which was set aside for the rabbi."

As Lansky's grandfather told him, the fortunes of Grodno declined when it fell under the rule of the czars. "Yet the community struggled to survive," Lansky went on. "It had a great tradition. For instance, the first Hebrew books for that area had been printed in Grodno. And in spite of restrictions the Jewish businessmen had built a textile mill and a tobacco factory that employed not only Jews but other people. But then conditions deteriorated rapidly in the nineteenth century, in my grandfather's lifetime. By this time Jews lived in 40 percent of the houses in Grodno and some of them also owned land. Then the pogroms broke out and some of the Jews decided to emigrate.

"The worst time for the Jews in Grodno and other ghetto communities was always at Easter and the Passover," Lansky said. "I remember the scenes from my own childhood. When I was four years old a great many frightened Jews came to stay in Grodno. They had fled from Bialystock, which was not far away. Even though I was so young I remember the stories they told about their wives and daughters being raped and murdered, though I didn't really understand what they meant. These refugees told how their homes had been burned down by the Cossacks and all their possessions stolen. Others were thrown naked into the snow and froze to death. The authorities encouraged the pogrom fever and it spread to Grodno. I saw myself how the peasants used to go into the little Jewish shops and look at the goods. They used to say, 'Jews. Christ killers. Don't sell us anything. Some night we'll come and take all your things and kill you at the same time.' They would hit the old Jews and push the women around, and they would laugh while they put their hands on the women's private parts and squeezed them. There was nobody to protect the Jews.

"My grandfather told me that the worst times of all occurred when he was a youngster, during the reign of Nicholas I of Russia. This 'dreadful anti-Semitic despot,' as my grandfather called him, brought in hundreds of anti-Jewish laws. For no reason whatsoever Jews were expelled from villages where they had lived for hundreds of years. Yiddish and Hebrew books were torn up. The Cossacks snatched little Jewish boys away from their parents for the czar's army. My grandfather used to have tears in his eyes when he told me about a couple he knew who were refugees in Grodno. They had twin boys, their only children. Just before their Bar Mitzvah, Russian soldiers arrived in the village and went from house to house grabbing all the Jewish boys. Mothers ran in the streets crying, begging them not to take away their sons. The Russian soldiers only laughed and the officers drew out their swords and threatened to kill anyone who interfered. Women flung themselves at their feet screaming and begging, and the officers, the Cossack ones at least, hit them while they cringed in the mud, begging for their children's lives.

"The twins were grabbed as well, though the parents tried to hide them in the cow barn. The Russians found the boys and took them both. The parents knew that if they survived the terrible journey to Siberia they would be converted into Christians and would have to serve for twenty-five years in the czar's army. The woman tried to protect her sons but was beaten senseless. When the Jews were expelled from that village the couple came to Grodno. By this time the poor mother had lost her reason. She used to sit in a chair swaying gently and moaning, and she died shortly afterward."

Jews continued to flock from the shtetls into towns like Grodno, Jewish writer Alexander Herzen, who remembered a Russian officer telling him about the "cursed little Jewish boys of eight or villages were always pointed out to me as the newcomers in is such a frail weakly creature . . . he is not used to tramping in the mud for ten hours a day . . . they cough and cough until they cough except the clothes they had on. They were refugees from the countryside, really, just as the Jews who went to America were refugees from the whole of eastern Europe.

"When Nicholas I died there was much joy among the Jewish people," Lansky went on. "Grandfather Benjamin told me that Alexander II was a 'good man.' He allowed a quota of Jews access to higher education and they were also allowed to travel outside the Pale on business. The serfs were freed early in his reign, and this benefited the Jews who lived in the shtetls because of the more liberal atmosphere. Perhaps most important of all for the Jewish population, he cut the military service for Jewish boys from twenty-five to five years.

"Then came a terrible calamity," Lansky said gently. "In 1881 Alexander II was assassinated by young Russian and Jewish terrorists. Why a Jew should assassinate Alexander was something my grandfather never understood. But this was a terrible time for the Jews who were living in the Pale of Settlement, the area where Jews were allowed to live legally in czarist Russia." The Pale stretched from the Black Sea to the Baltic, and more than 90 percent of Russian Jews, or about five million, lived in this area in the mid-nineteenth century.

"Suddenly there were 'bad times' again, as Alexander III came to power, and in the period between the death of Alexander II and the First World War, more than a third of the Jews who lived in eastern Europe left their homes and sought refuge elsewhere."

Just why there was not a similar exodus during the equally cruel reign of Nicholas has not been entirely explained, but in those earlier days there were fewer means of escape, and the promise of America was less well known. Zionism too, with its powerful impetus for immigration to Palestine, reached its height only in the 1880s. The catalyst for this great mass exodus was the pogroms that swept through the Pale after Alexander III became czar. Hundreds of anti-Jewish laws were passed. Jews were expelled from major Russian cities, and there were dreadful massacres.

On another day Lansky spoke of the pogroms he had witnessed himself. "It was when I was a boy that they got worse and worse," he said, "and the whole countryside was full of riots against the Jews in our ghettos. One man—I don't remember his name but I wish I did—held a meeting in my grandfather's house.

" 'Jews!' he shouted at the people who had gathered there. 'Why do you just sit around like stupid sheep and allow them to come and kill you, steal your money, kill your sons and rape your daughters. Aren't you ashamed? You must stand up and fight. You are men like other men. I have been a soldier in the Turkish army. I was taught to fight. A Jew can fight. I will teach you how. We have no arms, but it doesn't matter. We can use sticks and stones. Even if you're going to die, at least do it with honor. Fight back! Stop being cowards. Stop lying down like stupid sheep. Don't be frightened. Hit them and they'll run. If you are going to die, then die fighting. Protect your beloved ones. Your womenfolk should be able to rely on you.' " Lansky's voice was louder now. The words still thrilled him.

"That speech is burned into my memory to this day. I was not supposed to be listening and had been sent to bed, but I crawled out to eavesdrop. I carried this soldier's words with me when I finally traveled with my mother to America and the Lower East Side. I remember every single word and exactly how he sounded—even his accent. He wasn't from our area and had a different way of talking. I remembered his words when I fought back at the Irish and sometimes the Italians as a boy on the East Side. They were like flaming arrows in my head. That's why I always fought back, and why I started my own gang of fellow Jews to protect ourselves.

"This young Jewish soldier at once became my hero, but he had a lot of opposition in Grodno. The older Jews said he was a troublemaker. They said it was better if we kept quiet, as they had always done. Then maybe the Cossacks and the priests would leave us alone. That was the view of the older people. The soldier shouted and screamed at them, calling them cowards and chickens and worse. But a good many of the younger men and boys agreed with him, and so he started self-defense groups. I was too young to be included but I knew the older boys were going out into the woods and training with the young soldier.

"That fall, near Yom Kippur, we heard that there was going to be a big pogrom. We had advance warning from a friendly Christian. The people were very frightened, but the soldier told us not to run away, that we mustn't be frightened. We must stand up and not lie in our beds and tremble. He organized a self-defense team for each street, and even middle-aged and older people joined them. I remember he gave orders for us to board up our windows with heavy wooden planks and told us to hide our gold and other valuables in the woods, where the marauding Russians wouldn't find them. Then he got different groups to go to prepared positions in our ghetto. He worked day and night organizing, telling us all where to stand and how to ambush the peasants or the priests when they came to burn down our houses and steal our possessions. I was very excited, even though at four or so I couldn't fully understand what was going on. I remember wanting to join in, but my grandfather told me to stay in the house. Grandfather himself finally agreed with the young Jews who were fighting and said if he was not so old he would join them."

Meyer Lansky knows the history of Grodno very well. In the early 1900s it became the center of the Jewish underground—the first place where the Jews of eastern Europe stood up to resist their tormentors. Jews were not legally permitted to have arms, but the Jews of Grodno somehow amassed 250 revolvers and rifles. Those who did not have arms were given sharpened iron bars, knives, or wooden sticks. When a police inspector, a Russian, visited Grodno he was killed by one of the "commandos" from the self-defense groups. This was a revenge killing, solemnly discussed and organized in advance by the underground leaders because the official was touring the whole region organizing pogroms. There was no evidence against anybody, but the authorities were furious and the ghetto had to pay a heavy fine.

Despite the efforts of the self-defense groups, many Jews saw the writing on the wall and began to leave Grodno in increasing numbers during Meyer Lansky's early childhood. "At this time we had some awful arguments in our house," Lansky remembers. "My grandfather wanted to emigrate to Palestine. My father said the future lay in America. My grandfather kept reminding us of the terrible times of the past and saying that the same thing would happen in America someday. It was a Jew's duty, as the Bible said, to go to Jerusalem. He reminded us how they used to close down the cheders and the other Jewish schools, and repeated his stories of the horrible treatment of kidnaped Jewish boys.

"I was too young then to understand how the arguments going on in the house would affect my life. Again and again my grandfather said he didn't like the idea of America. 'What for America? There will be other ghettos there. The Torah teaches us that good Jews go to Jerusalem. That's where I will go and where I will spend my last days.'

"Eventually grandfather Benjamin got tired of the rows and said to my father, 'Max, you do what you want to. I am determined to die in the Land of Israel.'

"He and my grandmother Basha left Grodno in the middle of another pogrom. My grandfather had to abandon his business and his house. There were no buyers—the Russians would take everything for nothing after the Jews were gone. He packed what he could in bundles and left.

"My father, still disagreeing, went off to America. He promised to send for my mother and us children when he could save up enough money for the fares."

By 1913 more than two thousand Jews from Grodno, including Benjamin and Basha Suchowljansky, had made the hazardous journey overland and by ship to Palestine, and many more were going to the United States. Finally, two years after his father left Grodno, it was the turn of Meyer Lansky and his mother, brother, and sister to pack their possessions and head for America.

On the same day the Suchowljansky family made their last sad farewells, another group, their friends and neighbors the Pikovitches, also left Grodno forever. The two families embraced, shook hands, and wept together. They were never to see each other again. The Pikovitch family went to Palestine, and the grandson of the old man who left at that time became famous as Yigal Allon, Israel's foreign minister. The Suchowljansky heir of one generation earlier—whose name was to become Meyer Lansky—chose a very different destiny, that of becoming one of the most powerful leaders of the American underworld.

3 Harsh Paradise

"I was ten years old when I set out on the journey to America with my mother. The trip was a nightmare for us all. My mother was cheated out of most of the little money she had. We trusted a Jew who met us and he took the money to buy us a ticket. We never saw him again. Alone and bewildered, we were rescued by a Jewish lady who took us along to an official charity house, that's what they called it. They separated the children and the grownups, and I was worried because I thought I might not get back to my mother. I knew it was my duty to protect her. She was in tears most of the time.

"Finally we were taken to a ship, the S.S. *Kursk*. I was sick a lot. I remember how confused my mother was. She wept more than ever. We were in steerage, of course, and I slept in a wooden bunk. The worst part was when the sea got rough and people were vomiting all over the place. To this day I can still feel that awful smell in my nose. I would go out on the deck, though I had promised my mother I wouldn't. For some reason she thought I was going to fall overboard, in spite of the railing. It was better out there in the open. I felt ashamed for the people who lay in their bunks and were sick and didn't do anything about it. I didn't want anybody to see me in the same condition. I used to put my head through the railings and vomit straight into the water.

"The food came to us in big wooden buckets. My mother wouldn't eat, she was so worried and ill. But I did. I think I knew instinctively that I had to keep up my strength and that the only way to do it was to eat, even if most of it came back up.

"Then we came to a place they told us was called Ellis Island. It was April 3, 1911. That was America. It didn't look exactly like a paradise to me.

"I remember a doctor examining me and looking into my eyes and my throat with strange instruments. We had to wait, my mother and I, standing on long lines along iron railings, holding on to my little brother and sister. Everybody was very busy. Nobody spoke Yiddish and we couldn't speak English.

"As I remember, I can't say the authorities at Ellis Island were bad. It wasn't easy for them with all those foreigners arriving and all as bewildered as we were. But it wasn't easy for us either. Most of the people were frightened and thought maybe they would be sent back to Russia.

"After the first few minutes I wasn't frightened any more. When people spoke to me in Grodno about the paradise of America I always had visions of angels—I don't know why, but I thought America would be somewhat like heaven. These weren't angels, these strange men in uniforms and in white coats, but apparently they weren't devils either. I was still pretty bewildered but in a way I felt more at ease than my mother. I seemed to adapt more quickly than she did. But of course that was because I was a child. The immigration people put down my date of birth as July 4, 1902—maybe because I was small—but I know from my mother that I was ten. I guess they wanted to make a patriot of me.

"They asked my mother a lot of questions through an interpreter. By then some Jewish people had turned up who could speak both English and Yiddish. One of them told us what to say and not to be scared. It was not too bad for us really, because my mother told the authorities the truth—that my father had sent money for us and was waiting for us.

"Sometimes these days I go for a walk on the Lower East Side to see where I used to live. The streets looked bigger to me as a boy. I thought of my grandfather Benjamin as soon as I got there. I knew immediately he was the one who'd been right. This was not paradise. The streets were even dirtier than those in Grodno. It was very hot. Men with bundles on their heads tried to sell us things, and my mother didn't know what to say.

"We went to the address my father had sent us. He hadn't known when we would land. It was a great thrill for my mother to find him at home, which was two small rooms in somebody's apartment. My father looked different from the way I remembered him. Older. He and my mother were in tears. My younger brother and sister were bewildered by everything. I don't even remember the address of our first home, because we moved shortly afterward. My father was always trying to find us a better place to live.

"One of the first places my father took me to was the 'pig market,' the 'chozzer mark,' on Hester Street, near Ludlow, where everybody was milling around hoping to be called for a job. I liked it very much then. I didn't mind all the people—so many people."

Lansky was to realize later that when he was a boy the Lower East Side had a greater intensity of population crowded into a small area than anywhere else in the world. There were "so many people" in every block from Fourteenth Street down to Canal.

"I loved to walk around and see things I had never seen before, like peaches and bananas and other exotic fruits. I had no money and couldn't buy anything. I saw some boys stealing but I always remembered my mother telling me not to touch anything that did not belong to me. I always obeyed her—at least in those years I did.

"The overpowering memory of my childhood in New York is that we were always poor. My father had expected his parents to leave him a considerable amount of money—before they left Grodno for Palestine they were considered wealthy. But after we settled in New York we got word that my grandparents had died leaving nothing, and this disappointment on top of his present poverty was a terrible blow." Apparently Max Suchowljansky never fully recovered. He was unable to climb out of the grueling poverty of the Lower East Side and was a minor influence in the lives of his children.

Lansky's strongest illustration of the family's poverty had to do with the Sabbath. "Every Friday my mother used to send me to the baker to have him cook the cholent, which she always prepared for the Sabbath. I loved eating the special dish, traditionally prepared to eat cold on the Jewish Sabbath, the day of rest when no cooking was allowed. She would make the cholent with a great deal of care and attention, using beans and potatoes and brown eggs and vegetables. When we had the money she would add meat.

"You could always tell our financial situation that week by the quality of the meat she bought for the cholent. If times were comparatively prosperous she would get a good piece of beef from the butcher, a large chunk. But most of the time it was scraggly pieces, which were all she could afford. Sometimes, when the situation was very bad, there was no meat at all. I could tell by the look on her face how much meat there would be in the cholent when she handed me the dish to take to the baker. There were many weeks when she looked miserable. She hated seeing us go hungry, and she was always ready to give us her share because, like every Jewish mother in the neighborhood, she gladly sacrificed herself for the children. Even as a little boy I remember swearing to myself that when I grew up I'd be very rich, and I'd make sure that for the rest of her days my mother had only the best. In my childish mind I saw us all having a cholent with lots of meat every Friday night for the rest of our lives, a Sabbath dish with the best beef in the world. That was what I dreamed for the future, and I have a feeling that my desire to be rich, to have the best of everything, stems from those Fridays when I saw my mother's face as she handed me the cholent dish.

"I was very proud that the big family dish was placed in my care. It made me feel a man—responsible. With the nickel for the baker in my pocket I would go off to the neighborhood bakery, for the good reason that she didn't have an oven large enough to cook the cholent. The other boys from the neighborhood were at the bakery too, each one handing over his mother's cholent. Every dish was different, so the baker knew which cholent belonged to each family. When it was baked it was also my job to collect the cholent and bring it home.

"Then the whole family would sit down for the Sabbath meal. The rich smell of the cholent, with all its memories of the one period of rest for us, remains with me to this very day. I find it amusing that this traditional dish of poor Jews has now become a delicacy that wealthy people like to enjoy from time to time. It has become comparatively expensive, and that really makes me smile. I'll never forget the line of thin little kids, like me, carrying the poor man's cholent to the baker."

Lansky smiled. "I have another strong memory about the cholent that you may consider significant. My gambling instinct—it must have been in my blood since I was born—first came to the surface during those Friday afternoon errands.

"On the way to the bakery with the cholent held firmly in both hands, for I knew it would be a terrible disaster if I ever dropped it, I used to go along Delancey Street and other streets where the gamblers were shooting craps on the sidewalk.

"I must admit I was fascinated. I'd watch the players, Irish,

Italians, Jews, and who knows who else. I could feel a rush of excitement as I watched them gambling. It was mostly nickels, dimes, and quarters, but in the aggregate they looked like a fortune to me.

"One day the temptation to try my luck was too much for me. With the five cents my mother had carefully hoarded during the week, I decided to try to win a fortune. I handed the money over to the crap game banker, sure I was going to win—and to my dismay, I lost it! Nobody in the game paid any attention to me, and I stumbled away. For a long time I couldn't go home. I just didn't know how I would face my mother. I wandered around those streets, carrying the cholent, in total despair. I felt worse than a criminal. I had let the family down.

"Finally I decided that I had to go home and tell my mother. I walked straight home with the cholent in my hands, opened the door, marched into the kitchen, and told her exactly what had happened. My mother didn't shout at me but simply burst out crying. The tears ran down her face as she swayed from side to side, not moving, just crying, weeping, and not saying a word to me.

"I was very much ashamed of myself—I think maybe that was the worst moment of my life. My mother had no money left at all, not even another five cents so she could send me back to the bakery, and she was far too proud to ask any of her friends for help.

"That Sabbath was the worst, the most miserable one we had ever known. Nobody rebuked me. The crime had been so immense that there were simply no words, no punishment which could possibly compare with the misery I felt myself.

"To tell the truth, thinking about it now, I was genuinely concerned at the way I had upset my family, but what troubled me more than anything else was the fact that I had lost that money. My cheeks burned with the thought that I had been a loser, and that night before I went to bed I swore to myself that one day I would be a winner—I would beat them all. I was going to be the guy who ended up on top, whether as a gambler or by any other means didn't matter at that stage.

"I also decided that nobody would ever have the power to make me lose again, and for the next few weeks I went every day after school and in the evenings to watch the street gamblers play. I wanted to know the secret of how it was done. Slowly I began to notice that the men who actually ran the dice games and street gambling with cards were only the pawns. Other men, well dressed and looking much more prosperous, used to come and watch from time to time. I could see secret signs pass between the rich bosses and the men running the game. I used to follow them, making sure they didn't notice me. I would see the banker pull out of his pockets all the money he had won from the suckers, as they called the gamblers, and hand it over to the man with the good suit and the nice clean shoes.

"Once down an alley I saw the man who collected the money hit the banker across the face and scream at him, 'So you want to cheat us! Next time you'll get a bullet in the head.' Two men with him pulled out knives and slashed the gambler across the face. As he fell to the ground pleading for his life, with the blood streaming all over his clothes, the one with the silk suit stepped back and shouted at him, 'You pig! Your blood has stained my trousers.' Then he kicked the bleeding man hard in the ribs and in the genitals. As the man on the ground coughed up blood, the silk-suited man and his two assistants laughed and walked away as if nothing in the world had happened. I was too frightened to come out from behind the garbage can where I was hiding until they had gone.

"And then I ran away without trying to help the man on the ground, who was now very still and not making any noise at all. The blood kept oozing out of his mouth onto a piece of old iron that was against his face. It wasn't very noble to leave him there, but on the Lower East Side you learned to mind your own business when things like that happened. I ran. Nobody saw me, and if the police had stopped me I would have sworn that I had seen nothing and heard nothing. That was standard behavior, unless you were a relative or friend of the person who was hurt. Then you had to help him, of course. But my instincts of self-preservation warned me to keep clear. If they had seen me, the men would have attacked me too. They didn't want a witness to what had happened and they might well have killed me. I ran as fast as I could all the way home.

"The scare did not cure me. I watched the gamblers for weeks. I saw how they attracted customers by getting a member of the gang—pretending to be an innocent bystander—to encourage them to come in and play for small stakes. To his delight the sucker would win. They always let him win at first to encourage him. Then he would get greedy and ambitious and start putting larger bills down, and they would make him lose. Sometimes, to tempt him more, they would let him win all his original stake back. Finally, when the sucker lost his head and started putting down his whole week's wages, they would make sure he lost it all.

"With the gamblers it was the same every time. No matter how much they lost, they kept on trying in the hope of winning it all back. And when they lost everything they had, they would borrow. But all the time they lost. You could encourage them by letting them win just once or twice, and they were hooked from then on.

"I kept my eyes wide open and soon understood the tricks. Then I decided it was time for me to try my own luck again. This time I knew the rules and I understood exactly how they were doing it.

"I arrived one Friday evening with the cholent in my hands and the nickel in my pocket. I watched for a while and waited for the moment when the come-on man put down his money. He was going to win to encourage the suckers to try their luck, and that was the moment for me to strike. I was trembling all over. I was going to risk the cholent money and I knew I couldn't face my mother again if I lost it.

"That was one of the most fateful moments of my life. It may sound very strange when only a nickel was at stake, but it was truly a turning point. I waited for the second just before the banker threw the dice, and then suddenly bent down and placed my five-cent bet. I saw the banker give me a black look, but of course five cents wasn't very much and he didn't try to stop me. The suckers would have smelled a rat if the dice thrower had said something to me. My timing was perfect, but my hands trembled so much that I thought I was going to drop the cholent dish. But I won. I knew I would.

"That victory taught me a great lesson: that if you think ahead and carefully plan whatever you are going to do, whatever activity it is, then you can win. It's the fools who rush in unprepared, who try to get rich because they're greedy—they are life's suckers. That was a golden moment, a lesson that has lasted me to this very day. I was hooked on gambling from that moment on, and I have remained a gambler ever since. The difference of course is that I gamble only when I know I can win, when the odds are stacked in my favor. And that's the only way you can win. There's no such thing as a lucky gambler, there are just the winners and the losers. The winners are those who control the game, the professionals who know what they're doing. All the rest are the suckers.

"Week after week I used my winnings to play in dice games all over the Lower East Side. I moved around from street to street, going to places I didn't know, so that the players and the gangs wouldn't get used to recognizing my face. I never gambled with the cholent money again. I didn't have to, because I saved up my winnings in a secret hole I had made in the corner of my mattress.

"And then I began to notice something. The men who came to collect the money were all Italians. The same men were all around the Lower East Side. They used to write things down in little books every time they made a collection. Those well-dressed men never gambled with the dice themselves. They just watched, their eyes following every move, counting every dollar that passed to the banker. They would stand at the back of the crowd pretending to be passers-by, but I got so I recognized them. I drew my own conclusions: the ones who make the money are not the gamblers, not the men who manipulate the dice or the cards. And I realized too that the Italians who were collecting the money were the servants or messengers of somebody bigger. So it must be very big business, gambling with dimes and quarters on the sidewalks of the Lower East Side.

"Now my mind was made up. Once I was older and was sure I knew how to do it, I would become one of the men who ran the gambling. I could see no reason why it should be only the Italians who were making money out of gambling. What any Italian could do, I, Meyer Lansky, could do as well.

"It was a vow—and I have kept it all my life. For it is no secret that I became a very famous gambler in the United States and in Cuba. The advice I always give my friends and family and anyone who wants to listen is: Never play the dice or the cards or the roulette wheel or anything else if you dislike losing. Games of chance are for those who are greedy. The only man who wins is the boss in charge of either the little corner crap game or the multimillion-dollar casino. The owners are the only winners."

Lansky learned fast. "Once in Delancey Street," he said, "there was a terrible fight between two groups who were running gambling games. Most of the participants and kibitzers ran away, but I hid behind a pile of vegetable crates and watched it all. They were using knives, stabbing and kicking each other and screaming. Then one pulled out a gun and started shooting wildly. When the police came a little later there were two bodies on the sidewalk. The Irish cops shrugged their shoulders and didn't even try to find out what had happened from possible witnesses, knowing that everybody would swear he hadn't noticed anything unusual. The cops covered the bodies with their own coats until they were taken away. They threw the bodies into the wagon like chunks of meat. When they had all gone I crept out and went to the spot where I had seen one of the dice go flying in the middle of the fight.

"It was smeared with blood. I looked around to see that nobody was watching, then picked it up and slipped it into my pocket. I was taking it home for a souvenir, as any child would. Late that night I woke up and realized what an idiot I was. If the police found that die on me they would think I had been involved in the killing.

"I crept out of the house in the darkness, making sure not to wake my parents. Once I had reached the street I made sure I was alone. Then I took the die out of my pocket and flung it as far as I could over the roof of a building. I went home and went back to sleep. I was twelve years old."

A view of Orchard Street, on the Lower East Side of New York City, not long before Meyer Lansky and his family arrived there.

One of the original "Moustache Petes," Giuseppe (Joseph) Masseria, known as "Joe the Boss," led the Mafia in the 1920s—and always distrusted both Lansky and Luciano.

UPI

Arnold Rothstein, notorious gambler, bootlegger, and Lansky's mentor, at the height of his prosperity and fame.

Born Salvatore Lucania, Charles "Lucky" Luciano (named "Lucky" by Lansky) was one of the major figures in the American underworld until his deportation to Italy in 1946. Lansky and he remained close associates and friends until his death.

OPPOSITE PAGE

ABOVE LEFT After a visit to Cuba to confer with Lansky, Lucky Luciano was deported from the island. He was apprehended by Italian police at Genoa and escorted back to Sicily and exile.

ABOVE RIGHT An informal shot of Lucky Luciano taken just before his death in Italy.

BELOW The body of Lucky Luciano is lifted into a coffin at Naples Airport in 1962, after he collapsed and died there from a heart attack at the age of sixty-five.

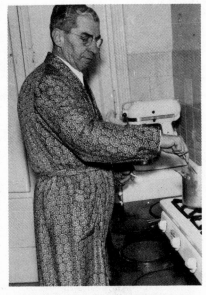

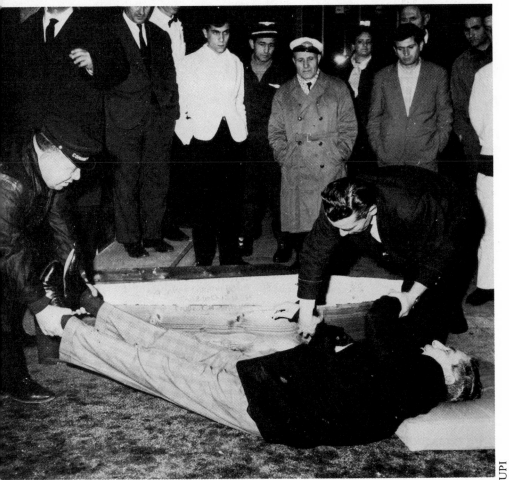

ABOVE Benjamin "Bugsy" Siegel, an original teenage member of the Lansky gang, was famous as a Hollywood playboy in the 1940s.

RIGHT Siegel was shot in a Mafia ambush in Beverly Hills in 1947. His bullet-ridden body lay at the morgue, identified by a toe tag.

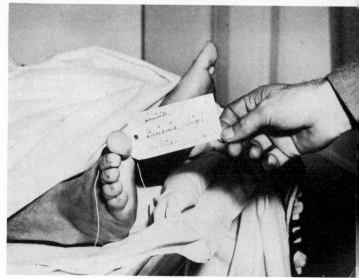

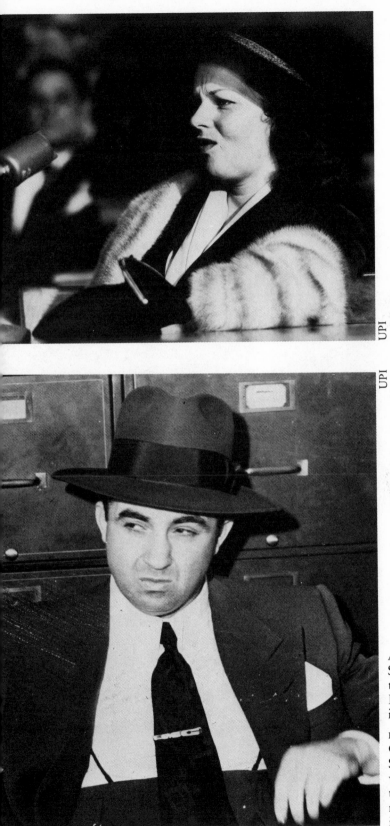

ABOVE Virginia Hill, Siegel's lover, testifying before the Kefauver Committee in 1951.

BELOW Mickey Cohen, once Bugsy Siegel's bodyguard, waits to appear before the Kefauver Committee in Los Angeles in 1951.

Costello walked away from the final inquiry session of the Kefauver Committee in New York City, March 1951, after refusing to disclose how much he was worth.

OPPOSITE PAGE

ABOVE LEFT Arthur Flegenheimer—"Dutch Schultz"—belonged to the Bergen Avenue mob in his teens and later joined Lansky in his bootlegging enterprises. He was shot by mob assassins in 1935, just before he was due to go on trial for income tax evasion.

ABOVE RIGHT Abner "Longie" Zwillman, an early member of the Lansky gang and long-time Lansky associate.

BELOW Frank Costello refused to testify at a Kefauver Committee hearing in 1951: he was too ill to answer questions.

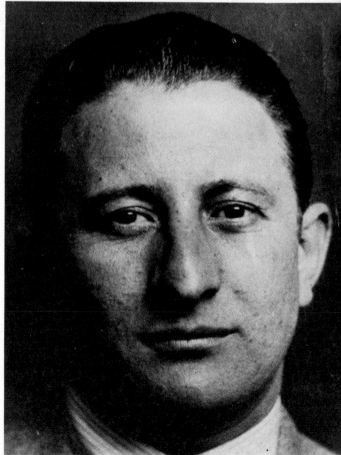

ABOVE LEFT Another
Luciano associate, Vito
Genovese waits to testify
before a grand jury probe
following the police raid of
the gangland convention at
Apalachin, New York, in
1957. Lansky was con-
spicuously absent from
the convention.

ABOVE RIGHT "Joe
Adonis" (Giuseppe
Antonio Doto) leaves
prison after serving twenty-
six months of a gambling
sentence.

RIGHT Carlo Gambino in
the 1930s. A member of
Luciano's gang, he later
took over Anastasia's
territory in New York.

LEFT Albert Anastasia appears as a witness before the Kefauver Committee in 1951.

BELOW The Park Sheraton Hotel barber shop in New York City was the scene of Anastasia's murder in 1957.

OPPOSITE PAGE

ABOVE Johnny Torrio, "the Fox," a Chicago gangland leader in the 1920s, was said to earn millions of dollars a year from bootlegging alone.

BELOW Al Capone, Torrio's well-known associate, plays cards with a U.S. marshal en route to the federal penitentiary in Atlanta in 1932. He was convicted of income tax evasion.

LEFT Joe "Socks" Lanza, a New York racketeer, had total control of the Fulton Fish Market. He was involved with Lansky in the Mafia's wartime links with the U.S. Navy.

BELOW Lanza (second from right) at a Latin Quarter nightclub party in New York, 1957.

UPI

ABOVE Joseph "Doc" Stacher, Lansky's link man with Batista for gambling operations in Cuba, retired to spend his last years in Israel.

RIGHT Stacher caught by a photographer in a men's washroom in Tel Aviv.

BELOW Al Smith (left) is sworn in as governor of New York in 1923.

BELOW RIGHT Fulgencio Batista, dictator of Cuba and friend of Lansky, shown in conversation with Richard Nixon in 1955.

BOTTOM Special Prosecutor Thomas Dewey (right) and Assistant Prosecutor Murray Gurfein arrive at the County Court House in New York City in 1935, during their attempts to crush racketeering.

UPI

UPI

4 Rachel of Delancey Street

Lansky not only loves to gamble—in his fashion—he loves to talk about gambling. The next morning he picked up the story. "I started having trouble with these gangs of gamblers. They began to recognize me and yell things like 'Go away, Jew boy.' I was too small to argue and I would simply do that—vanish. One man, a fat, slow-moving Italian, threatened to kick me and beat me up if I ever came near his game again. I waited in ambush for him one evening, and when he stopped on the sidewalk I darted out from behind a car, kicked him hard in the shins, and shouted, 'Dirty Italian!' Then I ran for my life. I heard him scream; I had kicked him very hard. That was my revenge for his calling me a Jew boy. I didn't go back to that street for a long time after that. I knew he would get me if he ever spotted me again."

Meyer's passion for gambling developed during his pre-teen years. He studied the ways of the dice and card players around the neighborhood. Sometimes, to his mother's distress, he would stay out all night, keeping his ears and eyes open—and his mouth shut. He had studied hard at Public School 34 and had learned English in a hurry, but now his studies suffered. Exploring the world of the petty criminals he knew, he was also trying to puzzle out how the big boys organized their gangs and carried off the profits of their various rackets. His younger brother, Jake, often went with him. Powerfully built and broad-shouldered, even then Jake towered over the older boy, but he worshiped Meyer and always tried to protect him, although the firstborn rarely needed looking after even as a child.

It was about this time that Meyer realized that his family name was unusually difficult for people to pronounce, and he began to call himself Lansky. Apparently his influence was already strong enough so that his family eventually followed suit. As his naturalization papers put it long afterward, Lansky was "the name by which he had been known since childhood."

His favorite pastime remained studying the dice games on Delancey Street. For hours he would watch the gamblers among the passing crowds. The religious Jews were conspicuous in their black coats, their wide-brimmed hats, their black beards and side curls, hurrying off to the synagogue or to their yeshivas to study the Torah, just as they did back in Grodno. Meyer realized that to these Jews New York meant nothing. Their lives centered on their religion and the study of their holy books. They might as well have remained back in eastern Europe—with one very important difference, that in New York they were free to study as they pleased and there was no danger of being caught in a pogrom.

Young Meyer also watched the Jewish peddlers struggling for a living, selling their pitiful wares. He watched the perplexed look of the "greenhorns," the new immigrants, who wandered around the grimy streets of New York which were not at all paved with gold as they had been promised. Instead they were littered with the debris of city living: old newspapers, broken glass, banana peels, dirty scraps of cloth, junk of every kind.

And everyone was poor except the big-shot gamblers. "I always remember how poor we were in those early days. Most families had three or four people sleeping in the same room. They took in boarders, greenhorns, people just off the boat. They used to sleep on iron cots or on mattresses on the floor. At one stage we had two boarders at our house, but my mother never liked that. She tried to manage without taking in such people. Some of our neighbors used to have whole groups of boarders. When one got up to go to work somebody else would come and sleep in his bed. In some places three men shared one tiny bed. They could only sleep certain hours of the day.

"Toilet facilities were awful and always stank. Several families had to share them. The whole building smelled filthy. Of course it didn't worry me so much at the time—I thought it was normal. It was only later that I understood what living in a nice apartment meant.

"A lot of people couldn't stand the strain and the crowded

conditions. There were many who committed suicide. And of course tuberculosis, which we called the 'tailors' disease' or the 'white plague,' was something we all dreaded—so many people seemed to catch it."

In those early days the only object that distracted Lansky's attention from gambling—"Schiessen dice"—was the figure of a young woman whose name, he had discovered, was Rachel. To the boy she seemed a mature woman, but he realized later that she could not have been more than eighteen or nineteen.

Usually wearing bright-colored, figure-hugging skirts or dresses, but sometimes in black, Rachel had her beat along a narrow strip of Delancey Street just off Essex. She always wore very high heels, and her jet-black hair, her dark brown melancholy eyes, and her well-developed bosom thrusting firmly through the tight white blouses she favored, haunted Meyer for months. Once when she caught him looking at her as she passed by, the girl smiled at the youth. He blushed deeply and hurried on, afraid that she might speak to him. But he dreamed of her that night.

One evening, with a mixture of morbid curiosity, excitement, and swelling adolescent frustration, he followed her after an elderly man had engaged her in conversation. The couple stopped near a building where she wanted to take him to a room which appeared to be at her disposal. There was a sharp argument in fierce low tones. The boy could not catch the exact words, but clearly a bargain had been struck. The customer wanted to make a small economy by not using the room.

The old man handed over some money, which Rachel insisted on in advance, then followed her up a dark alley. After a few moments Meyer crouched low and cautiously followed them, groping his way along the wall and avoiding kicking over the piles of bottles and other rubbish that littered the dark passage. Finally he found the couple. They had not heard him, even though he was now so close he could almost stretch out a hand and touch the girl. He hid behind a tall iron pillar and watched.

Rachel had lifted up her skirt. She was holding it high, at arm's length, up above her neck. She was leaning backward, supporting herself on one elbow, half seated on a garbage can. One leg was wrapped around the old man, whose trousers had fallen below his ankles.

"Come on," the girl said in irritation. "Get on with it. What are you waiting for?" As the elderly client complained about Rachel's not being in the right position for him, she swore back at him angrily, saying, "You didn't want to pay for the room, so what do you want me to do, stand on my head?"

Finally in a hoarse, agitated voice the old man told Rachel to turn around, so that she was face down across two garbage cans. She lay on them parallel to the ground with her legs stretched out, feet touching the ground, still wearing her high-heeled shoes. The old man leaned over her but still found it difficult going.

Whether it was the stench of the decaying fish in the heaped-up garbage in the alley, the grunts of the old man, or simply the sight of him thrusting his body into the buttocks of the outstretched Rachel, Meyer felt a wave of nausea sweep over him. He covered his mouth as he gagged; the couple must not hear him.

A few minutes of effort and the quick act of purchased love was over. Rachel lifted herself from her bed of garbage, and in the faint light from a tiny window in a wall overlooking the alley, Meyer saw her take her pants from her handbag and slip them on. Then she took out a brush and tried to straighten her hair.

The old man struggled for a minute or two to raise his trousers and then in a pathetic voice said pleadingly, "I've lost my shoes. I can't see."

Said the prostitute, "Our business is finished. Go get your wife to help you," and off she strode, almost brushing against the crouching boy as she went back into the street. The old man got down on his hands and knees in the alley, cursing "that filthy whore" as he groped among the debris looking for his misplaced shoes.

The boy left him with his problems and went back to Delancey Street, where he saw Rachel looking as beautiful as ever, leaning against a shop window and chatting calmly with another street-walker. Shame welled up inside him. How could she look just the same and even laugh as she chatted?

Lansky knew that Rachel handed over her earnings or at least part of them to a pimp who "protected" her. He was a tall, thin young man with a pinched face who had a reputation in the neighborhood for slashing the face of any of his string of girls who stepped out of line or tried to cheat him.

After the incident in the alley Meyer carefully avoided walking near Rachel, terrified that she would see in his face his shame and embarrassment for her. He could not stop his dreams of pure lovemaking and tender kisses with Rachel, but the horror of seeing her with the old man nauseated him.

Two weeks later young Meyer Lansky witnessed another scene that he would never forget. As he walked toward home one night, he heard a fearful shriek and cries for help. The boy recognized the voice immediately—it was Rachel's. Passers-by hurried on without even turning their heads. Screams and cries were not uncommon in the streets of the Lower East Side. As Meyer knew, you always minded your own business if you wanted to keep out of trouble.

With a mounting feeling of dread, the boy forgot all the lessons he had learned about surviving on the Lower East Side and rushed toward the sound. He knew precisely where the scream came from. It was the same alley where Rachel sold her love to clients who could not or would not afford the price of a bed.

As he ran toward the dark passage, his heart beating wildly, two men came tearing out of it, running as fast as their legs could carry them. In the light of the street lamp Meyer recognized one of them as the rat-faced pimp whom he knew so well by sight. Rachel's "protector." The two men passed so close that one bumped into the boy and almost knocked him over, cursing him for getting in the way.

A few feet into the alley he found the girl. As if under a spotlight, every detail imprinted itself in his memory. She lay on the ground, her head at a grotesque angle, her legs half bent under her, her skirt exposing her black-stockinged thighs, blood oozing from her neck and shoulders. She lay there still and very, very quiet. The boy was experienced enough to be almost sure the lovely Rachel was dead. She had crossed her pimp once too often and had paid the price. As a punishment, but also, as is the way of the world of whores, as a terrible warning to the other girls to keep in line, Rachel was now a corpse.

For the second time in two weeks Meyer Lansky was physically sick in that dreadful alleyway. Despite his anguish, however, he kept his head. He made himself look at Rachel once more, to see her face and to make really certain that she was dead. If she were injured, no matter how badly, he would have to run for help. But his glance confirmed what he already knew. Rachel would never again stroll up and down Delancey Street with that beautiful smile and those eyes that burned their way into the imagination.

Within minutes the police would be on the spot, asking who he had seen in the neighborhood. Meyer Lansky moved cautiously out of the alley and casually, so as not to attract attention, sauntered away, picking up speed only after he had turned a corner.

As Lansky grew up and became closer to the criminal world, he made one vow which he never broke: he would never become mixed up with prostitution in any form. He early acquired a reputation among his Italian friends of being a prude. They knew that talk of whores and making use of their services would always bring a stern look of rebuke to his face. They joked about Lansky's "morals," but never in front of him: he was soon so respected and feared that only a very foolish man would challenge his authority or poke fun at him. As an adult Lansky certainly had numerous love affairs, but he never discussed his mistresses with even his closest friends.

The young girl whom Lansky fell in love with as a teenager was obviously not the only prostitute in the Jewish community, as he knew even then. In the time and place of Lansky's youth, when any member of the Jewish community became a black sheep it was the convention to pretend he or she did not exist. If a young man turned to crime the community did all it could to keep the matter from reaching the outside world. "Why give them ammunition for anti-Semitism?" The many Yiddish and Hebrew newspapers of the time paid as little attention as possible to the Jewish gangsters and criminals of the Lower East Side. It was a kind of self-censorship which was built into the Jewish spirit.

In fact, hundreds of young Jewish women became whores, just as women in other impoverished neighborhoods did. One particularly poor area not far from the old Third Avenue El was well known for its "houses of iniquity," as pious Jews called them at the time. But even so, a very small proportion of Jewish women turned to this quick way of making money. For the Jewish families of this area it was a shameful and tragic thing, and there were bitter recriminations among immigrants who began to regret ever leaving Europe when they saw one of their girls or boys turn to crime in the promised land of America.

5 "My Name Is Meyer, Not Mike"

"The Irish were our worst enemies," Lansky said. "They hated Jews. They used to yell 'Christ killers' at us. The cops were mainly Irish, and whenever there was a fight between Irish and Italians, or an incident involving Irish with Jews, the cops would always take the side of the Irish, even if they were known hoodlums. The Italians were Catholics too, of course, but on the East Side the Irish considered them inferior.

"The Irish gangs used to come into our area and jostle and stop the old men, pull their beards, and scream insults at them. Whole gangs of these Irish boys and young men used to come into our streets and stop boys like me and make them take down their trousers to see if they were circumcised. The Irish policemen used to laugh when Jewish shopkeepers complained about being robbed by Irish boys. The Irish would walk into their shops and take what they wanted without paying for anything.

"I used to feel ashamed and angry at the way the Jews passively accepted such treatment. I kept thinking back to the days in Grodno and that young soldier shouting at Jews to stand up and fight. I remember his words so clearly: 'Fight back! Even if you're going to die, at least do it with honor.'

"One day when I was carrying the cholent home from the bakery for my mother, half a dozen Irish boys suddenly surrounded me. 'What are you carrying there, Jew boy?' the leader demanded. 'Have you got the body of a Christian baby there to suck out its blood? Are you going to make matzos with its flesh?'

"He pulled a knife and yelled, 'Take down his trousers! We'll see if he's cut properly, and if he isn't maybe we can help him lose a little more.'"

Lansky remembers the rest of the story, but when asked what happened next he says it was just one incident among many. He mentioned it only as an example. But the old peddler with the scared face and the blue sunglasses, the boyhood friend who still lives in the neighborhood, recalls the encounter vividly. "It was talked about for months afterward and became part of our folklore. It was probably the first step in making Meyer Lansky a legend." As he tells it, "Meyer was small and skinny as a matchstick. He looked like anybody could break him in half. I saw the Irish boys around him. They were older and bigger—they must have been seventeen or eighteen and Meyer was just my age, fourteen. Maybe not even that. We had both had our Bar Mitzvahs the year before, but I can't remember which one of us was first.

"The Irish boys were laughing and dancing around him, poking fun and threatening. It was a game to them. I don't think they were serious about using the knife, but the leader was really vicious—I had seen him before. So I was very frightened when I saw the knife gleaming there in the sun. Maybe he would have killed little Meyer. He looked pretty crazy and Meyer looked completely pathetic, standing there with the hot cholent in his hands.

"Suddenly, without any warning, Meyer lifted the cholent dish high over his head and with a great effort smashed it into the face of the Irish boy with the knife. He did it with all the force he had in his skinny arms. The boy was so tall that Meyer had to reach up high, but the dish struck the Irish hoodlum in the face. He screamed and dropped the knife. The gravy and vegetables and meat were all over his head and shoulders, because the force of the blow smashed the dish. It cut him badly, too. I could see the blood flowing down his collar. The boy dropped to the ground and rolled over into the gutter, banging his head on the curb while he was doing it. He was screaming in pain.

"Then Meyer jumped at one of the other boys and punched and kicked him like a wild creature. The Irish all attacked him together but Meyer managed to pick up the knife as they knocked him down. I saw him swing it twice, slashing one boy's leg and another's back before they kicked it out of his hand. They couldn't hold him down even though he was so small. He was fighting with his hands and his feet and even with his teeth.

"They beat him and beat him. They were all on him now. I think they would have killed him if the police hadn't arrived just by chance. The gang ran off except for the one with the hot cholent in his face. They had to take him to the hospital in the end, but as the two cops bent over him—he was still screaming—Meyer got to his feet. He could hardly walk. His clothes were torn, his face cut and bleeding too. He looked dizzy and fell down once but he realized that he had to get away while the cops had their attention diverted. Otherwise they would arrest him for sure. And he did manage to run away. They saw him go but he ignored their shouts to come back. One cop chased him but Meyer ran into the big market and disappeared in the crowd. The cops shouted for people to stop the boy but they took no notice, they acted as if neither the cops nor Meyer existed.

"When he got home Meyer's mother took one look at him and nearly fainted. He looked at her calmly as they stood there in the kitchen and said, 'Don't worry, Mama. I'm really all right. There is no cholent but I don't want you to worry. Wait a minute.'

"Meyer went to his bedroom and took some dollar bills from his hiding place. When he went back to the kitchen he gravely handed over the money to his mother and said, 'I want you to go and buy some food for our cholent.'

"His mother stared at him, but, without any explanation of what the fight had been about or where he had got the money, Meyer walked over to the sink and washed the blood off his face. He waved her away when she tried to help him."

As Mrs. Yetta Suchowljansky looked at her fourteen-year-old son, she must have known that Meyer was no longer a child. Perhaps for the first time she sensed the boy's aura of authority. She went out and bought a meal for the family. They ate it in silence that evening. There was no comment about Meyer's cut and battered face.

Lansky says today: "My conviction that a Jew should lead a normal life and a proud life stayed with me all the days of my childhood. I am not and never pretended to be an Orthodox Jew—I don't go around with a yarmulke on my head. But I've been ready at any time in my life to defend myself against insults to Jews or to me as a Jew."

Some weeks later the Irish gang came seeking their revenge. Again Lansky tells some of the story. "I'd gone with my friends to the East River to swim. We put our clothes on the bank as usual and dived in. None of us could afford bathing suits in those days. We used to leave one boy on the bank to guard our clothes, because the Irish liked to find our things and throw them in the water. Or they would jump in with us and try to hold our heads under. We had already had several river fights with them. While I was in the water I saw the Irish gang leader on the bank. I knew there was going to be trouble. He and his friends took their clothes off and came after us."

There are several versions of what happened next. As it happened, a gang of Italian boys had also decided to take a dip in the East River to cool off. Some of the Italians were schoolmates of Meyer's friends, and the two ethnic groups, though they were not close friends, were swimming around peacefully. There was no love lost between the Italians and the Irish on the Lower East Side, so the fight in the water became a straightforward conflict of Irish versus Jews and Italians. Somebody had taken a knife into the water, and suddenly, above the sounds of kicking, splashing, and punching, there was a scream.

The water around one swimmer suddenly became stained with red, and when the rest of the boys saw it they hurriedly swam to shore, grabbed their clothes, and ran. It was not until late that evening that the body of the leader of the Irish gang was washed up on the bank downriver. Who actually took the murder weapon into the water and who struck the fatal blow is not known. As usual, nobody had seen or heard anything to tell the police, and not a boy on the East Side would even admit that he had gone swimming that day.

The death of the Irish boy is not the only reason Lansky remembers the day he went swimming with his friends. The fight in the water also involved the leader of a tough Italian gang, a youth Meyer had encountered before and who would one day become his friend and ally in spite of ethnic divisions.

Before he turned fifteen Meyer Lansky had built a considerable reputation among the boys in the neighborhood. Even the Italians and the Irish had learned to respect his fierce courage. Despite his size he was good at school sports, especially basketball.

"One day some Irish boys invited me to come and play with them. They knew me from school and they knew I was the best player there, even though the other boys were taller and older. I agreed to play on their team and I was enjoying the game." Then came another "incident." "The gym was in an Irish area and one of the spectators got mad when he saw me playing with the Irish. He started to shout insults like 'Jew boy! Go home and eat your kosher pig food.' I walked off the court at the end of a quarter and went straight up to him. I told him to apologize or I'd smash his head."

When the Irish spectator, who was much larger and older than Lansky, refused to apologize, the others formed a circle around the two contestants. Clearly there was only one way to settle this dispute. The fight lasted for a full twenty minutes, as Lansky recalls to this day.

"He hurt me a lot, but I was in good condition and quicker too. We fought until we were both nearly exhausted and bleeding from punches to the nose and mouth. I got in the last punch just before we were both ready to fall down, but because he fell first and I fell on top of him I was the winner.

"The Irish respected me after that and I had no more trouble with them. They invited me to play with them regularly and I did. One day the captain came up to me and said he wanted me to become a permanent member of the team. We respected each other and he spoke to me in a friendly way." The captain had a brilliant idea. "It would be much better," he told Meyer, "if we called you Mike when we're playing. That way they won't know you're a Jew. They'll think you're one of us. It will keep you from having to fight every time you go on the court and somebody insults you."

"I knew he wasn't trying to offend me," Lansky said. "He was giving me, in his eyes, the best compliment he could—that I was as good as any of the Irish and not just a dirty Jew.

"I said to him, 'My name is Meyer, not Mike. It's the only name I have.'"

6 The Italian Alliance

Young Lansky had won a measure of respect, but his troubles with the Irish were far from over. "The day the Sicilian boy who was to become my lifelong friend sought me out for a handshake is one I will never forget," he said reflectively one evening as he sipped a Turkish coffee in the small Arab restaurant, the Siam, near Jerusalem's Jaffa Gate. Bearded Jews, black-robed Armenian monks, tourists, nuns, a never ending stream of humanity wandered by outside, in the narrow cobbled streets. Occasionally an armed patrol of Israeli soldiers or police sauntered along, casual but alert. Perhaps it was the holy city that sent the mind of a nonreligious man back to the time when he first made an alliance with someone outside his family's faith, and made it with a Catholic against other Catholics. Unrecognized as the man whom newspapers call "the secret boss of the Mafia," Meyer Lansky in 1971 described his early encounters with the boy who grew up to be known as Lucky Luciano.

The young Sicilian, whose parents, Antonio and Rosalie Lucania, had christened him Salvatore shortly after his birth in 1897, in the tiny hillside village of Lercara Friddi, had a background very similar to Meyer Lansky's, though their religion and customs were worlds apart. Beckoned by the great American dream of unlimited opportunity—a better life than could ever be achieved in a poor Sicilian sulphur-mining village—the family came to the United States in 1906 and settled among other Sicilians on the Lower East Side.

Disliking his school lessons, Salvatore Lucania took to the streets early and was soon involved in gang fights against other

Sicilians as well as the Irish. Once or twice young Lucania joined in the attacks on the Jewish boys as they went to and from school, but he quickly outgrew this kind of hooliganism. Lucania was not good at his lessons and had problems studying English, but he was sharp and intelligent. He was first puzzled and then impressed by the fact that most of the Jewish boys studied harder than the other pupils. As he watched his parents and other impoverished Italians struggle to make a living without hope of improving their hard lives, Lucania was quick to grasp the importance of learning and book knowledge as one sure path to success and prosperity in adulthood.

His respect for his Jewish classmates' accomplishments did not, however, keep him from exploiting their weakness against bullying by the Irish and Italian gangs. Instead of beating up the Jewish boys, Lucania had a more practical idea: he would sell them protection. In return for a few pennies handed over on a weekly basis, he promised that nobody would beat them up or tear up their schoolbooks. Just as Meyer Lansky became a leader at a young age, so Salvatore Lucania quickly became the boss of the boys in his neighborhood. He warned them all that the Jewish boys under his "protection" must never be touched, and although he was not physically big, his authority went unquestioned.

The day he met Meyer Lansky was a fateful one for both boys. For eventually a close friendship grew between them, a friendship that led them to become the two most powerful men in the criminal world. Nobody would have guessed their future relationship, however, when they first came face to face in Hester Street. By then Lucania was the leader of his own gang of Italian toughs and they had decided to walk boldly right into the heart of the Jewish area to find more customers for their growing protection business.

Lansky remembers that it was a bitterly cold January day. Fresh snow was falling onto the dirty gray sludge of the previous night's fall. Meyer was walking along with no buddies around when he suddenly found himself surrounded by a gang of Sicilian boys, all older and much bigger than he.

"If you wanna keep alive, Jew boy, you gotta pay us five cents a week protection money," the leader told the puny-looking victim. Salvatore was sure the kid was so frightened he was wetting his pants. But Lucania was mistaken.

Looking at the menacing faces that surrounded him, and hearing their leader's heavy accent, Meyer stared back and replied, "Go fuck yourself."

As Lucania liked to tell it, "He stood there, just a little punk. I was five years or so older than him and could have smashed him to pieces in a few seconds. But he stood there staring me straight in the face, just defying me and telling me to stick my protection up my ass. He was ready to fight. His fists were clenched at his sides. There was seven of us and any one could have given him the hiding of his life. In fact one of my gang stepped forward to grab him and teach him a lesson he wouldn't forget.

"For some reason I took a liking to this kid. He was very gutsy standing there and telling me to go fuck myself. Instead of being angry I wanted to laugh, but I didn't show my feelings because it would have meant losing face in front of my gang. I told the boy that was going to beat him, 'Forget it.' Then I stood looking at this young Jew boy and I said to him, 'We'll come back for you when milk from your mother's tits has dried on your face.'

"He didn't say anything but just looked at me hard. I was giving him an insult but he knew and I knew I didn't mean it. We both had a kind of instant understanding. It was something that never left us. Later we didn't always have to talk to explain things to each other. He knew I was getting him off the hook and insulting him purely to keep my gang members quiet. He detected the tone of sympathy in my voice, though none of my gang could pick it up. In the later days I would think something and he would have the same thought at the same time, you know how it is with some women sometimes, but of course we were men. The feeling was still the same though, it was as though we were twins and our minds were connected in some way. It may sound crazy, but if anybody wants to use the expression 'blood brothers,' then surely Meyer and I were like that even though we had come from totally different backgrounds."

A few months later Lucania and Meyer met again, when they went swimming in the East River with their respective friends. That was the occasion when the Irish attacked the Jewish boys in revenge for Meyer's exploit with the Sabbath dish. Whether Lucania—later to be better known as Lucky Luciano, Capo Di Tutti Capi, Boss of all the Bosses in the Mafia hierarchy—decided to grant unpaid and unsolicited protection to the kid he had taken a liking to is not known. But everyone knew that the Italians were more likely to carry knives than the Jewish kids, and it would have behooved their leader to take on the roughest work himself.

The two boys did not talk to each other that day, but the wars of both Italian and Jewish street gangs with the Irish intensified, and Meyer Lansky's reputation as a fighter grew. During the winter after the swimming incident, Lucania sought out Meyer Lansky and, to the smaller boy's great surprise, shook his hand warmly. "He and his buddies had heard all about how we Jewish kids were finally standing up for ourselves," Lansky said.

The meeting took place when no one else was around. The Sicilian was not going to show anyone who knew him his feelings of respect for a little Jewish boy. But after that the two became firm friends. By now Meyer had put together a gang of his own, several tough Jewish youngsters who were ready to use their fists when necessary, and he and Salvatore soon agreed to combine forces when there was conflict with the Irish. Their followers went along on the basis that the enemy of my enemy is my friend. As far as is known, this teenagers' mutual defense pact was the first time that the Jewish and Italian groups got together for joint action on the Lower East Side.

The right-hand "man" in Lansky's forces was a tall, attractive boy named Benny Siegel, whose parents had made the long journey from Kiev in Russia to escape the pogroms. The Siegels had been close neighbors of another Jewish family that also immigrated to the United States. The daughter of these neighbors later became one of Israel's most prominent leaders, Golda Meir, and it was she whom Lansky would ask for asylum when, fifty years later, their paths crossed thousands of miles from Delancey Street.

If Golda was to become a kind of rebel far in the future, the Siegel family found Benny a handful from the start. By the time he reached his teens they feared for him. Handsome, a smooth talker, he seduced every girl he could find—Jewish, Italian, even Irish. Hotheaded Benny Siegel was not interested in going to school and studying hard to be a doctor or a lawyer, the ambition the Siegels, like nearly every East Side Jewish family, had for their sons.

Even as a teenager, Siegel was feared. He was thought of as a *chaye,* an animal, by fellow Lower East Siders who joined the Lansky outfit. But they never called him that to his face, for he had a quick temper. The only man who ever addressed him this way was Meyer himself when he was angry with Benny. Sometimes in a good mood Lansky would put an arm around the broad-shouldered Benny and playfully say, "If you let me drive your new Yom Kippur Clipper, I will even forgive you for being such a *chaye.*" The rest of the outfit would smile, but a little nervously. It was one thing for the boss to make a little joke, but another for them to take liberties with the dangerous Benny Siegel.

As with the girls so with stickups and store robberies: Benny drew no ethnic distinctions. Once he had laid hands on a gun, he was ready to shoot to kill for money or anything else he wanted.

Meyer had first met the younger boy one day when he was studying a crap game. He had noticed that newcomers had suddenly moved into his neighborhood. Each group of players, each gang, traditionally had its own well-defined area of influence where only it had the right to operate. As he stood wondering who these new bankers were, the men who had always controlled the dice games moved in to evict them.

Knives were drawn and passers-by scattered as a fierce fight broke out. A dozen toughs who had been waiting up the street suddenly threw themselves into the battle—and Meyer quickly realized that the whole operation had been a setup. The game was a trap. As the five regulars struck indignantly to evict the newcomers, they were in turn ambushed by the waiting men. Guns came out and, amid the screams of women shoppers, bullets began to fly in all directions.

Curious, Meyer took cover behind a fruit stand to watch the outcome. The fruit peddler had fled in panic. The boy watched as the dozen newcomers battered the remaining victims into a pulp with kicks and iron bars.

Just then another boy rushed into the middle of the carnage. Weaving his way among the battling men, he went straight for a revolver which had fallen to the ground. Just as his fingers reached for the weapon came the sound of police whistles. At the same time one of the gang members leaped at the boy and tried to grab back the revolver. The police were now running straight for the contestants. The youngster held his ground and took careful aim at the gangster. He was about to pull the trigger when Meyer jumped out of his hiding place and took hold of his arm.

Lansky had suddenly recognized the boy as the son of a woman his mother knew. She used to cry and complain about the problems she was having with her Benny. "You're crazy," he shouted, holding on to Benny Siegel. "Drop that gun and run." Obeying without question, the young boy flung down the weapon and scampered away with Meyer, dodging around the cops. Minutes later, when they had lost themselves in the crowded market, Meyer was astonished to hear the boy curse him. "Why didn't you let me kill that bastard?" he said. "I needed that gun."

Meyer answered calmly, "The police were right on the scene. If you'd been caught with the gun you'd be in deep trouble. Only an idiot, a shlimazel, would shoot with the cops in sight. Use your head." Still complaining bitterly, Benny went home, but from that moment on the two boys were friends.

"When I decided the Jewish boys in the neighborhood should organize their own gangs to protect themselves as the Italians did against the Irish, I went to see Benny Siegel," Lansky remembers. "I told little Benny he could become my number two. He was young but very brave. He liked guns. His big problem was that he was always ready to rush in first and shoot—to act without thinking. That always got him into trouble. I explained patiently to him again and again that if you're going to succeed, it's better to work from behind the scenes. There are hundreds of people who can use guns and go into the firing line, but there are only a few who can organize and direct them to do it effectively," said Lansky to Uri Dan during one of their conversations, this time in the Dan restaurant on Tel Aviv's Ben Yehuda Street, where they ate chopped liver and gefilte fish, which Lansky likes because they remind him of the Lower East Side.

Lansky took particular pains to emphasize his feelings about violence, and to elaborate his claim that he had always tried to avoid the use of guns. "It's always much better not to shoot if you can help it. It's better to use reason—or if that fails, threats. You learn as a leader to direct others, and it's far more efficient to stay out of trouble. There has to be a way of getting what you want without violence. I admit that sometimes you have to take direct action, but then you do it positively, properly. Don't rush in like an idiot. You have to think before you act and work out exactly what you're going to do. And always limit the amount of violence—it's a poor substitute for brains." Thus Lansky's philosophy, which alas his second in command was never to learn.

Meyer and Benny became so close that the teenage group of boys they enrolled became known as "Lansky and Siegel's mob." The brains behind the gang were undoubtedly Lansky's, but he was never able to bring Benny under total control. To the day he died, himself under a Mafia death sentence, Siegel was only too ready to shoot first and ask questions afterward. Meyer's advice that "it's better to lose a battle and make sure you win the war" often fell on deaf ears.

It was his violent and impetuous nature that earned him the nickname Bugsy. As Lansky explained, "Everybody said he was crazy as a bedbug. But I loved him and as long as he listened to me he stayed out of trouble. When we were in a fight Benny would never hesitate. He was even quicker to take action than those hot-blooded Sicilians, the first to start punching and shooting. Nobody reacted faster than Benny." And indeed, Lansky and his associates would have their lives saved many times in later years by Bugsy Siegel's fearless action. "Doc" Stacher, another early member of Lansky's group, remembered that when they were running truckloads of bootleg liquor all over the United States in the twenties, Bugsy never hesitated when danger threatened. "While we tried to figure out what the best move was, Bugsy was already shooting. When it came to action there was no one better. I've seen him charge ten men single-handed and they would all turn and run. I never knew a man who had more guts. And the Sicilians felt the same way."

Besides Doc Stacher, the early Lansky-Siegel gang included Red Levine; a cousin of Lansky's named Irving Sandler, known as Tabbo; Abner "Longie" Zwillman; Lansky's younger brother Jake; Louis (Lepke) Buchalter; Yudie Albert; Dutch Goldberg; and later on Dutch Schultz, whose real name was Arthur Flegenheimer. Most of the gang had been boyhood friends. Stacher, for instance, lived around the corner from the Zwillman brothers, Abner and Irving. They used to play basketball together, and when he was in Israel in the 1970s Stacher still remembered, "Meyer always says he was the star. I guess his memory plays him tricks. I was the champ." Stacher dropped out of his Charlton Street public school at an early age and never attended high school. He got a job selling newspapers on the street corner and then, struggling to earn a living for himself and his parents, he worked in a shipyard and a fur processors'. He went into business on his own, driving out into the country to buy produce from farmers and selling it from a stall on the Lower East Side, but couldn't make a go of it. When America entered the First World War he tried to enlist in the Army but was turned down because "I was too skinny. I ate a lot of bananas to put on weight, but they made me sick."

In Israel, where he found asylum after a bout with the U.S. Internal Revenue Service, Stacher reminisced to Uri Dan even more freely than Lansky, once the boss had given him permission.

Stacher and the other early gang members remained loyal to Lansky all their lives. With the Italian group under Lucania, they formed the nucleus of the underworld organization that was to play a major part in American life through the next decades.

7 The Bonds of Friendship

"In those days my family still had very little money. Actually we were almost starving," said Lansky.

"I look around me here in Israel and see children all happily going to school, good schools with big athletic fields. It wasn't like that on the Lower East Side when I was growing up. Of course my mother always insisted that I attend school and do my lessons properly. I liked school anyway. But it wasn't easy. You had to go out of your little neighborhood where you knew everybody and walk along streets where there were Irish or Italians. Many boys dreaded the daily walk to and from school. Gangs used to attack the Jewish boys and you never knew when you were going to be in a fight.

"I realized quickly that I had to learn to speak English well and I read a lot and listened to my teachers. I respected them and I understood quickly that if I wanted to get on in life I must study. My grandfather told me: 'All the secrets of life are locked up in books.' I think he meant the Bible, but now I could see that books and the knowledge they contained were the key to open all doors in America.

"I also went to cheder until my Bar Mitzvah, but then I stopped going although my mother wanted me to continue my studies. If my grandfather had been there it might have been different, but my own father was too busy trying to make a living, working long hours in a sweatshop somewhere to try to get enough money to bring us up. I didn't see him that often, maybe only on weekends.

"In the earlier days he and my grandfather used to quarrel, and I loved my grandfather. Now Benjamin was not there and I took no notice of my parents' wish that I keep on at cheder. I preferred to go into the street and watch the crap games. Sometimes I would think of my grandfather. I knew he wouldn't have liked what I was doing, running around instead of studying.

"I was small and skinny even in my teens, but I had made a good many friends and I discovered that they looked up to me for leadership. I didn't deliberately set out to become a leader, but I guess it came naturally to me. When I finished the eighth grade in 1917 I had to leave school. That was a huge change in my life."

Lansky thought carefully about what he should do, how he could use the qualities he knew he had. "My parents wished I could go on with my studies and become a doctor or something like that. I was only fifteen at the time, but even then I knew I had to get a job and bring in some money. I was very good with my hands. I got a job in a tool-and-die shop, where the foreman used to say, 'Meyer, you have golden hands. In twenty years you'll be a professional worker and make good money. You'll earn a dollar an hour.'

"It was my father who managed to get me that job, thanks to a relative. He was determined not to let me work in the sweatshops. The garment industry was flourishing all over the Lower East Side then, and it needed a lot of unskilled as well as semiskilled labor. The factories were soon full of thousands of Jewish men, women, and children making clothes under the most terrible conditions. There were little factories everywhere on the Lower East Side, in people's homes, in converted stables, everywhere. These people got very low wages, and a lot of the work was piecework. People worked seventeen or eighteen hours a day seven days a week. They worked on the fire escapes and out on the sidewalks when it was hot. It was a terrible life and my father said, 'I'll never let you do that. You'll die young from the tailors' disease.' That's why he got me a job working with my hands as a toolmaker, although that wasn't the sort of job most Jews thought of as being suitable at the time."

Meyer's father had gone into the "shmattes" business—the rag trade, as the garment industry was called—when he first arrived in America, and for the rest of his life he drifted from job to job, one of the vast numbers who toiled in the sweatshops of the Lower East Side. "My father said I must stay away from the shmattes business and never go near it," Lansky explained on one of those rare occasions when he spoke about his father. "He wanted me to become a mechanical engineer. Somehow he had got it into his head that this was a career with a fine future. It was not the sort of job Jews thought about much in those days. But my father was told it was a good clean profession where you worked in a nice office. That's what he wanted for me. And that's why he got me the job as a tool-and-die maker.

"People forget," Lansky said, "but times were very bad in the early 1900s. There was huge unemployment. People were hungry and many actually died from lack of food. I was lucky to get a job outside the horrible shmattes sweatshops."

When his foreman had remarked a few times on his "golden hands," Meyer Lansky carefully weighed the words of the kindly man who promised that his earning capacity would rise to eight dollars for a full working day. "But for better or worse I decided that would not be my path in life," said the son of the Grodno immigrant family. Six years after they reached the land of opportunity, they were still on the verge of starvation. There was only one way Meyer could think of to acquire power and wealth. He would have to do it by following the path of gambling. And even though he could not admit it at the time, that meant he would become totally involved in the world of crime.

At almost the same moment Meyer Lansky was deciding that the life of a skilled worker earning a dollar an hour was not for him, his Sicilian friend and ally was deciding his own future. Salvatore Lucania was stepping out of the gates of Hampton Farms Penitentiary after imprisonment for possession of heroin. The youth had been recruited as a runner in a drug ring and had been betrayed by one of the Irish boys who was involved in the famous water battle in the East River. The heroin was found in the band of a hat which Lucania was carrying as part of his legitimate job as a delivery boy for a hat factory. A tip-off to the police led to his arrest.

The moment Lansky heard about the sentence passed on his newfound friend he decided to come to his aid. He was well aware that the Italian had saved him from a bad beating after that first clash on the street corner. And quite possibly Salvatore had saved him again during the fight in the East River.

Meyer Lansky has always had the reputation of being a man who keeps his word and is totally loyal to his allies. In the underworld, where treachery and the double-cross are professional hazards to be expected at all times, the "Little Man," as Lucania liked to call him, was known for never letting down a friend in need and never stabbing a partner in the back. Ruthless with his enemies, Lansky gave complete support to his friends.

Lansky demonstrated his loyalty and decisiveness when he helped Salvatore Lucania. In July 1916 he called at the home of the Sicilian's Jewish employer, Max Goodman, and pleaded with him to do all he could. No threats were necessary, for Goodman had taken a liking to Salvatore and had even invited him home for meals. After that Goodman paid frequent visits to Hampton Farms and urged his dejected messenger boy to avoid trouble in prison and make sure he remained a model inmate. He also pleaded with the authorities, and it was partly because of the promises he made to reemploy the youth and to act as his "second father" that Salvatore Lucania—now called Charlie because his Jewish friends found pronouncing his first name a problem—was paroled after six months, cutting his sentence in half.

When Meyer Lansky met him the first night he was free, the Sicilian showed no remorse about being labeled a criminal. "My only mistake was that I got caught," Charlie said firmly. Like Meyer Lansky he had made up his mind. Just as tough, just as ruthless, just as ambitious as the son of Max and Yetta Suchowljansky, Salvatore Lucania was determined to achieve wealth and power any way he could; and if that meant crime, then so be it. Lucania had learned his lesson, and learned it well from his first mistake; he was not to be caught and imprisoned again for twenty years.

At the meeting after his release from the penitentiary the bonds between Meyer Lansky and Charlie were sealed for all time. Henceforth they were to work in close harmony, Lucania as the front man, with his name and photograph frequently in the newspapers. Ebullient and extroverted, he fully enjoyed the publicity which surrounded his image of being America's number one gangster through the twenties and thirties. As long as he was "above the law," notoriety was his dish.

For his part Meyer Lansky early decided he preferred the shadows of anonymity. He liked to work discreetly behind the scenes. He was the brains, the cool head, the calculating businessman who weighed the risks carefully like the manager of any other large company. He restrained the Italian allies who ranged themselves behind Lucania; brought order into their frequently chaotic criminal activities; and saw to it they worked together for everyone's benefit. And ultimately he ranged behind him the Jewish *unterweltnikes*—underworld—not only in New York but in other major American cities.

Yet Meyer Lansky was never strictly a desk man. He was quite ready to ride shotgun with the liquor convoys during Prohibition and he was prepared to use a gun if called upon. And this aspect of his character was needed in his reunion with Lucania, for the Sicilian at once told Lansky about his suspicion that it was the Irish son of a New York policeman who had given information to the police about his being a heroin carrier. Charlie was ready to go out immediately and tackle the Irish youth, but Meyer advocated caution. "If anything happens to him now, the finger will be pointed straight at you," he said. "You know his father is a cop. They all know he was the one who gave the tip-off that you would stop at the poolroom on East Fourteenth Street where they trapped you. If anything happens to that Irish hoodlum they'll jump on you and you'll be back behind bars before you know it. This is something Bugsy and I can handle. But not now. We'll wait till the time is ripe."

Lucania took his pal's advice and waited a year for revenge. Meyer Lansky refuses to talk about the affair, but as Doc Stacher told it, thirteen months after Charlie Lucania got out of prison there was a widespread search for a missing nineteen-year-old Irish youth. The police made a strenuous effort to find him, for the boy was the son of one of their own. Charlie was questioned repeatedly, but at the time of the disappearance he had been out of town. What was more, he was able to give precise and verifiable details of all his movements. The Irish boy's parents never heard from him again and his body was never found.

It was now early 1917, and as the United States went into the First World War the friendship between Meyer Lansky and Charlie Lucania flowered. At the time neither saw themselves as future big shots in the underworld. They had sprung from poor immigrant families, their education had been limited. The two sought easy money by robbing shops, warehouses, private homes. Roaming farther and farther afield, into East Harlem and the rest of Manhattan, they held up prosperous-looking citizens anywhere. Any qualms that Charlie Lucania's Italian friends had about working in partnership with Jews were quickly dispelled as both Meyer and Bugsy Siegel proved that they were as bold as anybody. The two were ready to use their fists or knives when beating up night watchmen or whoever got in their way.

Forty years later Daniel Francis Ahearn, an early associate of Lansky, gave a remarkable glimpse of Lansky's first ventures into crime. Breaking the code of silence, the *omerta,* which has surrounded Lansky all his life, Ahearn admitted on March 15, 1957, that he was hopeful about being favorably considered for parole if he testified about Lansky in a denaturalization proceeding against him. Ahearn's confession was not only about Meyer Lansky's gambling activities. His words cast light on other aspects of crime in that period on the Lower East Side.

Ahearn, a year older than Lansky, vividly remembered their first meeting. He recalled that Lansky was known as Johnny Eggs but he didn't know why. Possibly that nickname had something to do with the way Lansky had smashed the Irishman's head with his cholent, which always had eggs in it.

Ahearn had met Lansky on Jackson Street between Front and South streets, in 1917 or 1918. "I was introduced to him by a fellow by the name of Johnny Barrett . . . Muggins. . . . There was some little tiff . . . over a little girl . . . called 'Red-headed Gertie.'. . ." A day or so after they met, Lansky and Ahearn broke into a loft of the Puritan Building, on the corner of Broome and Goerck streets, and took "some piece goods." Ahearn estimated that during the first year of their friendship they teamed up for perhaps six similar jobs, stealing merchandise from "different lofts, trucks."

"I would have died for [Lansky] at the time," Ahearn went on. "I really liked him a great deal. . . . And whatever money I had or whatever money I would steal from trucks I would always share, give him an equal share."

Ahearn was caught and sentenced to Elmira Reformatory, where he served fifteen months. He saw Lansky the first night he was back in New York, and noted that Lansky was carrying a gun. Lansky told him he was "connected with crap games" and was "making some money, with unions and so forth."

Lansky then took Ahearn to Essex and Rivington streets, where they talked with "Meyer Albert and Yudie Albert and Zeigie" and went to a "cabaret" on Rivington Street. They put Ahearn on the payroll of a floating crap game—"I think it was 10 percent of that game."

Ahearn's memories were to be useful to government prosecutors both then and later, especially in subsequent denaturalization attempts in the 1970s.

8 Apprenticeship

Both managements and unions used gangsters in the vicious labor disputes of the early decades of the twentieth century.

It was the bosses who first introduced criminals, signing them up personally or hiring them from detective agencies, turning a blind eye to the violent records of the men who came on the company payroll. In many cases these toughs were recruited for protection against workers who threatened to burn down factories or smash machinery when a fight for higher pay and better conditions reached bitter heights. The more ruthless employers gave their hoodlums carte blanche to attack strikers, and they followed these instructions with such enthusiasm that many union organizers were murdered or crippled for life.

In self-defense the unions turned to the underworld too, and hired their own gunmen to break the power of the toughs working for the bosses. From this "cooperation" it was an easy step for the gangsters to exert influence among union officials. In many instances they took over the unions and ran them, making fortunes for themselves by milking union funds and starting protection rackets. Recalcitrant employers would be forced to pay weekly or monthly fees for insuring that their businesses were not plagued by strikes. For further financial considerations the criminals who entwined themselves in the union organization could also put competitors out of business by blowing up factories or terrorizing both management and key workers.

In Chicago in the 1920s, for instance, gangsters were involved in most of the city's day-to-day activities. With Al Capone and his fellow Mafia chiefs running the city, some sixty trades and professions were under the iron thumb of the gangsters. These included such humdrum areas as the dry-cleaning industry. Anyone who wanted a skirt cleaned or trousers pressed paid a fifty-cent "service" charge, which was the cut handed over by frightened shopkeepers into the unlovely hands of small-time criminal collectors working for powerful bosses. The union heavies were just as ruthless in serving their masters as the thugs working for the bosses. They attacked factories and killed or maimed workers who refused to strike or join the union.

New York was not much different. In the garment industry especially, rival gangs of men employed by both sides clashed fiercely. Both Lansky and Bugsy Siegel were drawn into this murky world of terror and counterterror.

Again Ahearn's testimony gives a rare picture of the times, though Lansky fiercely denies every word of it. "The authorities were determined to indict me," Lansky says, "and when I went to Israel they again used a sworn statement by Ahearn in an effort to have me extradited. Ahearn was serving a twenty-years-to-life sentence for robbery and the immigration authorities, who were trying to revoke my naturalization, bribed him by promising him parole in exchange for a recital of lies aimed at besmirching my character."

Ahearn's deposition, made in the United States District Court, Southern District of New York, in 1957, was resurrected on March 10, 1971, in the Southern District Court of Florida in a grand jury investigation headed "United States of America vs. Meyer Lansky, Tel Aviv, Israel." Ahearn's confession was certified by Robert J. Campbell, Attorney in Charge, Strike Force 18, Organized Crime and Racketeering Section. In it Ahearn claimed that he and Lansky had been involved in several acts of violence on behalf of union organizers during the 1920s.

In one incident he and Lansky had met a union organizer at a Russian cabaret on Allen Street and had been sent upstate, to Peekskill, to burn down a factory. The union's affairs became more complicated and two weeks later, still in Peekskill, their orders were changed.

Meantime, "we would walk around that shop and these here scabs . . . were suspicious . . . of anyone approaching, especially strangers, and we had to be most careful . . . these scabs sometimes would holler, and naturally we would have to run away . . . we tried walking around there at night and most of these scabs were sleeping in the shop."

The organizer came to see Lansky and Ahearn and pointed out the "main mechanic, a Jewish person," and gave them his home address in Brooklyn. "If we can get rid of him," said the organizer, "it will slow up the production in that there factory." Ahearn went on to explain how it was done:

> . . . we trailed this guy, went on the train with him, but we lost him in the shuffle at Grand Central, getting off. But we had his address. We beat him out there. We went in a cab. He lived in the Williamsburg section. He lived in this house, and we stayed on the other side of the street, and naturally, when we saw him getting out of the cab—there were some people standing in front of the building—we didn't want to take a chance going over there to hurt him. We figured we would catch him in his house. . . .
>
> I knocked on the door and a woman responded . . . and she said, "Who do you want? Who is there?"
>
> I says, "Telegram." So she opened the door.
>
> When she opened the door I pushed it right in and I went right into their apartment and Meyer started going to work on the male there. That was the mechanic. . . .
>
> [Lansky] had a pipe in his hand. . . . He hit [the mechanic]. The man went down.
>
> [We were in the apartment] maybe two minutes, maybe less. . . .
>
> [Then] we met with the organizer and he gave us five [hundred]—he told us what a good piece of work we done. The mechanic won't come back no more. The wife won't let her husband go back to Peekskill to work in that shop no more. . . .
>
> We worked many jobs like that . . . going into factories, breaking up machines, throwing acid on goods and assaulting them workers, them scabs. It went on for . . . nine months or it could be longer . . . [in the] latter part of 1921 or in the early part of 1922. . . .
>
> [Lansky and I] were always close friends. [We worked together in] bootlegging—stealing out of drugstores, alcohol. . . .

Ahearn stated that during this time he and Lansky continued to be involved in crap games. Ahearn's duties were "more or less just like to keep order, be on the lookout in case they crash us, the cops, and so forth . . . sometimes we would carry guns . . . we were paid a salary and 10 percent of the winnings after all the overhead was taken care of."

At the same time the Lower East Siders were broadening their bootlegging operations:

> We met [Waxey Gordon, later to become a major partner in the bootlegging business] at Manny Wolf's [restaurant], I remember, and he seemed to like us two kids, and once in a while we would get some beer off him. . . . But we seemed to be more or less getting our own money at the time. . . . [We sold the beer] in case lots . . . to speakeasies if they bought it in lots. . . .

Later on Ahearn and Lansky "got liquor from boats," but "I never went out on them boats, though. I used to advise Meyer not to go out. I . . . was afraid he would get drowned or something out there. And I used to beg him to stay off the boats."

Ahearn gave a detailed account of how he became involved in a murder charge in the mid-twenties and of the help Lansky gave him:

> . . . it was one of them neighborhood gorillas [Hughie Gallaher], and seemed to have hot nuts for little Meyer . . . always abusing him with that foul language, like "you Jew bastard," when he would get drunk. "Get up against the wall. I want to try my guns on you," and so forth. And I liked Meyer very much, and I didn't like hearing this, see.
>
> "[It was around 2:30 on a Monday morning.] I was in a store on Madison Street with Meyer's cousin Tabbo, and [Gallaher] thought maybe he could find Meyer in there. . . . He was half in the bag, drunk, and when he recognized Tabbo he insulted him, called him "Jew bastard" . . . and he wound up pushing him. He was a great fist fighter, this Gallaher, see.
>
> So I told him, "Listen you, if you want to fight why the hell don't you go outside and fight? People are sleeping upstairs and you're making a lot of noise here. . . ."
>
> So he kept more or less abusing Tabbo and then he hit Tabbo . . . he had a knife, see, threatening him . . . anyway Tabbo went down, and he picked up something, it could have been a hunk of iron . . . and I remember he hit him.
>
> I started pushing them both out. . . . I told them, "Come

outside if you want to fight. For chrissake, we are going to blow this joint," because we had a little crap game that used to take place there and there was no crap game in session because it was just Tabbo and I, and Red Levine was sleeping in the bed.

The three men went out to a lot across the way, on Madison Street, where Gallaher "picked up a stick or a hunk of iron." Ahearn said, "Why don't you put down the stick?" and Gallaher said, "You shut up, too, you cocksucker."

So when he said that, he started swinging at me, and when he started swinging . . . I punched him and grabbed it out of his hand and I remember I hit him on the back of the head or the back of the neck.

When he went down Tabbo started picking up stuff and banging him and banging him, and then put him under . . . a load of wood in this here lot. . . .

Naturally we ran away . . . to Meyer's house on Columbia Street. . . .

I had a little blood on my shirt and [Lansky] says, "Jeez, take the shirt off," and he had a hell of a mother. His mother liked me very much, and my people, and I respected her, and still respect her, for that matter. Anyway, I got another shirt and put it on. So he says, "Let's get out of here," and we went to Tabbo's house on Lewis and Grand Street. . . .

His sister got up and she started hollering, "I got to get up in the morning" . . . and we figure we will go out, Meyer and I. So we told Tabbo, "We will see you later." . . .

And as Meyer and I were going down the staircase, two gentlemen were coming up the staircase. So I remember putting a handkerchief up to make believe I was blowing my nose. Anyway, we got by these two guys, and I later learned they were two bulls. . . .

Meyer says, "Come on, we will go down to French Bakers on Grand Street and get some coffee," and we went into this here bakery and had some coffee and doughnuts or something and we now learned in there that, jeez, Madison Street is loaded with cops and photographers and they are taking pictures there; that Hughie Gallaher is killed.

So he says, "Jeez, let's get out of here." So we went up to

Fourteenth Street . . . and sat there . . . just sitting and walking around . . . Union Square Park. And he says, "You stay here and I will go over and make a telephone call. I'll try and reach Yudie Albert down at Essex Street Market at Second Avenue."

He came back and told me . . . to go away, go uptown somewhere, lose myself. . . .

We went to Washington Street, [to a firm of fruit truckers, and from there] Meyer and I, we went to New Jersey . . . and I stayed at that house and [Meyer] would come over to see me occasionally.

Eventually Ahearn was arrested—after, as he claimed, Lansky arranged the details of how he was to surrender. He was taken to the Clinton Street police station, where he encountered "a detective . . . Bill Burns, who happened to be in the detective room. He says, 'You son of a bitch, I nearly got you there that night down on Ridge Street, you and that little Jew bastard.'. . ."

Ahearn was booked for the murder of Hughie Gallaher, but the charge was dismissed "for lack of evidence." Then he was arrested a second time for the same murder, after Lansky and Yudie Albert again told him he would have to give himself up. While he was in the Tombs awaiting trial, Lansky "would always come in the Tombs and see me and tell me what was happening . . . he told me how he is working over there at this machine shop, his cousin's place . . .

"I was taken before . . . Judge McIntyre. I was told that for counsel to represent me the Judge is going to work out a connection . . . Meyer . . . told me that it's going to cost a few bucks."

The second indictment was also dismissed.

Ahearn also told what he said was the true story of the man he knew as John Barrett, whose run-in with Lansky and Siegel was to provide further ammunition for the government's denaturalization campaign against Lansky. Meyer's brother Jake had a job with a Bronx fur-dressing company and the gang had got away with a lot of very valuable furs. When the Lanksy brothers examined the loot, they realized that some of the furs were missing. Apparently they first thought Ahearn had helped himself to the items, but later decided it was Barrett. They held a meeting and Lepke accused Barrett of stealing from them. Barrett confessed, claiming that he was unhappy about the split—Meyer and Bugsy Siegel were getting too big a share of the spoils whenever a robbery was carried out.

According to Ahearn:

. . . one day I met Meyer in front of my house, No. 500 Grand Street. Meyer told me that I had missed the party . . . the shooting of Barrett. . . . [Lansky] said he was in the car, but . . . he never told me he shot him. He just said he had him in the car, and this Johnny Barrett sensed something was wrong, I guess, on account of the conversations that were taking place . . . and he opened up the door of the car and he started running through the fields—he was a hell of a runner, this guy—and they started firing at him. They hit him four times, I recall—three or four times in the head. . . .

The Bug was driving, [and] Red Levine . . . And I believe Jimmy Coggiano.

[Lansky] told me, "What a lucky bastard. He came all the way from Long Island to New York in a taxicab with four bullets in the head and he is laying in Gouverneur Hospital.

"That would be a good place to clip him, right up in that ward . . ."

Ahearn then said that he himself had been shot by Bugsy Siegel not long before, and that Lansky had told him Barrett was "more or less the one who was responsible for you being shot."

And [Lansky] said . . . "I'll tell you what, here's a good idea: Let's go down to Mott Street. I know some ginzo down there, and we can get a juiced-up [poisoned] chicken. . . . His wife knows I was in the car, I can't give him the chicken, but you could pull the gag and give him the chicken . . ."

So we went down to Mott Street and we got this chicken, which was juiced up. I will admit it, I was hot for Barrett at the time, knowing . . . I was shot for nothing. And I met his wife, Grace, I believe her name was . . .

She says, "I am going down to see him. . . ."

I says, "Seeing you are going to the hospital to see him, here, give him this and don't even tell him it's from me. Surprise him." . . .

So she took the chicken and she headed for the hospital. . . .

I met her later and she started calling me all kinds of names . . . because when . . . he asked her, "Who gave you the chicken?" [she told him]. He took the chicken and winged it out of the window.

Two attempts to kill Barrett had failed, but he was still a doomed man until his uncle, as Ahearn went on to explain, pleaded on his behalf. After returning the stolen furs to the rest of the Lansky gang, Barrett was forgiven.

Danny Ahearn, however, never forgave Bugsy Siegel for shooting him, or having him shot, not long before. Precisely why Ahearn was hit is not known, but he was convinced that Barrett had told lies about him to Siegel and it was these lies that had caused him to be shot. In any event, soon after the Barrett shooting there was an apology of a kind for Ahearn from Lansky's friends. Perhaps realizing that Ahearn had been wronged and Barrett was the guilty party, Lepke invited Ahearn to a *bris* ceremony for his newborn son. The circumcision is a traditional occasion for family and friends to gather and congratulate the proud parents on the birth of a son.

Danny Ahearn, however, did not relish the prospect of coming face to face with Bugsy Siegel, who was also on the invitation list. As delicately as possible he declined, explaining that he "had something else to do on that particular day—a Sunday." Another reason why Ahearn decided to stay away from the circumcision ceremony was that Red Levine, a well-known killer for the Lower East Side outfit, would be present. Levine was a strange and unusual man. He was known to be a devout Jew and would pray every Saturday morning at his synagogue in New York, as he had done in his home town of Toledo. He took part in many operations when guns were needed, and was one of the most dangerous of all the Lansky-Lucania gunmen.

Not surprisingly, when interviewed about Barrett by FBI men many years later, Red Levine couldn't recall the incident and had nothing to say about Ahearn's recollections. But the shots fired at John Barrett during Meyer Lansky's youth were to haunt Lansky all his life. Nearly forty years later, in Jerusalem, he fiercely denied having anything to do with the incident, but the U.S. Justice Department, in its bid to have Lansky's naturalization papers revoked in the 1950s, instigated a long and thorough investigation into every possible aspect of Meyer's early life, including of course the Barrett episode. FBI agents tracked down John Barrett, who had changed his name from John Barth after his mother remarried.

Barrett said he had known Lansky from the time they worked together as tool-and-die makers, near the end of the First World War. He also remembered Lansky and Siegel as running speakeasies on Broome and Lewis streets.

"Lansky was very close to the Albert Brothers, Yudie and Willie, who operated a crap game over a tavern at Essex and Rivington streets." Meyer was "the watcher and strong-arm man," Barrett said. Although he was reluctant to talk, Barrett is alleged to have told the investigators that he had been shot by either Bugsy Siegel or Meyer Lansky when he "was taken for a ride after a party at Louis Lepke's house. Present on that ride were Lansky, Siegel and Red Levine." Barrett refused to testify for the authorities and "requested that the Service not call my house" because "I don't want to be bothered any more by anyone."

Barrett denied that he was shot because he had told the police the whereabouts of a load of stolen goods that Lansky and Siegel had hidden. But "he admitted," wrote the agent who interviewed him, that "Lansky and Siegel had been responsible for the robbery of a warehouse shortly before they shot him." Barrett claimed that he had not seen who fired at him, but said that Lansky and Siegel were both in the rear seat of the vehicle and that he was seated in front, next to the driver, Red Levine. He had jumped out of the car, hailed a cab, and gone to a friend's house. From there he was taken to a hospital, where he named Lansky and Bugsy Siegel as his assailants. Later, however, he refused to identify either of them because, he said, he feared for the safety of his two brothers.

Also in the 1950s Benjamin B. Edelstein, acting for the U.S. Immigration and Naturalization Service, went to see Joseph P. Heinrich, who had interviewed John Barrett in the hospital after he was "taken for a ride." Heinrich, at his home in Rosedale, Long Island, confirmed that Barrett told him Bugsy Siegel, Meyer Lansky, Red Levine, and another man were in the car. "When I arrested Meyer Lansky I knew him to be a member of a criminal combination engaged in illicit activities and that he was not gainfully employed in any legitimate enterprise," Heinrich recalled. He also confirmed that when Barrett was brought to court as a witness he refused to sign a complaint against Lansky and would not testify against him. The charges against Lansky were accordingly dismissed.

9 Building Up the Business

By the time the First World War ended, in 1918, Lansky had collected around him a group that was to remain loyal to him for the rest of their lives. He had the talent for demanding and getting total obedience and his friends were ready to die for him if necessary.

Charlie Lucania was moving in the same direction, recruiting Sicilians and other Italians until the two men had a nucleus of some twenty men who were both ruthless and reliable. Just as Lansky had picked Bugsy Siegel as his right-hand man, so Charlie chose a fellow Italian, Francesco Castiglia, a Calabrian, as his first lieutenant. Castiglia, who became better known as Frank Costello, was as ruthless as Bugsy, and just as quick to use his gun. He was also an extremely intelligent and resourceful man, able to move easily in all social circles.

Nobody was safe from the Italian-Jewish gang. Moneylenders, pawnbrokers, and insurance men collecting their weekly dime and quarter premiums from families in the Italian and Jewish ghettos were easy and frequent hit targets. These particular victims had ready cash on them, and that meant no hassle with fences, no negotiating or squabbling over the price of stolen goods.

Unlike the vast majority of other hoodlums, who quickly spent every cent they got from their crimes on "booze and women," as Lansky put it, Lucania and Meyer decided to set aside a part of their proceeds for a special fund. Neither man was sure how to use this accumulating capital, but both shrewdly realized that if ever they were going to get into the big time they would need money behind them. They decided to concentrate every effort on building up a large capital sum and later on in life see about enjoying the fruits of their labors. As prudent businessmen they were planning for expansion.

At this stage Meyer was reading every library book he could find on business management and finance. The first idea that crossed his mind was to put the growing volume of cash into a bank.

Deciding to patronize the biggest one in the neighborhood, he sent Bugsy Siegel to have a look at the place from the inside. The youngster (still in his teens) came back disgusted. "I'm not putting any of my money there," he said indignantly. The premises were guarded by one aged, half-blind security man, and "anybody can bust in and steal every dime in the place," Bugsy reported.

Instead of investing their money in the elegant branch bank, the gang raided it two weeks later and made off with eight thousand dollars.

Lansky never forgot his first love, gambling, but he was quick to see that the pickings from crap games on a local level were limited. Illegal off-track betting was already a flourishing business, and the two young men from the Lower East Side decided to move into this field. But here the up-and-coming Lansky-Lucania group had to tread carefully, for major mobsters were dominant in this nation-wide racket. There was big money to be made, however, and Meyer and Charlie cautiously began to buy their way into established "books," paying the bookmakers shares out of their savings.

To insure that their growing interest in bookmaking would be immune from police raids, the two young leaders began to make regular payments to the cops on the beat and the officers at police headquarters. Costello was given the task of finding ways to make the payments and was quite successful in the districts where they were operating. The gang also began to make pay-offs to local politicians who needed the cash to buy favors at the local ward level with gifts of cigars, food, and other tangible goods in return for votes. The gang leaders discovered that they had a commodity everybody seemed to want: hard cash.

Then in the following year, 1919, suddenly and almost simul-taneously came two events which were to be major factors in their future. The first involved one of the crap games that Meyer had organized and that was under his protection. The players were in the midst of the game in an old tenement building when six men burst into the room and began to lash out with their iron bars at the organizers, their bodyguards, and the suckers. Four people were badly beaten up before the assailants left. As they did so their leader, an Italian, shouted, "This is a warning. Next time we'll kill you!"

Meyer immediately set out to avenge the assault. When he tracked down the Italian who had led it, he was somewhat taken aback at what he heard. "Take it easy," he was told. "I was sent by Joe Masseria. If you touch me there'll be big trouble for you, sonny boy."

This was Lansky's first clash with Joe "the Boss" Masseria, one of the big names in the old Mafia hierarchy. Masseria had decided to take the Lower East Side under his wing, demanding a cut on every gambling activity there, right down to the smallest game in a private home for a few cents. This was part of his bid to build a power base as he strove to fill a vacuum created by the jailing of the leading Mafia chief in New York, Ignazio Saietta, known as Lupo, the Wolf.

Although he realized that he was taking on a gangster who was feared throughout the city, Meyer Lansky went on the attack. Backed by his own toughs under the leadership of Bugsy Siegel, he returned to the man who had led the raid on his crap game. That time the Masseria underling and his colleagues were thoroughly defeated. The fight spilled out onto the sidewalk, sending passers-by scattering in all directions. When the police came, Lansky was arrested and fined two dollars for disorderly conduct. To the surprise of local underworld figures, however, Joe Masseria did not seek immediate revenge. Clearly these Jewish toughs, allied to those of Lucania, were becoming a force to be reckoned with. The message had been received: "Keep your hands off the Lower East Side. This is our territory."

This gave both Lansky and Lucania—upstarts really—a growing sense of confidence in their powers, but caution advised them to play it very cool. Joe Masseria was a formidable opponent and the tiny group under Meyer and Charlie was no match for the several-hundred-strong group of hoodlums who took orders from Joe the Boss. In any open conflict between the young men from the Lower East Side and the established Mafia boss, Lansky and Charlie would have been wiped out. Still, Masseria kept his distance.

The second event that was to make such an impact on the lives of Meyer Lansky and Charlie Lucania was the ratification in January 1919 of the Eighteenth Amendment to the Constitution of the United States, which banned the general manufacture, sale, and transportation of intoxicating liquors and beers.

To the world this meant just one word: "Prohibition."

This huge social experiment was aimed at banning forever the "evils of drink." It would become an important chapter in the history of the United States. For men like Lansky and Lucania it signified a golden path to unimagined wealth, power, and influence.

Prohibition was the triumph of the old-fashioned virtues of an American countryside fighting to maintain its traditional way of life against the growing power of the cities. In particular the voice of American rural womanhood, represented by such bodies as the powerful Women's Christian Temperance Union and the Anti-Saloon League, passionately preached against the evils of drink. There was a widespread dread and hatred among rural and small-town women of the power of the saloons, where their husbands spent their hard-earned wages and where prostitution flourished. To them the abolition of alcohol meant that all other crime, all other evils, would disappear overnight. Poverty itself would vanish. Some Drys demanded that those who trafficked in it should "be hung by their tongues alive beneath an aeroplane and be carried right across the United States as an example to others to refrain from selling alcohol."

The Protestant church found its strength in the countryside. Its hostility to the city was based not only on the fact that the saloon was the offspring of urban living, but also on the knowledge that the Roman Catholic church found most of its adherents there. This was largely a matter of chance, for from the mid-nineteenth century onward most of the immigrants who crossed the Atlantic to seek a new life in the new world happened to be Roman Catholics. Thus the cry "The City is the home of rum and Rome" was in fact based on truth. It was no accident, then, that the powerful, almost exclusively rural, evangelical Protestant voice, including the Methodists, the Presbyterians, and the Baptists, allied with such groups as the Mormons, the Christian Scientists, and the Disciples of Christ, were in the forefront of the campaign for Prohibition. It was part of the war against Rome.

The urban Roman Catholics and Jews opposed Prohibition or were apathetic about it. Many of them saw the dangers that would spring from trying to ban alcohol by law. The Drys, however, were supported by many of the rich and powerful families in the United States who thought it might be a generally "good thing" if the saloons were shut down. The workingman, the customer of the evil, dirty saloon, might then become more responsible, not leave his wife and children to be burdens on private charity, and work harder.

The rich also drank, of course, and enjoyed their alcohol. But they reasoned that they were "responsible about it." They drank at home. After all, if you have a charming residence you do not have to seek solace in some crowded saloon. Many labor leaders, frequently against the wishes of their members, also supported the Drys; they saw whiskey and rum as the ally of the capitalist and a weapon used by the ruling class to keep the workers "subdued and crushed." Karl Marx had said that religion was the opiate of the masses. Many labor leaders believed that in the United States liquor had taken the place of religion in keeping the working class drugged and subdued.

There was no doubt that immense misery was caused by drinking in the American cities, just as in Britain and other countries which went through a rapid industrialization. The moderate voice of such American social reformers as Charles Stelzle, who said that "poverty causes alcoholism as much as alcoholism causes poverty," was ignored. He pointed out repeatedly that the best paid workers with the most leisure spent the least time in saloons: "The answer is to shorten working hours and paying employees a living wage." The way to combat the evil of drink was to raise the earning capacity of workers, not to outlaw alcohol. But the voice of the Drys was so fierce and so powerful that the Wets hardly raised a protest when on January 16, 1920, the Volstead Act prohibited the manufacture, sale, or transportation of any intoxicating liquor. It was not illegal to buy or actually drink booze, but the Volstead Act aimed at preventing any trade in liquor.

The Drys considered the bootleggers, the men who made and distributed illegal liquor—which went under such exotic names as canned heat, hooch, moonshine, smoke, and of course straightforward bootleg—worse than murderers. Some suggested that the authorities should even deliberately sell poisoned liquor. Although it would obviously result in the death of thousands of Americans, this was a small price to pay as it would discourage others from breaking the law and buying illegal alcohol from genuine bootleggers.

In hindsight it is easy to see that Prohibition was likely to be a total failure. No power on earth could stop people who were determined to drink from seeking out alcohol of one kind or another and paying any price for it. The fourteen years of American Prohibition did not stop drinking, but it did produce a vast array of new social problems.

10 Arnold Rothstein, Ph.D.

Arnold Rothstein was the despair of his family. Born in 1882, he had an excellent education and his well-to-do, middle-class relatives were convinced that his brilliance and intelligence would take him a long and honorable way in life. But instead of following the path of honest toil, Rothstein took to gambling and crime like a duck to water. By 1920 he was at the peak of his career. In the underworld his name was held in awe as he organized gigantic Wall Street bond frauds and the like, but his favorite sport was high-stakes gambling in his hotel suite and on the transatlantic liners favored by the rich. His quick mind won him the nickname "The Brain."

More than anybody else Rothstein was quick to see the glittering prospects held out by the passing of the Eighteenth Amendment. He saw immediately the opportunities and profits which the sale of illegal liquor would bring about, and rightly anticipated that the city population of America would see nothing wrong in drinking. Even law-abiding citizens who would never consider themselves law-breakers would not hesitate to buy bootleg whiskey.

On the Lower East Side, Italian racketeers had for years been involved in bootlegging in a minor way. In thousands of poor Italian homes illegal distilleries were a traditional way of life. At the time when Prohibition was introduced, this particular activity in New York was under Masseria's control. He immediately began to organize an increased supply of liquor from the distilleries secreted in the tenements of the Little Italys and the Little Bohemias of the slums. A whole army of such "alky cookers" (distillers of homemade alcohol) and booze runners was organized to cope with the expected demand for illegal alcohol. And just as predicted, there sprang up in New York, as in most other American cities, a number of speakeasies—or illegal drinking places. They flourished almost from the day the act became law.

The imaginative Arnold Rothstein quickly realized that this type of operation, even if expanded to its limit, was child's play compared to organizing bootlegging on a proper businesslike basis. As the ship bringing him back to New York came within sight of the Statue of Liberty, he heard over the radio the news of Prohibition. Then and there he worked out the broad outlines of a scheme whose scope was staggering. Making his plans while he organized future poker games on shore for his gullible and wealthy fellow passengers, he knew he was going to need allies for the new scheme. His thoughts turned to a small, lean, hungry-looking young man he had met quite by chance at the Bar Mitzvah of the son of old family friends in Brooklyn.

The young man had struck Rothstein as being smart and ambitious. The well-groomed gambler was highly amused as Lansky told him how much he envied his sophistication and way of life. Lansky confided to Rothstein that he read about his exploits in the newspapers and admired the way he had crashed upper-class New York society and become a powerful figure in it. The young man had implied that he too had dreams of becoming a man of power, a man as successful as Rothstein. Arnold Rothstein had forgotten the name of the youth. He glanced at his notebook and read the name he had scrawled: "Meyer Lansky."

That moment was another turning point in the life of the boy from Grodno, who was still working as a tool-and-die maker by day and at night building up his loyal following.

"I admit quite frankly that I made a fortune from bootlegging," Meyer Lansky said as he drove with Uri Dan through the hills of Judea for another visit to Jerusalem. "Everybody I knew treated Prohibition with contempt. The most important people in the country—respectable businessmen, politicians, senators, congressmen—they all bought illegal booze from me or from other men in the business.

"There are big companies in the United States today that had their beginnings in running illegal liquor into the country. What about Sam Bronfman, who ran it from Canada across Lake Erie, which we called the Jewish lake? Lewis Rosenstiel had an enormous bootleg business that became the Schenley Corporation when

Prohibition was finally repealed. You can buy shares in such companies on Wall Street today, and it's all very respectable."

As Lansky said, the close connection between bootleggers and today's highly respectable liquor manufacturers can be traced back to those early days of Prohibition. For instance, Bronfman, who became head of the international Seagram Company, was linked to one of Lansky's closest lieutenants, Abner "Longie" Zwillman. Like the Lansky family, the Bronfmans were part of the exodus from the pogroms of eastern Europe, but they made their new home in Canada. They became one of the wealthiest families in the whole of North America—and there is no doubt that the foundation for their wealth was laid by selling liquor to the United States during Prohibition. (Sam Bronfman's brother-in-law, Paul Matoff, was shot during a battle between rival bootleggers in Saskatchewan in 1922.) Yet it must be said that the Bronfmans were doing nothing illegal. It was legal to manufacture liquor in Canada, and it was also perfectly legal to sell it to anybody who was prepared to buy it. As Sam Bronfman later told *Fortune* magazine, "We loaded a carload of goods, got our cash, and shipped it. We shipped a lot of goods. I never went on the other side of the border to count the empty Seagram's bottles."

Lansky and his friends as well as other American bootleggers took delivery of Bronfman whiskey in a variety of ways in different parts of the United States. The liquor was sent by ship to destinations on both the West and East coasts; in fast speedboats crossing the St. Lawrence–Great Lakes waterways and across the border to New York, Michigan, Montana, and North Dakota. The islands of Miquelon and St. Pierre, not far from the coast of Newfoundland, became one of the chief nerve centers for this immensely profitable trade.

At the end of Prohibition the U.S. Secretary of the Treasury, Henry Morgenthau, Jr., claimed that Canadian distillers like Bronfman owed the United States approximately $60,000,000 in customs duties and excise taxes on the alcohol they had illegally dispatched to the United States in the previous fourteen years. A furious row between Canada and the United States resulted, with Morgenthau threatening to stop importation of all Canadian goods until a settlement was made. Finally the Ottawa authorities agreed to settle for a bill of $3,000,000—5 percent of the $60,000,000 demanded. The Bronfman family agreed to pay half, and handed over a check for one and a half million.

Another example Lansky cites is the Prendergast and Davis Company, set up in New York just a few weeks before repeal. Among its founders was Herbert Heller, a brother-in-law of Lewis Rosenstiel, head of Schenley Distilleries. Rosenstiel owned the premises where Prendergast and Davis was located. Lansky was a good friend of Lewis Rosenstiel's. Another man connected with Prendergast and Davis was Johnny Torrio, also a close friend of Meyer Lansky. Both the Rosenstiel and the Bronfman families became important figures in the United States after repeal; both were known for their philanthropy.

With a certain bitterness in his voice Lansky asks, "So why am I considered the criminal today because I was also part of the bootlegging business? Why is Lansky a 'gangster' and not the Bronfman and Rosenstiel families? I was involved with all of them in the 1920s, although they do not like to talk about it today and change the subject when my name is mentioned."

Back in 1920, however, Arnold Rothstein was only too happy to talk about his plans with the flattered Meyer Lansky. Here was the legendary millionaire gambler and underworld figure—tall, handsome, with liquid dark eyes—discussing a business deal: Lansky remembers that he kept cool and tried not to show his disbelief. It may seem eccentric of Rothstein to have turned to the raw and totally unknown young man as a prospective partner, but it was a calculated move. Rothstein neither liked nor trusted the old-time Mafia chiefs like Masseria and his archrival Salvatore Maranzano. For a start the two Italians were deeply prejudiced against Jews, especially Jewish upstarts like Rothstein. They were set in their ways and shortsightedly greedy, more concerned with maintaining their "family honor" than with money management. They hadn't the imagination to grasp the concept that Rothstein had worked out.

"Rothstein taught me some valuable business lessons that day we met," said Lansky. "He invited me to dinner at the Park Central Hotel and we sat talking for six hours. It was a big surprise to me. Rothstein told me quite frankly that he had picked me because I was ambitious and 'hungry.'

"But I felt I had nothing to lose. He knew I was working with Charlie Lucania—as he was still known—and that we could call upon our friends, the mixture of Jews and Italians who were loyal to us."

Two of Lansky's friends were to be especially useful in Rothstein's plans. Arthur Flegenheimer, known as "Dutch Schultz," was to take over the bootlegging empire in the Bronx under the direction of Rothstein and Lansky. Abner "Longie" Zwillman was part of the Lansky-Lucania operation that controlled the sale of illegal liquor in northern New Jersey.

Zwillman and Lansky became particularly close friends. Under Abner's guidance Meyer began to read avidly, for he was always very conscious of the enormous gaps in his education. Zwillman was a studious and religious man who studied the Bible and loved good literature. He guided Lansky's reading, frequently giving him books as presents. It was to Zwillman that Lansky confided his past and discussed the important role of his grandfather in his life.

Rothstein knew something about Lansky's friends and realized they were the troops he needed. The eighteen-year-old listened respectfully at their first business meeting and many subsequent ones as the older man lectured him about his ideas.

"There's going to be a growing demand for good whiskey in the United States," Rothstein said at the outset. "And when I say good whiskey that is exactly what I mean. I'm not talking about the rotgut rubbish your Italian friends are busy making in their chamber pots right now on the Lower East Side. That's O.K. for the poor creatures who don't know any better.

"I'm talking about the best Scotch whiskey from Britain. There's a fortune to be made from importing the stuff into the United States. I don't mean just the odd dozen cases or partial shipment now and then. Prohibition is going to last a long time and then one day it'll be abandoned. But it's going to be with us for quite a while, that's for sure. I can see that more and more people are going to ignore the law, and they're going to pay anything you ask to get their hands on good-quality liquor. I know what I'm talking about, because as you know I mix with society people who have money. It's going to be the chic thing to have good whiskey when you have guests. The rich will vie with one another to be lavish with the Scotch. That's where our opportunity is—to provide them with all the liquor they can possibly pass on to their guests or guzzle themselves. And we can make a fortune meeting this need.

"I want to set up a sound business for importing and distributing Scotch. It is illegal, of course, and will require running risks, but I don't think you mind that. I have the contacts to buy the stuff. I know the Scottish distillers and they know me. I've played poker with them. I've taken a lot of money from them. We're very good friends and there's no problem there. Would you like to discuss this with your Italian friends and let me know? But we have to move quickly. Other people are going to get on the bandwagon."

The matter was discussed the very next day with Charlie Lucania, who was then introduced to Rothstein. The young Sicilian was as impressed as Lansky by the suave and sophisticated gambler, and the three men developed a surprisingly close and genuine triangular friendship. Within a short time Lucania was imitating Rothstein's way of dress, and he was forever seeking the older man's advice about "how to behave when I meet classy broads," as he once put it to Rothstein's immense amusement. Arnold Rothstein didn't know it, but the leaders of the Lower East Side outfit called him the Ph.D., an abbreviation of the Yiddish expression "Papa hat gelt" (Father has money, or dough). And in truth he educated his younger associates in both crime and high living.

The gambler met the rest of Meyer's and Charlie's friends too. They included vain, good-looking Giuseppe Antonio Doto, born near Naples and called Joe Adonis or Joe A; and Vito Genovese, a small, muscular young man who at times objected to so many Jews being included in the organization. Relations between Vito and Lansky were always cool and distant. Carlo Gambino was in Lucania's group; and so was the sinister Albert Anastasia, whose real name was Albert Anastasio. He had altered it slightly to avoid shaming his family when the newspapers referred to him as a gangster. Convicted of murder but released from Sing Sing after the disappearance of vital witnesses, Anastasia was one of the toughest and most ruthless killers in the organization.

The proposition that Rothstein put to his young friends was simplicity itself: "I will travel to London and Edinburgh and other major European cities and see the Scotch distillers. I'll lay out hard cash and ask them to deliver their top-quality whiskey to us. We'll have crews we can trust and ships to bring it across the Atlantic. The total cargo will be the Scotch I will buy from the distillers. We'll avoid running risks by unloading the cargo at sea and taking delivery outside the American three-mile limit. We'll have to hire or buy a fleet of small fast speedboats and that type of thing, so the cargo can be distributed at night to special places we'll set up on the coast. Either they can let us have the whiskey on the ocean that way, or we can take delivery from one of the nearby Caribbean islands—Cuba may be a good place. It will be your job to smuggle the Scotch into the United States and then distribute it.

"But first I want to lay down an important principle, and this is something I want to be very clear about: We must maintain a reputation for having only the very best whiskey. There are two ways of making money out of this, as I see it. There's the quick and rather stupid way—we could get cheap rotgut whiskey or open the cases and bottles we import, dilute it, and mix it with the cheap stuff being produced over here. We could certainly make very high profits for a while that way. But we would simply get a reputation like your pal Masseria as being merchants of cheap, disgusting booze which might even kill people. We'd have only the lowest kind of clientele. I want to go for the society people, because that's where the big money is."

The reference to Joe Masseria was deliberate. Rothstein knew that the Mafia chief and Lansky had already crossed swords over the right to run the gambling in Lansky's neighborhood. And Charlie Lucania had nothing but contempt for men like Masseria and Maranzano, the "old-time Mafia Moustache Petes."

"In my opinion," Rothstein went on, "we should sell the whiskey as it reaches us—in the original bottles, unadulterated and untouched. This way you'll reach a discerning clientele who will come and seek you out for more supplies. You'll be known as reputable merchants, for nobody really considers selling bootleg whiskey illegal or immoral. You'll find that the best customers will come pouring in with their orders, and they'll open their front doors to you as well. This is a very big opportunity for you to make your names—and your fortunes. You'll be introduced to America's most famous men. And a very important consideration is that no stigma will be attached to you as being real criminals, the sort of stigma you would get if you dealt in drugs or prostitution or other rackets. Believe me, it's the right way for you to set out on your careers. You can make a fortune for yourselves and at the same time become very popular with the people who count in this country."

Neither Meyer Lansky nor Charlie Lucania, heads swimming at the dizzy prospects opening up before them, wasted any time debating the matter. The path ahead was clear as daylight. The two of them looked at each other and with a single voice told Rothstein, "Count us in." And thus was launched one of the largest and most profitable crime operations in the history of the United States.

11 The War with Waxey Gordon

Within months, as they established themselves as big-time bootleg operators, Charlie Lucania and Meyer Lansky spread their wings beyond their local borders in New York and across the United States.

A Philadelphia friend of Rothstein's named Irving Wexler, more commonly known as Waxey Gordon, had come to the same conclusion as the New York gambler at almost the same time; that there was a fortune to be made by smuggling the best Scotch whiskey into the United States. Rothstein and Gordon made a separate partnership. Part of the deal was that the Philadelphia man would allow Lansky and his New York friends first call on the liquor Rothstein smuggled in from Europe. There was to be a link between the groups in the two cities, and each would give the other first preference at all times. It was also agreed that they would not work with third parties without consulting each other.

As their self-confidence grew, Lansky and Lucania went into partnership with other gangsters, such as Lucky Johnson, who ruled Atlantic City as effectively as a Roman Caesar. It was in this area that a very large proportion of the bootleg Scotch was landed. Moe Dalitz and Johnny Scalise, the bootleg princes of Cleveland, and Solly Weissman of Kansas City were quickly brought in to join the Rothstein-Lansky-Lucania organization. Soon tens of thousands of cases of whiskey were being transported all over the country to meet the unquenchable demand for good-quality liquor. Under the skillful guidance of Rothstein, who introduced Lansky to modern business methods used by leading American firms, the bootlegging operation took on the appearance of a formal business corporation.

"The only difference between us and, say, an ordinary legitimate organization or business was that we dealt basically in cash. We also had another very powerful advantage," Lansky added. Nobody had to worry about paying taxes. The profits from bootlegging were enormous and the risks minimal, and there was no public hostility of any importance. Bootlegging was not considered antisocial. Most Americans did not regard the men who engaged in this trade as real criminals.

The mood of the times was symbolized by Groucho Marx's wisecrack: "I was a teetotaler until Prohibition." And in Chicago Al Capone expressed the bootleggers' philosophy when he said, "I make my money by public demand. If I break the law my customers, who number thousands of the best people in Chicago, are as guilty as I am. The only difference between us is that I sell and they buy. Everybody calls me a racketeer. I call myself a businessman. When I sell liquor it's bootlegging. When my patrons serve it on a silver tray it's called elegant hospitality."

Lansky and Lucania quickly realized that even if their employees were caught, the penalties for bootlegging would be small. Most judges were reluctant to enforce the full rigor of the law because they and others involved with the law drank alcohol. They were uneasily aware that when they were offered whiskey at the homes of friends it had clearly been illegally sold and distributed in the United States, possibly by the very men who appeared before them for sentencing.

There were relatively few arrests, however, partly because Lansky and Lucania had their front man, Frank Costello, to bribe customs officers, policemen, judges, and politicians. This corruption, fed with the profits of Prohibition, was viewed by the bootleggers as "unavoidable business expenses."

One of the bootleggers' major problems was the question of physically moving the whiskey from city to city. The gang bought dozens of trucks but soon these vehicles themselves became targets for other criminals who wanted a slice of the cake. Not everybody had Rothstein's connections with Scottish distillers and the captains of British industry, and it seemed logical enough to simply grab the whiskey that belonged to the New York bootleggers, rather than try to import it themselves.

Lansky had no further need for the money he earned as a tool-and-die maker, but for a time he kept that job as a legitimate front in case the police became curious about the way he earned his livelihood. Then he decided to quit this work and become an automobile mechanic—at least for part of the day. He had long been fascinated by cars and this interest lasted. Even when he became extremely wealthy he would tinker with automobile engines for hours. He became expert at maintenance and tuning engines, and many of the getaway cars his Italian and Jewish associates used were maintained and serviced by Lansky himself.

"I realized the importance of the car very quickly," he explained. "You mustn't forget that in those days the car was a comparative novelty in the United States. But Rothstein taught us that mass production of cars would revolutionize many things in America. I realized myself how important it could become in our particular kind of business." If Lansky and his outfit had a fleet of automobiles serviced by themselves and adapted for their purposes, their efficiency would be greatly increased.

The distribution of liquor was just one problem they resolved by using modern transport methods. Such methods also helped them enlarge their area of activity. Crimes could be carried out quickly and fast departures from the scene were easy. Law enforcement officers simply couldn't keep up. Together with the telephone, the automobile enabled men like Lansky and Lucania to extend their activities throughout the United States.

But other bootleggers had fast transport too, and the menace of hijackers had to be faced. Young Lansky met the challenge in typical direct fashion, determined to follow his precept that leaders should lead from the front. With Bugsy Siegel at his side and a group of armed men to back them up, Lansky rode shotgun, protecting the convoys of their precious Scotch whiskey. Meyer's men were more than ready to fire on any would-be highwaymen who tried to stop them, and not averse to engaging in a little hijacking of their own.

Lansky remembers one of these coups with particular satisfaction. It was organized by Bugsy Siegel, who got wind of a boatload of whiskey being landed in Atlantic City and, eyes gleaming, told Lansky, "The stuff belongs to Joe Masseria."

The two young Lower East Siders still had a score to settle with the Mafia boss. Heavily armed and masked, the "Bug and Meyer" gang, this time without the benefit of the Lucania men, drove down to Atlantic City and carefully prepared an ambush on a back road. A two-thousand-dollar bribe had paved the way; Siegel knew the precise time and route of the four truckloads of whiskey.

Total secrecy surrounded this particular raid, because Masseria's cargo was due to be delivered to Rothstein's business partner, Waxey Gordon, and to be mixed with cheap alcohol in a distillery in Philadelphia. The Philadelphia bootlegger would be intensely displeased if he found out that his goods had been stolen by his so-called friends from New York.

The Lansky men chopped down a tree and casually laid it across the road, as if it had just blown down. Then they waited in the darkness.

Exactly on time, at three-thirty in the morning, the convoy came in sight. It was guarded by ten Masseria men. The front truck ground to a halt as the driver spotted the tree, and several men jumped off the trucks behind to move the obstacle off the road. As soon as they started pulling the trunk out of the way, a volley of shots sent them running to the roadside in panic. Within seconds three bodies were sprawled on the ground and to these corpses were soon added the limp bodies of five badly wounded drivers and guards. The rest quickly surrendered as Bugsy Siegel and his men surrounded the convoy.

The victors could not resist giving the Masseria guards who were still on their feet a beating with fists, feet, and wooden clubs. This was to prove their undoing, for one of the victims recognized Lansky and eventually the news of the identity of the attackers came to the ears of Joe the Boss back in New York. The Sicilian did not take action against Lansky and Siegel at the time because he was trying to persuade Charlie Lucania to join forces with his own organization, and he knew that Lansky and Siegel were closely allied with Lucania. But he vowed secretly that as soon as that arrangement was made he would deal with Lansky and Siegel in his own way.

The information about who the hijackers were also got back to Waxey Gordon in Philadelphia, and he was furious at being robbed of his share in the profitable deal arranged with Joe Masseria. Gordon held his tongue because he did not want Arnold Rothstein to know that he was also working with the Mafia chieftain, whom Rothstein despised. But from that moment there was a bitter feud between Lansky and the man from Philadelphia.

Soon afterward the two men began to quarrel openly, much to the embarrassment of their various partners. The dispute reached such bitter proportions that they accused each other of being double-crossers and liars. Once they came to blows, but Charlie Lucania stepped between them and told them both to "behave." The feud was long-lasting and by 1931 had become known in the underworld as the "War of the Jews." Finally Charlie Lucania decided to take stronger action, because the dispute between his two friends threatened to disrupt their business. This was the only situation he had ever seen in which the passions of the "Little Man" seemed to conquer his normal common sense, and it was obvious that the organization could not contain both Meyer and Waxey.

Loyal to his partner from their youthful days, Lucania bided his time and hatched a careful plot that hinged on Lansky's brother. Jake Lansky was by now a valued member of the gang, complete with nickname. When the brothers were teenagers, Jake used to believe that Meyer was upset about being so small. When they were walking together Jake would slouch, with his shoulders hunched forward, pretending to be shorter than he really was. As a result he was called Jake the Hunchback by the other members of the outfit, although normally he walked perfectly upright. On the Lower East Side the Lansky brothers were called "David and Goliath" by everybody who knew them.

Jake traveled to Philadelphia with a sheaf of papers in his attaché case. The documents were handed over to startled but highly grateful Internal Revenue officials. They were just what was needed to complete a rather sketchy case against Waxey Gordon. The gangster was then arrested and convicted for income tax evasion, totally unaware that his partners in New York had betrayed him. Waxey Gordon was sent to prison in 1933. When he was released he was unable to make a comeback as a major figure in the underworld. He tried his hand at wartime black-marketeering but was caught and again sent to prison. He tried to push drugs after his release but a tip-off to the police resulted in yet another prison sentence. Lucania and the Lanskys had long memories.

The dethroning of Waxey Gordon made life easier for all the Lower East Siders. The far more compliant Nig Rosen (real name Harry Stromberg) and Max "Boo-Boo" Hoff took his place in Philadelphia.

12 Cash on the Barrelhead

Very soon after they began working with Rothstein, Lansky and Lucania were both wealthy. Rothstein introduced them to the most affluent society circles, where they were warmly welcomed. A certain glamor and excitement was attached to them as being bootleggers. Wealthy and influential people enjoyed drinking the good whiskey their somewhat shady guests smuggled into the United States, and invited them to the famous parties of the twenties.

Lucania enjoyed mingling with the most famous names in American society, with politicians, industrialists, businessmen, and multimillionaires. He learned manners and dress from Rothstein and plunged into the glamorous life. Lansky attended one or two of these parties but soon declined to attend any more. Even then, when the temptation to see and be seen must have been great, Lansky preferred to remain discreetly behind the scenes. He didn't want to be known as a bootlegger and he managed to remain little known among the people who drank the Scotch he and Rothstein provided.

Although both men were still in their twenties, Lansky and Lucania were now running a sizable business. Rothstein was carrying out his grand scheme, making frequent trips to Europe to buy the whiskey and paying cash every time. As planned, the goods were shipped across the Atlantic and landed in Canada as well as the Bahamas and Cuba. Lansky and Lucania were not the only bootleggers, of course, but they had a handsome share of the total business. Whiskey imports to Canada from Scotland rose by something like 400 percent in the late 1920s, while Canadian consumption, according to government reports, fell to half its former amount during the years of Prohibition.

The whiskey which was landed on islands of the West Indies was transported to the ships of "Rum Row," along the three-mile limit from Boston to Atlantic City. The smugglers would try to dodge the U.S. Navy and Coast Guard vessels keeping watch along the shoreline while the bootleggers met the Rum Row middlemen with their own fleet of speedboats, transferring the cargo at night. The dangers at sea were high. From time to time whole cargoes were lost to the Navy or the Coast Guard. Rival hijackers sometimes stole shiploads on the high seas or seized cargoes with violence and bloodshed after they had landed on the East Coast. And every now and again the customs and police also seized truckloads of illegal whiskey. Bootleggers were sometimes killed in what became a hazardous operation, as the gangs vied for the supplies coming into the United States. But for those involved, the risks seemed entirely worthwhile, because the profits were enormous.

A case of twelve bottles of Scotch cost the bootleggers around twenty-five dollars, including the cost of bribing guards, hiring sailors, and paying off the men who did the loading and unloading. The Scotch distillers took advantage of the situation by raising their prices. Still, the final profit to men like Lansky and Lucania was in the region of a thousand dollars per case. Although much of the whiskey was sold in its original bottle—at perhaps thirty dollars a fifth, with the overall cost to the bootlegger just over two dollars a fifth—Lansky and Lucania had hit on an ingenious method of tripling the profit on each bottle of imported Scotch.

Lansky explains: "There was a major loophole in the Volstead Act. You couldn't sell liquor, but if a doctor said you needed alcohol because of health problems (and it is amazing how many doctors gave their patients prescriptions for booze), you were allowed quite legally to buy alcohol. Naturally this liquor had to come from somewhere, to help all those poor unhealthy Americans who could not be cured by taking aspirin or other drugs like that. The government licensed certain firms in different cities to make alcohol for sale as medicine."

What Lansky and Lucania did was repeated by other underworld figures. They simply became partners of the owners of the alcohol-producing factories. The owners had no choice in the matter even if they wanted to resist the "offers" made to them. Men like Lansky and Lucania had very effective ways of enforcing cooperation. Some legitimate operators tried to resist but ended up with broken bones or worse. The message soon got across, and after that very few tried to resist. Indeed, many owners welcomed their new partners when they saw how much everybody's profits increased.

Behind the locked doors of these legally operated distilleries the alcohol produced on the premises was mixed with the bootlegged Scotch, which usually arrived in the middle of the night. Cheap unaged whiskey was judiciously added, along with prune juice, caramel, or other ingredients that would produce the right color. Rothstein probably never knew his junior partners had revised his methods. He remained firmly convinced that their customers should always get the real McCoy. Lansky and company, however, were careful to employ chemists and other experts who were skillful at mixing and disguising the true taste of the product they were selling. Few people could detect that they were not getting genuine Scotch.

The process of diluting the whiskey enabled the bootleggers to convert one bottle of genuine mature Scotch into three or four bottles of the mildly doctored drink. It was estimated by U.S. government officials that something like sixteen million gallons of industrial alcohol a year was used by bootleggers for this process at the height of Prohibition.

Much of this dilution of whiskey and jacking up of profits was done by Waxey Gordon and his successors, who controlled a whole string of legal distilleries in the Philadelphia area. "But it was not as simple as it sounds," Lansky remembers. "We had to get bottles that looked like the real thing. It was too risky to order them from ordinary plants, so we bought companies and went into the manufacture of bottles. Then we had to buy expensive printing machines to make the labels, which were a precise copy of the famous Scotch names like Johnny Walker or Haig or Dewar's. We even had to get involved in the real estate business, buying warehouses where we could store all the bottles and whiskey.

"We became a big business corporation employing hundreds of people who frequently didn't have the faintest idea who their employers were. This was a legitimate business and I had to read lots of books about how to run such an organization properly, because we were buying ink and paper and glass from legitimate firms and we couldn't arouse suspicion about our real activities. We had to hire accountants and other administrators to make sure that we never ran into trouble with the authorities, and we always paid our bills and taxes promptly."

Not only did Lansky and Lucania learn fast, but the "Little Man" evolved some original business practices. He employed scores of bookkeepers and accountants, all of whom had to have at least two qualities above all others. First, they had to know how to work without talking about the business. Second, the figures and other details of the work had to be stored in their heads. Lansky did all he could to prevent his accountants from writing things down. He didn't want evidence ever to be produced that could be used against him. As a result most of the administration was simplified and carried out orally. No books as such were kept, and when it was essential that paper and pen be used, the lynx-eyed employer and a few of his trusted lieutenants saw that all such documents and papers were destroyed the minute they were no longer needed.

"We had no filing system," Lansky said dryly. "I never saw any point in keeping records of past business deals. Either you knew what you were doing or you didn't. And if you didn't know what was going on, or what was happening in your business, you deserved to go bankrupt anyway."

By now the gang's whiskey was being drunk in the very best speakeasies in New York. It was distributed in a fleet of trucks all along the East Coast in a sophisticated manner, with supplies kept in reserve and rushed to any city that might suddenly find itself running short. The network grew quickly as links were made with bootleg bosses. Al Capone in Chicago was one of the closest allies of the Lansky-Lucania organization. Although the name Capone is synonymous with Chicago Mafia legend, Al Capone had started his career in New York.

"It was Bugsy Siegel who knew him well when Capone lived and worked on the Lower East Side," Lansky said, discussing the connection between Italians and Jews in the American underworld. "Capone had a bad reputation in New York and was known as a killer. He found himself in great difficulties when the police got out a warrant for him on a murder charge—he had beat up a Brooklyn bartender so badly that he died. Bugsy Siegel was a close enough friend of Capone's to hide him out with one of his aunts, somewhere on East Fourteenth Street."

Alphonse Capone was lucky he had good friends to keep him away from the cops, but they all realized that he couldn't stay in New York indefinitely without being arrested. "The heat really was on him," as Lansky says. So he was sent to Chicago and given a job with Johnny Torrio, who had also come from New York to try his luck in Chicago. Torrio, known as the Fox, was struggling to take over the leadership of the Mafia in Chicago, and was opposed by one of the famous old-time "Moustache Petes," Big Jim Colosimo. Within a short time Al Capone became the Fox's right-hand man, a move that delighted the Rothstein-Lansky-Lucania syndicate because Capone was very much their man. Although Capone eventually became his own master in Chicago, running scores of rackets and criminal operations, his loyalty to his New York friends was so firm that Lansky and Lucania knew they could always count on him.

Colosimo made a major mistake when he remarked to Torrio that he was "better off in Chicago." Asked what he meant, Big Jim said, "If you go back to New York you'll have to mix with those dirty Jews like Lansky and Bugsy Siegel. I can't understand why Charlie Lucania mixes with them. I sometimes have a suspicion that he must have some Jewish blood in his veins—otherwise he wouldn't have anything to do with that scum."

This comment pleased neither Lucania nor his Jewish allies. Bugsy was all for going straight to Chicago and killing Colosimo. He was restrained only by the cautious Lansky, who with Lucania was planning to use Torrio to set up a bootlegging operation in Chicago which could be under their firm control. It was wiser not to start a shooting war there until Torrio was better established.

Colosimo then made an even worse mistake than sneering at the "Hebes" of New York. He told Torrio that there was "no future in bootlegging" and insisted that the traditional rackets—drugs, prostitution, and loansharking—were the best businesses to be in. He saw no reason to change his habits.

This sealed Colosimo's fate. For what troubled Lansky more than anything else was Big Jim's poor judgment. Anti-Semitic remarks were nothing new from the Italian members of the underworld. What both he and Lucania feared was that other mobsters would take advantage of Jim Colosimo's lack of interest and start rival bootleg-liquor networks in the city. A council of war was held in New York, and Frankie Yale, a killer who had thrown in his lot with Lucania, was sent to Chicago with orders to settle the "Colosimo problem" once and for all. He did it by blowing the Mafia chief's brains out with a single shot.

Meyer, Bugsy, and Rothstein solemnly sent an enormous

wreath, the largest one on display at the well-attended funeral. Only Johnny Torrio understood the irony of the beautifully hand-painted card attached to the flowers. It read: "From the sorrowing Jew boys of New York."

Such sorrow did not last long. Johnny Torrio took over the Mafia empire in Chicago with Al Capone as his right-hand man, and the Lansky-Lucania outfit began sending a flood of illegal whiskey. The profits were shared equally, for the bosses of the rapidly expanding Lower East Side gang always treated their partners well. They saw to it that allies were paid promptly and fairly, especially in time of need, and earned the reputation of never cheating their friends. This generated a fierce sense of loyalty, which was to be of great value to Lansky and Lucania in the years ahead.

13 Company Chairman

"It all happened a long time ago," said the old Lower East Side peddler who knew Meyer Lansky. "But I remember it so clearly.

"Meyer was small—about five foot five when he was full grown—but he became a very big man. This was the time when he used to walk around in his silk suits and Bugsy Siegel was even more expensively dressed. Meyer always looked well groomed and discreet, like a real businessman. Bugsy was different. He talked loud and his clothes were loud too. He always had beautiful girls with him. He was a legend with those girls. They were dancers and actresses and models and girls like that. I never saw him more than once with the same woman, blond, redhead, dark—every kind. We called it a scandal, the way he behaved, but to tell you the truth we were all rather jealous of him.

"Meyer was respected. He was kind and generous but it was no secret that he was the boss. He was so little, but when he walked people got out of his way and were polite and careful how they talked to him. It wasn't that they were scared of him, for I never knew of him hitting or killing anybody. Maybe he did, but I don't know of any example personally.

"Meyer always looked as if he knew what he was doing—like a company chairman used to getting his own way and having his orders obeyed without question. At this time he was just in his twenties, the same age as me, but even older men respected him, the Orthodox people. They knew he wasn't earning his money as a motor mechanic, but even so they admired him."

The admiration of his fellow Jews on the Lower East Side clearly reflected one aspect of the character of Meyer Lansky as he rose in the world. He not only made a fortune for himself; he also reveled in the power and influence his status brought him.

Charlie Lucania was lording it with equal success in his own Italian ghetto of the Lower East Side, but the style of the two men remained poles apart. Lansky avoided publicity and would not mix with the showgirls and society women who were now eagerly inviting Lucania to their homes. It was considered an exciting thing for wealthy women to be seen with the tantalizingly sinister Sicilian and to boast afterward that they had been seduced by the "gangster" from the slums of New York.

Outsiders believed, understandably, that it was Lucania who ran the organization. In fact the leadership was shared equally, with decisions reached only after full discussion among Lansky, Siegel, Costello, and a few other lieutenants. But the authority and leadership of both Lucania and Lansky was such that they generally dominated all their colleagues. They were clearly the joint "brains," and their orders were obeyed without question or reservation—particularly at a time of crisis when there was no time for democratic discussion. Both men were ruthless, tough, determined, and now they were full-fledged criminals—even if not all the population considered bootlegging a "real crime."

The two men were to set up other rackets, including dice games, card games, and roulette in back rooms all over New York City. They bought control of uncountable legitimate businesses; corrupted politicians on both a local and national level; bought the protection of policemen and high ranking officers. If Lansky appeared to be a "kind and reasonable young man" to his fellow Jews on the Lower East Side, he was smart enough and ambitious enough to work his way up in the world of crime quickly and efficiently. He fully lived up to Rothstein's hunch that he would become one of the most powerful members of America's underworld.

Lansky was harsh on those who crossed him, and this was made clear not only in the behind-the-scenes role he played in extending his "company's" influence into Chicago, but also in the way he dealt with those who tried to cheat him or Lucania.

Chicago turned out to be one of the most profitable investments made by the board of directors that Meyer and Charlie ruled. The hard-driving Al Capone and John Torrio, using the tactics that their friends in New York were perfecting, poured a steady supply of dollars into the eager hands of the corrupt administration there, under Mayor William Hale "Big Bill" Thompson. They provided "protection" to their allies in the distillery and brewing businesses and then bought their way onto the boards of several legitimate companies. By 1924 Capone and Torrio were making several million dollars a year from bootlegging alone. And of course a cut was always sent to the New York outfit.

However much Al Capone might say he was merely a "businessman" with his partner Johnny Torrio, he could insure a successful operation only by corrupting politicians and police officials on a vast scale, by blackmail threats, and by killing rivals who dared try to muscle in on his monopoly in the city. In the 1920s there were not hundreds but thousands of unsolved murders, and most of them were carried out by gangsters settling scores and competing fiercely among themselves. There were over a hundred bomb explosions in the business premises or homes of people who dared stand in the way of the Capone gunmen. Innocent people were badly injured, beaten up, and sometimes killed, as an example to others not to resist.

Neither Capone nor Johnny Torrio shared their predecessor's anti-Semitism, and they included in their organization a number of Jews, one of whom was named Samuel Bloom. Like Rothstein, Bloom was cultivated and highly intelligent, and like the New York gambler he did not think much of the idea of spending his life as a doctor or businessman. Bloom at first made a handsome living in Chicago by bribing doctors to give him prescriptions for alcohol. This legally acquired "medicine" helped swell the profits of the bootleg trade when it was blended with Rothstein's Scotch.

Then, as Lansky tells the story, Bloom came up with a brilliant idea. He and Rothstein had set up a poker game with a wealthy Scotsman. After letting him win a few hands, the gamblers suggested that they play for "real stakes." Feeling that he was onto a good thing, the Scot agreed.

The result was that within a few hours he found himself stone broke. And that meant a profit for the two gangsters of just over $50,000. It was a good night's work. Samuel Bloom later commiserated with the mug he had carefully nursed before emptying his wallet so professionally. The Scotsman, however, kept the stiff upper lip he had learned at his public school, and showed no ill feeling. He told Bloom, "There's plenty more where that came from."

When he added that he had a controlling interest in a big Scottish distillery that made a first-quality whiskey called King's Ransom, Bloom could hardly believe his luck. He quickly suggested that his friend from the Scottish Highlands could recoup his losses by going into partnership with "some friends of mine who might be interested in importing your whiskey into the United States."

Lansky said, "Bloom rushed to see us about the deal and we told him to go ahead. But we insisted that he tell his British pal we wanted a total monopoly of his whiskey. We would buy whole shiploads if he could guarantee us permanent exclusive rights to his King's Ransom label. Even then it was clear to Rothstein and me that Prohibition wasn't going to last forever. It couldn't; the whole country was breaking the law. When that happens either the law gets changed or the country collapses, and I was sure the United States wasn't going to collapse.

"So I was thinking of the day when Prohibition would be over. We had set up an elegant distribution system. Why shouldn't we keep the business going legally when the Prohibition laws were repealed? If we could create good will and obtain the contracts now, right at the height of Prohibition, then we could keep the whole business going when it became lawful."

Lansky's partners fully agreed with him, but what excited Bloom for the short term was that King's Ransom turned out to be ideal for bootlegging. It had a rich, heavy flavor and could be blended with generous quantities of cheaper whiskeys and medicinal alcohol without losing its taste. Profits would be enormous.

The Scotsman was handed $100,000 in cash as an initial deposit and Bloom was instructed to refuse a receipt, a gesture that impressed the distillery owner tremendously. Bloom said simply: "We will work on trust." Rothstein and Bloom let their new friend win back some of his losses at poker games in New York, but he never recovered the bulk of his $50,000. That, of course, had provided half of the deposit.

The Scotsman was true to his word. Within weeks whole shiploads of King's Ransom were being nationally distributed along the Lansky-Lucania pipeline. The bulk of it went to the very wealthiest and most discerning of their clients. And when repeal came, for a number of years the Lower East Side outfit, through a company controlled by Frank Costello, was the U.S. importer of King's Ransom.

But poor Bloom overreached himself. Basking in the congratulations of his Chicago and New York friends, he let his gambling mania rip. He had always loved every kind of gambling, and now, feeling that his luck was running with him, he went wild. In a single poker game in Rothstein's suite at the Park Central Hotel, he lost over $100,000. He continued to lose and was soon in a desperate situation, unable to raise money quickly enough to avoid getting a bad name as a nonpayer.

A few days later Lansky and Lucania were worrying over a major setback. A convoy of trucks loaded with King's Ransom whiskey had vanished on its way south from Boston. Their Boston partner, "King" Solomon, was outraged when he was accused of carelessly letting 15,000 cases of the best Scotch get itself hijacked.

Lansky went to Boston to question Solomon and find out why the system had sprung such a leak. It had cost the company a loss of over a million dollars in potential profits, let alone the loss of the money paid in advance for the shipment. Lansky returned to New York with disturbing news—news that was to be Sam Bloom's death warrant. It was absolutely clear that he had sold the details of the convoy's route to a rival gang of hoodlums who had hijacked the entire shipment. Lansky had proof of Bloom's betrayal and he also knew the identity of the hijackers.

It was decided to take no action against the robbers—they were really only small-time crooks who had struck it lucky. Charlie Lucania said reasonably, "We would have acted the same way if we could have got our hands on somebody else's big load."

But it was clear that Bloom's involvement could not be ignored, and here rose a matter of protocol. Lucania knew there was an unwritten code which made his Jewish colleagues reluctant to shoot a coreligionist.

There was silence in the room as the Sicilians present looked at Lansky's poker face.

Lansky rose and left the room to telephone Rothstein. When he returned to the council meeting he told Lucania in a flat voice, "Bloom has just settled his debt. He paid up the $100,000 he lost in Rothstein's rooms." This was exactly a week after the hijack. The gamblers at Rothstein's had been surprised at Bloom's having the money, because everybody knew his luck had been bad.

Bugsy Siegel rose without a word and left the room, and after that nothing further was ever said about Bloom's betrayal.

When Bloom's Scottish friend asked after him at a poker game a few weeks later, he was gravely told, "Sam's in Europe studying Renaissance art."

The distiller replied, "He is such a cultivated gentleman. I was hoping to invite him to join me for grouse shooting in Scotland next year."

Bloom was in no position to play poker ever again, or to join the shoot in the Scottish Highlands. His body, encased in cement, lay at the bottom of the Hudson.

The mystery of who had killed Bloom was never solved, but in the 1950s, when the government undertook its massive probe into Lansky's past, FBI agent Edelstein unearthed some clues. One man interviewed was Benjamin B. Baron, who had worked as a railroad inspector between 1926 and 1934. Baron had discovered that contraband shipments of alcohol were being made at his place of work, and when he tried to "notify his superiors by telegram he found that these telegrams were intercepted by persons who were engaged in the illegal transportation of liquor. He succumbed to incessant proposals that were made to him to help a certain combine involved in the transportation of liquor. The man who bribed him was 'Yasha' Jack Katzenberg, who was head of an organization which received shipments from Sol [sic] Bloom of Chicago. Bloom represented a Florida and South Carolina group who imported approximately 10,000 cases of whiskey on each trip from Nassau, Bahamas. Bloom had hired Lansky and Bugsy Siegel to protect him against kidnaping and hijacking."

Edelstein reported that Baron told him:

> In the pursuance of the duties of the Subject [Meyer Lansky] Jack Lansky and "Bugs" Siegel [were] "Protectionists," murder and kidnaping was their forte. When the three discovered that they were "immune" to arrest for the commission of these crimes, they commenced kidnaping activities on their own and received in the form of ransom cash payments and interests in illicit liquor groups and in that way eventually became part owners of combines in the illegal liquor racket. [Baron] is further reported to have mentioned that among the victims of the Lansky-Siegel combination were included Sam Lee, who was

murdered in 1934 and who was a partner of "Yasha" Katzenberg and Harry "Sweeney" Rosenberg. A Jack Levinson, who was also a member of one of the bootlegging groups, was the victim of kidnaping by the Lanskys and Siegel; that Sol [sic] Bloom of Chicago, the source of the liquor shipped to the Katzenberg group, was kidnaped by the Lanskys and Siegel and as a result of this kidnaping they apparently took over the Bloom interests in Chicago.

According to Edelstein, Baron did not want his name to be disclosed; he said he "wished to live and did not want to be murdered."

In 1959 other investigators found Baron at the Long Island Jewish Hospital, being treated for a "spinal and arthritic condition." Fearing that his children would learn about his past, Baron refused to divulge further details about Lansky's career: "It has been 27 years since I have seen any of these people and I have forgotten a lot."

The roles of employer and employee in Baron's statement were reversed by the testimony of Carlos M. Bernstein, a former special investigator for the Bureau of Alcohol, Tobacco and Firearms of the Treasury Department. Bernstein had interviewed Yasha Katzenberg, "who was then involved in bootlegging and narcotics," and had been told that Lansky and Siegel had financed him "in shipments of liquor and narcotics."

Another FBI agent reported:

In August, 1938, Yasha Katzenberg, who at that time was under indictment in the Southern District of New York, charged with violation of the narcotics laws, along with Buchalter and 28 others, furnished information to the effect that the head of the organized racketeer syndicate with headquarters in New York City and nationwide ramifications was Meyer Lansky. Other members were Abner Zwillman, "Moe Dimples" (Morris) Wolensky, Cuddy Cutlow, Joe Adonis and others whose names were not mentioned. According to Katzenberg, this syndicate secretly owned and controlled the liquor importing firm of Thomas J. Malloy and Company, 601 West 26th Street, New York City, and other legitimate businesses, as well as the Revere Race Track in East Boston, Massachusetts, and other race tracks in California. He stated that the syndicate was engaged in a program of "muscling in" on all larger professional gambling activities throughout the United States.

An FBI document dated August 24, 1971, reveals that one of its investigators reported:

> Just prior to the repeal of the 18th Amendment, the Kings Ransom Distilling Company was controlled by Siegel, Frank Costello and Meyer Lansky. The White House Scotch Distilling Company was controlled by Siegel and Lansky. Capital Distillers was controlled by Siegel and Lansky together with one Levinson, whose identity is not known.

King's Ransom whiskey, though lucrative, did not bring good luck to its first two importers. Like Sam Bloom, Arnold Rothstein himself finally fell victim to the gambling passion. His murder deeply upset his friends from the Lower East Side.

As Lansky put it, "We all admired him. He was always totally honest with us and he taught us a great deal. We got on well right from the beginning—like me he was a gambler from the cradle. It was in the blood with both of us. Rothstein seems to have had a gift for figures too, and he used to practice by asking his friends to fire off random numbers at him. He would multiply, divide, add, or subtract these numbers and produce the answers instantaneously. He had an ice-cold nerve and even when playing for the highest stakes, with hundreds of thousands of dollars at risk, he never lost his head."

The legendary Arnold Rothstein's career seemed glamorous indeed to his young East Side allies. And it is easy to see why Rothstein took to Lansky. In his early youth Rothstein too had loved street crap shooting and a popular gambling game known as "Stuss," a variation of faro.

It was Rothstein who brought about a link between Lansky and Lucania and the New York politician Al Smith. Both Lansky and Lucania admired Al Smith, as many people on the Lower East Side did. Although he was Irish, Al Smith too was the son of a poor family and had worked in the Fulton Fish Market. A poor boy who made good, he had not lost the common touch.

Smith had become a member of the State Assembly in 1903, and in 1918, by then a power in Tammany Hall, he was elected governor. He introduced a great deal of legislation to help the poor people of the Lower East Side. Bills he was able to get passed included those limiting child labor and insuring the rights of workers.

As a teenager Rothstein had worked for a Tammany boss called Big Tim Sullivan. At that time and for some years afterward, Tammany, the Democratic Party organization in Manhattan, was totally under the control of the Irish. Later the Italians participated in control of the organization, and the Jews too found some foothold. But when Rothstein became involved with Big Tim Sullivan he was one of the first Jews to do so.

Jewish involvement in political corruption via Tammany Hall is hardly surprising. The vast majority of the two million Jews who reached America between 1880 and 1914 were of course hard-working, law-abiding members of society. In spite of anti-Semitism, especially in the professional schools and the banking and insurance business, most Jewish immigrants found ways to support themselves on the right side of the law. As with other ethnic groups, it was a minority that took illegal shortcuts to wealth and power.

This criminal minority had flourished even before Lansky came to America, and he knows some of the facts and folklore about it. At the time he arrived almost a third of all juvenile delinquents who appeared in the New York courts were boys and girls from homes of Jewish immigrants. This did not necessarily imply serious lawbreaking. In many cases their criminal activities were petty theft and other minor peccadilloes, and many other children were homeless or removed from troubled families.

Rothstein, of the generation just preceding Lansky's—but by no means a typical member of the delinquent minority—went into gambling in a big way when he was still in his twenties, setting up a fashionable casino in Manhattan. His close friend Nicky Arnstein, Fanny Brice's lover and also a big-time gambler, once asked him why he spent so much money and time on gambling when he was already a multimillionaire. Rothstein shrugged and said, "Why do you eat every day? I can't help it. It's part of me. I just can't stop. I don't know what it is that drives me but I'll gamble to the day that I die. I wouldn't want it any other way."

Nicky Arnstein was unhappy at his friend's behavior. It wasn't just the gambling. Rothstein apparently couldn't stop engaging in criminal activities of every kind. He stole from his gambling partners and on several occasions was nearly killed when he was caught cheating them. Arnstein frequently talked with Rothstein's father, a respected businessman and merchant. Rothstein Senior had stern ethics; indeed, he was called Rothstein the Honest. He shared Arnstein's concern about the family black sheep, especially after 1919, the year his son made the biggest headlines of his whole notorious career.

Arnold Rothstein was responsible for the strangest scandal that ever rocked America's sporting world. "Buying" eight players of the Chicago White Sox baseball team, he tried to "fix" the 1919 World Series. Rothstein gave $100,000—acquired in one poker game, according to legend—to his loyal lieutenant Abe Attell. Attell gave it to the ballplayers, who in return agreed to lose the first few games of the series. Rothstein and his friends bet heavily and planned to win millions. But somehow the story leaked out and American sports lovers were up in arms. Rothstein, a genius at dodging the law, managed to extricate himself from the scandal although no one had any doubt about his complicity.

In 1928 Arnie Rothstein began to lose at his fabulous poker games. As stories spread around New York that he had lost vast sums to other gamblers such as the Californians "Nigger Nate" Raymond and "Titanic" Thompson, Charlie Lucania and Meyer Lansky grew alarmed. They talked several times with Rothstein, assuring him that if he did have money problems they would be glad to help him out. In any event he was sharing in their bootlegging profits, and the two younger men couldn't figure out why he should be short of money. They knew that his weekly take from bootlegging alone sometimes totaled hundreds of thousands of dollars. But the gossip didn't stop, and Lansky and Lucania held a number of meetings with Rothstein's other friends, trying to discover why he seemed to be suddenly going to pieces.

According to Lansky, "The gambling fever that was always part of Arnie's make-up appears to have gone to his brain. It was like a disease and he was now in its last stages. He gambled wildly—even bet half a million dollars on the 1928 presidential election. His money was on Herbert Hoover to beat Al Smith, and of course he won. But this did not seem to help him. He started to look like a man suffering from some terrible sickness. Gambling really is a disease. It becomes part of a man and takes over his life even if he's winning. And there's something else I learned very quickly about gambling. There is only one way to win—and that is not to play. Every player, even Arnie Rothstein, king of them all, loses in the end, whether it's the horses, craps, blackjack, roulette, or anything else. Only the house or the bank or the casino wins. That's why I gave up firsthand gambling at a very early age. I ran crap games and dice games, I set up gambling joints and casinos. I knew I would always win that way. And I knew I would not end up like Rothstein."

Despite the aid Rothstein's friends offered him, he continued on his reckless, self-destructive course. "He was only forty-six when I saw him last, but he looked like an old man, as if some great disaster had torn his life to pieces."

A few days later, on November 4, 1928, Rothstein was shot in his suite at the Park Central and was rushed to the hospital. He lived a few hours, but although the police pressed him hard to say who his murderers were, he refused to give any names. The secret went to the grave with him.

14 The Feud with Joseph Kennedy

Like any other businessmen, Meyer Lansky and Charlie Lucania needed office space, and about 1924 they leased a permanent suite in the elegant Claridge Hotel. Their operations had reached the level of a major concern, and their suppliers knew it.

"The Scottish distillers took full advantage of the demand for their product," Lansky says, "and they knew they were dealing with men who weren't in a legal business. Those fine upright men in Britain kept squeezing us for higher prices; they knew there was never enough booze coming in to meet the demand. If the so-called bootleggers like me are called criminals today, then those lords and other gentlemen from Scotland and Canada must be called the same thing. They took full advantage of Prohibition to line their pockets. I don't blame them, you understand. I'm sure I would have done the same. But we had to streamline our operations.

"To cut costs and increase efficiency, we chartered our own ships to bring the Scotch across the Atlantic. This meant a lot of administrative work—sending our own employees to Europe to organize the chartering and to hire the right kind of crews.

"I must say in all modesty that we ran things well, avoiding bureaucratic paperwork as much as possible and finding ways to simplify our dealings with the Europeans. They were surprised at the way we worked, but when you pay cash in advance as we did, people are usually happy to do it your way. When we turned up to do business over there we were treated like kings.

"By the middle twenties we were running the most efficient international shipping business in the world. Those guys in Europe told us so, too. We always hired the best brains. Importers, exporters, lawyers—we got them all for each branch of the business. I checked what they were doing and got them to change their ways to suit our business, to speed things up and avoid the red tape they were used to.

"Rothstein had the most remarkable brain. He understood business instinctively, and I'm sure if he had been a legitimate financier he would have been just as rich as he became with his gambling and the other rackets he ran. He could go right to the heart of any financial problem and resolve it unerringly. I tried to keep up with Rothstein in reducing every business or financial operation to its basics. I asked his advice, asked questions, read as much as I could, and introduced some methods I worked out on my own.

" 'Trust your memory,' I used to tell my employees. 'Keep your business in your hat. And if you want to work with us, make sure your memory doesn't let you or us down.' Sometimes people are tempted to cheat a little when they know you haven't got bits of paper to refer to, but I was very careful about this. If anybody did try to put one over on us, he was caught very soon.

"And we paid more than anyone else and paid in cash. It's remarkable how loyal people will be when you look after them as well as we did. We gave them incentives and rewards for good work. When they came up with useful proposals we praised them and lined their pockets too. If people involved with us had domestic problems, or anything else was bothering them, they could come to us any time. We'd help out with money, if it was needed, or sometimes by having one of our boys go and talk to whoever was causing the trouble."

As another good business tactic, Lansky and Lucania put aside their earlier hatred for the Irish. They made an alliance through Costello with Big Bill Dwyer, who had once worked on the docks in New York and, also seeing rather early that Prohibition could be profitable, had set up his own bootleg network.

But not all the Irish were allies. In 1927 there was an incident between two rival gangs that cost the lives of eleven men. A convoy of whiskey shipped in from Ireland to Boston was hijacked by a gang of men waiting along the roadside in southern New England. The guards resisted fiercely, and in the bloody battle nearly every one of them was killed or wounded. The gang that carried out the ambush was part of the Lansky-Lucania organization. They grabbed the liquor but they had bungled the operation, and the leader would have been punished severely if he had not died of his wounds.

According to Doc Stacher, the men from the Lower East Side found out later that Joseph Kennedy was involved in the shipment from Ireland, and they believed he knew who the hijackers were. Kennedy lost a fortune in the hijack, and for months afterward he was beset by pleas for financial help from the widows and relatives of the guards who were supposed to protect the cargo.

As Siegel said angrily when Lansky demanded an explanation for the bloodshed, "It really wasn't our fault. Those Irish idiots hire amateurs as guards."

Stacher explained the principle: "If there was a chance of getting out of an ambush, then of course you had to fight. But if you were outnumbered or outgunned, and in a position where you couldn't do anything about it, our soldiers were always told to run or surrender. We could get more whiskey, but blood and corpses lying all over the road meant police investigations and other problems. It wasn't always easy to hire good gunmen or guards, but we tried to preserve lives whenever possible." And Lansky had the same philosophy. The armed men who rode the convoys were there to warn off potential hijackers. They had orders to avoid shooting if possible. The most important consideration was to keep the business running smoothly.

Joseph Kennedy held his grudge, according to Stacher, and members of the Lower East Side outfit like Meyer Lansky and Joe Stacher were convinced, as they repeatedly told the authors, that he passed his hostility on to his sons. Like most underworld figures, they seemed to take the Kennedys' crime-busting attempts as personal attacks. "They were out to get us. They had a personal grudge."

Stacher added bitterly that when Joseph Kennedy was the American ambassador to Britain he advised President Roosevelt that the Nazis were going to win the Second World War. Certainly there is no doubt that Ambassador Kennedy was an unpopular ambassador in London in the days just before the war. His pro-German, anti-British approach won him few friends, although he did find some champions among the circle of aristocratic families who wanted to appease Hitler.

In Israel, long afterward, Stacher claimed: "A young FBI attorney told me bluntly one day, 'We're going to get you, Stacher, and your buddies like Meyer Lansky too.'"

Stacher got the message loud and clear, as he put it, and decided to get out of America. He told the authors: "The full weight of the American government is against me, and even if I were as innocent as a baby—which I am not—there's no point in fighting the administration. The Kennedy family is thirsting for my blood, and in such circumstances I decided there was no point in arguing."

15 Back to the Shmattes Business

Almost by accident and as a by-product of their lucrative bootlegging, the Lower East Siders diversified their business by getting into the New York garment trade. "I grew up knowing all about this business," Lansky says. "When I was a boy I got to know the slave trade, as we called it, only too well. In the middle of the nineteenth century, before the eastern European Jews arrived, it was the German Jews who were involved in making clothes. Most of the clothes used to be manufactured by hand, and among the immigrants there were thousands of cheap laborers, men, women, and children, who could be hired to make all these clothes.

"Garment industries grew up in other cities—Chicago, Boston, Philadelphia—all places where Jews settled. But New York was where the industry really boomed. Of course there were Irish and German workers too, but more and more the Jews, partly because of their tradition of being tailors, became the cheap laborers in the garment industry.

"In my early teens I used to see people working on fire escapes and in the streets, especially when it was hot. The men and women hunched over their machines morning, noon and night. They were always working, their machines whirring away. The grandfather and grandmother might do light work, like pressing the finished jackets or the pants or the women's clothes. The children helped their parents.

"Another reason why so many newcomers went into this business was that it required relatively little capital. All you needed

111

was a sewing machine you carried on your back. In a tenement I lived in as a boy, there was a flat that was always packed with people working over the tables and on the sewing machines. The noise and smell were terrible. I used to go past and feel the heat come out around the doors. There was virtually no light and no ventilation. The place was filthy. People used to eat over their machines, and the crumbs and other debris just lay there on the floor. The only toilet was very primitive, and it was a mess.

"People said that the contractors were just bosses, but it was hard for them too. They worked as hard as any of the people they employed. From day to day they never knew how many people they would need, and I remember people gathering in the Hester Street 'pig market' early in the morning, greenhorns and others. They would stand around waiting for the contractors, not knowing each morning who they were going to work for or how much work was available. You could buy anything in that market, from spectacles to old clothes to men and women who were looking for work. The only thing you couldn't buy was a pig."

Lansky added soberly: "Every time I go to New York I pay a visit to the corner of Greene Street and Washington Place. You can read the inscription on the wall of the New York University building that stands there now: 'On this site, 146 workers lost their lives in the Triangle Shirtwaist Company fire on March 25, 1911. Out of their martyrdom came new concepts of social responsibility and labor legislation that have helped make American working conditions the finest in the world.'

"I know exactly what that's all about. I know it by heart. The Triangle Shirtwaist Company was in a large building. The fire happened only a month before we landed. Everybody was still talking about it, and the parents were still mourning bitterly.

"Everybody had rushed to the fire, yelling, 'Triangle is burning! They're trapped inside!' Thousands of people ran there, and when they arrived there was the most terrible scene. The factory occupied three floors and employed Jewish and Italian girls, mostly teenagers. There were about six hundred of them. It had quite a good reputation as those places went, but now the six hundred girls were trapped. Some of them escaped down a stairway, and others climbed onto the roof. The problem was that the doors to the main stairway were locked and the elevators stopped functioning. Many girls were killed by the smoke as they sat next to their machines. And then the most horrible thing started happening. The girls crowded to the windows and to escape from the inferno coming up behind them they started jumping from the eighth, the ninth, and the tenth floors. They just jumped. And of course they all died as they hit the street. The firemen were there, and although they spread nets this didn't help. The girls' weight crashing down was too much for the nets to hold and they died on the ground all the same. The ladders the firemen brought were not tall enough and only reached up to about the fourth or fifth floor. The hoses weren't powerful enough to do the job and never even reached the fire.

"The girls' relatives were screaming as the flames grew worse and more and more jumped. The firemen were very brave but they could do nothing. Stores and houses nearby were turned into emergency hospitals, and the bodies were carried into rooms of some of the houses. Most of the dead, a hundred and forty-six, were young girls, although some men workers also died."

The Triangle disaster did not prevent New York from becoming the dynamic center of the garment industry. It was a volatile high-risk business, with fashions changing rapidly and competing manufacturers trying to guess what sort of clothes the public would buy. The old system of making clothes by hand was swept aside as a vast market for ready-made clothes, manufactured by the most modern machinery, was created.

A vital element in the manufacturers' competition was how to catch the eye of the buyers who flocked to New York at least twice a year from all over the United States. They came to purchase vast quantities of clothes for department stores, chain stores, and wholesalers who supplied both large and small retailers. The buyers exercised tremendous power, and the manufacturers spent liberally and frantically to sway or bribe them. It was good business to cater to the visiting men and women who held the order books. Whether it was sex, tickets for the best shows, or any other favors that might swing an order their way, the manufacturers were ready to oblige.

Naturally, the most glittering prize for the buyers during Prohibition was bottles or cases of whiskey—not the rotgut that almost anybody could buy in the local speakeasies, but the real stuff, brought all the way from the Highlands of Scotland. And it was here that Louis Buchalter, or Lepke—he got his name from the fond diminutive, "Lepkele," that his mother used—came up with his idea. The very fact that this member of the gang could actually think from time to time always surprised Lansky and Rothstein; Lepke's contributions were primarily ruthlessness, courage, and loyalty.

Even his greatest friends and admirers admitted that he was mostly a strong-arm with not much brain.

Still, it was Lepke who suggested, "Listen. We can get in big with the garment business by selling them whiskey at special rates. Only the ones that buy our protection will get this bonus, of course."

Both Lansky and Lucania were quick to appreciate Lepke's idea. They knew he was an expert on the way the garment industry was run.

"Lepke was the biggest name in the protection racket in the clothing world, though he used to be rather crude about how he handled it," Lansky said, remembering the days when he first came into contact with Lepke. "What he would do was approach some garment manufacturer and tell him that he must pay so many dollars a week, depending on the size of his business, for protection. When he was asked who they were being protected against, Lepke would look the clothing boss straight in the eyes and just say, 'Gangsters.' "

Unless the protection money was handed over, Lepke's friends would beat the manufacturer up, frighten his key workers, throw acid on his goods, or if necessary burn the place down. When the braver owners sought police protection, Lepke's mob had been known to settle the matter once and for all by planting a bomb on the premises.

Several clothing manufacturers were killed or badly maimed by Lepke and his hoodlums before he joined the ranks of Lansky and Lucania. The young co-leaders were opposed to unnecessary violence but allowed their various lieutenants to run their own businesses as they thought fit. As long as they accepted orders and paid a percentage of the take, they were given a free hand. Lucania in particular was determined not to operate in the fashion of the old "Moustache Petes," demanding total control over everything. As a businessman who delegated power, he was surrounded very quickly by underworld bosses who were only too happy to work under his protection. They appreciated the fact that he didn't always try to muscle in and dominate them. Yet in another way, as Lansky sees it, this proved to be his downfall when later on, in the 1930s, he was found guilty of carrying on a prostitution business. Lansky insists that Charlie had no control whatever over this vice trade and was unaware that some of his lieutenants were running brothels in his name.

At any rate, Lansky and Lucania saw at once that they would have to take Lepke in hand. In 1924, at their first "merger" meeting—held in the Claridge Hotel—they told the puzzled new-comer, "You're an idiot. We'll have to teach you to use your brains, not your trigger finger. This is the only condition we impose on you. A policy of a stick and carrot and a quiet word is far better than killing or beating up, and if you join us it will have to be on our terms."

And so they showed Buchalter that by wearing a suit and tie and calling on the manufacturers in a friendly way, cooperation could be far more quickly and efficiently achieved. "What these garment manufacturers want is money, that's the carrot. We can give them ready cash when they need it."

Lansky and Lucania knew that banks were reluctant to lend money to the garment industry, whose methods were regarded with suspicion and mistrust. Bankers were conservative and distrusted the modern mass-production methods the garment makers used. To keep up with the changing world of fashion the most up-to-date equipment had to be continually found and bought. Manufac-turers who wanted to keep ahead of their rivals had to find the money somewhere to pay for the new machines, frequently im-ported from Europe. Sometimes they had to design equipment themselves and then have it made. But all this meant an enormous outlay in instant capital.

Lepke was told to offer loans to the manufacturers, loans whose interest rates would naturally be higher than those available on the financial markets, but which would be much more easily obtained. The subject of protection was no longer mentioned when Lepke first called, and when a firm could not meet its interest payments on time, the influence of Lansky's thinking was apparent.

"We won't worry about the nonpayment of interest for a while," Lepke was told to say. "Don't worry," Lansky went on. "Our money will be repaid all right. We should offer to forget about the loan altogether and even give them back their interest if they've paid any. Instead we should suggest that we become silent partners in their business. You must explain that we will not interfere in the way they run the business. But we'll draw up proper legal documents giving us a share of the business with the profits divided up fairly. Louis, you must tell them: 'This way we will all benefit. With your knowledge of the industry and with our financing, nothing can keep us from growing. And when you need more capital you can always come back to us for fresh supplies. We'll give any request a sympathetic hearing.' "

If Lepke was not always able to express the terms as eloquently as they were explained slowly to him over several sessions, once he had grasped the new philosophy of how to run a racket in a modern way, he put it into operation most efficiently.

As far as Lansky and Lucania were concerned, the loan idea was not only an excellent way of generating new business and diversifying into a fresh field. It also solved one of their major problems: What was to be done with the vast cash profit they were raking in from Prohibition?

It could not be deposited in banks because that would arouse the curiosity of the tax authorities as well as the police. Money handed over in cash solved many problems for the organization as well as the clothing manufacturers. And the lack of receipts carried no risk. Any businessman who had ideas about making off with the money lent him by Lansky and Lucania, or claiming that he had never received it, was quickly made aware of the iron fist: the toughs who worked for Lepke, and if necessary others on the payroll, were given a free hand. After one or two unpleasant incidents in the garment industry, the message was heard all over this closed world where everyone knew everyone else. There were very few problems after that.

Lepke's hold over the garment industry spread rapidly. Now and again he ignored his new partners' orders to avoid violence and reverted to his old methods when confronting firms that did not want his loans. Here he employed the traditional Mafia-style protection violence to make sure that the recalcitrant manufacturer contributed something or other to "our business funds." He had learned this expression at Claridge's and thoroughly enjoyed using it at every opportunity thereafter. But in general Lepke used Lansky's sophisticated techniques quite successfully.

And Lepke's inspiration was a credit to the whole organization. Favored clients in the garment industry were sold cases of Scotch at cut rate. Some even got them free. The profits were so enormous that this generosity cost hardly anything. On the contrary, manufacturers who had somehow resisted both Lepke's soldiers and the offer of loans began to plead for their own supplies. They could not compete with rivals who had as much good whiskey as they wanted.

Naturally, when these manufacturers pleaded to be able to buy Scotch, Lansky drove a very hard bargain indeed, and the manufacturers had to accept it. Major orders often hinged on whether or not the buyer could go back to his home town with a case or two of good whiskey. Some of it remained in the hands of the buyer, but the bulk of it went to his bosses. There is no question that the success of many garment businesses in New York during Prohibition was due more to their generosity with Rothstein's Scotch than to the quality of their goods.

After Lansky and Lucania merged with Lepke and thus with the clothing industry, their fame spread through the underworld. Because the two young men operated in New York, they received the special notice of the traditional Sicilian-born "dons." The veterans strongly disapproved of the way Jews and Italians, including such despised Neapolitans as Vito Genovese, were becoming big names in the world of crime. They resented all these non-Sicilians becoming involved in the rackets which they had so long dominated themselves.

Until the time of Prohibition the Moustache Petes were not much troubled by the activities of the newer gangs. Lucania had only a few members in his organization and they were careful not to interfere with the rackets of the dons, who, for instance, had cornered the market on traditional Italian food like olive oil, artichokes, cheese, and other imported goods. They also controlled gambling in the Italian ghettos and they manufactured illicit alcohol on a small scale. Now these old-timers saw the younger Italian-Americans and their Jewish allies carving an increasingly large chunk from the profits on the sale of liquor, and also moving into their traditional fields of criminal activity. To them this meant war.

And war to the death it proved to be.

16 The Moustache Petes

As he stood outside the Intercontinental Hotel overlooking the Mount of Olives, with the walls of Jerusalem below, Lansky said thoughtfully, "When you see an old city like this, with its ruins and the excavations taking place, and you can pinpoint the exact site where David conquered the Old City of Jerusalem from the Jebusites thousands of years ago, you learn to appreciate things in a historical sense.

"I've seen history in the United States during my lifetime, and I'm thinking back now to the late 1920s and the early 30s, when what was known as the Castellammarese War occurred, called after Castellammare del Golfe, the town where Salvatore Maranzano was born. Several hundred gangsters and gunmen were killed in that war, in New York and other places. According to the newspapers, the public regarded this as simply a settling of scores between rival Mafia gangs. People shrugged their shoulders and said, 'So what? Let the hoodlums kill each other and the streets of our cities will be free of crime.' Men were shot in their homes and blasted in the streets of New York. Some were tortured very badly and their bodies dumped in the ocean or a river. Nobody really knows how many people died, but hundreds is probably a low estimate.

"In effect, this wasn't so much gang warfare as a historic moment in the life of America, certainly a turning point in the history of crime. Up to that time the old-style Mafia boss controlled Italian life. I grew up with the Italians. I got to know all about the Mafia and the tradition the Sicilians brought with them. I learned about it from the more educated Italians I became friendly with.

"In the old days, many centuries ago, the Mafia really meant a place of refuge in Sicily. The Sicilians don't forget how badly they were treated by the Romans—the same Romans who conquered Jerusalem used the Sicilians as slaves. Then it was the turn of the Christians. The Catholic church owned huge estates and the Sicilians were the exploited workers on their lands. When the great Muslim invasion of the Mediterranean took place, the Sicilians were freed, but after the victory of the Christians over the Arabs, new waves of invaders conquered Sicily and turned the peasants back into slaves. There were the Normans, the Byzantines, the Anjous, the Spaniards, and of course Italians like the Neapolitans.

"To defend themselves the Sicilians set up their 'Cosa Nostra,' what we call the Mafia today, to defend themselves. They had a code of honor—it was them against the rest of the world. They were Robin Hoods, robbing the rich to help the poor. They had the old traditions, including the famous *omerta*. Those were cruel times and the concept of the vendetta, people killing their enemies because of family feuds, became part of their tradition.

"My Sicilian friends have told me that Sicily was conquered something like sixteen times. Again and again they fought tyrants. They helped the famous Garibaldi when he set out to free Italy and unite the country. They fought against Mussolini because he was an Italian outsider.

"Like the Jews who came from eastern Europe, the Italians from Sicily and southern Italy brought their old traditions and attitudes with them. Whereas the Jews were frightened of authority because of the history of the ghettos, the Italians had only contempt for all forms of lawful authority and all forms of government. It was quite natural that the Sicilians formed Mafia organizations in America. The older generation quickly gained control of the waterfront in New York, and there it was like the old country—nobody in the Italian community could make a move without paying the money, the tribute. But the idea of helping the poor against the rich and the weak against the strong went wrong. The Mafia exploited their own kind. The Black Hand extortion gangs of the turn of the century made fellow Italians pay them money, and if they didn't hand over their miserable earnings somebody was tortured or killed.

"It used to make me laugh when the older Italians I knew spoke about the Mafia and its code of honor; the idea that the powerful were helping the poor was a bad joke. I used to tease my Italian friends about the Mafia. They were so honorable that no one in the

Mafia ever trusted anyone else. They lied to each other, cheated each other and killed each other. The crime in the Italian ghettos was in fact carried out by gangsters who called themselves Mafia but didn't even know what it meant. There were dozens of 'Mafia' gangs, not only in New York but in other American cities where the Italians settled, like Chicago. When I grew up I knew their leaders. They were people who had come from Italy and all the immigrants feared them.

"Prohibition changed all that. I would say that Prohibition was the biggest single factor that allowed really major crime to develop in the United States. When the sale of liquor was made illegal the old-time Mafia leaders reacted the way they always did, by looking inward. They forced the Italian families who had their little private stills to produce more liquor and to sell this poisonous moonshine in cheap speakeasies. It took a man like Arnold Rothstein to see the potential of bootlegging on a major scale. The old Mafia leaders didn't have the sophistication or the contacts, at first, to do the same thing. Later on they began to imitate us and import whiskey themselves. But they still depended mostly on bootleg liquor made in the United States. This was profitable but nothing like the money-making business of importing the stuff in quantity. They envied the people like Rothstein and tried to muscle in by hijacking our convoys.

"When that didn't work they decided to take over the younger men in the business, and that's how the Castellammarese War started. It was a clash between the old Mafia leaders and the young men like Charlie Lucania and the people who had grown up in America.

"The Moustache Petes lost out, the young men took over, and although they carry the name of Mafia to this very day, the situation was completely changed. Charlie Lucania had nothing to do with the old traditions of Sicily. Our Lower East Side group included Jews and mainland Italians, whom the Sicilians scorned. My friends were the sons of immigrants; young men who adopted new American styles and did away with most of the old customs, though sometimes they still paid lip service to them. Crime moved out of the small ghettos and became nationwide under the new leaders."

Whether he wanted to be or not, Meyer Lansky was dragged into the Mafia war because of his association with Charlie Lucania. The two most powerful Mafia leaders in the country, Salvatore

Maranzano and Giuseppe Masseria, both feared the growing power of the Lucania-Lansky organization and envied its profits.

Masseria, short, fat, earthy, tough-talking, and dangerous, suggested to Lucania that he join his own well-established organization. Masseria had hundreds of men ready to kill for him and he ruled part of New York with an iron fist, controlling gambling, prostitution, and drug peddling as well as the liquor made by the poor Italian families who paid homage to him. If Lucania joined him, he would have to ditch his Jewish associates. Masseria told Charlie he couldn't understand why a nice Sicilian boy would deal with Jews. This stipulation was no surprise to Lansky, who had already clashed with Joe the Boss. Salvatore Maranzano, a Sicilian who was the chief of the Castellammare clan, also wooed Lucania. Maranzano resented Masseria's power and wanted the title "boss of all the bosses" for himself. If Maranzano was more subtle in his approach than Joe the Boss, this was because he was a more sophisticated man. Well educated, he had traveled widely and claimed to be fluent in several languages.

Lucania reported all these moves to his partners, Lansky and Bugsy Siegel, and told them candidly that both men wanted him to get rid of his Jewish connections. It was clear to Lansky, as well as the other partners, that one day a war would break out, but the old-timers' organizations were vastly superior to theirs. The younger group decided to play for time and try to follow a policy of divide and rule.

Knowing the Sicilians, Lansky began to prepare for the inevitable conflict. He had to steer a delicate course, because if either Sicilian chief felt that Charlie was going to join the rival camp, neither would have the slightest compunction about killing the whole leadership of the younger outfit.

Both Masseria and Maranzano made tempting offers to Lucania. They promised him the role of first lieutenant in their organization, and as a further inducement he would share in profits from all their rackets.

Lansky warned his friend, "Once you accept such an offer you'll find yourself under their total control. Neither will hesitate to kill you the minute he thinks you've stepped out of line. Each of these guys wants to maintain his own empires and squeeze the life out of the other. You're the pawn in their game. Only it isn't a game. Our lives are at stake."

Bugsy Siegel was all for going to war immediately against one or the other or both at the same time. Lansky and Lucania said the moment was not yet ripe and patiently set out to build up their own organization, seeking new recruits and allies among the other young Italian and Jewish gangsters they made contact with in New York and other cities. Their major motivation was not trying to take control of the underworld but simply making money. Old-fashioned feuds wasted energy and resources that could be more profitably used in creating more wealth for themselves out of bootlegging, gambling, and their related rackets.

"We were in business like the Ford Motor Company," as Lansky puts it. "Shooting and killing was an inefficient way of doing business. Ford salesmen didn't shoot Chevrolet salesmen. They tried to outbid them. We had long ago decided to follow the same principles, to use guns or violence as infrequently as possible, or better still, never to use violence at all. Our friends who worked with us, our boys, were given strict orders to behave properly. They were not even supposed to wear loud clothes. We tried to keep them from fighting and showing off. When they drove the outfit cars, for instance, they had to keep clear of the cops by not committing traffic offenses. We tried to get them to be disciplined. We were very strict with our outfit."

Even so, the thieves and gunmen who were the soldiers of the gang could not be controlled that easily. They were not employees in an insurance office nor did they have the mentality of white-collar workers afraid of losing their jobs and pension rights. They were men with criminal mentalities who set up little sideshows of their own, carrying out robberies and stickups and running private rackets. As a result they frequently got into trouble. Lansky and Lucania made it an iron rule that they would never abandon any of their men, no matter how much they had disobeyed orders. Every effort was made to bail out a gang member who had gotten arrested, and a full-time staff of lawyers was kept on the payroll to insure that every known or invented legal device was available for even the most lowly member. Members who strayed were disciplined, but they were always given a chance to redeem themselves. They were not shot or tortured or beaten up as in the traditional Mafia outfit. Instead Lansky imposed a system of fines, which stung in a more practical fashion.

By 1924 the Lower East Siders began to feel increasing pressure from the two old dons. Both Sicilians pressured Lucania by increasing the number of hijacking attacks on the convoys. Tip-offs were given to federal Prohibition agents by Masseria's lieutenants. The Lucania-Lansky outfit took serious losses but they quickly rose to the challenge. They increased the number of armed guards on their convoys, and the leaders themselves went out to help protect the bigger shipments.

The younger group got the better of the exchanges and the hijacking attempts were abandoned. But at a council of war Lansky coldly warned, "We'll play for time, but it's not a question of which Sicilian we join, it's a question of both of them being eliminated. If they don't kill each other, we'll have to do the job ourselves."

Negotiations between Lucania and the two Sicilians dragged on by design. The old chiefs became so desperate to recruit him that they were finally prepared to let him keep his Jewish associates. Then spies in the enemy camp reported that Masseria's patience had finally run out, and that unless Charlie joined up immediately, the full might of the Sicilian's organization would be turned against his gang.

As a tactical move Lucania agreed to become Joe the Boss's henchman, but he stipulated that although he would share in the profits of the old Sicilian's rackets, the entire bootlegging empire remained his private concern, to be run by himself and Lansky.

Lucania took up his headquarters next door to Masseria's offices at the Hotel Pennsylvania. He streamlined the old man's organization, but his real work was done during the hours he met with Lansky and the other leaders of the Lower East Side outfit. The biggest problem was that they did not have enough guns to support them. Without advertising what he was doing, but taking full advantage of the friendships and business links he had developed through their bootleg operation, Lansky scurried around the country. He was assured of support from Al Capone in Chicago. In Philadelphia Waxey Gordon was still obliged to back him, and so was the emerging force there, Nig Rosen. Another Philadelphia bootlegger, Bitsy Bitz, did the same. In Detroit the Purple Gang, led by Jewish gangsters, also pledged support. The main bootlegger in Cleveland, Moe Dalitz, was also ready to side with Lansky.

Just after Lansky's trip, open warfare broke out between the Sicilians, as he had hoped. Several hoodlums on both sides were killed, and as the vendetta grew so did the violence. Lucania kept away from the firing line and his troops, under the firm command of Bugsy Siegel, kept off the streets.

As Lansky put it, "As long as they were killing each other they were doing our job for us." Lansky and Lucania knew they had to move very carefully indeed if they weren't to be caught in the crossfire between the two gangs.

"Divide and rule," said Lansky, and secret negotiations with Maranzano were begun. The plan was to pretend to throw in their lot with each of the warring Sicilians, at least until the dust settled and they could see who the winner was. This was a clever but dangerous plan. And it backfired—because of circumstances that neither Lansky nor Lucania had foreseen.

Lansky was planning to be married, and because his attention was distracted from the conflict, the entire leadership was nearly wiped out.

Meyer had known Anna Citron since childhood. His father and Moses Citron had been good friends, and for years the parents had hoped their two children would one day marry. Lucania frequently teased Meyer about his apparent lack of interest in girls, but it was not so much lack of interest as discretion. Even Lansky's closest friend, Bugsy Siegel, never knew the identity of Lansky's girl friends, either before or after marriage, though it was believed that he invariably chose Jewish girls because he had sworn at an early age to obey his mother's plea to go with girls of his own faith.

Lansky thought hard and long before proposing to Anna. She was an attractive girl, dark-haired and dark-eyed, but he could see from her mother's ample form that she too would probably be fat. But she had been brought up in a devout Jewish family and was an excellent cook. More important, her adoration of Meyer was total and unreserved. Moses Citron was troubled by the rumors that surrounded Meyer's name, but when the young man finally proposed to his daughter she was so happy that he did not have the heart to try to stop the marriage.

Meyer's prospective in-laws were surprised to discover that the man who was going to marry their daughter had never bothered to become a naturalized American. There were some raised eyebrows, and Meyer hastily explained that when he was nineteen he had in fact filed a Declaration of Intention to become naturalized. The document which proved this was numbered 100973 and stamped with the date August 9, 1921. On September 27, 1929, some eight months before his marriage, Meyer became a citizen of the United States in the U.S. District Court for the Eastern District of New York, and he proudly showed Anna his certificate, Number 2-517-814.

Deciding not to make unnecessary complications for himself so near the date of his wedding, particularly when his future father-in-law seemed to consider his naturalization so important, Lansky did not mention to the naturalization examiner that he had been in trouble with the police several times during his youth. His papers were marked with the notation NCR, no criminal record. He also listed his occupation as machinist, although in truth he had long since abandoned this profession for more lucrative fields.

Both these irregularities were to cause him immense problems in later years, when the FBI checked up on his past, and every pressure was being exerted on the Israeli government to have him sent back to the United States.

The first witness at Lansky's naturalization hearing, in 1929, was Irving Sandler, the son of Max Lansky's sister. The two boys had grown up together and Sandler, known as Tabbo, had been a founding member of the Lansky-Lucania outfit. The second witness was Jacob Klein, who worked at the time as a post office clerk. Klein was a cousin of Meyer Lansky's by marriage. He was later to tell investigators that Lansky had lived on Columbia Street and on South Third Street in Brooklyn in his youth. Klein agreed to be a witness when Lansky's father asked him to do so, and at the time he was not sure of Meyer's profession, believing him to be a "furrier" or a "machinist." (In 1926 Meyer Lansky had officially listed his occupation as that of a chauffeur.) It was no secret that Meyer was involved with running bootleg whiskey, but neither the Lanskys nor the Citrons had the faintest idea to what extent Meyer was connected with illegal enterprises. And as to bootlegging itself, Jews as a group had never been enthusiastic Drys. Drinking was not a major problem among them, and the traditional Passover wine was part of their religious celebration. There was not much social opprobrium attached to the "liquor supply profession," as Lansky has called it.

Both families made elaborate arrangements for the wedding, which was primarily a family affair. Charlie Lucania was the only outsider invited, and he fully appreciated the honor. The ceremony took place on May 9, 1929.

Lansky told his friends that just before the wedding Moses Citron had a long, serious talk with his prospective son-in-law, offering him a partnership in his own fairly successful business, called Kreig, Spector, and Citron, which dealt in produce on Monroe Street in the New Jersey port town of Hoboken. Meyer solemnly thanked his prospective father-in-law and agreed to accept a minor executive role. The salary of fifty dollars a week was more than adequate, he said.

After his marriage Lansky did spend a good deal of time working in his father-in-law's business. This was not merely to please his relieved father-in-law but because he realized that by having a proper front as a businessman he could more easily hide his other activities. He took some time out from the incipient war with the dons and brought his sharp business sense to bear on the company to such good effect that its affairs prospered as never before. The totally innocent father-in-law soon found that Meyer was setting up Jewish companies, such as the Lansky Food Company Inc., the Elaine Produce and Food Company, and, later on, a company intriguingly called Molaska, Inc., with the ostensible purpose of making powdered molasses as a sugar substitute.

Moses Citron and Meyer became close friends, despite the fact that Meyer and Anna early developed marital problems. The two men's friendship was to outlast the marriage. Possibly suspecting the type of business his son-in-law was engaged in, the father-in-law did not ask questions and preferred to turn a deaf ear to what his daughter must have hinted about business methods that involved absences in the middle of the night.

It was Anna's religious scruples—she was always sincerely devout—that caused problems for Meyer. She was an intelligent and law-abiding woman who married Lansky believing he was a machinist running an auto rental business in partnership with Siegel. It did not take her long to realize that her husband was going against the tenets of their religion by associating and working with gangsters. Charlie and Bugsy and other gang members came to visit the Lanskys, and Anna received them cordially at first. But when she realized these men were carrying revolvers and were known criminals, she refused to have them in her home. Meyer spent less and less time there himself, and more and more with his friends at their hotel headquarters and at their own homes.

Once in a rare moment of unburdening himself to Lucania as they dined with Doc Stacher on Mulberry Street, Meyer complained bitterly about the way his wife was interfering with his business. "Why can't she be like your Italian friends' wives?" he said. "They know their place, they stay at home and never question what their husbands are doing. Anna keeps asking me why I carry a gun and why I meet with Italians and why I don't work full time for the family firm." Charlie knew that in speaking about his personal problems Lansky was clearing his own mind. He offered no advice and Lansky sought none. He was a man who always thought out his problems alone and quietly, then he would announce his decision and nothing would ever make him go back on it.

Anna soon became pregnant, and during the early months, which were physically difficult for her, she and Meyer became close again. They both looked forward eagerly to the birth of their first child. Anna remained at home or visited her parents and for a while chose to ignore her husband's illegal activities. Meyer spent more time that he could really afford working for his father-in-law, hoping to please his wife and take some of the pressure off their marriage.

The Mafia war was at its height in 1929, and Lansky's inattention put his whole gang in danger. Bugsy Siegel was naturally the one who first took the bull by the horns. He warned his friend with the bluntness that was part of his personality: "Listen, Meyer, you're taking your eye off the ball, and you may be the world's greatest hitter but if you're not watching the ball we're going to lose the Series." Lansky understood the message, but he was desperate to keep his marriage going. He really did love Anna and he took the idea of fatherhood very seriously.

While Lansky was preoccupied at home, Lucania had to cope with a sudden crisis. Two Lansky-Lucania gunmen, Abraham "Bo" Weinberg and Charlie "the Bug" Workman, had infiltrated the top squad of killers surrounding Masseria with orders to turn their guns on Masseria if necessary. Suspecting something like this, Masseria sent them on a mission and then betrayed them to the police. They were both arrested, and Lucania, though this may have revealed his real intentions, had them freed through Frank Costello's influence.

Masseria then provoked a showdown with young Lucania. At a stormy meeting he demanded that Charlie get rid of all his Jewish connections once and for all, and also throw the bootlegging empire in with the other Masseria rackets, thus giving the Sicilian a share in its profits. Knowing this was a moment for decisive action, Lucania turned to Lansky, only to find his friend preoccupied with Anna's pregnancy, spending most of his time at home.

Almost daily there were shooting incidents as the gunmen of Maranzano and Masseria tracked each other and killed on orders. Masseria's gunmen struck a heavy blow against their rivals by murdering Gaspare Milazzo, a major crime figure in Detroit and a power in the Maranzano organization. As Lansky knew, this meant that it would be a fight to the finish, because Milazzo was a close childhood friend of Maranzano from Castellammare. Now Maranzano would take bloody revenge. He did not, however, as the newspapers reported, plan to send his man into the streets with guns blazing. Instead, as Lansky anticipated, he employed the cunning for which he was famous. He ordered his gunmen off the streets and began to make secret approaches to Masseria's lieutenants, promising them promotions and financial rewards if they joined him. He approached them one by one through emissaries, hoping to break his rival by pulling down the pillars that supported him.

One of the men thus approached was Tom Reina, who ran his own criminal organization in ie Bronx. Reina's second in command was Tommy Lucchese, ᴜ close friend of both Lucania and Lansky known as Three-Fingers Brown. It was through Lucchese that the Lower East Side men had a finger in the bootlegging in the Bronx. As Reina toyed with the idea of joining up with Maranzano, Lansky warned Charlie: "Lucchese and Reina have both signed their death warrants. They've both talked too much. Joe the Boss is going to know about the secret talks, and if Reina isn't on the death list already he soon will be."

In a desperate move to save Lucchese's life, Lucania reported to Joe Masseria that Tommy was his own spy in the opposite camp. This was the only thing that could save him, because Masseria had already ordered him killed too. There was a hasty meeting in Lucania's new headquarters, the Barbizon Plaza Hotel, and a unanimous decision that Masseria would have to be killed. How this could best be done had to be worked out.

Lansky came to the meeting but hurried home afterward. Anna had phoned in the middle of the meeting to tell him that she was having premature labor pains. White and trembling, Lansky rushed off, only to find that it was another false alarm. Anna was nearly hysterical these days. She couldn't bear to have her husband away from home.

Shortly after Lansky left, a message came from Maranzano demanding a meeting with Lucania. He insisted on an immediate conference and suggested that they meet on Staten Island. This island in New York Harbor was neutral territory, or so Lucania thought. A childhood friend of his named Joe Profaci controlled Staten Island, and although he worked for Maranzano he had secretly sworn loyalty to Lucania.

Convinced that he could trust Profaci to see that his interests were guarded, Lucania agreed to the meeting. He decided not to consult Lansky because of the rough time he was having at home. The only man who knew Lucania was going to meet with Maranzano was Vito Genovese, who was opposed to the get-together. Genovese tried to reach Lansky to warn him of what he thought was a trap, but he couldn't get Lansky on the phone. Following orders, Genovese drove Lucania to the Staten Island ferry late in the evening of October 17, 1929.

Many conflicting stories have been told about what happened to Lucania that October night. Some were invented by newspapermen and some were spread by Charlie and his friends. They had no wish then or even years afterward for the authorities to get an idea of what really happened. As Lansky tells it, however, Charlie did meet Maranzano that night in a deserted garage on Staten Island. Maranzano had decided to teach the young Sicilian a lesson for daring to become allied to his Sicilian rival. Lucania, through lack of experience, had underrated the cunning of the old fox. He had trusted Maranzano to be a man of honor and had arrived alone and unarmed.

For a while Maranzano spoke quietly, gently chiding Lucania for not following his original advice and joining him. Suddenly the door of the garage burst open and a dozen masked men surrounded Lucania. Maranzano got up from his seat and gave his orders: "Beat him. But I don't want him dead. I want him to be taught a lesson he'll never forget."

The experienced Maranzano hoodlums at once got to work on the young Sicilian and beat him to within an inch of his life. Lucania was strung up from a rafter by his thumbs and kicked and punched time and time again. As Lansky was told later, each time Lucania was knocked senseless a bucket of cold dirty water was thrown in his face.

Finally, after he regained consciousness for the third or fourth time, Maranzano came up to him and said, "Now listen, Charlie, I don't want you to ever forget what happened here tonight. I'm going to kill you unless you obey instructions from me from now on. You'll become my second in command. But first I want you to do one thing. You have to go and kill Masseria."

In great pain and knowing that he might have to pay for this with his life, Lucania spat in Maranzano's face and said, "Fuck you. So much for your Sicilian honor."

The enraged Maranzano took a knife from one of his henchmen and deliberately slashed Lucania's face from his right cheek up to just under his eye. It was a cut which was to leave Lucania with a scar he took to the grave. Maranzano then had the unconscious Lucania loaded into the back of his car and dumped on Huguenot Beach on the island. Driving along on nearby Hylan Boulevard, a patrol car found him late that night. The police took him to a hospital, and although at first he was thought to be dead, his life was saved.

Policemen stood by the bedside waiting for Lucania to recover consciousness—and name his would-be assassins. Charlie Lucania pretended to be dazed and gave several versions of what had happened, none of them the truth. In pain as he was, he kept his head and even then was planning revenge. Not believing any of the stories Lucania told them, the police threatened to book him for car theft. When he was told about the charge of grand larceny, Lucania smiled and solemnly said, "I'll send for my lawyer."

It was not until three o'clock on the morning of the 18th that word finally reached Lansky that his friend had gone to meet Maranzano. "That was one of the worst moments of my life," Lansky remembers. "If I'd been around, Charlie would never have gone on that lonely ride when Maranzano nearly killed him." Lansky's anger at Genovese for leaving Lucania alone with Maranzano marked the deepening of hostilities between the two men.

Afraid Lucania was dead, Lansky ordered every gang member to search for him and his killers, and later that day they discovered that Charlie was in the hospital. Thinking quickly, Lansky realized that having his men rampaging through the streets seeking revenge was a futile exercise. Bugsy Siegel wanted to go in with guns blazing and blast Maranzano and his whole gang, but Lansky ordered his and Lucania's troops to go home and do nothing until further orders. All of them, even Bugsy, obeyed and vanished from the streets.

None of Charlie's friends visited him in the hospital, knowing full well that his room would have a police guard. They waited for him to recover, and when he was brought home by ambulance they kept away a few days longer. When a council of war was finally held at the bedside, Lucania was still swathed in bandages. He told his friends that it had taken fifty-five stitches to sew him together again.

Lansky made one of his rare jokes: "From now on we're going to call you 'Lucky,' because you ought to be dead." The nickname stuck, and soon afterward Lucania changed his surname to Luciano to make it easier for his American associates and his society friends to pronounce.

After the beating Lansky figured out the real reason why Maranzano had not killed his friend Charlie: "Maranzano knows his own men would have a very hard time getting close enough to Joe Masseria to bump him off. They know you're supposed to be his assistant and they're sure you'll get the message and kill him for them. Beating you up was a warning and your life was saved only because Maranzano wants you to do his dirty work for him."

Luciano had worked this out for himself but hadn't mentioned it. He joked to Lansky, "You should have been born a Sicilian. You think as crooked as any one of us."

With a straight face Lansky retorted, "With my Jewish brains I'm just one ahead of you—you see I can look right around the Sicilian bends."

Although Lansky had rallied to Luciano's side, he was so busy with Anna in the later stages of her pregnancy that as Luciano recovered, Lansky virtually disappeared from active leadership. Bugsy Siegel took his place, and being a man of action said that it was time the group used its muscle—"But we must do it in an intelligent way." Orders were given to kill Tom Reina, who Tommy Lucchese reported was about to switch camps from Masseria to Maranzano. Bugsy Siegel was all for handling the matter himself, but it was decided that the killing had to be done by a Sicilian. Vito Genovese was chosen to make the hit, and on February 26, 1930, Reina was killed while visiting his aunt in the Bronx. As the police were later to report, Reina's head was blown off with a shotgun.

The plan was to stir up trouble between the two Mafia rivals, and it worked well. Maranzano thought the killing had been ordered by Masseria, and although Joe the Boss had no idea who had carried out the assassination he immediately fell into the trap of pretending that he had ordered it. He also appointed one of his friends, Joseph Pinzolo, the new boss of the Reina family's holdings. Although Reina had not had much say in the bootlegging business, he was very deep into other rackets, including control of the ice distribution trade. Refrigerators were not in common use and the sale of ice was an important industry in the area. Every delivery had been controlled by Reina and a fee was handed over to his men for such deliveries.

The Lower East Side outfit ordered Reina's old lieutenants like Tommy Lucchese to play along and accept Pinzolo's orders "for the time being."

Pinzolo was a close friend and would not betray Joe the Boss, but meantime secret negotiations should continue between Reina's logical heirs and Maranzano. Both Lucky and Lansky had made up their minds that they had to kill Masseria before they finally dealt with Maranzano.

Two Reina gunmen, Tom Gagliano and Dominic "the Gap" Petrilli, were then assigned to kill Pinzolo. The actual hit was made by Petrilli, who shot Pinzolo in his offices near Times Square. With Pinzolo out of the way, Tommy Lucchese and the other ex-Reina lieutenants resumed negotiations with Maranzano, arranging the transfer of allegiance and assets to him. Many of the negotiations took place at Peter Luger's, a famous steak house in Brooklyn, where both Luciano and Lansky often went too. Now, however, they kept away from Peter Luger's, not to disturb negotiations.

The net was closing in on Masseria. Again not using their Jewish gunmen, the Lower East Siders turned to Anastasia and Frank Scalise to gun down Peter Morello, Masseria's chief bodyguard. Morello was murdered in East Harlem and the message that went back to Masseria was that the killing had been carried out by Maranzano's men. Joe the Boss then began to hire outside killers to help him wipe out his enemy.

The war spread to Chicago, where Joseph Aiello, an enemy of Al Capone and a friend of Maranzano, was killed by Masseria's gunmen. The blame was placed on Capone, but he indignantly professed innocence. No one believed him, for he was fighting viciously on the Chicago front of the war.

One after another the gunmen of both Maranzano and Masseria were slain in the streets of New York, and what disturbed Lansky's men most of all was that the feuding was distracting them from their main business of making money, as well as drawing public attention to the underworld.

On January 15, 1930, Anna Lansky gave birth to the couple's first child. The boy, named Bernard, was found to be a cripple. Lansky's sorrow was compounded by the fact that his wife was still deeply disturbed and blamed him for calling down the wrath of God on them and their child. They had been punished for his wicked way of life.

The crisis nearly broke Lansky. He fled from his home and disappeared. When he heard of this, Lucky sent their friend Vincent Alo to find Lansky, and Alo tracked him down to a hideout they had used in the past in Boston. Alo's nickname was Jimmy Blue Eyes.

He had the knack of getting on with most people and being a good listener. Luciano knew that if he had sent Bugsy Siegel or if he himself had gone to try to console Lansky, neither would have had the patience to really help him.

For nearly a week Vincent Alo sat with Lansky as the grief-stricken "Little Man" struggled with his emotions, providing his friend with bottle after bottle of their own bootleg whiskey. Then after six days Lansky suddenly showered, shaved, had a meal, and went out to his car without a glance at his companion. He drove straight back to New York, with Jimmy Blue Eyes seated beside him, and resumed his life.

Lansky had surmounted the greatest personal crisis of his life. From then on he was even more taciturn and withdrawn than before, except with his closest friends. He kept his marriage going but now refused to listen to his wife's pleas that he change his way of living. He spent less and less time at home, and Anna devoted nearly all her time to her disabled son. She became almost totally immersed in caring for him. Lansky never mentioned his son to his friends and they tactfully never spoke about his family problems.

In any event, they had the inevitable gang showdown on their minds. At a key meeting on a fishing boat Costello owned in Oyster Bay, Long Island, the leaders made some crucial decisions. They agreed that Maranzano was getting the better of Joe the Boss, and Luciano coolly decided that he should pretend to throw in his lot with Maranzano in spite of his desire for quick revenge. Luciano and his troops had one priceless advantage: neither of the old Moustache Petes had the faintest idea just how powerful the Jewish section of the organization was. For this reason it was decided to keep Bugsy Siegel and his sharpshooters off the streets, ready to swing into action as a surprise element when required.

Lansky, however, refused to allow Luciano to meet Maranzano on his own and insisted that Siegel must attend the new merger meeting and not for a second leave Lucky's side. To avoid another double-cross the get-together was arranged at the Bronx Zoo. The two men, followed by their personal bodyguards, carried out their discussions as they walked around the zoo tossing peanuts to the monkeys. They finally shook hands on an agreement near the lion house.

Lucky was to become number two in the Maranzano organization. He had the right to retain his Jewish lieutenants and to share in all the spoils of the Sicilian's rackets. The one condition he must fulfill was to kill Masseria. Without a second's hesitation Luciano agreed to the stipulation.

Less than an hour later he was back with Masseria in one of Masseria's offices on lower Second Avenue, explaining how he had worked out a plan to wipe out the whole Maranzano hierarchy. It was April 15, 1931, a spring day, and to finish off the good day's work Luciano suggested they all drive out to Coney Island to celebrate the bloodbath about to be launched against Masseria's bitter enemy. Unknown to Joe the Boss, the restaurant—the Nuova Villa Tammaro, at 2715 West Fifteenth Street—belonged to one of Luciano's good friends, Gerardo Scarpato. As Luciano later told his Lower East Side friends, the Sicilian boss was plied with red wine and enormous servings of the specialties of the house. Masseria had always been a greedy eater, and as Luciano watched him bolting down his food and drinking what seemed gallons of the wine, he wondered whether Masseria might not kill himself first from overeating. For three hours Joe the Boss drank and swept the plates clean.

Finally, when all the other guests had left and even Masseria's appetite was beginning to fade, Luciano excused himself and went to the toilet. He locked himself in and sat down, as planned. One of the Lower East Side outfit's black cars, especially overhauled the day before by both Meyer and Lucky, drew up outside. In it were four gunmen, the four most trusted killers in the organization—Joe Adonis, Albert Anastasia, Vito Genovese, and, leading the squad, Bugsy Siegel.

As the four burst into the restaurant, Joe Masseria half rose to his feet, desperately looking for an escape route. Bugsy Siegel opened fire first, followed split seconds later by his three fellow assassins. Six bullets crashed into the body of "the Boss" and fourteen other bullets were embedded in the walls and floor of the restaurant.

Legend has it that just before he was killed, Joe the Boss was playing cards with Lucky, but Luciano always said this was simply not true. The only thing Masseria had in his hands was the tablecloth, which he pulled around him as he fell over in his chair, staining it with his blood.

The four gunmen ran for their car. Their driver, Ciro Terranova, was so nervous that he stalled the vehicle twice. Bugsy Siegel punched him and shoved him aside, then took the wheel himself and calmly drove off at high speed. The innocent Luciano pulled the chain on the toilet, emerged, and called the police. Lucky went into great detail about the stomach-ache that had kept him in the toilet. He had no idea whatever about the identity of the killers.

Next day there were roars of laughter as newspapermen delicately retold the story, avoiding Luciano's graphic description of how he had answered a call of nature. American readers learned that he had been washing his hands when the shooting took place.

Maranzano was delighted at the news. With his chief rival out of the way, he decided to organize a crowning ceremony, making himself Boss of all the Bosses, at a banquet hall on the Grand Concourse in the Bronx. This turned out to be the last manifestation of the old style of Mafia "emperor anointing," as Lansky calls it.

17 The Caesar of the Bronx

Lansky had read up on Julius Caesar, who was Maranzano's hero. He was sure Maranzano was going to crown himself emperor in the style of ancient Rome. But a spy planted as a servant in Maranzano's home reported that the new Mafia chief had books about the life of Charlemagne spread out on his study table, with passages underlined that described how Charlemagne had crowned himself Holy Roman Emperor in Rome. As Lansky joked to Lucky Luciano, "He's going to do the same thing in the Bronx, and you'll have to go down on your knees and pay homage to him like one of those obedient warriors." Luciano would play along with the farce—it would be foolish to disrupt the old man's game.

In the ceremony Maranzano, as expected, demanded and got the promise of total obedience from all those present. Lucky later told an amused Lansky, "He was there as you predicted, acting like an emperor. He told us he was the supreme ruler. He would give everybody their orders and in the future they would all have to accept his rule and share their profits with him. He set up five major families in New York. They aren't allowed to fight one another but each will run his own part of the city—all coming and kissing his ass from time to time." Luciano was appointed the head or capo of one of the five groups, and he was to take over the former Masseria domain. Tom Gagliano was head of another family. Joe Bonanno, Joe Profaci, and Vincent Mangano were to be the other New York bosses.

"He got the setup from the way Caesar ran the Roman legions.

Each commander has a second in command and then there's another range of bosses under him and a man in charge of ordinary legionnaires arranged in groups of ten, just like Caesar did with his legions," Luciano reported. "The whole place was decorated with the most amazing display of crosses, virgins, and pictures of saints. I didn't know there were so many saints.

"The only thing missing was a crown. I looked everywhere for it. But his chair was bigger than everyone else's and he sat on it like a throne. He gave us a long lecture and talked for what seemed like hours about Julius Caesar and stuff like that. He even had the nerve to pat me on the head when he asked me to come and sit next to him as his chief lieutenant." Naturally, neither Bugsy Siegel nor Lansky was allowed to witness the ceremony. Non-Sicilian Italians were admitted but made to feel second best.

It was from this grandiose meeting, at which strict rules were laid down, that the legends of the modern Mafia or Cosa Nostra grew. Each participant had to swear not to talk about the organization even to his wife or children; to obey without question all orders of his leaders; and not to attack any other member no matter how much he was provoked. All past grievances had to be forgiven and a total amnesty for past deeds enforced. They were all to work together harmoniously and—a fine touch of traditional Sicilian honor—nobody was allowed to eye any other man's wife or woo his daughter unless accompanied by a suitable chaperone. None of the younger men in the hall took seriously what they called "that Sicilian mumbo-jumbo crap." They were nonetheless compelled to follow the tradition of coming up to Maranzano and giving him an envelope with hard cash inside as a symbol of their loyalty. At that one meeting Maranzano raked in more than a million dollars from his acquiescent audience. Few people in the room, however, had the faintest illusion that the new setup would last very long. Most were uninterested in the panoply of power and its meaningless traditions as Maranzano explained them.

As he sat beside the new "chief of all chiefs," Luciano himself was busy figuring out how to destroy him and take his place. Quite as much as Lansky, he considered the crowning ceremony a temporary aberration to be forgotten when the moment was right.

Like two generals before a major campaign, Luciano and Meyer Lansky spent the weeks after Masseria's death planning the downfall of Maranzano. More spies were planted. Every available detail of Maranzano's life, including his early training for priesthood, the list of languages he knew, his girl friends, his eating habits, and the names of his bodyguards, was carefully listed. As the chief crime figure in the country now, Maranzano had to be taken even more seriously.

At dinner one evening in Ratner's restaurant on Delancey Street, Lansky told Luciano, "He's punch drunk. I think he really believes he's Julius Caesar or Charlemagne. He's making one major mistake—he's underestimating us." Luciano hardly needed Lansky to tell him that Maranzano had got so full of his own importance that he genuinely believed Lucky had forgiven the beating.

With trusted bodyguards Lansky toured the country again, seeking support. Siegel was with him, and both asked for the help or at least neutrality of their Jewish colleagues when the showdown with Maranzano came. At the same time Luciano sought alliances with Italians and Sicilians who didn't care for Maranzano. In Pittsburgh they were promised the allegiance of Salvatore Calderone, a Sicilian who ran his own show in western Pennsylvania. In Cleveland John Scalise and Moe Dalitz threw in their lot with Lucky and Lansky; and Frankie Milano, the Ohio Mafia leader, promised to join them. Santos Trafficante gave his support from Florida, and so did Capone from Chicago.

Maranzano was apparently so arrogant now that he neglected the elementary intelligence operation of checking up on Lansky and Luciano. He felt that after the terrible beating Luciano would cower forever; and he was totally ignorant of the power of Meyer Lansky, Bugsy Siegel, and their nationwide army. But soon Lansky and Luciano, seeing the tide running in their favor, became overconfident and spoke too openly about their plans to wipe out Maranzano and his loyalists. Word got back to Maranzano and the wily old man decided to strike first.

The first inkling the younger men had of what Maranzano was planning came from one of Lansky's friends in Philadelphia, Nig Rosen. Again Maranzano was ignoring the strength of the Jewish part of the underworld, the Lower East Siders' secret weapon.

Nig Rosen had been suspicious when his lieutenants in Philadelphia reported that one of Maranzano's lieutenants, a man called Angie Caruso, was in town. He saw to it that a tall blond dancer was introduced to the impressionable Caruso, and that night in bed Angie bragged to her about his forthcoming role in a master plot that would net him thirty thousand dollars. The girl laughed at him, and as Caruso tried to persuade her to go off with him to South America she taunted him: "You're just a big talker, a guy from New York who thinks he's fooling around with a hick." Caruso had eaten and drunk too well, and to prove his point and demonstrate his importance he explained that he himself was going to kill two men in New York, one of them Vito Genovese. The dancer persuaded Angie to give her more details, and when she reported the conversation to Rosen he realized that Maranzano had drawn up a death list.

Several days later one of the spies in Maranzano's household staff confirmed that Luciano and his friends were all due for execution. The spy produced a complete list, and to the surprise of the Lower East Side leaders, not a single Jewish name was on it, not even that of Bugsy Siegel, who was well known in New York as a killer. If confirmation was needed that Maranzano had completely neglected the powerful muscle of the Jewish part of the gang, here it was.

It was clearly a race against time. Who would kill first, Maranzano or Luciano? Lansky and Luciano were convinced that they could strike first. They had so many spies in the old Sicilian's organization and had bribed so many of his palace guards, the gunmen who would be sent out against them, that they became overconfident again.

Maranzano outwitted Luciano and Lansky for a time by the simple expedient of hiring freelance killers to carry out his executions. One of them, a lone wolf called Mad Dog Vincent Coll, was ready to kill Italians, Jews, or anyone else if the price was right. Coll came back to New York from Chicago to work for Maranzano, with the chief assignment of killing Luciano. Meantime the old boss surrounded himself night and day with his most trusted bodyguards, changing his movements frequently, switching his headquarters and using tasters for everything he ate. His home was a fortress surrounded by dozens of his soldiers. A squad of men traveled in his own car and a fleet of vehicles drove ahead and behind when he moved around the city. Still self-confident, Maranzano now opened elegant offices at 230 Park Avenue, where he conducted his legitimate businesses, an import-export concern and a real-estate company called the Eagle Building Corporation. These two operations were run quite legally; Maranzano paid taxes on them and employed accountants to make sure no mistakes were made.

Before Maranzano's hit list could be acted upon, Meyer Lansky and Lucky Luciano put their plan into operation, a plan to liquidate the only man who now stood between them and total domination of the underworld. The plan they made in the summer of 1931 was based on Maranzano's Achilles heel, his anti-Semitism. The last thing he would expect would be getting shot by Jewish gunmen. His bodyguards had been used to facing only Italian or Sicilian rivals for so long that they wouldn't dream of outsiders getting at their boss, and there were Jewish gunmen available, Lansky's undercover reserves, whose faces were totally unfamiliar to Maranzano or his men.

The head of the commando group was Lansky's trusted chief driver, Red Levine. He and four other men were kept isolated in a house in the Bronx, and Bugsy Siegel rehearsed them in the killing until each one was letter perfect in his part. Siegel had decided that the murder would take place in Maranzano's new office on Park Avenue, which he was very proud of. The spies had reported that he loved to strut around from window to window and gaze down at the traffic below. That would be the place he would least expect his enemies.

Internal Revenue agents, genuine ones, called at Maranzano's offices from time to time to examine his books, and the Mafia capo would produce his records and proudly show them that all was aboveboard. He didn't know it was Lansky's brother Jake who had tipped off the government men that they could find irregularities. The Internal Revenue men had so far found nothing amiss, but because of these investigations there was no great surprise when four men knocked at Maranzano's office doors on September 10, 1931, identified themselves as federal agents, and demanded to see the books.

They were let in promptly, and the unsuspecting staff—including Maranzano's bodyguards—were facing revolvers. They had no choice but to raise their arms and let themselves be disarmed and tied up. Then the killers stabbed Maranzano again and again before finally putting him out of his agony by firing six shots into his heart.

After this display, Maranzano's staff at once offered their allegiance to their boss's killers, showing no remorse about their change of loyalty. The only man who swore vengeance was the killer Vincent Coll. He sent out a message that he would gun down Bugsy Siegel, Red Levine, and the other four men who had killed Maranzano.

It was a rash act. Less than six months later, Coll was killed while making a call in a Manhattan telephone booth. The man who tracked him down and got the drop on him was Bugsy Siegel, who had decided to pick up the challenge despite requests from his friends that he leave this work to underlings and to Dutch Schultz's boys.

Maranzano's murder was a public sensation, and there were lurid newspaper stories about gang warfare in which scores of Sicilians and Italians died on the same day as Maranzano. Yet as Bugsy Siegel well knew, only one man had died that day. By cultivating allies in advance and then cutting off the head of the serpent, the young men from the Lower East Side had insured that the other crime chieftains, not only in New York but in other cities, would immediately switch their allegiance.

True to old-style Mafia traditions, Maranzano was given an extravagant funeral, with enormous wreaths of flowers and a full complement of the largest black limousines that could be hired. Lucky Luciano and his Italian friends followed the hearse to the graveside. Out of delicacy the Jewish contingent stayed away from the proceedings. They were perhaps not as moving as those for Charlemagne or Julius Caesar, but it was the best the mob could do.

18 Under New Management

By late 1931, with the last of the old-time Mafia leaders gone, thirty-four-year-old Lucky Luciano, with Lansky at his shoulder, stood at the pinnacle of organized crime in the United States. The two young men from the Lower East Side were determined to stop what Lansky, then aged twenty-nine, was already calling "the wasteful wars between jealous Sicilians and Italians." They had learned that there was an immense fortune to be made from crime, and that to become rich and powerful did not require the use of indiscriminate violence. Bootlegging, gambling, and moneylending-protection could be run with rewards, threats, and bribes; these methods would draw less attention from the public and the authorities.

With their bodyguards, Lansky and Luciano toured the country, visiting each gangland chief in turn and spelling out the new way of thinking. There was to be no new capo di tutti capi. Every underworld leader would run his own empire any way he wanted to. There would, however, be coordination among them. It didn't matter much to Luciano and Lansky what the organization was called. As they told Doc Stacher, "What difference does it make? Whether it's the Mafia, the Cosa Nostra, the Unione Siciliano, or the Kosher Connection just isn't important. The names mean nothing to us. What we want to do is get on with the business."

When the two men went to Chicago they reluctantly agreed to appear at a large meeting given in their honor by Al Capone. An old and trusted ally, the Chicago hoodlum was nearing the end of his reign and was soon to go to prison for income tax evasion. To show off his power to his New York friends, Capone reserved the best rooms in leading hotels like the Congress and the Blackstone for his gangster friends from New York and elsewhere.

If ever there was a truly representative meeting of American criminal leaders, this was it. In Chicago in the fall of 1931 there were, of course, the traditional Sicilian chiefs who turned up, but what was new was that the meeting hall contained many men who had grown up in the United States. Men like Bugsy Siegel, Dalitz, and Dutch Schultz mingled easily with Irish Catholics and others whose origins were not so obvious. Later on, blacks and Spanish-speaking criminals from Puerto Rico and Latin America were to take their place in the American underworld, but in 1931 the leaders were white-skinned sons of Europeans who had settled in the United States.

Because of the difference in temperament it was Charlie Luciano who took the spotlight, but discerning members of the audience noticed that Meyer Lansky was never far away from him. As Bugsy Siegel once said to Stacher, "They were more than brothers, they were like lovers, Charlie Luciano and Meyer, although of course there was nothing sexual between them. They would just look at each other and you would know that a few minutes later one would say what the other was thinking. I never heard them argue. I never heard them quarrel. They were always in agreement with each other. Charlie was tough and ruthless in an open way. Meyer was just as tough, just as ruthless, but he never showed it. Charlie was the brains of the organization and he knew how to handle the gunmen and the soldiers who worked for us. Lansky was the financial genius and could keep in his head how to move from one business to another, what to do with the money and where the future prospects lay. They were an unbeatable team. I often quarreled with both of them, but I always knew that they would prove to me in the end that I was wrong. You couldn't beat them. Nobody could have. I suppose if they had wanted to they could have conquered the whole of the United States, starting anywhere they wanted to. If they had become President and Vice-President of the United States, they would have run the place far better than the idiot politicians that did it."

It was Luciano's job to spell out the philosophy of the Lower East Side to the underworld figures who had come from all over the United States. Lucky refused the offers to accept money in sealed envelopes, as Mafia tradition laid down. "He just told the men gathered there, and there were hundreds of them, that the old Mafia traditions were fine for Sicily but not for the United States," said Doc Stacher, who was at the gathering. " 'Talking about putting a crown on my head is kid stuff,' he told them. 'It's time we grew up.'

"Some of the older men didn't like that kind of talk. They thought it disrespectful. But the majority of them liked it fine.

"Luciano told them that we had to use modern methods to 'earn a nice living.' That's how he put it. That speech got him a lot of cheers. 'We'll all work for each other, but everybody running his own outfit,' said Lucky. 'We all need each other. And enough of killing. Let's use our brains instead of our guns.' It was the same kind of speech I always heard Meyer make, only Lucky was speaking as one of the boys.

"Lucky even said it would be better, more democratic, if the ordinary guys in the outfits had more say. 'Everybody must feel that he belongs and everybody must have a chance to speak,' he said. 'It's O.K. to give orders, but the smallest man in every outfit should always be given a chance to talk to the boss if he has a grievance.' "

Living up to his new status, as well as his gay-blade temperament, Charlie Luciano moved into the privately run Waldorf Towers section of the Waldorf Astoria Hotel, on Park Avenue. He lived there as Charles Ross, holding meetings with his lieutenants from time to time. Meyer Lansky did not like calling at this famous hotel, full of celebrities from all over the world, and when the two men had business to discuss they would meet either at the home of Frank Costello on Central Park West or in one of their favorite Italian or Jewish restaurants. They went to Miller's Delicatessen and to Lucky's favorite spots in Little Italy. And they met often after their power was consolidated. Besides day-to-day business, they were planning for the future. They expected Prohibition to end with the next presidential administration.

The cornerstone of the Lower East Side outfit's present success had been laid in 1929, when Lansky left his puzzled bride to attend a conference of underworld figures in Atlantic City only a week or two after his marriage. So many men attended this gathering that they took over two hotels, the Ritz and the Ambassador. It was here that the "Kosher Connection" or the "Group of Seven" was set up in a somewhat formal way. There were more than seven men who worked out future strategy concerning the coordination of bootlegging, and they were not all Jews, but the names stuck. This meeting was the basis for all their future expansion.

The participants at Atlantic City were mainly bootlegging chiefs, and they represented the new brand of criminals. Men like Maranzano and Masseria had not even been invited, something which offended them deeply. Waxey Gordon and Nig Rosen were there from Philadelphia. Moe Dalitz came from Cleveland and so did his cohorts, Lou Rothkopf and a man named Leo Berkowitz, who preferred to be called Charlie Polizzi. Also present was "King" Solomon from Boston, a man almost as noted for clashes with Meyer Lansky as Gordon was. Three years later Solomon was murdered in his own Cotton Club, by an unidentified killer. The Detroit Purple Gang, ruled by Abe Bernstein, was also represented. Longie Zwillman and Dutch Schultz were present, of course, along with Al Capone; Willie Moretti, from New Jersey; and, from New York, Albert Anastasia, Frank Costello, Ace Mangano, and Frank Scalise.

A lot of time was devoted to social gatherings and huge meals. But the real business was done away from the hotels as the men strolled along the beach. They agreed to keep in touch to insure a good supply of liquor across the country and its more efficient distribution for the benefit of all. Lansky's other favorite topic of conversation was how to increase the return from their gambling interests. Lansky and Luciano missed their mentor Arnold Rothstein, who had just been killed in New York. Both men accepted Frank Erickson, who had been Rothstein's right-hand man.

Erickson had concentrated on bookmaking in New York, in partnership with Frank Costello. This had developed so successfully that it too was extremely profitable for the Lower East Side leaders. In Atlantic City, Erickson came up with the idea of turning his local bookmaking business into a national one. In partnership with Moses Annenberg from Chicago, a country-wide wire service for bettors was organized which enabled bookmakers to synchronize their activities and lay off big bets across the United States. From this grew the underworld's massive investments in race tracks and in betting on other sports.

Now Meyer Lansky was able to devote the bulk of his time to the great passion of his life, gambling.

"People all over the world in all periods of history have had two great passions—besides the normal one for sex," Lansky told Uri

Dan. "One passion is wanting to drink alcohol and the other is to try one's luck at gambling. I know you Israelis don't have gambling, but it's true all the same. My childhood sent me toward the second passion."

The Lower East Siders turned their minds to making money out of another kind of gambling which went on in poorer parts of New York. Street betting flourished everywhere even though it was illegal. Lansky and Luciano decided to organize this business on a "proper basis" but with Erickson still in charge. Many store owners were in the habit of taking bets from their customers and passing the stake on to runners who would take the bets to bookmakers in the district. It was a hazardous sideline, because the shopkeepers never knew when they were likely to be caught and arrested. And although they got a cut from each bet, the income from week to week for the shopkeepers was uncertain.

It was Lansky who came up with an idea that was soon to make the Lower East Side outfit the unchallenged kings of bookmaking in the Jewish and Italian slum areas, and a man who remembers it clearly is the old peddler on the Lower East Side. "It happened in my youth and I remember it because it changed the lives of so many poor people. I knew Meyer Lansky was behind it. Everybody knew that. Who else had the brains to think up such an idea?

"What happened was that his men went around to hundreds of small shopkeepers—bakers and grocers, delicatessens and candy stores—all those that had a cash business. The shopkeepers were given a salary, a hundred and fifty dollars a week. That was a lot of money in those days, I can tell you that. They would get their pay every Friday about lunchtime all year round, and I remember that Fridays became the happiest day of the whole week for many people.

"All the shopkeeper had to do was accept his customer's bet and then pick up the telephone and call it in. Meyer's boys installed the phones at their own expense. And on top of that, the cops who used to raid the stores whenever they felt like it, to check up if betting was taking place, all kept away. They were bribed—in other words this was what they call a protected racket. Meyer's men removed the danger for the shopkeepers. They didn't have to worry about being arrested. Of course they didn't have a percentage of the bet any more, the way they did in the old days, and they had to pay their own phone bills. But they had phones installed free for nothing and they were guaranteed a steady income. Some people used to make more than a hundred and fifty dollars a week the old way, but it was very uncertain and they were glad to settle for security.

"It was a popular system that Lansky's men introduced. People would beg the collectors to choose them to handle the business. That extra hundred and fifty a week made a big difference to a lot of people who lived here. Being a small shopkeeper was no great honor—you worked long and hard for very little profit. The betting money used to buy extra things. Parents would save up the money to pay for their sons and daughters to go to college to become doctors and lawyers and teachers. Sometimes they would use some of the money for vacations or nice clothes. Nobody ever saw any harm in gambling, nobody ever understood why it was such a crime. If you're rich and have the time and money to bet at the race track, it's all legal. So if the rich could do it, why not the poor? Why were we discriminated against?"

It was not always possible to install telephones, and runners were still needed by the men operating the bookmaking business. Lansky and Luciano turned to the peddlers who used to tramp up and down the stairs of the Lower East Side tenements and along the grimy streets selling their wares from door to door. These peddlers had long been part of the colorful parade which was the street life of the Lower East Side. They sold everything from tin mugs to secondhand clothes to combs, vegetables, and any other merchandise they could possibly carry. They were the poorest of the poor, poorer than the street peddlers, who might at least own their own carts. Profits were minuscule; most housewives would slam their door in the face of a peddler trying to sell his cheap and frequently shoddy goods.

Now the peddlers were recruited by gang members to carry betting slips from individuals to bookmakers. They were glad to earn an extra income as they made their weary rounds, and their trade was perfect for these errands. It was nearly impossible for even the most zealous policeman to keep track of them. The outfit also recruited the men who peddled ices in the summer, walking the streets with little handcarts selling flavored drinks cooled with chunks of ice. Moving from street to street, they gathered in the bets.

The gambling network also spread into upper Manhattan and other boroughs of New York. Before a move into a new area was made, the first step was to approach the local police and arrange a proper scale of bribe money to be handed over each week in cash—always on time and always as prearranged, because the Lansky-Luciano gang valued their reputation of keeping their word and paying on the dot. Very soon there were hundreds of these police-protected "hand books" under Lansky's and Luciano's control. At the same time they also owned or had a share in bookmaking "banks," where individual bookies—both hired and independent—could lay off bets when too much money was being offered for a particularly favored horse. The risk of a major loss if too many people backed a winner was avoided by sharing it out.

Lansky and Luciano themselves left nothing to chance. The offer of a hundred and fifty dollars a week to the shopkeepers seemed generous, but in reality this figure had been carefully calculated with the aid of Arnold Rothstein's arithmetical genius. By averaging out losses and gains over a trial period of several weeks, they knew precisely what their profits would amount to, taking into account all expenses—including wages, telephones, payoffs to police, and renting premises for the bookmakers. They also hired bookkeepers and accountants to keep track of the money, and Lansky, Stacher, and their friends made quite sure these employees never cheated them.

Within a year the bookmaking business was grossing millions of dollars a month, and with the constant flow of cash that their small-time betting was producing for them, the Lower East Side outfit moved on to high society, which also liked to gamble on the horses.

As Lansky explained, "A lot of wealthy people didn't want the bother of going to the track or maybe didn't have the time. So we provided nice premises where they could come and relax and bet as much as they liked. We called these places horse parlors. It cost us a great deal of money to have them decorated. We made these establishments the finest in America. We bought the best furniture, so the society ladies would be comfortable, and the atmosphere was like a living room in a rich house. We provided good food and installed telephones and loud-speakers. We even had some of the places painted and decorated to look like a race track, with fancy pictures of horses, and we installed betting windows, just the way you see them at a race track. And we made sure everything was legitimate. We never cheated the customers—we didn't have to. The minute the results of each race were known, the management would put up the winning names on a board or announce them over a loud-speaker. We gave the same odds as the tracks. We always had an excellent reputation, so people trusted us and invited their friends and relatives. There was no limit to what they could bet, and that meant there was no limit to the amount of money we made. Because bookmakers never lose. Just the suckers who bet on the horses."

What helped make the horse parlors especially popular was the good bootleg Scotch. Regular customers were served free; occasional customers got reasonable prices.

At the same time they set up their elegant horse parlors the Lower East Side outfit decided to open their own speakeasies. Selling direct to the customers and avoiding the middleman multiplied the profits. In addition, the Lansky and Luciano speakeasies had miniature casinos fitted out with roulette and crap tables as well as slot machines. These very superior speakeasies were immediately popular, not only in New York but in outlying districts as well.

By the middle twenties the financial rewards of crime were enormous for the Lansky-Luciano group. They had lost nothing by concentrating on the more socially acceptable activities of bootlegging and gambling, and their public reputations were not as notorious as those of the traditional Mafia criminals who were known for prostitution and drug running. Neither Lansky nor anyone else involved in these activities has ever been specific about profit figures during the Roaring Twenties. Their reticence is understandable. They did not pay taxes on the vast capital they accumulated. It is true that they did make out tax returns, but the figures were a joke; they described themselves as chauffeurs, taxi drivers, or traders, with front businesses whose books were immaculately kept and always available for inspection. Lansky and Siegel, for example, were partners in a "car rental agency." Even these "legal" operations showed reasonable profits, but of course the vast bulk of their private fortune was stashed in other companies through a financial maze that was virtually impenetrable.

Later, when they became more sophisticated, the Lower East Side leaders would open Swiss bank accounts, but in the 1920s this was not thought of. Financial experts and government officials have calculated that men like Luciano and Lansky must have been making four or five million dollars a year each from their bootlegging operations, and this was in addition to their share of the take from other forms of crime that their partners and lieutenants managed on their own initiative, which included prostitution and drug running.

With the success of the bookmaking and horse parlor networks assured, it was time for another expansion. What of the people who could not afford to visit a horse parlor or did not have enough know-how to place a bet with the local bookmaker? Lansky hit on the idea of helping those who could not afford to bet more than a few cents at a time to enjoy the thrill of trying to get rich quick, and to enjoy it every day of their lives, not just when the horses were running.

From this idea, breathtaking in its simplicity, came the pervasive, popular, and apparently ineradicable numbers racket.

"I used to bet myself," said the Lower East Side peddler. "Every day there would be a lucky number. It had three digits from 000 to 999. They would always tell you in advance where they would get the numbers. For instance one day they would say that the numbers of the horses that would win certain races would be the combination. Or it would be the score of a football or baseball game, or maybe the closing stock exchange index for the day. The number was always something you could check yourself and nobody could know in advance. You knew that the thing wasn't crooked and that everybody had a fair chance.

"You could bet just a dime or a quarter or even a penny, so what did you have to lose? If you had the good luck to pick all three numbers in the right order you got back six hundred times the amount you bet. That was a very tempting proposition, not only for me but for everybody else I knew. Housewives and kids used to bet their pennies or dimes or quarters. There was always a chance of making a fortune."

The numbers racket was first tried out in Harlem as early as 1925. The blacks who had begun to populate the upper part of Manhattan were mostly very poor and the white gangs did not consider them smart enough to begin to understand how remote the chances of winning were. The old-style Mafia bosses sneered at the "penny gambling" Lansky instituted with the enthusiastic cooperation of his partners—particularly Frank Costello, who for many years was to run Harlem like a Roman consul. But the old dons' smiles were soon wiped off as virtually every man, woman, and child in Harlem became a numbers addict, betting every day. True, it was only pennies at a time, but the money poured in. And although the odds of six hundred to one sounded fantastic to the bettors, the real odds of a thousand to one meant vast profits for the promoters of the scheme.

Acting quickly, to keep imitators from getting a foothold, the Lower East Side outfit spread the numbers operations—or as they came to call it, "policy"—to other areas of New York and on across the country. Special policy banks were set up to deal with the huge number of bettors and the cascades of money. Everyone in the two-to-three-hundred-member outfit was given a share in the profits and was expected to take an active role in running the organization in his territory and to hire his own aides for the menial work. Thousands of people were hired to keep the numbers racket working efficiently, and in the 1920s and especially the 30s, during the Great Depression, most of them needed the job. As usual, everybody was paid promptly and in cash.

19 Playing Politics

Unlike most Americans, Meyer Lansky found 1932 a very good year. Lansky's second son, Paul, was born in September 1932. The news from the doctors that the boy was physically all right made him very happy. His first son, Bernard—called Buddy—was permanently crippled, and though Lansky was fond of the older boy, Buddy could not fulfill all his paternal dreams. These even included having a son at West Point one day, and from the moment of the child's first cries, Lansky planned his second son's schooling and launching into American life.

In the same year Lansky began investigating gambling possibilities in Florida and Cuba, and initiated a relationship with Fulgencio Batista, soon to become dictator of Cuba.

Also in 1932, in good time before the Democratic and Republican party conventions, Charlie Luciano and Meyer Lansky convened an important meeting of their out-of-town allies and lieutenants at Claridge's in New York. Repeal was not long off, and the Roaring Twenties which had treated the Lower East Siders so well were gone forever. Many people had been ruined by the great Wall Street crash of 1929 and its after-shocks. Unemployment was severe, and the public was crying out for change. Sensing the mood of the country, Lansky and Luciano decided to expand and diversify on a larger scale and at a faster pace, and to make this easier they sought to take a more active part in national politics. From their earliest days they had learned how easy it was to bribe police and local politicians, and their voices were now powerful in the ranks of the New York Democrats. With some of the people's national representatives on their side, the ambitious duo could operate even more freely. Bribes, not bullets, continued to be their watchword.

For this reason the participants at Claridge's agreed that they would try to influence the coming presidential election. At the time Herbert Hoover was the Republican President of the United States. He was hoping to serve another four years, but it was clear to most observers that the Republicans were tarnished with the Depression and were going to be swept away in a Democratic landslide. One of the potential Democratic contenders would certainly be Al Smith, no longer governor of New York but still a political power. Smith had wanted to be a candidate in 1924 but had failed. The Democratic Convention had passed him over. He had been nominated in 1928 but Hoover had defeated him. In 1932 he felt his great chance was coming, and he turned to his friends in the underworld for assistance.

According to Lansky, Frank Costello, who as part of his job for the Lower East Siders had kept in touch with Smith after Rothstein died, arranged a meeting between Lansky, Luciano, and Governor Smith at the home of multimillionaire John J. Raskob as early as 1928. Lansky missed the meeting, but Charlie spelled out to him the details of the deal the governor had suggested. Smith needed to make sure he had full Tammany and Democratic Party backing from the vital areas of Manhattan, the Bronx, and Brooklyn, and he knew that the politicians in these areas were being bribed by the young gangsters from the Lower East Side. They did back him, and so did "their" politicians, and Smith did in fact carry the Democratic Convention. They also backed him in the election, which he lost partly because of anti-Catholicism and perhaps also because the country was not eager for change during the apparently prosperous year of 1928.

Now in 1932, with the Democratic Convention scheduled for Chicago in June, Al Smith was again determined to throw everything he had into the struggle to become President. Once more he turned to the Italians and other Catholics of New York's underworld and asked Luciano for his full backing at the convention.

Lansky, however, warned his friends at the Claridge Hotel meeting that there was no certainty of Al Smith's winning the nomination. The present governor of New York, Franklin D. Roosevelt, looked like the stronger candidate. Lansky also felt that Smith's Catholicism would still be a powerful barrier to his winning the election even if he got the nomination. He insisted that a way must be found to back Roosevelt as well as Smith, so that if Roosevelt became President the underworld would still be in a position to influence the White House.

The Lower East Side leaders went to Chicago to exert direct influence on the convention. Their muscle was based on the corruption that existed in New York during the administration of Mayor James J. Walker, a man who made no secret of his friendship with leading criminals. Lansky, Costello, and Luciano were so at ease in their power that they went to Chicago quite openly, traveling with the New York City delegation. Luciano moved into a large suite at the Drake Hotel with Al Marinelli, a Tammany leader who was an old friend. It was from this suite that the main thrust for Al Smith as presidential candidate was launched. Frank Costello took another hotel suite and shared it with a different Tammany leader, Jimmy Hines, who was backing Roosevelt. Costello worked closely with Hines, in case Roosevelt should be successful. Thus the Lower East Side men had a foot in both camps. Meyer Lansky, avoiding the limelight as always, took a third suite and assigned Longie Zwillman to hurry from delegate to delegate, keeping his finger on the pulse of the convention. Lansky operated behind the scenes and was rarely seen by delegates or newspapermen.

But while Lansky remained in the background, the rest of his group threw their weight around, showing both contenders that they had vast resources for use in getting to the White House. And as they made it clear they were ready to pour money into the presidential campaign, they also provided enormous quantities of bootleg whiskey to the guests they invited to their suites. There was twenty-four-hour hospitality, with food and liquor in generous helpings to the delegates and their wives and friends. In return for the flow of money and other promised support, the gang leaders made it clear that they expected in return an easy ride in the future, with little pressure or hindrance to their activities.

At Lansky's suggestion the underworld representatives declined to say who they would support. It was deemed politic to keep their cards close to the chest until they saw which of the two candidates was going to be nominated. Albert Marinelli, with his keen political sense, first sniffed the tide running in favor of Roosevelt, and he suggested to Lansky and Luciano that the full weight of their backing be thrown behind FDR. What finally persuaded the leaders to switch firmly to Roosevelt was a promise that supposedly came down from FDR that he would be "kind"—Lansky's word—to them in exchange for their backing. Roosevelt later denied making any such promise, and many gangsters were prosecuted and jailed during his administration. Roosevelt ordered the FBI and other law enforcement agencies to crack down hard on crime, and he pushed them to follow through. Roosevelt was also to break the power of Tammany Hall. Jimmy Walker was forced to resign and fled to Europe, and a number of Tammany leaders, including Jimmy Hines, went to prison.

Al Smith warned the gang at the time, according to Lansky, that they would be double-crossed, but they nevertheless stuck with Roosevelt. Many years later, discussing the matter with Doc Stacher in Israel, Meyer Lansky admitted that the switch away from Al Smith had been a terrible mistake. "I should have stuck with Arnie Rothstein's advice. He told me from the first that Al Smith was a great guy and that I could trust him like a brother if he gave his word.

"Smith always understood the problems of the Jews and the Italians on the Lower East Side, as well as his own kind. He used to campaign in our area and he had a genuine sympathy for the poor. He spoke like us. He acted like us. He was one of us. I should have known better than to switch to Roosevelt.

"In a way we had no choice—we were convinced in Chicago that Roosevelt was going to win that nomination. But it was a mistake to abandon Al Smith. My experience of life is that it is always wrong to be disloyal to a friend. You pay for it in the end, the way we did with Roosevelt. He forgot his promises and he ruthlessly attacked people like Lucky.

"In a way I guess that was to be expected. When you become President of the United States you do your duty. I had no quarrel with Roosevelt for taking action against crime, or what he and his law enforcement people said was crime.

"Where I quarreled with Roosevelt was later on, when the Second World War began. There was a great outcry about the way Jews were being treated in Germany and Roosevelt refused to listen to pleas from Jewish leaders to let more refugees into the United States. Thousands of Jews who were killed in the concentration camps might have been saved if he had taken a more liberal approach. I heard that Mrs. Roosevelt pleaded with her husband to let Jews under threat of death come to the United States, but FDR dodged the issue."

At the 1932 Democratic Convention Lansky and his colleagues did not spend all their time playing politics. They had other important business. Long talks were held with Moe Dalitz and other Midwestern associates about expanding the gambling aspects of their business. Contact was made with Huey "Kingfish" Long, the colorful governor of Louisiana, and he promised to help them open up gambling casinos in his state. As always, the Kingfish could use the money he would get in return. Lansky outlined what they wanted—to introduce slot machines and other nickel-and-dime games for ordinary citizens in Louisiana, particularly in New Orleans, and also permission to open luxuriously equipped casinos where people from all over the country could gamble for high stakes. One of Arnold Rothstein's former partners, the sophisticated but aging Dandy Phil Kastel, was put in overall charge of the Louisiana operation.

To back up Kastel and make sure everything was businesslike, Lansky appointed one of his brightest young men, Seymour Weiss. Weiss set up headquarters in the Roosevelt Hotel in New Orleans.

Later Lansky went to New Orleans himself to draw up the financial details of the deal, taking Doc Stacher with him. Huey Long was worried about how to get his bribe money without the authorities finding out. By this time Roosevelt was in power, and although the Kingfish had backed him to the hilt, tax inspectors were beginning to hound Long. Lansky listened patiently as the Louisiana governor railed against Roosevelt for double-crossing him. "He promised me he would take the tax people off my back if I backed him. His promises were worthless and they're onto me now like a pack of wolves," he said indignantly.

Lansky and Stacher calmed him down by saying that they were ready to pay three to four million dollars a year to him in cash. The money would be sent to a numbered account in Switzerland, where not even the long arm of Internal Revenue could find it.

Stacher added, "You have nothing to worry about. We'll take the money there for you with our special couriers and nobody but you and us will know your number. And only you will be able to draw on the account. Your signature and secret code which you will give the bank—you don't even have to tell us—will be your protection. To put the money in, all we need is the number. To draw it out, you need the code that only you will know. You must never write it down. Keep it in your head."

Deeply impressed by this sophistication, the governor gave his visitors from New York carte blanche. The opening of the famous Blue Room at the Roosevelt Hotel and of the Beverly Country Club, also in New Orleans, was the beginning of the nationwide development of casinos. From there Lansky and his associates expanded into Hot Springs, Arkansas, where the loyal Owney "Killer" Madden was put in charge. This famous health spa became an especially lucrative gambling center.

Indeed, the atmosphere in Hot Springs was so friendly to the underworld that when gangsters were on the run, or ill, or suffering from battle wounds, they knew they could recover there without problems with local authorities. Madden ran the Hot Springs casinos with quiet expertise, assisted by Carlos Marcello, a Tunisian who was one of the few Lansky lieutenants who was neither a Jew nor an Italian.

From Arkansas, Lansky's attention moved to Covington and Newport, in Kentucky, but more and more he began to think of Florida as the place to concentrate on.

Lansky had been interested in Miami since the early days of running bootleg liquor from the Caribbean, and he thought Miami was ripe for plucking now. America's favorite vacation spot was drawing ever increasing numbers of wealthy people, and those who went there for the sun were often bored. If casinos could be set up in the city, instant profits would come tumbling in. Moving into Miami itself would not be easy, since it was already controlled by Little Augie Carfano. Working cautiously but carefully Lansky bought hotels and clubs close to Miami, in Broward and Dade counties. With the aid of his good friend Moses Annenberg, he brought in a wire service for the local race tracks that was used by bookmakers all over the country. The local gambling bosses had to use the service. Underworld money, shrewdly directed by Lansky, poured into the area, and entrenched racketeers like Carfano were swept aside as the ruthless combination of Lansky and his colleagues from New York outmaneuvered them.

Lansky obtained control of the Miami area with one of his favorite techniques, the careful use of front men. For example, when he was buying the Tropical Park race track, just south of Miami, he used relatives of Owney Madden; Frank Erickson, who had taken over Arnold Rothstein's gambling business; Herman Stark, a loyal lieutenant who was later involved with the casinos in Havana; and good friends from Chicago who had been associated with Al Capone.

Front men, cash on the line, and the ability to plan and assign every detail—these would soon put Lansky and his colleagues in control of Miami and Miami Beach.

20 The Mob on the Run

Just before Christmas of 1933, Prohibition was finally swept away. For fourteen years Americans had wrestled with their consciences over whether or not to break the law and drink illegally or remain upright citizens and go thirsty. The desire for alcohol had won, and the major beneficiaries had been the bootleggers and their underworld associates.

Now that the sale of illegal alcohol was no longer an important source of income, many underworld leaders moved to gambling, prostitution, and drug running. But the shrewder criminals like the Lower East Side outfit had long since made their plans to move also into the legitimate business of importing whiskey, as Rothstein had predicted. Lansky went the other leaders one better, for although he joined his partners in setting up legitimate companies dealing in alcohol—including import businesses as well as the transformation of speakeasies into restaurants and night clubs—he realized that the sale of untaxed liquor could still be a highly profitable operation. Legal whiskey was heavily taxed; the bootleg equivalent could be sold more cheaply and more profitably. Lansky had set up the Molaska Corporation partly with this in mind. Incorporated in Ohio by Lansky and his amiable father-in-law in 1933, the firm had as its stated purpose the processing of dehydrated molasses to be used as a substitute for sugar. Other unofficial partners in the business included Moe Dalitz, Charles Polizzi, known as Chuck, and Sam Tucker. Citron took an active part, investing over $120,000 in Molaska. The real business purpose, of course, was to use the

159

molasses in alcohol; it is an excellent flavoring agent. There were Molaska plants in various places, including New Jersey and Ohio. The business was skillfully operated and the premises were moved from time to time to avoid detection by the Alcohol, Tobacco and Firearms Bureau.

Even so, occasionally one of the distilleries was raided. After the discovery of one of Molaska's plants in New Jersey, the *New York Times* told its readers that enough illicit alcohol had been found there to flood New York and New Jersey. The journalist's figure of speech gave an inkling of the size of the enterprise. Millions of gallons of illegal booze were produced, and much of it was sold to the legitimate firms set up by underworld leaders who were, of course, close friends of Lansky.

Lansky's cautious nature was becoming more and more evident. In Molaska he surrounded himself with colleagues and employees who acted as his front men, and he distanced himself from his gambling and other enterprises by operating farther and farther away from the scene of the action. He was cushioned by his friends, and his own name was rarely mentioned in the newspapers.

Charlie Luciano, on the other hand, now began to pay the price for his enjoyment of publicity, as Roosevelt's war against criminals started up in earnest. Turning ruthlessly on the underworld, FDR gave all the backing he could to the new wave of law enforcement officers who were determined to smash crime and win reputations.

One such enthusiastic wielder of the sword of justice was Thomas E. Dewey, U.S. Attorney for the Southern District of New York. He had already struck at the underworld by jailing Waxey Gordon, who was prosecuted in New York. Now he launched an all-out attack against one of the men allied with Lansky and Luciano. Stockily built, the blue-eyed, Bronx-born gangster known as Dutch Schultz had started out as a printer but joined a gang of criminals called the Bergen Avenue mob when he was still in his teens. Hold-ups and burglaries were his initial plunge into crime before he became associated with Lansky and Phil Kastel as well as Luciano. Schultz had been Lansky's partner since the very early bootlegging days.

When Dewey sent out the message that he was gunning for every major Mafia figure in New York, he made it clear that his first target was Dutch Schultz but that he was also after Lucky Luciano.

Dewey found a powerful ally in the new mayor of New York, the "Little Flower" Fiorello La Guardia, who was elected in

January 1934 on a Fusion platform that promised a fight against Tammany corruption as well as the New York underworld. No sooner was La Guardia in office than he ordered his police commissioner, Lewis J. Valentine, to make war against the criminals his number one priority.

It was clear to the Lower East Siders that both Dewey and La Guardia meant business, and that they had strong public support for their aims. The underworld tried to set up defenses against attack and at the same time continue their highly profitable activities. Dutch Schultz went into hiding and Lansky and Luciano, with Zwillman, Adonis, Lepke, Lucchese, and Genovese, conferred about how to neutralize Tom Dewey.

Dutch Schultz had already given his partners a lot of trouble because he sometimes declined to follow their modern approach of down-pedaling violence and operating on a businesslike basis. One of Schultz's notorious specialties was to threaten restaurant owners with death or with their premises being blown up if they didn't pay him protection money. Even while on the run from the police, he went on killing people he considered his rivals, including Jack "Legs" Diamond, who may have been encroaching on Schultz's protection territory in the Bronx and parts of Manhattan.

Besides Schultz's recent murders, what alarmed the Lower East Side leaders far more was that he was openly declaring that the only way to escape Dewey's clutches was to kill him. And if that happened, the leaders knew that the public and the authorities would turn venomously against them. The whole array of American law enforcement agencies would be forced by public pressure to bring them all to trial.

Meantime Dutch Schultz's behavior became more and more unpredictable and erratic. Perhaps the strain of hiding out and the fear of capture was telling on a man used to tough direct action. To the surprise of his fellow Jews in the underworld he decided to convert to Roman Catholicism. This was accepted with raised eyebrows, but after that he made the unpardonable error of having one of Lansky's closest friends, Abraham "Bo" Weinberg, killed. The Dutchman, as he was known, had decided that Weinberg was working behind his back to divide up his holdings among the rest of the Lower East Side gangsters.

"Schultz was ranting and raving," Doc Stacher remembered. "I was the one who had kept close to him even in the previous months, when there was already great hostility between him and the rest of our guys. I tried to reason and argue with Schultz but I think he was going crazy. He thought Lansky, Luciano, Bugsy Siegel, Zwillman, and all the rest of us were combining against him and were going to steal his money. And even worse, he told me straight out that if Dewey did manage to get him and put him behind bars he would talk his head off. I reported this to Lansky and the others and we knew there was only one thing to do—we'd have to get him before Dewey did."

There was a warrant out for Schultz, but so far, thanks to his friends from the Lower East Side, he had evaded capture. Dewey had declared that he was determined to nail him, but a year had gone by with no results. Now the leaders of the Lower East Side outfit decided to handle the "rogue elephant," as Stacher called him, in their own way.

"And that meant his death warrant was signed. All of us met and agreed that he had to die. At first Albert Anastasia, the most efficient killer of all, was supposed to do the job. But even though Dutch Schultz had become a Catholic, our Italian partners looked at us and we all knew that this was an internal Jewish matter. It was the understanding we had with each other and the Italians like Charlie Luciano respected our wishes to keep this in the family.

"Bugsy Siegel was all for handling the matter personally. But there was another problem—Dutch Schultz's bodyguards were Jewish too. One of the men was a close friend of Bugsy's called Otto 'Abbadabba' Berman. He had the nickname because he was always eating a kind of candy bar that had that name. It was clear that to get Dutch Schultz his bodyguards would have to be killed as well. Bugsy went pale when he thought about his boyhood buddy Abbadabba, but he was still ready to do it. We all agreed, however, that we should step aside and leave it to Charlie 'the Bug' Workman to organize the execution. The Bug had been in the organization right from the beginning and in my opinion he was just as cold and ruthless when he was ordered to carry out a shooting operation as Anastasia or any of the others.

"Charlie Workman was called in and joined us a couple of hours later. We told him what he had to do. He nodded and left the room.

"Later we learned the full details of how it was done. It wasn't difficult, really, because the Bug knew most of the people around Dutch Schultz—after all, we'd all been together in the rackets since our teens—and knew exactly where the Dutchman hung out. The Bug didn't waste time. It was October 23, 1935. He got his guys together—Mendy Weiss and a third man whose identity we were not told. They went down to the Palace Chop House and Tavern in Newark. The three of them walked straight in, guns blazing, and killed Dutch's three bodyguards, Ab Landau, Bernard 'Lulu' Rosencranz, and, of course, Abbadabba Berman. All three were dead in seconds. Dutch Schultz was in the toilet at the time. Bug Workman walked straight in there and killed Dutch Schultz with a single shot. He didn't die right away and we heard later that before he left this life he was given the Catholic last rites. But Dewey never got him—and Dutch Schultz never ratted on us.

"Later Charlie Workman was sentenced to life for the killing. Too many people knew he had been involved. He was finally freed on parole in 1964," Stacher ended the story.

The Lower East Side leaders had rid themselves of a man who had become dangerous to them, but they had also removed a name from the top of Dewey's list. The prosecutor switched his major attention to Luciano, thinking that Luciano's flamboyance would make it easier to get him behind bars than any of the rest of the Lower East Side mob.

Luciano was intelligent and well protected. His only weakness was his notoriety. He was so widely known as a gangster and as number one in the underworld that the public was ready to believe anything evil about him. A member of Dewey's staff, Assistant District Attorney Eunice Carter, is credited with the plan to trap Luciano. The prostitution business in New York was controlled by a number of Luciano's underlings and, according to Lansky, without the knowledge of the boss. "Charlie had the same revulsion about running brothels that I did. He believed no respectable man should ever make money out of women in that horrible way. I would never have anything to do with it and I know perfectly well that neither did Charlie."

By this time Luciano was so busy in so many areas, and the organization had become so huge, that there was no way to keep track of everything everyone else was doing on the side. How could the manager of a big corporation know what his employees are up to in their spare time? Besides, the new management had the business principle of each man being responsible for his own territory.

"A number of them were involved in prostitution," Lansky says, "but Charlie couldn't know that."

Finally, in February 1936, Dewey struck. Patrolmen, detectives, and special members of the vice squad arrested several of

Luciano's lieutenants and simultaneously pulled in hundreds of prostitutes. Dewey's men interrogated them one by one. One of the key attorneys on his staff was Murray Gurfein, who was later to use his special knowledge of the mob for the benefit of the federal government.

A powerful case was built up, showing that prostitution was an organized racket in New York. There was no direct link to Luciano but the evidence clearly indicated it was his troops who were running the brothels and pimping for hundreds of prostitutes. On April 1, Dewey declared that Charlie Luciano was "Public Enemy No. 1 in New York," and he issued orders for the Sicilian to be arrested on sight.

Lansky and Siegel agreed that Luciano would be wise to pay a visit to Hot Springs, where he would be protected by Owney Madden's excellent relations with the local authorities. Dewey applied pressure both publicly and through the FBI, and there was a national outcry about justice being hindered in Hot Springs. Even so, Luciano was safe for several months. Finally twenty armed Arkansas Rangers were sent to Hot Springs to arrest Luciano and take him to Little Rock, the state capital, and from there he was extradited to New York.

The case against Luciano opened in New York State Supreme Court in downtown Manhattan on May 13, 1936. During the next three weeks some sixty prostitutes and madams—including Muriel Ryan, Rose Cohen, Helen Kelly, Jenny the Factory, and Nigger Ruth—told how they had been exploited. Again and again Dewey, now special prosecutor for New York, emphasized that the exploiting gangsters were associated with Charlie Luciano and had been acting under his orders. Then Dewey produced his star turn, a girl named Florence Brown, who related that under her professional name of Cokey Flo she had become a prostitute and that she herself had heard Charlie Luciano give orders to beat up, torture, threaten, and drug girls to force them to work for the organization. Cokey Flo was followed by Nancy Presser, who had been a prostitute since her early teens and who claimed that she had been the mistress of Waxey Gordon, Dutch Schultz, and Joe Adonis. She then testified that she had also shared Luciano's bed, and to add insult to injury added that Luciano had been unable to make love to her.

In Lansky's view, "The whole thing was a frame-up. Dewey had decided to get Lucky Luciano and the only way he could do it was through the girls. They built up a phony case against him and everybody must have known that the girls were lying. They had been told exactly what to say. I never believed a word of it, and nobody who knew Charlie believed it either. But because of his reputation and a hostile judge, the jury were prepared to believe anything. Lucky was paying the price for the publicity he had enjoyed so much."

On June 7, Judge Philip J. McCook sentenced Luciano to thirty to fifty years in prison, the longest sentence ever given in the United States for compulsory prostitution. The dozen small fry tried with him were also convicted. Luciano was sent first to Sing Sing and then to Dannemora Prison in Upstate New York.

After the trial Dewey virtually admitted that the charges of prostitution were only a means to the end of getting Luciano behind bars. He told the press that "this was not a vice trial. It was a racket prosecution. The control of all organized prostitution in New York by the convicted defendants was one of the lesser rackets. The prostitution racket was merely the vehicle by which these men were convicted." He went on to say that Luciano controlled narcotics, policy, loan-sharking, and other criminal activities in New York.

As Luciano was led off to prison, Lansky gave silent thanks for the decision he had made many years before, to avoid public notice whenever he could.

Even Lansky had some narrow escapes, however. Earlier, in late 1931, he had called an important meeting of his closest aides at the Franconia Hotel, on Manhattan's Upper West Side. Somebody tipped off the police and they raided the hotel. By chance Lansky was not at the meeting, and Stacher was in charge. When the police lined up the men they found in the suite, Lansky was conspicuously missing from Police Captain Michael McDermott's official photograph of the event. Those whose names and faces were recorded included Bugsy Siegel, Louis Lepke (Buchalter), a man called Phil "The Stick," and Little Farvel, whose real name was Philip Kovolick. Little Farvel was the most devoted of all Lansky's followers. At various times he served as bodyguard, chauffeur, and in any other capacity the boss needed him for. Kovolick had known Lansky since they were teenagers, and in their various scrapes on the Lower East Side as well as the famous occasion when Lansky's budding group of gangsters clashed with Joe Masseria's tough men, it was Little Farvel who was in the forefront of the fight.

The others in this remarkable group photograph were Joseph "Doc" Stacher, Harry "Big Greenie" Greenberg, Hyman "Curly"

Holtz, Harry Teitelbaum, and Lewis "Shadows" Kravitz. Despite lengthy interrogation all the men were released without charges, according to Lansky.

That situation would change soon, especially for Louis Lepke, as Dewey's mills continued to grind. Before Lepke joined Lansky and Luciano he had been arrested several times for such things as robbing elderly peddlers in the streets of the Lower East Side. Then, with another criminal named Jacob Gurrah Shapiro, he began his major career by corrupting union officials and setting up protection rackets. Both were good at blackmail backed by the ruthless use of fists, feet, and firearms. When he came under the control of Lansky and Luciano, Lepke became more or less a "respectable" criminal and used force less often, but his basically violent character was sometimes too much for even Lansky to handle. Despite repeated warnings not to become involved with drugs, Lepke became a major figure in narcotics, along with his own personal gang—Jacob Katzenberg, Louis Stark, Tootsie Feinstein, Solly Gross, and Benny Harris. They had their own opium-making plant on Seymour Avenue, in Brooklyn, which blew up in February 1935 and put the Narcotics Bureau on their trail. From then on Lepke became one of the bureau's chief targets. It was discovered that he had been smuggling in opium from Hongkong and other Chinese ports, bribing customs officials as necessary. During one period of a few weeks, six shipments of heroin arrived from China, the government found, netting Lepke over $10,000,000 in clear profit.

With the narcotics men on his trail, and his penchant for violence far from curbed, Lepke was an embarrassment to Lansky. And after Luciano went to prison, when Lepke insisted that he run his own rackets and declined to pay his dues to the men who recruited him, he became a menace. Even in prison Luciano still shared in the organization's profits, and Lansky and the others were scrupulous about collecting his share as well as their own. Only Lepke refused to cooperate.

Meantime Dewey decided to make Lepke his next major target. Describing him as the worst industrial racketeer in America, Dewey offered a $25,000 reward for his arrest. The FBI chief, J. Edgar Hoover, called him "the most dangerous criminal in the United States" but offered a lesser reward of $5,000.

In 1937 Lepke disappeared, and for two years his friends in the underworld helped him hide. But instead of being grateful, he made increasing financial demands and at the same time ordered his gunmen to kill several people he thought might give evidence against him if he was caught.

The Lower East Side group met to decide what to do about Lepke, and, according to Doc Stacher, it was agreed that he would have to be sacrificed. Bugsy Siegel, now managing the organization's West Coast gambling interests, had come in from California for the meeting. He, of course, was all for going out to shoot him at once. "It was Lansky who persuaded Lepke's closest friend, Moe 'Dimples' Wolensky, to set a trap for Lepke where he would land himself in jail. We had made up our minds that the days of shooting people like the Dutch Schultz business were over. Bugsy was disgusted at this kind of talk, and yelled at us that we were all going soft. But we worked out a plan and Lepke walked straight into it. Wolensky told Lepke we had made a deal with J. Edgar Hoover. All Lepke had to do was give himself up. He would get a light sentence in return and the heat would be off all of us. We got the newspaperman Walter Winchell into the scheme by promising him a scoop for his paper.

"Lepke, not very bright, finally accepted the plan. On the night of August 24, 1939—a very hot night—Lepke came out of his hideout on Third Street in Brooklyn and climbed into a waiting car to go to a meeting at the corner of Fifth Avenue and Twenty-eighth Street, over in Manhattan. Anastasia was our driver. He handed him over to Hoover, and with Winchell driving the car they took him straight to prison."

Lepke got a sentence of fourteen years for his narcotics offenses. Then, despite all his friends' promises, he was handed over to the hungry Tom Dewey and sentenced to a further thirty years.

Greenie Greenberg, who had been a loyal member of the Lansky-Luciano outfit from the early days, was one of Lepke's suspects. Convinced that Greenberg had talked to the FBI about his narcotics activities, Lepke put him on his death list. Knowing Lepke's ruthlessness, Greenberg fled to Canada, but he had forgotten to take the precaution of hiding money there and soon was desperately broke. He got in touch with his pals in New York and threatened that unless money was sent to him he would come back to New York and tell the considerable amount he knew about the Lower East Side outfit.

As Stacher put it, there was no hesitation in the discussion about how to deal with Greenberg. "We all liked Big Greenie, but this was disloyalty and Allie Tannenbaum was told to bump him off. Allie immediately went to Canada, but Greenberg realized there was a gunman on his trail and vanished. Apparently he eventually found some money because in late 1939 he surfaced on the West Coast—Bugsy found out that he was living at 1094 Vista Del Mar, in Los Angeles. Bugsy was very excited and wanted to shoot Greenie himself. Longie Zwillman got the weapons to do the job and Allie took them to California.

"We all begged Bugsy to keep out of the shooting. He was too big a man by this time to become personally involved. But Bugsy wouldn't listen. He wouldn't even listen to Lansky the way he used to. He said Greenberg was a menace to all of us and if the cops grabbed him he could tell the whole story of our outfit back to the 1920s."

Siegel, Tannenbaum, and another gunman named Frankie Carbo made up the hit squad. As Greenberg came back to his apartment after buying a paper on the night of November 22, 1939, Siegel and Carbo shot and killed him on the spot.

While the gang had been pursuing Greenberg to keep him from talking, another Lansky gunman had actually begun to talk. Dewey had arrested Abe Reles, who had the nickname "Kid Twist." Reles was told that a man he had known named Harry Rudolph was now alleging that Reles was one of the gunmen who had murdered a certain Alex Alpert back in 1933. Reles was threatened with the electric chair, and the threat worked. Reles dictated a long, very detailed account of the activities of the Lansky-Luciano gang, from the early 1920s up to the present.

As Stacher remembered it, "We heard that Dewey's mouth was watering when Reles told how Bugsy Siegel and Allie Tannenbaum had bumped off Big Greenie in Los Angeles."

Tannenbaum was arrested immediately and also started talking. Bugsy Siegel went into hiding. If he were brought into court with Reles and Tannenbaum giving evidence against him, he would go straight to the electric chair.

The wheel then turned back to Lepke when both Tannenbaum and Reles testified that in 1936 Lepke had murdered a store owner named Joseph Rosen. Rosen had been a brave man: when Lepke threatened him he had said he would complain to the authorities. Lepke had immediately sent three of his killers, Mendy Weiss, Louis Capone, and Pittsburgh Phil Strauss, to shoot him. At last Dewey had his murder charge.

Doc Stacher said, "This meant the end of Lepke. To be quite

honest we were sorry for Lepke, who had been the victim of his own stupidity and who was now completely crazy as far as we could see. However, there's not much room for sentiment in these matters."

Lepke was indeed done for. With other former Lansky gunmen giving evidence in court against them, in November 1941 Lepke, Louis Capone, and Weiss were found guilty and sentenced to the electric chair. The third gunman, Phil Strauss, was doomed anyway. He had been found guilty of killing a gambler, Irving "Puggy" Feinstein, who had made the mistake of trying to cheat Albert Anastasia by refusing to pay a debt. Strauss and a gangster called Bugsy Goldstein were both betrayed by the "singing" Reles.

Lepke and his loyal gunmen Mendy Weiss and Louis Capone were executed at Sing Sing on March 4, 1944. Stacher said, "We decided to do nothing to help Lepke. In fact there was nothing that could have been done, once all that testimony came out. But Bugsy Siegel was a very different case. He was a close friend and Lansky's right-hand man right from the time they were boys. We spent a fortune in California to save Bugsy from the chair.

"Dewey was determined to get Siegel back to New York. We heard that Abe Reles was grilled all the time to find out if Bugsy had committed any murders on the Lower East Side. Meantime, the key to whether he'd be tried for the Greenberg shooting lay with Abe Reles too. The cops were hiding him in the Half Moon Hotel, on Coney Island. The California authorities had indicted Siegel and Carbo for murder, but both men were already in hiding.

"We brought Bugsy to New York for a top-level meeting on how to deal with the threat against him, and Meyer used some pretty harsh words when he and Siegel first got together. It was the only time I ever saw Meyer so furious. He yelled at Bugsy, 'I've told you over and over, "Use your head instead of your gun." And you wouldn't listen—and look at the trouble you're in now.'

"Meyer finally calmed down and we started figuring out how to keep Abe Reles from dragging Bugsy to the chair. It was Frank Costello who came up with the plan. You mustn't forget that Frank's role all these years was to bribe the police and other officials—politicians in New York and later on in Washington and other places. Like the rest of us, Costello reasoned that if Reles could be silenced permanently, the case against Bugsy and maybe those against some of the others who were facing lesser charges would be thrown out of court. So he got to work and found out which room Reles was in at the Half Moon—not so hard because the cops had a round-the-clock guard on it. But then Frank really showed his muscle. He knew so many top-ranking cops that he got the names of the detectives who were guarding Reles. We never asked exactly how Costello did it, but one evening he came back with a smile and said, 'It's cost us a hundred grand, but Kid Twist Reles is about to join his maker.' "

On the morning of November 12, 1941, Abe "Kid Twist" Reles was found dead on a strip of concrete below the window of his hotel room. District Attorney William O'Dwyer and Dewey had been told that Reles was being guarded "better than the gold in Fort Knox." But Dewey's treasure was gone, and the heat was off Bugsy Siegel.

The mystery of what really happened to Abe Reles was never satisfactorily explained. Years later, when he was living in Italy, Lucky Luciano claimed that the police officer Frank Bals and others guarding Twist had been bribed directly by Costello. Bals asserted, as he had done at the time, that Reles' death was an accident that could not have been prevented. When O'Dwyer became mayor of New York in 1945, he rewarded Frank Bals for his services during investigations of crime in the city by making him deputy police commissioner. Luciano's claim that Bals had been bribed has never been substantiated. Many people in New York believe that from the safety of Italy he was merely trying to settle his own old scores with the New York police.

Stacher said simply, "The death of Reles was a great relief. Bugsy couldn't be tried and Albert Anastasia was off the hook too. Reles had told Dewey that Anastasia was the one responsible for shooting a Teamsters Union guy, Moishe Diamond, back in 1939. That killing shocked Lansky and me—it was totally unnecessary. Anastasia was demanding that the union pay some huge amounts of protection money and Moishe refused. He was a very brave man. Lansky told Anastasia to leave him alone, but Albert had his own way of doing things. He hired Allie Tannenbaum to kill Moishe, and he shot him I don't know how many times in a Brooklyn street in May of 1939. Reles told O'Dwyer about it but nobody else had talked."

Stacher added, "Reles' death let Anastasia breathe easier, but he was still worried that Dewey and O'Dwyer would come after him for some other crimes Reles had probably told him about. As soon as we got into the Second World War, in 1941, Meyer advised Albert to let himself be drafted and keep out of sight in the Army. Anastasia jumped at the idea, and damned if they didn't send him to a camp in

Pennsylvania somewhere to teach GIs to be longshoremen. He had started out on the Brooklyn docks, you know, and he knew all about longshoring. Of course he still gave the orders on the waterfront—even from camp."

Justice of a different kind eventually caught up with Albert Anastasia for the dozens of murders he ordered and carried out himself during his long reign of crime. Anastasia signed his own death warrant by threatening his fellow Mafia leaders in New York, intending to become a new boss of all the bosses. They reacted in the only way they knew. One day as he was having his regular shave in the basement barbershop of the Park Sheraton Hotel, two killers walked in and shot him in the head. Although hit ten times, Anastasia still struggled. The horrified barber said afterward, "He was bleeding but he still tried to grab the killers. He fell down. They shot him again. Then they ran away."

Anastasia died on October 25, 1957. His killers have never been apprehended, and although there have been many guesses about their identity, nobody is quite sure who carried out the execution.

21 "He Never Cheated Anybody"

Dewey's war against the underworld strengthened Lansky's determination to keep his own name as far from public attention as possible, and Luciano's imprisonment was an additional reason to stay out of the public eye. Always a private man, he was now a family man too, and he was delighted when his third child, a daughter whom he named Sandra, was born on December 6, 1937. Tremendously fond of his children, Lansky had an increasingly strained relationship with his wife. Hidden though they were, his underworld connections continued to plague her.

Lansky burrowed further and further away from view in the late 1930s, and the next public record of him was his registration with the Selective Service Board on February 14, 1942. He gave his age as forty. Although he registered in Los Angeles, Lansky gave his permanent address as 411 West End Avenue, in New York. It has been noted that one of his close neighbors was Thomas E. Dewey. Lansky told Los Angeles Local Board 242, "I work for Krieg, Spector and Citron at 727 Monroe Street, Hoboken, New Jersey." He explained that he was a vice-president in charge of personnel but suggested that he could best serve his country as a machine operator, since that had been his training as a young man. Lansky dutifully kept in touch with the Selective Service Board, informing them of changes of address such as his move to 211 Central Park West in 1943. Only five years from the upper age limit when he registered with the draft board, Lansky was never called up, though he said later that he would have been "glad to serve if needed."

Lansky's activities since Luciano went to jail in 1936 had been more complicated than any draft board form could show. He had been energetically building up the gambling empire which he and his friends considered the best way to increase the already immense capital acquired during the age of Prohibition. Concentrating on Florida and Cuba, the two favorite resorts of rich Americans, Lansky traveled often to both. He strengthened his ties of business and friendship with Batista and was the power behind casino gambling on the island.

When he went to Havana, Lansky always took his link man with the Cuban dictator, Doc Stacher. It was Stacher who actually handed over the cash bribes to Batista, and Stacher who supervised the couriers who took both Batista's money and the gambling profits from Cuba to Switzerland.

In 1937 Lansky organized one of the most luxurious casinos in the world in the Hotel Nacional in Havana. At about the same time he leased a highly profitable race track near Havana from the National City Bank in New York.

At the height of Dewey's campaign against the New York underworld, Lansky went first to Florida and then on to Cuba for what could not have been purely a business trip. He was in his suite at the Hotel Nacional for months. The FBI sent agents there to ask him for his cooperation in pinning down narcotics charges against Lepke and others. Lansky was polite but replied that he could not really help. He gave them his business address on Broadway, in New York, saying that if they needed any further information they could always reach him through the office. He offered them a drink, very politely, and with equal civility showed them the door.

According to Stacher, "Meyer was the first one to think about Cuba, way back in the early thirties. We knew the island through our bootlegging business, and what with the great weather and the good hotels and casinos we would build, rich people could easily be persuaded to fly over to an exotic 'foreign country' to enjoy themselves. Of course Meyer could have gone out on his own and set up a private gambling empire there. But that's not his way. He spoke to Lucky Luciano and other friends of ours from around the country at a meeting in the spring of 1933 in Luciano's Waldorf Towers suite. It was one of the few times when Meyer went there. Some of the group couldn't understand why our money should be invested in a place that wasn't even in America. Meyer explained very patiently and suggested that a large amount of money invested there now would make fortunes for all of us in the future.

"He said we needed somewhere safe to put the cash from the bootlegging. Our biggest problem was always where to invest the money. It didn't really appeal to any of us to take it to Switzerland and leave it there just earning interest. What Lansky suggested was that each of us put up $500,000 to start the Havana gambling operation. At the end of his speech Charlie said he was in on the deal and ten of the others, including Bugsy Siegel, Moe Dalitz, Phil Kastel, and Chuck Polizzi, also chipped in half a million bucks. Lansky and I flew to Havana with the money in suitcases and spoke to Batista, who hadn't quite believed we could raise that kind of money.

"Lansky took Batista straight back to our hotel, opened the suitcases, and pointed at the cash. Batista just stared at the money without saying a word. Then he and Meyer shook hands and Batista left. We had several meetings with him over the next week and I saw that Meyer and Batista understood each other very well. We gave Batista a guarantee of between three and five million dollars a year, as long as we had the monopoly on casinos at the Hotel Nacional and everywhere else on the island where we thought tourists would come. On top of that he was promised a cut of our profits.

"Later on we spread out to other parts of the Caribbean, but our biggest operation—and the one that pulled in the most money—was in Cuba. Meyer had all sorts of visions then, before the war, of spreading to Europe and starting up American-style casinos there, but the war put an end to that. We had enough on our hands anyway, in Florida and the Caribbean.

"Even after Charlie went to prison Meyer never forgot him. I went with Meyer to visit him in that horrible cell of his—we called Dannemora 'Siberia'—and Meyer told him all about the deal he made with Batista. Meyer told Charlie that his share of the profits would be kept for him and in his view the best place was to keep it in Switzerland. Charlie wanted some of the money in America for his family, and the two of them went into details on how it was to be cut. Meyer also told Charlie and the rest of us that he had one private deal with Batista. That involved the sugar he needed for his Molaska company. There was no problem about that. It had always been understood that this was a private business which had nothing to do with the rest of us. I think Lansky was really running it to keep his own family and his in-laws happy. He wanted to show them that he could be legitimate, which was funny in a way because the company was mostly turning out illegal alcohol."

Luciano's decision to hand over to Lansky the responsibility for handling all his financial affairs and the rackets he controlled was a signal to most other underworld characters that the Little Man was the one to trust with their money. "Meyer became, you might say, the bookkeeper but really the financial adviser for nearly all the important guys. They trusted him and never once through the years was there any suggestion that Meyer misused his power. He never cheated anybody. It was Meyer who organized our network for running money to Swiss banks through the Caribbean islands and countries in South America. We trusted him totally. I never heard anyone say anything disloyal about Meyer."

With all his responsibilities and his special interests in Cuba and Florida, Lansky did not forget the rest of the United States. In the mid-thirties he had suggested to Bugsy that it was time for him to move West. Siegel, who was fascinated by the West Coast and especially Hollywood, went off at once. What Lansky had in mind was that there were unexplored gambling opportunities not only in Los Angeles and other urban areas in California but in the relatively underdeveloped state of Nevada. Tall, good-looking, impetuous Benjamin Siegel did not intend to neglect his work but was equally interested in having fun among the movie stars. His brother, Maurice, and sisters, Esther, Ethel, and Bessie, were uneasy about his criminal activities, but in his wife's eyes Bugsy could do no wrong. When he explained to the former Esther Krakower that the climate in California would suit their two daughters, Millicent and Barbara, she loyally started packing.

Just before the Siegels moved to California, Lansky said to Bugsy with a smile, "Take it easy with those Hollywood broads, I know you've always wanted to get laid by actresses." As Bugsy Siegel said later, "Meyer didn't laugh very often. I was surprised at him. But I often thought Meyer knew me better than I knew myself."

Doc Stacher agreed: "Bugsy and Meyer were closer than blood brothers. Bugsy saved Meyer's life more than once. I remember when Waxey Gordon finally found out that it was Meyer who had sent his brother Jake to give the authorities the evidence that sent him to jail. Waxey was out of action by then, but Charlie 'Chink' Sherman decided to avenge his boss. Sherman came to New York with one of his hit men, Tony Fabrazzo, and they managed to get into the building on Grand Street where Bugsy and Meyer used to meet. Bugsy spotted the bomb they'd planted and flung it out the window, but it went off and he got hurt. But that didn't keep Bugsy from gunning for Meyer's enemies. He tracked Fabrazzo down in Brooklyn and killed him.

"But as time went on Bugsy became a little restless at always being second fiddle to Meyer, and I think that was one reason why Meyer set up the West Coast assignment specifically for Bugsy. And Bugsy was pretty hot in New York by then, too. It was only a matter of time before Dewey would get him on something."

Bugsy Siegel knew the actor George Raft, noted for his underworld roles, and the two of them were soon involved in several deals on behalf of the Lower East Side men. But Siegel's arrival caused some repercussions in the local underworld, which was controlled by Jack Dragna. Anticipating problems, Lansky went up to see Luciano in Dannemora and asked him to persuade Dragna not to cause trouble. His argument was that California was so wide open and so big that there was enough room for everybody. Luciano agreed and sent a message to Dragna asking him for "full cooperation" with Siegel, who would be "coming West for the good of his health and the health of all of us." Even from jail, Luciano's influence was such that Dragna agreed to respect his wishes. But all the same he resented the arrival of the brash, blue-eyed New Yorker and patiently waited for a chance to get rid of him.

As soon as he got to Hollywood, Bugsy Siegel rented a mansion owned by the famous singer Lawrence Tibbett, and within days he was involved in a wild romance with a French actress named Ketti Gallion. Soon he was seducing one starlet after another. He and Raft went to the Santa Anita race track almost daily, betting heavily.

It wasn't long before the flamboyant Bugsy was involved in a more serious love affair, this time with the Countess Dorothy Di Frasso, a very wealthy society woman. Bugsy and the friends from New York who visited him were on first-name terms with such famous actors as Cary Grant, Clark Gable, Gary Cooper, and, of course, Jean Harlow, who had been the lover of Longie Zwillman.

Despite his hectic social life, Siegel remembered that he had come West to make money. Arm in arm with the seemingly cooperative Dragna and the gunman Mickey Cohen—born in Brooklyn but an Angeleno since childhood—Bugsy in the late 1930s was masterminding gambling along the Los Angeles waterfront and involved in establishing a gambling ship known as the *Rex,* which operated off Los Angeles. But some of his so-called moneymaking schemes were far too antic to please Lansky. He went on an expedition with the equally flamboyant Countess Di Frasso, seeking Spanish treasure on Cocos Island, off the coast of Costa Rica, and returned treasureless after nearly blowing the island to pieces with dynamite. Then he went with his "fancy lady," as he called her, to Europe, where he met leading Nazis including Hermann Goering and Joseph Goebbels, both of whom he said he wanted to shoot. He went on to hit the high spots on the French Riviera with Raft, until a stern cable from Lansky brought him hurrying home, where he was told to get on with the business at hand and "stop thinking you're a movie star."

When Siegel was implicated in the murder of Big Greenie Greenberg and had to hide out, it only enhanced his glamorous reputation in Hollywood. It became almost compulsory for Hollywood personalities to include Bugsy Siegel in their circles.

But by 1941 Bugsy Siegel and his Hollywood friends had become less interesting to the American public. When the United States entered the Second World War in December 1941, attention was riveted on another type of hoodlum, the man who aimed to conquer the world under the crooked-cross swastika.

22 The Waterfront "Volunteers"

On November 9, 1942, when American forces had been in action less than a year and it looked as if Nazi Germany and its ally Italy had a good chance of winning the war, the former French liner *Normandie* suddenly burst into flames at its North River moorings on the West Side of Manhattan.

The transatlantic luxury vessel had once been the pride of France. It had won the coveted Blue Ribbon of the Atlantic. Caught in New York when France fell, the *Normandie* was being converted into a gigantic troop carrier, renamed the *Lafayette*. Its high speed would make it a difficult target for the German submarines that were patrolling the Atlantic and sinking hundreds of vessels carrying troops and vital supplies from the United States to Great Britain and the Soviet Union.

Fires burned fiercely all over the *Normandie*. It seemed that there had been arson in several different parts of the ship. And despite efforts to put out the flames, the French vessel finally rolled over at her mooring.

The wreck of this once handsome liner, highly visible on Manhattan's West Side waterfront, was a powerful psychological victory for the Axis powers. Had Nazi saboteurs penetrated New York so successfully that they could operate freely wherever they wanted? Or was someone from the work force on the piers responsible? Someone perhaps sympathetic to Mussolini and his Fascists?

The public was not informed that a state of near-panic reigned at

U.S. Navy headquarters in Washington, but it is easy to understand the alarm. The Port of New York handled nearly half of all United States foreign trade. The two hundred cargo docks, warehouses, and passenger ship piers of Manhattan, Queens, New Jersey, and Brooklyn covered nearly eight hundred miles of water frontage.

In the vast, sprawling area where every day motor trucks alone made something like 25,000 separate trips, where nearly 1,000 railroad cars and 2,000 trucks came and went in every twenty-four-hour period, it seemed impossible to insure total security. And what made it even more difficult to control the activities of possible saboteurs was the fact that thousands of longshoremen were required to load and unload the cargoes. Mechanization was still a long way off.

The International Longshoremen's Association, the East Coast dock workers' union, was Mafia dominated. A command from the underworld could close down or presumably damage the harbor. It was through the Port of New York that the guns, tanks, airplane parts, and food needed by the beleaguered Allies were flowing to Europe in ever increasing quantities. And even before the *Normandie* was lost, U.S. Naval Intelligence had become convinced that information about ship convoys was being signaled to submarines or directly to Germany by agents in New York. Even more disturbing was a report that shipping data and even assistance in refueling submarines might be traced to criminal elements among the Italian- or German-speaking people working on the waterfront of New York.

During 1942 the war at sea had gone from bad to worse. In March alone, fifty ships were sunk by the rampaging U-boats. Many of these undersea vessels were highly efficient IX-C long-range submarines operating from their deep concrete piers in the French ports of St. Nazaire and Lorient. Bombing raids against these bases proved futile. The victims in that bloody month included twenty-four American vessels and eight British ones. The others belonged to such countries as Norway. And in the three-month period before the *Normandie* disaster seventy-one merchant vessels had been torpedoed by Hitler's submarines.

These figures represented losses of men, matériel, and propaganda momentum comparable to Pearl Harbor itself. The Navy seemed totally unprepared to cope with the submarine menace. What was Naval Intelligence doing? Nothing, as far as anyone could see.

The Navy Department, under Secretary Frank Knox, went straight to President Roosevelt with the problem, and Roosevelt proposed setting up a special intelligence unit to handle security in the Third Naval District, which included New York, Connecticut, and northern New Jersey ports. It was to be directly under Knox's control and outside the normal security service hierarchy, which caused some irritation and anger among Navy brass but seemed the only way to repair the situation in a hurry.

There was tight secrecy around the work of this particular intelligence unit. After a lot of infighting, Naval Security managed to get its way and reports were made directly to it, then to Secretary Knox. But then and even long afterward, intelligence activities in the Third Naval District remained one of the best-kept secrets of the war.

One powerful reason for secrecy was that the intelligence men seem to have thought it imperative to work closely with the Mafia in their efforts to increase security. More than a hint of how much cooperation there was between gangsters and the naval authorities came not long after the war ended, when Thomas E. Dewey, now governor of New York, suddenly announced on January 3, 1946, that he was commuting Lucky Luciano's thirty-to-fifty-year sentence and that Luciano would be sent to Italy.

For years after Luciano's departure, rumors persisted about what role he and the mob had played in the war effort. In 1954, William B. Herlands, New York State Commissioner of Investigation, conducted an official but secret inquiry into the rumors for nine months. The naval authorities did all they could to block Herlands' efforts to get to the bottom of the story, but Rear Admiral Carl F. Espe, director of Naval Intelligence of the Department of the Navy, admitted, "We are advised that contacts made with Luciano and his influence on other criminal sources resulted in their cooperation with Naval Intelligence which was considered useful to the Navy."

After calling dozens of witnesses, including many reluctant naval officers, Herlands concluded in his official report: "The evidence demonstrates that Luciano's assistance and cooperation were secured by Naval Intelligence in the course of the evolving and expanding requirements of national security. No practical purpose would be served by debating the technical scope of Luciano's aid to the war effort. Over and beyond any precise rating is the crystal-clear fact that Luciano and his associates and contacts during a period when 'the outcome of the war appeared extremely grave' were responsible for a wide range of services which were considered 'useful to the Navy.' "

Less official observers have some evidence of a partnership which flourished mightily from its beginnings in 1942, when rather sinister-looking men, not at all Navy types, were often seen going furtively in and out of the Navy's New York headquarters, first at 90 Church Street, then at Number 50, in downtown Manhattan.

This was the headquarters of Lieutenant Commander Charles Radcliffe Haffenden, head of the B-3 (investigative) section of the Third Naval District's intelligence staff. He was an extroverted, unorthodox Navy man who had risen from the ranks during the First World War. During peacetime he had had a variety of jobs, including that of brick salesman. He quickly realized that he had the toughest job of all in Naval Intelligence. The admirals had turned their noses up at "playing spy" for far too long, and now they were paying the price for their shortsightedness.

The effort to enlist leaders of organized crime in securing the sea lanes to Europe was a desperate shortcut to compensate for years of neglect in the vital field of intelligence work. And in picking Haffenden the naval authorities had made a shrewd appointment. As one of his aides said of him, "He took no notice of regulations and red tape and other crap like that. He once told me, 'I'll talk to anybody, a priest, a bank manager, a gangster, the devil himself, if I can get the information I need. This is a war. American lives are at stake. It's not a college game where we have to look up the rule book every minute, and we're not running a headquarters office where regulations must be followed to the letter. I have a job to do.' "

Haffenden soon realized that his more notorious criminal contacts were rather shy about being seen on Church Street. He began inviting them to call at his hideaway offices at the Astor Hotel, in midtown Manhattan.

His predecessors in the New York office had not been so thoughtful. Their own security staff had run into a wall of silence on the docks. These fresh-faced, often inexperienced naval men from good families and good colleges could not speak the language of the docks. Longshoremen said, "We don't know nothin' " to all their earnest inquiries. Efforts to find out who had been behind the blaze on the *Normandie* made absolutely no progress. Nobody on the docks dared—even if they had wanted to be helpful—to speak to total strangers.

When Haffenden took charge it was clear to him that his staff would have to make contact with the Mafia leaders, people who had the authority to talk if they wished. The devil himself had to be consulted, because he alone could give the Navy the answers they were looking for. But the devil in the guise of the mob is not easy to find.

The Navy appealed to the offices of Manhattan District Attorney Thomas E. Dewey, the man who knew the most about gangsters in New York. Surely his knowledge of the underworld would help. Dewey ordered one of his dedicated and informed investigators, Murray Gurfein, to cooperate with Commander Haffenden and his "ferret squad."

Gurfein knew that if any cooperation with the Mafia was to result from his efforts, a message would have to be sent to the top echelons of the criminal world. No minor crime figure would talk to the authorities without orders from his top boss. As a first step he got in touch with Joseph "Socks" Lanza, the Mafia chief who ruled the Fulton Fish Market, the largest fresh seafood center in the world. No fishing boat, no matter how humble, landed its catch without paying homage to Lanza in the form of a hundred-dollar bill. No load left the market without another bill being slipped to one of Lanza's lieutenants. Even when Lanza was serving a prison sentence in Michigan before the Second World War, he still ran the place. Now "Socks," in and out of jail since childhood on charges of murder and other crimes, found himself being asked to cooperate with the authorities, his lifelong enemies.

In the tradition of spying and counterspying, Gurfein met Joe Socks one midnight in March 1942, on a bench in Riverside Park. Gurfein said to the astonished gangster, "We want you to help your country. We want to know what's going on. We want information from all the captains and sailors who know the coast. You're well aware of the little places where friends of yours used to land cargoes of liquor in the days of Prohibition. Now we want to know who's behind the sabotage and spying in the dock areas." A few days later the bemused Lanza found himself in the Astor Hotel, with a full-fledged naval commander in uniform complete with war ribbons shaking his hand and offering him a drink. "I'm Commander Haffenden. I'm going to ask you to be a patriotic American."

The voice of the U.S. Navy went on: "Right now we know that the sea is swarming with Italian and Portuguese fishermen hauling in the mackerel catch. We need to find out how the Germans are getting information about our ship movements to Europe. Can you and these fishermen help us? I'd like to send you some of my agents for you to disguise as ordinary fishermen aboard the boats going out."

Lanza said he would do what he could, and off he rushed to seek advice from an old friend he knew he could trust.

"The minute Joe spoke to me I knew it was a message for somebody higher up," said Lansky. "Naval Intelligence was hoping Joe would lead them directly to the spies who were working for the Nazis, but Gurfein knew better."

Murray Gurfein knew life was not that simple. He was well aware that nothing could be done without the cooperation and help of top Mafia leaders. Lanza ran the Fulton market but he was a pawn in a much larger game.

Lansky believes Gurfein picked his contact because he knew about Lanza's relationship with Joe Adonis and Frank Costello. Police had photographed them at Lanza's wedding in February 1941. Gurfein had also established that Lanza was known to Lucky Luciano through Lanza's brother-in-law, Prospero Vincent Viggiano, who was a Tammany boss. Lanza also had Tammany chief Albert Marinelli in his pocket. Gurfein hoped all this meant some connection with Luciano, however tenuous. It would probably take Lucky himself to give the order for cooperation that Gurfein needed.

"Joe Socks did the right thing by coming to me," said Lansky. "He knew I'd give him the right advice. Both of us went to see Frank Costello, who had been best man at Joe's wedding. But Gurfein's move had been even shrewder than he realized, because Lucky and I were close to Lanza ourselves. We got him out of a lot of trouble when he was a boy, and he never forgot how we helped him. His mother, Carmella Lanza, went to Frank Costello when Joe was arrested for killing a man on the South Street docks. Frank came to Lucky and me and there was pressure on the witnesses, who suddenly decided they hadn't seen anything. So Lanza was freed. Later on, Lucky sold Joe a house in Long Beach, out on Long Island, where he hid out when he had some other problems. Lanza stayed there for quite some time and I think he enjoyed it. He brought his girl friend—I remember her name, Rosie Sanganata—and didn't budge from Long Beach until things were quiet. So Lanza knew where his best interests were when he had a problem.

"Everybody in New York was laughing at the way those naïve

Navy agents were going around the docks. They went up to men working in the area and talked out of the corner of their mouths like they had seen in the movies, asking about spies.

"Only one man was going to give the O.K. to the Italians' talking to the Navy. If he said yes, there would be a deal. If he said no, no deal. Frank Costello was not going to move on his own and certainly Lanza wasn't. The key to the whole situation was in Charlie's prison cell," said Lansky.

"Sure, I'm the one who put Lucky and Naval Intelligence together. We both knew that when Mussolini went into the war some of the Italians in America were proud. They were second-class citizens in America—to be poor means you're automatically second class. It was very important for them that Mussolini was winning. It gave them pride. Even if he was a friend of Hitler they didn't care. This was a small minority of the Italian-Americans, you understand, but they did exist—and a few others were terrorized by Fascist agents."

Lansky thought a moment, then for the first time gave his version of the story for the record. "I want to make my situation clear," he said. "The reason why I cooperated was because of strong personal convictions. I wanted the Nazis beaten. I made this my number one priority even before the United States got into the war. I was a Jew and I felt for those Jews in Europe who were suffering. They were my brothers. I've never got used to the idea of being called a criminal, and I'd like to tell you how and when this label was first put on me. Maybe it will surprise you, but it started in the 1930s, after Hitler took power in Germany. Nazi sympathizers in the United States, some of them Americans of German origin and some not, set up what they called the German-American Bund, or Union.

"This was a pro-Nazi organization that spread Nazi-style anti-Semitic slogans. They strutted around the place and made threats, like throwing all Jews into concentration camps. I was always very sensitive about anti-Semitism, but during those years many other people also became worried. Important WASPs, as we would call them now, openly made anti-Semitic statements and some magazines and papers backed them. This worried Jewish leaders, including the most respected one of all, Rabbi Stephen Wise. He sent me a message asking me to do something about this dangerous trend. Another Jewish leader who was worried was a respected New York judge, an important member of the Republican

Party. We knew each other and one day in 1935 he came to see me and said, 'Nazism is flourishing in the United States. The Bund members are not ashamed to have their meetings in the most public places. We Jews should be more militant. Meyer, we want to take action against these Nazi sympathizers. We'll put money and legal assistance at your disposal, whatever you need. Can you organize the militant part for us?'

"I was very flattered and of course agreed to help. 'I'll fight these Nazis with my own resources,' I said. 'I don't need your cash. But I will ask you one thing, that after we go into action you'll try to make sure the Jewish press doesn't criticize me.

"The judge promised to try to do that, and for the next two or three years my friends and I saw some good action against the Brown Shirts around New York. I got my buddies like Bugsy Siegel—before he went to California—and some other young guys. We taught them how to use their fists and handle themselves in fights, and we didn't behave like gents. A lot of young men who had no connection with me came to see me quietly, without publicity, young guys in all kinds of occupations, and many not so young.

"The judge and his friends supplied the names of the big activists among the Nazi sympathizers. For instance, there was that famous affair in Yorkville, the center of the German colony in Manhattan. I was given the address where the Nazis were preparing a meeting, and Walter Winchell telephoned me about it and encouraged me to take action.

"Well, we got there that evening and found several hundred people dressed in their brown shirts. The stage was decorated with a swastika and pictures of Hitler. The speakers started ranting. There were only about fifteen of us, but we went into action. We attacked them in the hall and threw some of them out the windows. There were fist fights all over the place. Most of the Nazis panicked and ran out. We chased them and beat them up, and some of them were out of action for months. Yes, it was violence. We wanted to teach them a lesson. We wanted to show them that Jews would not always sit back and accept insults. I know that the judge and Rabbi Wise were pleased with us.

"Walter Winchell phoned to thank me for busting up that meeting and I told him he had nothing to thank me for because I was doing what had to be done anyway, and I also told him he had given me the wrong address, we had found the right place on our own.

"We operated against the Brown Shirts in a whole lot of places—in New York, New Jersey, and even farther away. We knew how to handle them, me and my friends. The Italians I knew offered to help, but as a matter of pride I wouldn't accept. I neglected my business many times to travel around and organize our counterattacks. I must say I enjoyed beating up those Nazis. There were times when we treated a Bund leader or other big anti-Semite in a very special way, but the main point was just to teach them that Jews couldn't be kicked around.

"But the Jewish leaders couldn't stop my mistreatment in the press, and would you believe, the Jewish press was the first to condemn us. When they reported our anti-Bund activities they referred to us as 'the Jewish gangsters.' I remember this was the way the *Morgen Journal,* the big Yiddish newspaper of the time, came out against us. In fact the Jewish papers were the first to call us the 'mob of Lansky and Bugsy Siegel.' This was the first time I was ever publicly mentioned as a gangster.

"Later the general press and the radio picked it up. When I asked journalists in New York to stop it, they answered me, 'Why do you say we shouldn't call you a gangster when your own Jewish press describes you and your friends that way? They must know what they're talking about.' I had no answer to that one.

"The Jewish press helped create a pressure group of influential political people in the Jewish community who objected to our direct action program. One day we got a message from Rabbi Wise to stop our activity—people were saying it was morally wrong to use the same violence the Nazis were using. I tried to argue, but if leaders like Rabbi Wise decided it was wrong, I had to respect their wishes.

"I really think our action against the Bund created an atmosphere in which my name was easily connected with gangsterism and the Mafia. During those years certain groups operated in the United States which became known as Murder Incorporated or other such extravagant titles. Of course there were criminals, but I had nothing to do with that kind of criminal violence. But as the years went on, people confused the issues. My name was connected with gangsterism and that was it. And I do believe some circles in America wanted to create the impression that all Jews were criminals. It was another form of anti-Semitism.

"At any rate, after we stopped our direct action against the local Nazis, I was still ready to do all I could to help America because it had adopted me. I was planning and wondering what I could do long before I was approached. But Gurfein knew that the Italians on the waterfront would not cooperate fully unless Lucky said it was O.K., and why should Lucky help the authorities who had sent him to that hideous prison?" In summer, as Lansky remembers Luciano telling him, "it's like a hothouse, and it stinks like a human being who's never washed in his life. In winter the wind comes right through you and you can see the ice forming on the inside walls. That's why we call it Siberia. It's the worst place in the world. In a way, Meyer, it would be better to be dead than to stay here."

After the initial contact with Lanza was on the grapevine, Gurfein used every other method he could to get to Luciano. His second contact was with Moses Polakoff, a lawyer who had represented both Luciano and Lansky. Polakoff had served as Assistant U.S. Attorney and for five years was chief of the Southern District's Criminal Division. From 1928 until 1932 he was on the staff of the New York State attorney general's office.

Polakoff, who had been a Navy seaman in the First World War, was especially sympathetic to those hundreds of Americans being drowned at sea in 1942. He recalled for the Herlands inquiry of 1954 that Gurfein had told him the intelligence agencies believed that "if sabotage was to be done, it might be done through the direction of the Germans, but by the Italian element." And "if Luciano made an honest effort to be of service in the future, they would bear that in mind."

Polakoff told Gurfein that he did not know Luciano "well enough to broach the subject to him on my own, but I knew the person who I had confidence in . . . I would like to discuss the matter with this person before I committed myself." Lansky was the man Polakoff had in mind.

Lansky takes up the story. "The big meeting was between Polakoff, Gurfein, and me. We had breakfast sometime in April 1942 at the Longchamps on West Fifty-eighth Street between Fifth and Sixth avenues. I told Gurfein that I loathed Adolf Hitler and that I was a patriot. I was grateful that America had given me a home and that America had been good to me through the years. But I did say, I remember it quite clearly, 'I must warn you. Mussolini is very important to some of the Italians in New York. He is a hero to them.' But I said that I'd do all I could to help the Navy or anybody else to win the war."

Gurfein told Lansky, "The Navy wants some prominent Italians to get active in a movement to stop sabotage."

Lansky replied, "The man you want is Lucky Luciano."

23 Escape from Siberia

Gurfein was not entirely surprised when Lansky turned the conversation to Luciano. This might be the breakthrough the armed forces needed. But he had to ask, "Can we trust him?"

"Sure you can," said Lansky. "I'll guarantee it. His family is all here, right in New York. They're proud to be Americans. Never mind about his crime record. His father and his brothers and sisters and their children—I know them all. I know they will do all they can to help us. And so will Charlie.

"But if you want me to talk to Lucky about this you have to help me as well. You have to make a gesture he'll understand and appreciate. Get him out of Siberia. He's cold and angry up there in Dannemora, and it's hard for me and his family to get there. I'm not going into the way you framed him with those vice girls, but you must realize there're going to be problems. If you bring Lucky to Sing Sing and then maybe set up the right atmosphere, we can do something. And there's another thing. If we're going to carry this off, the talks between Lucky and me had better be really private. Up there in Dannemora everybody in the prison sees every single person who arrives. People talk and the news will be back in New York in a few hours. That may not help our cause one little bit."

After the breakfast meeting, the three men went to the Astor Hotel, Room 196. "I shook hands with Commander Haffenden. He was very polite. Very hospitable. A real gentleman."

On Haffenden's desk was a dossier on Meyer Lansky which told the naval officer that Lansky was "bigger than Buchalter or Jacob

Shapiro. He is the equal of such gangsters as Bugsy Siegel and Mickey Cohen. He was a major figure in bootlegging operations and is concerned today with the manufacture, sale, distribution, and the gathering of money from juke boxes. He is a personal friend of every major Mafia leader and man of crime in America. He is deeply involved in illegal gambling."

Haffenden said, "You'll notice that I am not wearing my uniform and this is not my real office. That's downtown on Church Street. I'm going to be frank with you. I need your cooperation, not for myself but for the United States.

"I'm going to ask you to keep what I say a complete secret. I'm risking the lives of many men by mentioning it. A very large convoy of American troops is shortly going overseas from here. I want their safety to be absolutely guaranteed. We've got to make sure no word of this leaks out from the men who work the docks."

This was not the dreadful indiscretion it sounds like. Haffenden knew that the embarkation of large numbers of troops could not be kept a secret on the docks, and the soldiers would have to go regardless of security, because they were headed for the Allied landings in North Africa. And he probably had shrewdly guessed that the "Little Man" would rather die than betray such a confidence.

"During our talk Haffenden admitted to me that they were still worried about the *Normandie* incident. If sabotage could happen there it could happen again, maybe even a worse blow. Navy Intelligence was very upset, very worried about espionage on the waterfront. He told me what I already knew, that the Italians ran the waterfront unions and he was well aware that they could close the whole port down if they wanted to. He was quite frank and said that preliminary contacts had been made through Joe Lanza, as I also knew. He mentioned our work against the local Nazis, the Brown Shirts. He had obviously been well briefed about my background. I could see the dossier on his desk. He was very careful and polite with me. He said he knew I had a reputation as a gangster but he also knew I was strongly against the Nazis. He appealed to me to be a good American and to think of the Jews suffering in Europe.

"I replied right away that I knew what I had to do. I left his place and went straight to Frank Costello and told him he had to cooperate. He agreed, of course. The message went to Albert Anastasia too, and I told him face to face that he mustn't burn any more ships. He was sorry—not sorry he'd had the *Normandie* burned but sorry he couldn't get at the Navy again. Apparently he had learned in the Army to hate the Navy. 'Stuck-up bastards' he called them.

"Next thing Frank and I did was to get back to Joe Lanza. He took his orders like he always did. He kept going to the Astor Hotel and promising the agents he would help them all he could. These agents were still thinking they could get to the top Mafia leaders through Joe. Joe was uncomfortable with these naval men and they had some trouble understanding what he was saying, with his accent. But they were always polite. I was working out how to approach Lucky, and I told Joe Socks to keep his help on a low level in the meantime. He wanted to know how much money to take from the Navy. Frank and I told him not to be an idiot. 'You're going to be a patriot,' we said. 'You do it for nothing. Even your expenses have to come out of your own pocket.' Joe was very surprised but he didn't argue. He did what he was told. That's why he'd been put in charge of the fish market.

"Joe kept meeting those Naval Intelligence guys all over New York. They used to buy him lunches on Broadway and in restaurants in the Fulton Fish Market area. I wondered how they put it down on their expense vouchers." As part of the Navy-ordered coverup later, all documents—vouchers and other papers relating to the Mafia-Navy connection—were destroyed. Just how the agents coped with expense sheets listing names of Mafia leaders is still a mystery.

Lanza obeyed orders but it soon became clear to Commander Haffenden that the help of this minor chieftain was limited. "If the Navy was going to get the real information they wanted, they would have to deal with Lucky," Lansky says. "I kept telling them that because I knew it was the only way to get the job done."

The naval authorities' next move was to confer with New York State Correction Commissioner John A. Lyons. It was his suggestion that rather than send Luciano to Sing Sing, as Lansky had asked, he should be transferred to Great Meadow Prison, in Upstate New York near Comstock, which would be more pleasant than Sing Sing and more convenient for interviewing him.

John Lyons was a one-time police inspector who had a better insight than most people on how the underworld was run. He had led a crack squad of detectives that became known as the Lyons men. They were later the models for the famous television series "The Untouchables," and John Lyons himself was merged into a fictionalized Eliot Ness. Asked to give the Navy some major help, he did not hesitate. "I am in favor of the Naval Intelligence project and I intend giving Luciano every possible opportunity to aid and assist the United States intelligence services," he said. "I'd do it if it only saved the life of a single American soldier or a single American ship." Thus Luciano was quickly and quietly transferred to Great Meadow Prison.

Meyer Lansky's role in the deal between the Mafia and the authorities was understood by all concerned. In a letter to the warden of Great Meadow, Lyons wrote, "Dear Warden, This is to advise you that I have granted permission to Mr. Meyer Lansky to visit and interview Inmate Charles Luciano in your institution when accompanied by Mr. Polakoff, the inmate's attorney. . . . You are authorized to waive the usual fingerprint requirements and to grant Mr. Lansky and Mr. Polakoff the opportunity of interviewing the inmate privately."

"I was looking forward to seeing Charlie," said Lansky. "We went by train to Albany, then drove the sixty miles to the prison, Polakoff, Costello, and I.

"Charlie didn't know why he'd been moved and he was suspicious when they told him he had three visitors. They didn't tell him who we were. When he saw us he could hardly believe his eyes. He stretched out his arms and shouted, 'What are you doing here? I never expected to see you fellows here.'

"Charlie threw his arms around me and kissed me. He'd never done that before, but he was pretty carried away. He guessed at once that we'd had something to do with his getting out of Siberia. He told me he had a clean cell with hot water. It was a big change after Dannemora. He'd tried not to complain up there, but he couldn't help telling us that at Great Meadow he had decent toilet paper for the first time in six years.

"I handed him the food packages we'd brought along, some Italian sweets and pastrami and kosher pickles that I knew he liked. I waited while he had a snack, then I began to talk about the Navy situation. He heard me out and asked what Frank and I thought. Frank said he should cooperate with the government. I told him, 'It may very well help you, Lucky, and it certainly won't do you any harm.' I thought he ought to do it for patriotic reasons but it might also help him get out of jail eventually.

"We went over the legal aspects, as we'd done so often before— only this time we had some hope. Charlie wouldn't be eligible for parole until 1956 at the earliest, and I told him bluntly, 'If you cooperate you stand a chance to get out earlier—a commutation or whatever. Maybe they'll be lenient with you. Otherwise you've got no chance at all.'

"Charlie sat there for a while. Then he said he needed time to think it over. I wouldn't like it said that I made an offer to Charlie that he couldn't refuse. That's the sort of language that belongs to movies about the Mafia. We simply made him an honest and respectable proposal and reminded him that American lives were at stake. Then we went off and let him think about it.

"On our next visit Charlie told us he had made up his mind. He looked at me with a smile and said he was excited at the prospect of doing something useful and also at the possibility that he would be free before he was an old man. He said to me, 'I have no choice. Let's do it.'

"He was worried about one very important thing which the Navy hadn't mentioned. He was not an American citizen and there had been a deportation warrant against him since the time of his trial. It still stood. If he got a commutation he would likely get deported at the same time, and he was afraid that if he helped Americans against the Fascists he might be killed when he got back to Italy, no matter which side won the war.

"Charlie told us, 'Look, I'm going to be deported if I get out of here—whenever and however that happens. I want this deal kept quiet, absolutely top secret. All the contacts we'll have to arrange, all the orders, have got to be kept quiet. Otherwise I'll be a marked man when I get sent back. And there's no point in getting out of jail if I'm going to end up with a bullet in my head.' "

Luciano insisted that Lansky had to be the man who would go around New York and speak privately to his friends and underlings. He said that if a message was passed through Lansky the Italian community would accept it as authentic and honest. They would tell Lansky what the Navy needed to know and obey the orders he brought because they knew he spoke for Luciano. And the first order Lansky had to transmit was to come and confer with Luciano himself.

Polakoff confirmed that the naval authorities approved this arrangement between the prisoner and Lansky. "These people knew that if Lansky claimed he was acting for Luciano, that statement would not be questioned."

In the following weeks a series of Mafia overlords and their associates made their way in and out of the gates of Great Meadow Prison. Singly and in groups they came to the court of Lucky Luciano. Lansky was always with the Italian gangsters brought to receive orders on how and where and what influence was to be exerted in the port area of New York. Frequently Charlie and Lansky held meetings by themselves with only their lawyer present, for the prison authorities insisted that Polakoff be present at all times. Lansky and Luciano used these meetings to discuss their personal business.

"But Polakoff never took part in the discussions," Lansky said. "Some of the matters we had to talk about were not for him to listen to. We didn't want to embarrass him, so we would go to the other side of the room and he'd read his newspaper. He used to bring a pile of papers to catch up with what he had to read."

Within a month of the first get-together at Great Meadow Prison, Lansky was able to tell Naval Intelligence, "I can promise you one thing. There'll be no German submarines in the Port of New York. Every man down there who works in the harbor—all the sailors, all the fishermen, every longshoreman, every individual who has anything to do with the coming and going of ships to the United States—is now helping the fight against the Nazis. There is nowhere in the United States where you'll find a better brand of patriotism. I can give you a cast-iron guarantee on this, a guarantee backed by Charlie Luciano."

Lansky's visits to Luciano lasted longer and longer. The prison authorities were worried, for clearly the Allied war effort was not the only business the two men were discussing. After all, those in the know considered Lansky the "brains" behind Charlie Luciano and the two men seemed to have a vast amount of business to discuss. Plans for controlling and extending their joint criminal empire were certainly included in their agenda, though even some thirty years later Lansky still did not wish to talk about that aspect of the conversation.

Lansky was also a frequent visitor at naval headquarters. He saw Commander Haffenden almost daily, either at the Astor Hotel or openly at official headquarters on Church Street. "At first we got down to such details as the loading and unloading of ships at the piers," Lansky remembers. "How to prevent work stoppages and strikes and how to speed up loading. How to keep troop movements a secret. Who to trust and who not to trust. How to prevent sabotage. I didn't always know the answers to the questions they asked. They were very pressing about what they wanted to know, and came up with a lot of demands. But I could always pick up a telephone and get the information—either right away or, if I had to talk to several people, in a few hours.

"With Charlie's backing everything went smoothly. I must emphasize that none of this could have been done without him. His word in the Italian community was still total law. No one would disobey him.

"One big problem was getting the cooperation of the International Longshoremen's Association. I got hold of Johnny 'Cockeye' Dunn, who ran the West Side piers in Manhattan, and took him to meet Commander Haffenden. I mentioned Lucky's name and Cockeye came right along. I had to get him out of jail first, as it happened, but I told the Navy he was the man for the job and he came out on bail. The Navy saw to it—I know they went very high up to pull that one off. Cockeye didn't have any official position in the union and he'd been in prison a lot of times, for robbery and other crimes. But he was the power over there no matter what anybody said.

"Johnny was very grateful to be out. He helped the Navy so much that I think they gave him a code number and an official kind of title.

"I gave Cockeye his orders: 'You have to go down to the piers and find out who is loyal and who is not loyal. You have to see that there are no strikes and that the job is done quickly when military stuff is being loaded. And we have to make sure everybody keeps his mouth shut about troop movements. You've got to know at once if anybody is talking too much. That means going into the bars to see that the crews and the longshoremen don't start sounding off when they get drunk. If they start giving away important information you've got to stop them, and if you see anybody listening to them hard you have to find out who it is and tell Commander Haffenden.'

"Dunn came to me several times to complain about the way the Navy was doing things. 'I can suggest better methods than they're using,' he said. And what's more, he did.

"Dunn had a lot to do with stopping sabotage on the docks. He knew everybody and people were terrified of him. Haffenden used him a lot. For instance, there was the time when the Navy was suspicious about German agents at the Great Northern Hotel, where some of the waterfront people hung out. There was a leak there. So Cockeye got hold of some of his men and dressed them up as waiters and they listened to what the other waiters were saying. They took notes about the guests and who was listening to whom. He got his men dressed up as all kinds of staff in hotels and night clubs in Brooklyn and Manhattan.

"Old Cockeye didn't necessarily play by the rules. I remember once Commander Haffenden was upset about a couple of men who were staying at one of the West Side hotels. They were extremely interested in what the sailors were saying. Haffenden had no way of putting an end to this; he was sure they were spies but he had no proof. Cockeye didn't wait for proof, and the naval agents were very surprised when the two men vanished. They questioned Cockeye about it and he just said, 'They'll never bother us again.' They didn't press him for details but just asked him in future to consult them before he took any special action of his own. A great deal of this sort of thing went on with Cockeye. I don't say he killed many people but he certainly was an expert at strong-arm tactics. Don't forget, the docks are a very rough area and some pretty tough men work there. Cockeye knew how to handle them better than any man alive. And he kept the ships moving. Those war years were the best for him—violence in a good cause. Later on he went to the chair for murder."

Commander Haffenden met with many equally unsavory figures. His former secretary, Elizabeth Schwerin, told the Herlands inquiry that some of the biggest names in the underworld were there. Commander Haffenden would order drinks for them in his suite and Miss Schwerin would take them in herself. He was "very enthusiastic" about the cooperation they were giving him. "And he made the statement once: If he had not had this cooperation, he would not have been able to do many things for the Navy, government and country, either in preventing sabotage . . . getting cooperation or information, whatever it was that he needed."

Another man whom Lansky channeled to Haffenden was Jeremiah Sullivan, who had served ten years in Sing Sing on a second-degree murder charge. Known to most people as John McCue, he was the right-hand man of Joseph Ryan, president of the International Longshoremen's Association. Pleased to find himself mixing with such respectable people, the ex-convict could not help the naval authorities enough. In fact he embarrassed them with the amount of assistance he offered in keeping the port working smoothly—an embarrassment caused mainly by the strong-arm methods he preferred. Once or twice when Navy men reported difficulties with certain individuals on the docks, broken legs and broken arms brought instantaneous cooperation.

"I took all sorts of people to see Lucky," Lansky said. "Each guy I brought got a lecture on how he had to do his duty as an American citizen and cooperate with the military authorities.

"As a result of all this I met a lot of Italians I hadn't known before, and I took most of them to Commander Haffenden myself. I was shepherding so many people around that I began to feel like I was living in Grand Central Station. Somewhere along in there I was introduced to Haffenden's boss, Captain Roscoe MacFall, who was the intelligence officer for the whole Third Naval District. I was told that this was the man who had thought up the whole idea of roping in the Mafia to help the war effort."

Despite efforts by naval authorities to play down wartime cooperation between the armed forces and criminal elements, Captain MacFall later testified, "The use of underworld informants and characters, like the use of other extremely confidential investigative procedures, was . . . a calculated risk that I assumed as District Intelligence Officer. It was my responsibility to use my best judgment as to the ways and means of getting information. . . ."

24 The Navy and the Mafia

During 1942 and '43 Lansky stayed close to New York, helping the Navy as much as he could and giving much less attention than usual to his far-flung business interests. He had to limit his visits to Florida, where he had been concentrating his efforts during the past few years, and because of the war he no longer flew to Havana.

Then, as Lansky tells it, came one of the most exciting moments of his war. "I got a message from an Italian I knew. He insisted that I go to meet him myself because he was scared to talk to anyone else. Lucky had given orders that any Italian in the New York area who had information was to give it to somebody important in the Mafia. But this man insisted on talking to me because he was afraid his information might get back to a pro-Mussolini Italian, in which case he would be a dead man.

"He wouldn't even talk in the restaurant in Little Italy where we met. He insisted that we go for a walk. As we strolled along he explained that he had a brother who was a fisherman. The brother had been out on his boat the night before, off the coast of Long Island. What troubled the fisherman was that he himself was up to something illegal, but he had nevertheless confided what he saw to his brother. I promised that I would never reveal either of their names and I didn't ask what the illegal activity was. It didn't matter and my guess was that the real reason why they were so scared was not about the law but because they were going against somebody in the Mafia—catching fish and not paying the proper tribute to the local Mafia man, something like that. What did matter was that the fisherman saw a submarine rise out of the water. He was terrified and didn't move. He watched the submarine lid, as he called it, open up, and then some men got out. They pulled a rubber boat out of the submarine and the four men plus two sailors got into it and rowed to the shore. The oars were padded and it was all done very quietly.

"Then the four men climbed out of the boat with some suitcases and walked up on the beach. The boat went back with the two sailors and they and the small boat were hauled aboard. The submarine closed its lid and vanished out to sea.

"I thanked the man and offered to pay for his trip in to see me, but he was insulted at that. He only asked me to keep his secret and I promised again that nobody would know who had told me the story. It was three in the morning by then, but I rushed to see Commander Haffenden. He was very excited and told me he was going to handle this business in person, though he had over a hundred agents working for him. I told him the exact place where the submarine had come out of the water and the approximate time, everything the fisherman's brother had said, but with no names and no mention of illegalities.

"Not long afterward J. Edgar Hoover announced the arrest of eight German saboteurs in New York City and Chicago. It was a great victory for the United States. After the story came out, Commander Haffenden told me he had gone out to Long Island as he said he would, and that the fisherman's fantastic story was all true. Four Germans had landed there with dynamite and arms and other sabotage equipment. Their plan was to blow up factories making tanks and guns as well as bridges and ships. At about the same time four other German saboteurs had landed close to Ponte Vedra, in Florida, disguised as fishermen. They were captured in Chicago with names of contacts in America still on them. This led to the FBI tracking down quite a large number of Nazi agents in the United States.

"Haffenden showed me a German button that had come off the shirt of one of the Nazis who climbed out of that submarine. He had found it on the beach where they landed. It was evidently a souvenir he cherished very much. I noticed he carefully put it back in his pocket.

"That was a rewarding experience for me, but I also enjoyed helping the war effort on my own, rather than through collaboration with Charlie. I had kept in touch with a lot of the people who had helped in the fights against the Bund, and so I had a good deal of information to pass on to the Navy about the man who liked to call himself the American Hitler, Fritz Kuhn. A lot of Germans like him were in the Yorkville Bund, and they made no secret of the fact that they were supporting Hitler even though America was now in the war.

"Some of our information about that crowd came from another team of fake waiters. I persuaded some of the people who owned restaurants in Yorkville to hire friends of mine posing as waiters, so they could listen to what the customers were saying. And the commander found some German-speaking Navy agents to play the part.

"Then I got Joe Lanza to speak to one of his pals, William 'Tough Willy' McCabe, who was in charge of the numbers runners in Harlem. These are the guys who carry the money from the bettors to the syndicate. I thought having some waiters up there would be a good idea. Then Joe suggested that we get some Navy agents into the business of servicing the vending machines in the clubs. The people who did that job came in at odd times of the night and day to make their collections, and it would be a good cover. To see how it would operate, Commander Haffenden, his boss MacFall, and some of their guys went and had dinner at Roger's Corner, on upper Broadway. This was one of the places where the boys were going to work, because a lot of German sympathizers liked to eat there too.

"So we had naval officers being collectors for the Mafia. They handed over the money they collected and were always honest in their dealings. I think this must be the only time the U.S. Navy ever directly helped the Mafia," Lansky said dryly.

"My stand against the pro-Nazis also got me involved in what must have been one of the most sensitive problems the intelligence people had to deal with. Right in the middle of the war the Navy was worried—and so were some big shots in Washington—about some senator named Walsh. For some reason he had got into the habit of coming up to New York, and there was a strong suspicion that he was a regular patron of a brothel over near the Brooklyn Navy Yard. It was a homosexual joint but it was not the senator's preferences that were upsetting people. Everybody knew it was a hangout for Bundists. A lot of them were homosexuals. I was always amazed at how many of those bully-boy Nazis were not the slightest bit interested in women—mostly their tastes turned to other men or young boys.

"There were rumors that this particular brothel was a center for spies. Clients came from all over New York and Washington and elsewhere, and there were some important government people among them. It would be a good place for a spy, because if you got hold of the names of the patrons you could blackmail them to death. All you'd have to do would be to take some pictures through a hole in the wall or a trick mirror and then squeeze the victim for money or information.

"That's why Haffenden was asked to find out about this particular senator. Was he being blackmailed? It sounded like Walsh was more dangerous than the other politicians who dropped in from time to time. He had a big say in the Naval Affairs Committee and knew as much as anybody in Washington about that branch of the service. If he was being blackmailed, the Navy had no secrets.

"Haffenden first asked Polakoff for suggestions about what to do. Polakoff asked me and I got Mikey Lascari into it. I had known Mikey a long time—he was a childhood buddy of Charlie's—and I knew he was an expert on that part of Brooklyn. By the 1940s he was involved with the rackets in New Jersey, but I knew I could count on him.

"It didn't take us long to confirm the rumors. Twenty-four hours later we got the news from Mikey that, sure enough, there were bona fide spies operating out of that brothel. And in addition one of the male prostitutes had a customer whom he had to treat very special and who was known as the 'Senator.'

"Haffenden reported to his bosses and they told him to find out all he could about the man. Some of Mikey's boys showed the Navy team where to hide in the brothel and who to watch out for. They put surveillance on the place around the clock from the outside. Then one day Haffenden told me, 'Please take no further action. I don't want any of your associates involved from here on. There's probably going to be a big scandal but it'll be hushed up because it's wartime.'

"But of course we did keep our own men on the lookout. I was curious. I didn't want the Navy doing something without my knowing what they were up to. They weren't always efficient, as Cockeye said, and it's always worthwhile knowing what is going on.

"Well, they pulled in the owner of the place and threatened him until he told them who the spies in his brothel were. The authorities arrested five men and three of them were proved to be enemy agents.

The other two were released. I was surprised—I knew from our own network they were spying too. A couple of days later these two men were found dead. Nobody had seen anything and nobody ever got charged. We knew those men were spies, and if the authorities weren't going to handle them, then Charlie's men probably settled the matter themselves.

"The brothel owner went to prison to protect him from a revenge killing. He had talked a great deal and the police or the Navy or somebody handled the information in a rather ham-fisted way. Haffenden didn't want to discuss the case at all. I got the impression he was being gagged by his superiors. Mikey's boys and, I heard, some of the Washington press corps knew the story, but it was pretty much hushed up, just as Haffenden predicted. Once he tried to tell me that the senator was not Senator David Walsh but actually another Walsh who had once been a New York State senator. I looked Haffenden straight in the eye and said, 'That's funny. I know the guy you're asking me to believe is the guilty party and he's exactly eighty-seven years old. Are you kidding, he's going to a brothel four times in a week?' "

Lansky seemed to enjoy reminiscing about his wartime contributions more than any other period of his life. Once he was thoroughly involved in keeping the waterfront safe from saboteurs, he took on with equal enthusiasm its protection against union disruptions. The ILA, corrupt and Mafia-ridden but now patriotic to a fault, was glad to have his help in driving off attempts by the West Coast longshoremen's union to clean up the New York waterfront. So was the United States government. The International Longshoremen's and Warehousemen's Union was run by Harry Bridges, a tough, honest Australian whom the government had been trying for years to deport on charges of communism. He was the mortal enemy of Lanza, Anastasia, Adonis, and the other Lansky-Luciano associates who ran the waterfront as a set of fiefdoms, saved by money, violence, and the vicious shape-up system from any semblance of democratic unionism.

According to Lansky, once or twice during the war it looked as if the ILWU had a chance on the East Coast, and according to Lansky, he and his intelligence contacts agreed that Bridges had to be stopped.

"Commander Haffenden got word about this and told Polakoff that the last thing he wanted was labor strife in New York at a time when convoys were being loaded for Europe and North Africa.

There was a certain political aspect in the matter too, but I didn't get into that. I don't think Haffenden did either. His job was to keep the ships moving as safely as possible.

"Moses Polakoff came to me to say the commander was anxious about a rumor of a wildcat strike on the Brooklyn waterfront. Like most unions, the ILA had made a wartime no-strike pledge, but if the Mafia had wanted a strike there would have been one. Our boys had promised no strikes, but of course they had no control over the trouble Harry Bridges might cause. The Navy couldn't get mixed up in a labor dispute directly, not even in the middle of the war. I was surprised they didn't come straight to me, but I appreciated that maybe sometimes things were so complicated that the approach came through my lawyer.

"In fact it was no problem. I had a word with Frank Costello and there was no need to even get Lucky involved. On Frank's orders Joe Adonis simply picked up the phone and gave orders to Brooklyn that there mustn't be a strike, he would deal personally with any man who made trouble in the ILA. I can tell you there was no strike—not even a hint of one.

"A few days later the commander came specially to thank me and said, 'That was a swell job. You stopped that strike.' "

Undeterred by ILA and Mafia antagonism, the Australian union leader came to New York several times during the war years. Joe Lanza was told to deal with Bridges his own way—no questions asked. Lanza sought out the Australian and beat him up.

"Sure Joe belted him," says Lansky. "What did you expect him to do? Have an intellectual discussion with him? Joe wasn't that kind of man."

The means whereby the waterfront was kept quiet hardly fitted in with democratic concepts of legality or morality. Despite the Mafia's orders, however, there were troublemakers and some German sympathizers on the docks, as well as genuine spies and disgruntled individuals who tried to defy the Mafia, help the Nazi cause, or both. If the rebellion was a minor one, the underworld would have the individual fired from his job or beaten up as a warning. Real troublemakers and professional spies met a grimmer fate. The Mafia underlings who had orders from Luciano to make sure there was peace did not trouble the Navy about such men. Waterfront murders were frequent and mostly unsolved: nobody ever saw or heard anything that would help the police with their inquiries.

"There was peace on the waterfront," says Lansky. "It was kept with rough methods. But that's what the Navy asked us to do and that's what the Navy got.

"You can't deny it. The peace resulted from an unwritten agreement between the Mafia and the naval authorities. If they had wanted to, the Mafia could have paralyzed the dock area. I once asked Commander Haffenden what would happen if there was a shutdown there. He threw up his hands and said, 'Without the supplies we're sending to Russia and Britain the war could go on a lot longer. It could even change the course of the war.' So in the end the Mafia helped save the lives of Americans and of people in Europe.

"From the moment when I went to see Lucky and got his cooperation, nothing went wrong in the Port of New York. No sabotage, no strikes, no ships delayed. No enemy agents as far as I know ever got any important information from the men who worked there, and no suspicious characters were allowed anywhere near the loading docks."

Later Meyer Lansky was able to help not only Naval Intelligence but also other branches of the armed forces. The battle against the submarines was now beginning to swing the way of the Allies, and among the reasons, he believes, was the security network that he masterminded and the Mafia guaranteed. Another important development was the introduction of modern antisubmarine measures such as radar, which proved increasingly effective.

25 Sicilian Memories

The landings in North Africa were a success, and plans to invade the European mainland were stepped up.

"Commander Haffenden asked me to have dinner with him one evening," says Lansky. "He told me that they would soon go into Europe. This made my heart glad. It meant the final stage of the war against Hitler. The commander asked me if I could help him again. I didn't see how I could be of assistance in invading Europe—not Meyer Lansky. But the commander suggested that I begin collecting information from the Sicilians I knew. Sicily and the Italian mainland might well be invasion targets if—when—we opened a second front. The intelligence people wanted pictures and maps and details about the areas where the Navy would land the American soldiers. Haffenden was particularly interested in landscapes. What he wanted from me was to approach Sicilians in New York and get hold of their family photograph albums or postcards or anything that had to do with the Sicilian coastline. Obviously this sort of information had to come from the people who had emigrated from Sicily. He also asked me to find reliable contacts in Sicily itself.

"Navy headquarters were soon jammed with Sicilians and other Italians who had been told to go there to show their family mementos and tell what they could remember about the old country. The Navy also asked them to try to send word to relatives there that they should cooperate with the Allies."

Lansky may exaggerate the amount of reliance the naval authorities placed on their Mafia connections, but authoritative voices have confirmed many aspects of his story. Rear Admiral William S. Pye, president of the Naval War College, told a service audience after the war about the serious problems intelligence faced, elaborating on the difficulty his branch of the armed forces found itself in after the Casablanca Conference of January 1943. At that meeting Prime Minister Winston Churchill, President Roosevelt, and their military aides decided to defer an invasion of France across the English Channel, despite widespread calls for a second front. At this stage of the war the Allied forces gathering in the United Kingdom were not powerful or organized enough to attack Nazi-dominated western Europe, yet at the same time the "soft underbelly" of Europe had been opened up by the Allied conquest of North Africa. The Allied war leaders therefore decided to make landings in the Mediterranean area, both to force the Germans to disperse their forces and to put out of action Hitler's by now very unwilling junior partner, Benito Mussolini.

Admiral Pye went on to explain that the feeling that "intelligence duty is somewhat akin to spying and, therefore, in time of peace, is an undignified and unworthy occupation" had been a great hindrance. Hence the U.S. Navy found itself seriously deficient in the intelligence needed for the Allied campaigns; "especially in North Africa and in Italy, we found that we lacked much information required for the most effective planning."

By coincidence the first target on the "soft underbelly" was Sicily, the breeding ground of the Mafia. Lansky says, "There was a lot of pressure on me to keep trying to get people to provide names and addresses of relatives and friends who might be useful for the OSS agents who would land in Sicily even before the soldiers did, as well as the agents who were to go in with the first wave of assault troops." The Office of Strategic Services, wartime predecessor of the Central Intelligence Agency, had its own cadre of Italian-speaking spies and agents, but additional contacts on the spot would be of good use to them.

"The traditional Mafia still dominated the towns and villages of Sicily. Everyone knew that. And though Lucky and I had long since abandoned the Mafia trappings over here, family and clan ties with the old country were still close."

Captain MacFall himself gave this testimony to the Herlands inquiry: "Prior to the landing of United States forces in North Africa and also subsequent to that time, the District Intelligence Office concentrated a considerable portion of its forces on the collection of strategic intelligence in the North African theater and the Mediterranean basin. Lieutenant Commander Haffenden was taken from Section B-3 activities and placed in charge of F Section, which undertook the collection of strategic intelligence in aforesaid area.''

Said Lansky, ''I think one reason why they picked Sicily was that Mussolini was hated there. He had expelled many Sicilians in an effort to break the Mafia but of course it just made them dislike him more. I was very impressed at how thorough the Navy was. They kept looking for people who could give them information about tides, the kind of sand on the beaches, the roads leading in and out of villages, how wide they were, what kind of surface they were. Could the roads support heavy vehicles? Were there any bridges? What were they made of? The kinds of things only local people could know. We brought the Navy hundreds of Sicilians, and nobody we asked to cooperate ever refused. Some of them couldn't even speak English. They had to talk to Sicilian-speaking agents, and sometimes they rambled on and on, but the interpreters were usually very patient. They came with books and postcards and old travel brochures. I once told the commander his office looked like a library. There was so much stuff that he had to bring in Italian personnel to go through all that material. They used to work night and day at it. Haffenden was under enormous pressure. He began to look haggard and he lost weight. I knew he had to produce results—and quickly.

''Haffenden even telephoned Moses Polakoff to complain about lack of progress—he said he was being pressured to increase the flow of details. 'The lives of many Americans hang in the balance,' he said. 'There's a war on.' Haffenden kept me jumping, but I realized that Washington was on his back. We stepped up our campaign to the point where I don't think there was a Sicilian family in New York that wasn't questioned by my Italian friends and asked to look in their suitcases, trunks, and attics to see if they could find anything else.

''Polakoff came to see me again. He said, 'They're screaming for more information.' So I went to see Joe Adonis to tell him to push himself and make a big effort. I took Joe to the commander, who it turned out knew all about him. That wasn't surprising, because the commander's staff included people who used to work for Dewey when they were hell-bent on cracking the underworld in New York—Murray Gurfein was only one connection. Joe found the situation very funny. He was all smiles when he shook hands with the commander and some of his aides.

"The assistants weren't that enthusiastic; you could see the look of antagonism on their faces. One of them said, 'I know about you, Mr. Adonis. You've been arrested for a lot of crimes—assault, extortion, kidnaping, robbery, smuggling booze, and so on.' Joe listened to him quietly and the smile never left his face when he said, 'Nobody has ever put me in prison. You have yet to prove any of these things.' Joe really worked very hard to show he could be a patriotic American. He found some Italians we didn't even know existed.

"I was really curious to see what Commander Haffenden did with the Sicilians who came into his office. When Joe and I brought these people in he would pull open big maps and charts on the wall. When he and his staff discovered which village the Sicilians came from, they would show them little maps of that area and ask them to talk about the places they knew and which citizens might be friendly and those who might have some particular grudge against Mussolini. Haffenden was especially anxious to talk to people who had been fishermen, who knew where the rocks were and how the tides ran. Anyone connected with the sea was a bonus.

"Sometimes some of the Sicilians were very nervous. Joe would just mention the name of Lucky Luciano and say he had given them orders to talk. If the Sicilians were still reluctant, Joe would stop smiling and say, 'Lucky will not be pleased to hear that you have not been helpful.' Sometimes he said things in Sicilian dialect. Once Joe heard about a Sicilian who had been mayor of a village. For some reason he wouldn't come to see the commander. They sort of kidnaped him and took him to see Lucky, and after that he was very helpful. Joe Lanza found two old seamen who used to sail up and down the Sicilian coast. Joe was very proud to have dug them out of Brooklyn, where they were working on the piers.

"Then Joe got his pal Vincenzo Nangano involved. Nangano was in the import-export business before the war—cheese, wine, olive oil, and so on. My information was that he was also the chief contact between the Mafia in the United States and the parent organization. Nangano knew just about every Italian who had connections with Italy and he brought in a lot of people with bits of information.

"Dozens of extra staff came into Commander Haffenden's office as the time of the Sicily landings got nearer. Haffenden spent more and more time in Washington, consulting with the naval counter-intelligence people. Of course they weren't confiding in us then, but later on, when the campaign in Italy was well under way, Commander Haffenden told me that the names we provided were a big help.

"Lucky came up with a plan that I thought was pretty wild, but I passed it on to Haffenden. Lucky was enough in touch with things, through me and all his other visitors, to be fairly sure the Allies would go into southern Italy—probably Sicily—and he wanted to join up with the invading army. He thought he could go in as an ordinary soldier and be a kind of liaison or scout. He said he was ready to go with the first troops. He thought his presence would guarantee Sicilian cooperation. He didn't want anybody to think he was just trying to get out of prison; he was ready to risk his neck to prove his point. He said he was prepared to be parachuted onto the island, though he did say they ought to teach him a bit in advance about how to do that. 'I know nothing about parachuting,' he told me, as if it was news. I had to laugh at the thought of Charlie landing in a tree or on top of a church. Poor old Lucky—playboy to prisoner to paratrooper in his dreams.

"I toned down Charlie's proposal somewhat before I discussed it with Commander Haffenden. I began by suggesting that it might be a good idea to take along some nonmilitary Italians who had been born in Sicily if, as I thought, that was where the invasion would begin. 'These men can speak directly to the villagers,' I said. 'They could get information about troop movements and local conditions quicker than anybody in uniform. If they were Italians, or rather Sicilians, then the local people would trust them.'

"Then almost as an afterthought I said to the commander, 'Why not take along the best-known Sicilian of them all—a man who is a kind of king in his native country—Lucky Luciano? Maybe you could land him from a submarine in advance. He can get information in Sicily or southern Italy better than anybody in the world. I can guarantee that he'll get you what you need. And if you wish, he will surrender himself to you afterward. Luciano is a responsible man and eager for action.' "

Haffenden was interested in the idea and promised to take it to Washington, but soon afterward, according to Lansky, he said, "I did bring up the plan on my last visit to Washington. They rejected it. They're happy enough to get the information we send them, but the senior men at headquarters are playing ostrich and pretending they don't know where it comes from. They pointed out that there would be a major scandal if the public ever heard about our getting cooperation from criminals. I was told never to mention the possibility of Charlie Luciano going to Sicily with the troops again."

Haffenden was in fact officially rebuked, and a report on the incident praised his resourceful imagination but added that it was "not always balanced by good judgment." And so, despite the plan Luciano had made and Lansky had refined so carefully, Lucky Luciano did not land with the Allied forces like some underworld Errol Flynn on the beaches of Sicily.

Right in the middle of the very successful cooperation between the Mafia and the Navy there came a threat to the Mafia enforcers of that cooperation. "This came about," Lansky believes, "because Dewey took office as governor in January 1943, and he was still gunning for the Mafia. Joe Lanza was arrested and sentenced to seven and a half to fifteen years for extortion and conspiracy. They took no notice at all of his assistance to the Navy. 'No deals for any criminals' was their line. 'All Americans have a duty to help the war effort and shouldn't expect special rewards.'

"As you can imagine, a lot of Lanza's friends in the Mafia didn't want to cooperate with the Navy any more. Joe's friend Ben Espy was particularly angry about the way they treated him, and to make sure he didn't turn against us, I gave him a job with my juke-box organization, the Emby Distribution Company. But in fairness to them I must say that the Italians, even the bosses of the Mafia, did continue to cooperate, in spite of Joe's disgraceful treatment."

If Lanza was not to receive clemency because of his contributions to the war effort, Luciano was apparently in a somewhat different category. On February 8, 1943, Polakoff retained another attorney to initiate an official plea in the New York County Supreme Court on behalf of Lucky Luciano to modify his thirty-to-fifty-year sentence. The key to the request lay not only in Lucky's efforts to redeem himself by being a model prisoner but in his having been "cooperative in the war effort." To support this claim Commander Haffenden went to see Judge Philip McCook, the man who had imposed the sentence, and spoke to him privately in chambers.

The commander told Lansky, "I did speak on Charlie's behalf, but I couldn't go into intelligence details or make any recommendations. I would have liked to help Luciano because of his great efforts to help us—which I probably knew better than anybody else in the Navy—but I had my orders." To be quite sure that the Navy would not be officially involved in any controversy, Haffenden's chief, Captain MacFall, had told Haffenden to tell the judge that "Naval Intelligence had no interest one way or the other in the question of whether Luciano's sentence should be reduced."

Judge McCook turned down the application for modification of Luciano's sentence, although he indicated the way the wind was blowing when he wrote, "If the defendant is assisting the authorities and he continues to do so, and remains a model prisoner, Executive Clemency may become appropriate at some future date."

Lansky hurried up to see Luciano at once. "I knew he would be deeply upset by the decision. He was in a bad way, very depressed. I had to be tough with him. 'Listen,' I said, 'we got you out of your cell in Siberia into this nice warm prison where they treat you like a gentleman. Be patient. Judge McCook doesn't like you. If he were to say now that he was too severe with you he would lose face. That's why he rejected your appeal. But he's giving you a signal. He says he wants executive clemency for you someday—that means he hopes the governor will get him off the hook. And remember, they've got you over a barrel in any case. You still have to go on playing it right. There's no other way in the world for you to get out of here. If you stop helping now, while the war is still going on, you don't stand a chance. This is no time to act like a shmuck, my friend. You just keep on cooperating. They want to help you but not yet.'

"So I talked sense to him," Lansky says, "and he cheered up. He was in prison, remember, and some of his judgments couldn't be trusted because he'd been away from ordinary life for so long. When a man is alone in his cell he starts seeing things in a different way. Charlie reminded me that it was very hard being inside. He knew my advice was sound, and he would abide by it. But even if the conditions were not as bad as in Siberia, he hated being in prison. There was nothing I could say to that. We sat there for about ten minutes without a single word. Then he sighed and I shook hands and left."

Judge McCook's comments hinting at Luciano's assistance to the war effort were reported in the newspapers and the public got the first hint of official cooperation with the most notorious gangster in the country. The Navy put up a brave front and refused comment, but the brass were deeply concerned. A colleague reported that Rear Admiral Arthur Train, the director of Naval Intelligence, was "very disturbed," although there is no doubt that he had been aware what was going on in New York.

26 Invasion

"I heard on the radio about the Allied landings in Sicily," says Meyer Lansky, "and I knew I had played a part. Later on Commander Haffenden told me about an incident in Sicily that showed how important the intelligence work in New York had been.

"There were four officers, Commander Joachim Titolo, Paul Alfieri, Tony Marsloe, and James Murray, who had been working in New York. They all spoke Italian and I had seen them many times questioning the people we brought to headquarters. The four of them went in with the first wave of troops in Sicily, aboard Vice Admiral Hewitt's flagship *Monrovia*, and landed with the soldiers on the beaches at Gela and Licata.

"As I heard the story, while shooting and bombing was going on all around them, the agents ran right along the beaches with the maps our volunteers had helped them make. They knew exactly where to go and who to see. They visited relatives and friends of Italians in New York and brought greetings, sometimes even letters, and then they would ask the local people to come and show them where the Germans had planted mines near the landing beaches and in the port areas. And the local people cooperated.

"I was told that 'Mafia' and 'Lucky Luciano' were passwords. Maybe that sounds crazy right in the middle of the war, when all Italians were supposed to hate Americans, even Italian-Americans, but one of the agents told me later that those words were magic. People smiled and after that everything was easy.

"Commander Haffenden told me very proudly that our cooperation had saved the lives of hundreds of American soldiers. The villagers led the agents along paths where there were no mines. They showed them where the Germans and Italians had set up booby traps, and where their machine gun and artillery nests were, and the quickest way to get around these strongpoints. The agents found the fishermen who lived in the area and learned the exact places where the Germans had mined the harbors, so the landing craft could come in safely.

"I was asked to keep this story a secret, but later Commander Haffenden told me that some day, after it was all over, I could talk about one of Paul Alfieri's successes, which was thanks to a man Charlie had saved from the electric chair. I'm not going to mention his name because his children live in the United States now and they still carry their father's name. None of them have any connections with crime.

"He was a guy who did something stupid a long, long time ago. Some cops roughed him up on the Lower East Side, and, being only sixteen at the time, he went right out for revenge. He shot a policeman, who later died of the wounds. They got out a warrant for the kid, and his mother, who was a cousin of Lucky's, came to beg him to help. Lucky was very angry with the boy and was ready to let him be arrested. But the mother flung herself at his feet and cried and begged him to save her son. Lucky didn't want to get involved, but in the end he managed to get the boy out of New York to Canada and then had him sent to Sicily to live with relatives. He was warned that if he ever came back to New York Charlie would kill him. He didn't want any part of somebody who shot a cop. The guy kept his word and never returned to America. Instead he became an important citizen in Sicily, a leader of the local Mafia. He was responsible for keeping in touch with a number of Mafia men who had been deported from the United States or had left to avoid arrest. In Sicily they were very close to one another and they used to talk about the good old days in the United States. None of them could return; they were a little band of exiles. Lucky sent messages to them from time to time, and he had the necessary information about them passed along to Haffenden's boys, with the message that they must cooperate with the Americans or answer to him personally.

"Alfieri was the one who made contact with this particular man who had killed the cop. The Navy probably didn't know about his past, but it might not have mattered at that point. What Alfieri needed was the exact location of the secret headquarters of the Italian naval command. He came with written authorization from Lucky Luciano and he produced the piece of paper. The local man got his men together and took Alfieri to the house which was supposed to be top secret—except that everybody in Sicily knew where it was. The Mafia gang shot the German guards outside and then surrounded the place. Alfieri went inside and blew the safe open. Then, guarded by these friends of the ex-New York fugitive, he escaped with the documents he'd found. The local Mafia had told him a good deal of what the documents contained, and Alfieri found that they were right.

"The Navy man took the papers right back to his boss, who sent him over to the flagship of Vice Admiral Richard Connolly. The documents gave precise details of the entire German and Italian defense network on the island, right down to the radio codes. And there was a bonus, because among the plans was, so I was told, one of the greatest prizes that ever fell into Allied hands in the Mediterranean war. Documents showing the disposition of the Italian and German naval forces in the whole southern European war zone had been stored in this safe. There were detailed plans of mine fields and the 'safe routes' through them."

Naval Intelligence reported of that find: "These documents when transcribed were used successfully to accelerate the Italian surrender," and for that day's work Alfieri was awarded the Legion of Merit. His presidential citation stated, "By his resourcefulness and daring, his devotion to duty, he made available information of great value in planning future operations, thereby contributing in large measure to the success of our invasion forces."

In spite of all the help from local people, the fighting in Sicily was severe and the work of the naval agents there went on until all resistance on the island came to an end. The sixty thousand German forces, although heavily outnumbered by nearly half a million Allied troops, fought ferociously over the rugged mountainous terrain for more than five weeks.

Using their Mafia contacts, the New York intelligence men quickly established who were the key workers in the port areas of Sicily—the pilots, tug operators, and crane drivers. These people were persuaded to return to work to get the harbors into operation and expedite the Allied landings. They were also able to tell the Allied military government who could be trusted and who the Fascist sympathizers were. All four of the men acknowledged that their contacts among the Mafiosi of Sicily were of great assistance.

Meantime special commando units were sent to prisons on the island where Mussolini had incarcerated known Mafia chieftains. These men were freed along with other anti-Fascist prisoners. Then the Mafia leaders were put to work as scouts and propagandists, nearly always with good will on their part, once it had been explained to them that Charlie Luciano had ordered their coopera-tion.

In its official report at the end of the war, the OSS admitted that its own agents, recruited and trained in the United States, were not of great use. "In contrast, selected [Sicilians], recruited, trained and briefed on the spot, had not only natural cover for line-crossing, but also an intimate knowledge of the terrain." These were local Mafiosi who frequently acted as guides for Allied forces, risking their lives to do so. Many British and American agents were saved from falling into the hands of the Gestapo through quick action by the under-world in Sicily. These Mafiosi also carried out heroic actions against the German forces on their own initiative.

The cooperation between the American armed forces and the Mafia underworld has been bitterly criticized, but it was not the first time that men fighting for the highest ideals had turned for help to the ancient Mafia clans. Giuseppe Garibaldi landed at Marsala in 1860, on his way to fight for his dream of a united Italy. The local Mafia threw themselves wholeheartedly behind him and many Sicilians joined his campaigns on the mainland. In much the same way, the local people in 1943 took heart and fought to throw off those whom they saw as the latest in a long line of oppressors, the Germans.

Yet no sooner was the fighting over than old instincts resurfaced, in Sicily as elsewhere. Many of the Mafia heroes set up their own black-market networks, stealing Allied war supplies and pilfering scarce medicines like penicillin to sell at high prices to the local peasants.

The Mafia in America was no different. The men who were helping Navy Intelligence were at the same time exploiting war shortages and gas rationing to garner fortunes from black-market rackets. The underworld did not change its spots, merely its tactics. Its leaders were still masterminding criminal activities and exploit-ing society's every weakness.

This paradox, endemic in American as well as Sicilian society, contributed to the growing alarm at Allied headquarters about cooperation with the Italian and Sicilian underworld. A review committee was sent out from Washington and there was a thorough shake-up. Scores of intelligence agents working for Secret Intelligence were sent to other parts of the Mediterranean. An official report made at the time stated: "The SI Italy section was the principal unit investigated. Its personnel, predominantly Sicilian American, had tended to form a clique reluctant to concede authority to others."

As Lansky remembers it, "Commander Haffenden told me that many of the agents involved were bitter about the criticism of their methods. They were called down after the fighting and after the Allied forces had benefited from their Mafia contacts.

"Why was Sicily so important? That was the question I asked during the war. Haffenden's view was that the capture of the island was a great blow to the Axis alliance, because Hitler had sworn that no Allied troops would land successfully anywhere in Europe. 'The capture of Sicily was a dagger at Hitler's throat,' he said. And to make things worse for him, at the same time the Nazis were losing a big battle in Russia, the great Soviet victory at Kursk.

"Hitler wasn't beaten yet, but things looked a lot better for us, and certainly the surrender of the last Nazi forces in Sicily, in August 1943, spelled the end for Mussolini."

Twenty-one days later, on September 8, Italy surrendered to the British and Americans. The Germans fought on, however, and Lansky later learned that the Mafia connection played an important role in the bitter battle of Salerno. "Several naval agents I knew in New York, including Marsloe and Alfieri, came ashore with an advance group of American Marines. I can hardly believe they managed to get through alive. There was fierce fighting and the Germans bombarded the area with heavy machine-gun fire. The fighting went on for a week, and for a while it looked like the Americans were going to be thrown back into the sea. But over a hundred of these intelligence men kept at their work, sneaking through the defense lines somehow and scouting the countryside for information.

"Marsloe and Alfieri were the real heroes. They knew exactly who to go and see—as a result of information we had got from a man who ran a little delicatessen down on the Lower East Side. The man's brother lived near Paestum, an old ruined city near Salerno. Our contact told the agents in New York that his brother was an important Italian official and a reliable anti-Fascist.

"When the two Americans got there his house was under gunfire and in ruins, but they discovered the man they were looking for hiding in the cellar. Bombs and shells were falling all around, but they introduced themselves very courteously. As I heard the story, the two agents ignored the bombardment while they calmly explained to the man that they brought greetings from his brother. And sure enough, one of them fished in his pocket and brought out a letter signed by the delicatessen owner asking his brother to cooperate.

"It must have been a crazy scene, shaking hands in a cellar with bullets everywhere and the man's family hiding in the corner. The official burst into tears when he got the greeting from his brother. He kissed the two American agents and said they were better than 'friends of friends'—that's a kind of Mafia oath of loyalty. They were friends of a blood relative. The Italian official risked his life by climbing out of the cellar and taking the agents along a path and showing them a prize they had never even dreamed about. They dodged bullets to get there, and several times they had to fling themselves into the bushes to avoid dive bombers.

"The Italian showed the two American agents the most advanced kind of torpedo—it could turn in the water and go straight to any target no matter which way the ship moved trying to dodge it. He had seen the torpedo come ashore during a trial, and although the German and Italian Navy people searched for it, they never discovered the weapon, simply because he and some fishermen had covered it with tree branches and leaves. The Italian realized that it must be a very important weapon, because the Germans even asked local inhabitants to try to find it and offered a reward. But of course nobody in the area knew anything except the Italian official and his fishermen friends." This torpedo was the Italian Navy's advanced SIC torpedo. It was such an important discovery that it was flown to the United States within a few days.

"The same Italian official led the American agents to a group of Partisans, some of whom were Mafia members. The minute their friends in the United States were mentioned they promised total cooperation. They helped the two intelligence officers capture important maps. These documents showed how the mine fields had been set out in the farmlands around the beaches and where the artillery concentrations were. The Partisans told them where the German headquarters were, and a few hours later, after sending radio messages back to headquarters, the Marines captured the place."

In Sardinia, Lieutenant Titolo, using letters from relatives, found a number of fishermen, and with their help captured nineteen high-ranking German officers who were trying to rejoin the main Nazi forces on the mainland. He too knew who to see and whose name to mention in order to obtain unqualified aid and support.

"When these Navy men came back to the United States I heard about their adventures in Italy," said Lansky. "I was proud that I had laid the foundation for all this by bringing Lucky Luciano into the picture.

"I followed the war closely on the radio and heard about the battles for Naples and Monte Cassino. When the Italian-speaking naval boys got back I was amazed to hear that they had played a part in all these fights. In every single place, they had gone into the battlefield area days ahead to find out from local Italians where the German positions were. Once they gave proof that they were friends of friends, *gli amici,* all doors were open.

"In Rome, Marsloe was there in June 1944 before the city was captured. He went in with an advance group and used Mafia contacts to get hold of a high-ranking Italian officer. The man didn't want to cooperate at first, and the local Mafia who had guided the Americans to the man's home asked them to leave the room for a few minutes. The agents did as they were told, and although they were sitting in the next room they decided to cover their ears. Ten minutes later they were summoned back into the room where the Italian official was sitting in a chair, white as a sheet and trembling all over. 'Please,' he said, 'I will do anything you want. Please ask me for anything you need.'

"The frightened official took the two agents to a nearby house and pointed to an upstairs window fifty yards away. They sent for help and kept the place under close surveillance. A squad of heavily armed Americans came and stormed the house very suddenly— there was no shooting. Inside were four men who were about to set out on a spectacular mission to assassinate General Sir Harold Alexander, the British commander of the Allied ground forces. The house was a mere hundred yards from his army group headquarters, which had been set up in a tent."

Lansky went on, every detail of memory a pleasure. "For this and other exploits Marsloe was awarded the Bronze Medal for Valor of the Italian Underground Resistance. Later he told me he had used his Mafia connection to find and rescue an important Italian who had been working for the Allies secretly in the latter part of the war.

He was Franco Maugeri, a former chief of Italian Naval Intelligence. The Germans had got wind of his treason, and to save his life—as well as that of the Italian who led them to the four-man hit team—Marsloe had to grab him before the Nazis did. He then had to smuggle Maugeri through the front lines to safety."

Commander Titolo later confirmed that "I did seek out members of the criminal elements in the northern part of Italy." Indeed, Titolo was the commander in chief of a newly created combined U.S.-British intelligence unit which moved into Genoa as the fighting still raged in Italy. Not only Lansky but soon everybody was to know about the exploits of the naval Mafia, as Luciano called them.

Marsloe exploited his underworld contacts to score one brilliant intelligence coup after another. He was taken to the very building where carefully hidden away was a top-secret bifocal nocturnal periscope for use in submarines, an instrument that was far superior to anything in use at the time in the United States Navy. Marsloe also found a whole range of new types of mines and the entire sabotage equipment in use by the daring Italian frogmen who used to swim under water and blow up Allied ships. He was the man who "came across" the first jet-propelled midget submarine (the *campini*), which the Italian government planned to share with the Japanese for use against American vessels in the Pacific. Marsloe was awarded the Legion of Merit and at the end of the war joined the famous frogman Commander Buster Crabbe at the Allied Experimental Naval Center in Venice.

Said Lansky, "The happiest man of all was my friend Alfieri. It was not his two Legion of Merit medals that he was so proud of, but the lead he got that he said would put him in the history books. It happened right at the end of the war in Italy, just after Mussolini was caught with his mistress and strung up by the Partisans. A call went out from Allied headquarters to find all Mussolini's diaries and documents. The Germans were also after this material. They contained secrets that would have been damaging to the Axis powers. A message had been intercepted from Hitler himself saying that Mussolini's private papers must be destroyed at all costs."

To get this material became priority number one for Allied headquarters, and the Italian-speaking agents from New York were asked to help find it. "Alfieri used every bit of muscle Lucky Luciano and I had given him in New York," said Lansky. "He managed to get hold of some top Mafia men in Italy and pressured them about the documents. Twenty-four hours later they took Alfieri on a wild ride right across Italy. They didn't tell him their names, and knowing the score he never inquired. Alfieri didn't even ask these rough-looking Italians how they had managed to get hold of a brand-new American jeep, complete with instruments and weapons."

As Alfieri himself described the end of that journey, "I was driven straight to a villa overlooking Lake Garda. It was a pretty rough ride. There I was led to a room. The door was shoved open by my guide, who laughed and said, 'You are going to need a big truck for all that rubbish.' " Before the astonished eyes of the American Navy man were the Italian dictator's entire personal archives—one of the most dazzling prizes in the whole history of Mafia-U.S. Navy cooperation.

27 The Payoff

Lansky had told the Sicilian story with great pride. Now he reverted to the man who helped make the invasion a success. "Lucky Luciano was not going to wait a minute longer than necessary before he asked Moses Polakoff to start trying to get the payoff for the help he had given to men like Alfieri and other intelligence agents."

As church bells in Allied countries rang out the joyful news of peace on VE Day, May 9, 1945, Moses Polakoff was handing over a six-page document pleading for executive clemency for his infamous client.

Now that the war was over, there was no need for restraint any longer, the lawyer wrote, no inhibitions about such information "harming the war effort or damaging civilian morale . . . Charles Luciano has voluntarily caused to be furnished valuable, substantial and important aid to the United States military authorities, which information and aid were a conceded contribution to the prosecution of the war . . . and expressed a complete willingness without any reservations to aid in whatever manner he could. As a consequence," Polakoff's brief continued, "for approximately two years, the said Charles Luciano and, at a special request of said Charles Luciano, the friends of Charles Luciano furnished to Commander C. Radcliffe Haffenden of the United States Naval Information, information and performed other services which were valuable and substantial."

"But the minute peace came," Lansky says, "the Navy started

on their big cover-up. The war was over and they didn't need the Mafia any longer. Every time Polakoff tried to get some of them to send letters in support of Lucky for the help he had given, the naval authorities put a lid on it. They refused to let any of the men involved talk about the work we had done. But now the truth should be told, and that is why I'm telling you for the first time what really went on."

The key man in the Mafia connection was clearly Commander Haffenden, who said flatly that help from the Sicilian-Americans in New York was not only "of great value to the United States Navy but it was of equal value to the Army at the time of the Sicilian invasion."

Parole officers investigating Luciano came up against a wall of silent hostility in the Navy. Documents about the Mafia connection were said to have "vanished," but in fact the Navy ordered them destroyed at all costs. Haffenden was warned that he was not to give any interviews to civilian agencies, including those of the parole board, about Luciano's plea for clemency. Nor, of course, could he discuss the matter with the press.

Lansky remembers, "I really got mad at those Navy guys. They were trying to say that Lucky had nothing to do with helping them. They burned valuable documents we gave them. They stamped on any of the intelligence officers who had worked with us when they tried to talk to us again. They were forbidden to say a word.

"Then one day Commander Haffenden said something that really shocked me. This is what he told me and I can recall every word. 'Meyer, I have to warn you. They're going to deny that you had anything to do with us. One very senior naval officer in Washington told me that he was not going to give any kind of credit to any Jew sonofabitch.

" 'They're moving heaven and earth to close every avenue of information that shows the Navy had the help of the Mafia in winning the war. They're ashamed that they had to turn to the Mafia and they're going to deny it. I want you to know that I do not share their anti-Semitic feelings, which I haven't really talked much about. But I've always leveled with you as you have with me. That is why you must know what's going on. I can do nothing to support or defend you. I have to accept orders. I can't help Charlie Luciano or I'll be court-martialed.

" 'To keep up the pretense that Mafia cooperation is a myth they are going to press the parole board to keep Lucky in prison forever, to prove their point that there was no contact with criminal elements. It's the greatest double-cross of all time. And there's absolutely nothing you or I can do about it. I can't even talk about it to anyone except you.' "

Despite the Navy's efforts to prevent Haffenden from telling the story of wartime cooperation between the armed services and Mafia chiefs, the commander remained on very good personal terms with Lansky. The last time they met was at the wedding of Moses Polakoff's daughter in 1950, when "Haffenden said the Navy was giving him a hard time. They had warned him of all sorts of terrible consequences if he opened his mouth. He died two years later from some war wounds which had finally caught up with him."

Moses Polakoff was enraged at the Navy's attitude. He told the parole board through one of its officers, Joseph F. Healy, that Lansky's "services were all voluntarily given and that he had nothing to gain by the services except the service to his country." He told Healy that the officers of the Navy were "aristocratic snobs," thinking it beneath their dignity that they had turned to the underworld for help. And Polakoff was sure that Governor Dewey had given permission for such contacts to be made.

For his part Meyer Lansky was determined to see that the truth did reach the light of day. He went straight to Parole Officer Healy and told him the full story of the Navy's involvement with the Mafia right from the first meeting with Haffenden at the Astor Hotel in April 1942.

And despite every effort by the Navy to throw a blanket over what had happened in the war, Governor Dewey finally declared, "Upon the entry of the United States into the war, Luciano's aid was sought by the Armed Services in inducing others to provide information concerning possible enemy attacks. It appears that he cooperated in such effort, although the actual value of the information procured is not clear."

On January 4, 1946, inmate number 15684 of Great Meadow Prison was told that Governor Dewey had granted him "special commutation of sentence." He was transferred to Sing Sing prison, closer to New York, as the first step to his eventual liberty.

Later Dewey was to be a little more forthcoming about the matter: "Luciano's aid to the Navy in the war was extensive and valuable. Ten years is probably as long as anybody ever served for compulsory prostitution. And these factors led the parole board to recommend the commutation, combined with the fact that Luciano would be exiled for life, under law."

The authorities made sure that they got rid of Lucky very quickly and very quietly, as Lansky put it. "I wanted to go see him at Great Meadow, but before I could get there he had been taken away and was passing through Sing Sing. From there they rushed him to Ellis Island.

"I got special permission to visit him there. But first I met Frank Costello at Moore's Restaurant on Broadway and we made plans to give him a great send-off. I told Frank that the newspaper guys would be around and it was essential that Lucky be got out of the country without too much publicity. Not that he would mind, but if there was too much fuss, somebody in authority might change his mind. Costello told me, 'No journalist or photographer is going to get near him. I give you my word.'

"It was a strange feeling going back to Ellis Island," said Lansky. "It brought back memories of when I arrived with my mother. I was nearly in tears as the ferry took us across the water. Moses Polakoff and Mikey Lascari and I got a cab to the ferry terminal and met Frank there. We all had special passes to get through to Lucky, where he was being kept in isolation. When we saw him we all embraced and there was a lot of emotion. I went to see him a couple more times, to take him some clothes and other things he needed. And of course I took care of the money, cash and traveler's checks."

On February 8, Lansky and his friends and some of Luciano's family went over to Pier 7 at the Bush Terminal, on the Brooklyn waterfront, to say farewell to Luciano.

"The *Laura Keene* was not the most luxurious vessel in the world, but we did our best for Charlie. Costello and Albert Anastasia had done their job. The ship was guarded by about two hundred longshoremen with their baling hooks in their hands. They had been given orders to let nobody onto that ship except authorized friends of Lucky and the rest of the passengers—a dozen other guys being deported. We had a wonderful meal aboard, all kinds of seafood fresh from the Fulton Fish Market, and spaghetti and wine and a lot of kosher delicacies. They brought it in huge hampers, along with crates of French champagne. It was a great bon voyage party.

"Lucky also wanted us to bring some girls to take along with him on the ship to keep him company. I asked Adonis to do something about that, and Charlie joked, 'Little Man, I'm pleased we are not using your choice of women. That is one department in which you are not an expert.' Joe found three showgirls from the Copacabana Club and there was no difficulty in getting them aboard. The authorities cooperated even on that. Nobody going into exile ever had a better send-off.''

The Liberty ship *Laura Keene* had transported valuable supplies to Europe and then had brought American troops home from the war zone. Now this hardworking vessel was the setting for a nostalgic get-together of America's leading gangsters, underworld bosses who had come from all over America to pay homage to their chief. Naval authorities and port officials did nothing to stop this strange gathering. On the contrary they did all they could to help Luciano's friends and protect them from the attentions of journalists trying to break through the barrier of longshoremen.

The guest list for the sailing party reads like a gangsters' Who's Who. Bugsy Siegel, William Moretti, Moe Dalitz, Frank Costello, Tommy Lucchese, Joe Adonis, Steve Magaddino, Phil Kastel, Owney Madden, Joe Bonanno, Albert Anastasia, and of course Meyer Lansky helped Lucky Luciano with the turkey, the chickens and the vast display of delicacies. After years of prison food, the ex-convict could not eat much of the rich fare, but his friends did well by it while Luciano sipped champagne and joked with Meyer about the days when it was illegal and they were bringing liquor secretly across the Atlantic. There was a great deal of laughter and reminiscing and singing throughout the night, before the guests finally slipped ashore early on the morning of the *Laura Keene*'s departure.

On February 9, 1946, a wintry Sunday morning, the S.S. *Laura Keene* set sail for Genoa with the uncrowned king of the Mafia aboard. The U.S. Navy had needed his help and he had given it. Now the price was being paid, commutation combined with deportation. A dubious deal, obviously, but the soldiers and sailors whose lives had been saved through the Luciano-Lansky effort might well have considered it a justifiable bargain.

The farewell gathering aboard the *Laura Keene* not only reunited many of Charlie Luciano's friends. It was also the occasion of one of Bugsy Siegel's increasingly rare visits from the West Coast. Doc Stacher was at the party and remembered it fondly. "We were all there—it was like old times, though we were a little cramped in Charlie's cabin. Maybe the only shadow on the celebration was the coolness between Bugsy and Joe Adonis. Bugsy had taken over Joe's former girl friend, a gorgeous woman from Alabama named Virginia Hill, as his number one mistress. Bugsy was really in love with Virginia, the first time in his life he had fallen so hard—and that, I suppose, includes even his wife. And Virginia was crazy about him, though she'd had a lot of lovers before, including several of our guys. Except for that, and nobody made a big deal about it, everybody stood around talking a mile a minute and eating and drinking very sociably. I remember Meyer talking to Frank Costello in a corner; they were probably congratulating themselves about getting Lucky out, and maybe about the good party they had put together. Frank and Meyer had been close for a long time. Frank's real name was Francesco Castiglia, you know, and he was from Calabria. He had a rough, hoarse voice that he blamed on a 'bum doctor' who took out his tonsils and adenoids when he was a kid, but he was a very smooth man. Meyer had introduced Frank to his wife, a Jewish girl named Loretta. Frank was different from a lot of the guys. He was faithful to Loretta all his life.

"The conversations aboard the *Laura Keene* that night weren't all reminiscences about the good old days. Meyer told us about the terrible time he was having trying to get established in Las Vegas. Bugsy never had used all the opportunities he had to establish us in Nevada, where gambling was legal. In 1941 Meyer had ordered Bugsy to send Moe Sedway—Morris Sidwirz was his real name—to work in Las Vegas, and Meyer himself used to drive out there with Bugsy. At first Bugsy just couldn't see the potential—he was too busy being a Hollywood playboy—but Meyer persisted and eventually everybody realized that there were endless possibilities out there in the desert. During the war years, when expansion elsewhere was impossible, the organization concentrated on developing the business in continental USA, and there weren't any real road blocks except in Nevada."

As Lansky says, "Las Vegas today is an incredible place where big entertainment corporations make millions. We were in at the beginning, the pioneers. It wasn't fun driving back and forth across the desert to get the whole thing rolling. It was terribly hot and the cars were always overheating. There were times when I thought I would die in that desert, driving back and forth, keeping track of our emergency cans of gas and oil.

"When I went out there with Bugsy the first time, Vegas was a horrible place, really just a small oasis town where motorists could rest awhile and get gasoline and water and dry ice for the engine. At the time Reno was Nevada's most prosperous city because of the divorce laws and because of the gambling, but even Reno wasn't much. What I had in mind was to build the greatest, most luxurious hotel casino in the world and invite people from all over America—maybe the high rollers from all over the world—to come and spend their money there.

"We decided to build a hotel and casino and call it the Flamingo—we thought up the name one day when we were at the Hialeah Race Track, in Florida. There's a pretty little lake there and in the evening you can watch the flocks of pink flamingos rise in the sky. There's a local legend that flamingos are a sign of good luck and anyone who shoots the birds will have seven years of misfortune. So because of the good luck connection, Bugsy had the idea of naming our Las Vegas project.

"He and Virginia Hill spent a lot of time supervising the construction of our hotel, but it was very difficult to get construction materials, and workers had to be brought in to Las Vegas from California and the East. Everything was tremendously expensive. Bugsy had to bribe the Teamsters Union to get their men to haul the necessary supplies across the desert. I raised some more money for him in New York, and though some of the parties were reluctant they agreed to put up the extra millions we were going to need. It took much longer and was far more expensive than we anticipated. But there was no point in doing it at all if we didn't do it right. It had to have the best food, the best rooms, the finest entertainers. Our policy was that guests could come to Las Vegas and stay there quite reasonably, but with the best entertainment and comfort in the world. Our money would come from high-stakes gambling in the casino. The choice of the desert was deliberate; once you got tourists there, after they had eaten and drunk all they could there was only one thing left—to go gambling. There was some criticism that we were throwing money away, but I insisted and Bugsy agreed that we had to be superluxurious. As I remember, I promised at Charlie's farewell party that Bugsy and I would get the Flamingo going in just a few more months."

Lansky was not only dreaming of and working on the transformation of Las Vegas in early 1946. He was again developing his Cuban interests, which he had begun to revive as soon as the war was over, and aboard the *Laura Keene* he told Luciano in detail about developments in Cuba since Lucky had been in prison. It seemed to him the story might be especially useful to his old friend now.

Lansky's friendship with Batista had grown, and both men saw their gambling profits increase in the late thirties. Lansky found himself involved in Cuban politics as early as 1938, when Batista legalized the Communist Party in Cuba to solidify his control. Meyer argued fiercely with Batista over this move, warning him that he was going to run into problems with the American government if he cooperated with the "reds." Batista assured him that he had the Communists in his pocket, and indeed with their support Batista was elected president in 1940. Then came the war, and Lansky's enterprises in Cuba became dormant because few Americans could travel there. But in 1944, toward the end of the war, came new elections in which Lansky took more of an interest than his business directly required.

The American government became alarmed by intelligence reports that Batista was moving further to the left, and an approach was made to Lansky through his friends at Naval Intelligence. As Lansky tells the story, "I was told at one stage that President Roosevelt himself asked his intelligence men to get me to speak to Batista. Whether this was true or not I never found out—the agent from the Navy in New York didn't say so. It was made quite clear to me that the American government wouldn't let Batista go on running the island if there was any danger it might go Communist. I explained this to my good friend Batista, who was very reluctant to get out of politics. To console him I said we would keep up our own close ties. When the war was over we would reestablish Havana as a major gambling center for Americans and we would always give him his cut. Batista thought about this for a while and realized there was no point in fighting the American government. I'm sure that at this time the United States would not have hesitated to invade the island if Washington thought the Communists had any chance of coming to power. When the intelligence people told me that the U.S. government would not under any circumstances let him remain president in the 1944 elections, and that I was to pass on this information to him, I knew they were serious. My own opinion that Batista was a staunch anti-Communist counted for very little.

"Batista was very depressed until he realized he could just get himself a stooge to be his front man. He chose a well-known doctor, a man named Ramón Grau San Martín. The link between the two men was secret, and when Grau San Martín was elected people considered it a defeat for Batista. The American authorities gave Batista permission to come and live in Daytona Beach, in Florida. And sure enough, the minute the war was over we were back in business, opening up the casinos and welcoming the tourists back to the island.

"On the *Laura Keene* I reviewed all this with Lucky and told him I thought that although he was exiled to Italy, he didn't have to stay there forever. It would be impossible for him to come back to the United States, at least for the time being. 'But why not Cuba?' I said to Charlie. 'There's no reason why you shouldn't come and live in Havana. You could operate from the island the way you did in the old days. You'll be warmly welcomed there, I'll make sure of that. And there shouldn't be any flak from the American government, since I did exactly what Naval Intelligence asked me to in Cuba. It was my duty to do so, but you and I also know that a peaceful regime will be a lot better for our own interests. We don't want war or revolution there. All we need is peace, so that we can get on with the business we set up together. And with luck, you can help run it.' " As Lansky bade Charlie Luciano farewell, both men were determined that the parting would be a short one and that they would soon be reunited in Havana.

Luciano's arrival in Italy created problems for both the government in Rome and the American authorities. Neither expected Luciano to remain long in retirement. He was sent to his native village of Lercara Friddi, in Sicily, where exile was cushioned by the enthusiastic welcome of the local Mafia, and within days after his arrival he was organizing a black-market operation. Soon afterward he was installed in the Excelsior Hotel in Naples, masterminding the sale of food, cigarettes, and other goods stolen for him from American PX stores. He then moved to Rome, and lived in an apartment in the Excelsior Hotel on the Via Veneto.

But the former underworld leader was restless in Italy and waited impatiently for an opportunity to leave. Finally Lansky sent him a cable in the autumn of 1946 saying simply, "Hotel Nacional." The message was unmistakable. Meyer had arranged for his arrival in Cuba and was paving the way for him to reestablish himself in his former role.

28 The Unlucky Flamingo

The Second World War ended in August 1945, and the following year brought hectic times for Meyer Lansky. Besides running his New York operations, supervising Bugsy Siegel's work in Las Vegas, and reopening Cuba for American gambling, Lansky also had to worry about his friend Luciano, who was having problems with the Italian authorities, urged on as they were by the Americans.

To complicate his life even further, Meyer Lansky's marriage was on the rocks. The "Little Man" was always reluctant to speak of his domestic problems, but Doc Stacher, who saw a lot of the Lanskys, knew the situation. "Meyer was close to his children, crazy about them. If it hadn't been for them, he would have left Anna many years earlier. He wanted them to grow up in a family atmosphere even if he and Anna didn't get on. They never quarreled openly, as far as I could see, but there was a certain coolness between them. Anna was still very devout and opposed to everything Lansky stood for, but there was nothing she could do about it. She was terrified that the children would follow in his footsteps. Buddy, the older boy, was very close to his father and admired him tremendously. So in spite of Meyer's repeated assurances to Anna that he wouldn't let the children get involved, she had reason to worry, at least as far as Buddy was concerned. But what Meyer wanted for Paul, his second son, was for him to be fully integrated into American society. He really meant it about West Point. Anna didn't appreciate this either. She wanted Paul to be a rabbi. Meyer adored his daughter, Sandra, whom he called Sally. She was a very intelligent girl and Anna complained to me that Meyer was spoiling her, giving her everything she wanted. Mother and daughter didn't get on very well, and as a little girl Sally resented the way Anna kept telling Meyer to 'stop giving her so many presents.'

"In my opinion the couple should have separated a long time before they did, but Meyer had old-fashioned ideas about providing a proper home for the children. The strain told on Anna and she had some nervous breakdowns. Around the end of the war they put her in a mental institution, although this was kept very quiet. Anna got better when she was away from her family, and finally they decided to live apart. When he wasn't in Florida or Cuba or out West, Meyer stayed with his sister on Ocean Parkway, in Brooklyn, and Anna kept the apartment on Central Park West.

"In September of 1946 they were formally separated. Meyer didn't contest Anna's custody of the children, but they spent a lot of their time with his sister and his mother. Meyer still played a big part in bringing them up and selecting the schools he wanted them to go to. The boys were teenagers by then. He was always very generous and gave Anna as much money as she wanted. According to the separation agreement she was supposed to get three hundred dollars a week, but he gave her a lot more than that. Anna soon went to live in Miami Beach, as I remember, and Meyer moved back to the old apartment on Central Park West. Their divorce was finally granted on the fourteenth of February 1947, but Meyer remained very close to his children."

Lansky doesn't talk about the years with Anna but he loves to talk about the children. "I was very proud of Paul," he said, "and I did all I could to help him with his ambition to become an Army officer. I visited him at West Point quite a bit—it was a nice drive from New York—and he introduced me to his two roommates. They all enjoyed the delicatessen Paul liked for me to bring from the city. One of his roommates was the son of a Colonel Freeman, who was very close to General Eisenhower. When Eisenhower became president in 1952 I was very surprised to get an invitation from Colonel Freeman to attend the inauguration ceremony.

"I assumed this had been a mistake. Colonel Freeman probably didn't know the terrible reputation I had. I wrote to him with thanks and regrets, implying that the dignitaries there might find it inconvenient to have a man like me around. But I got a reply from Colonel Freeman saying something like 'Don't forget to come to the ceremony. Don't you know that in our clubs we play the same slot machines that you've got in your casinos, and that we used to drink your bootleg whiskey?' That certainly made me smile," said Lansky. "But I sent thanks and regrets again. Big public things just aren't my style.

"I know Paul won't mind my saying this now, but when he first went to West Point he found a lot of anti-Semitism there. He didn't tell me about it till several years later, but in his first week there he had several fist fights with fellow cadets who made anti-Jewish remarks. Paul challenged every one of them and took them on. After that they left him alone. When he told me I was so proud of him I nearly cried. It reminded me of my own days on the Lower East Side, and of course I thought of that courageous soldier of my childhood in Grodno.

"Paul had been flying since he was sixteen and he was a pilot, a captain in the Air Force, during the Korean war. At the beginning of the 1970s he went across the United States talking at university campuses urging volunteers to join the American army. He believed very firmly in the American role in Vietnam. And now that we're no longer involved, people are beginning to see the true situation. Paul was right. I've always shared his views about our role in Vietnam. Paul became an engineer after leaving the Air Force in 1963 and went to live in the state of Washington with his wife and children." Paul Lansky physically resembles his father although he is taller. As a boy he had a vacation job at the Singapore Resort Motel in Miami Beach, which belonged to Meyer's brother Jake. One of the features of this hotel, on Ninety-sixth Street and Collins Avenue, was a pair of parrots who lived in the branches of a tree in the lobby just above a pool. For years the parrots were a family joke to the Lanskys as they screamed out their favorite words, "Meyer and Jake, Meyer and Jake."

Sandra graduated from Pine Crest School in Fort Lauderdale, Florida. She married Marvin Rappaport, a young man she had known from her school days. It was a marriage that delighted her father. One of Marvin's relatives had been involved with King's Ransom whiskey since Prohibition days, and the family had been friends of Lansky's for years.

Lansky's family problems in 1946 did not keep him from preparing for Luciano's arrival in Cuba. From Italy Luciano traveled in a devious way by a ship which stopped first in Caracas. From there he took a plane to Mexico City and there he chartered a private plane to take him to Havana. He did not have to pass through normal customs control in Cuba, and obliging officials whisked him through VIP facilities before he drove to meet Lansky at the Hotel Nacional.

From their hotel Luciano moved to a villa Lansky had hired for him in Miramar, an elegant Havana suburb full of rich Cubans and Americans. Lansky had no problems in getting the Cuban minister of interior, Alfredo Pequeño, to grant permission for Luciano to stay on the island as long as he wished. Luciano also got permission to have an American car imported to Cuba without paying the import tax.

There was little time for Luciano to enjoy the easygoing way of life then much in evidence in Cuba. Soon he and Lansky were again involved in planning for the future, a future that envisaged Luciano's return to the United States.

As Doc Stacher remembered the reunion, "Both men were banking on the fact that Tom Dewey would run for president in 1948 as the Republican candidate. Although Luciano detested Dewey for sending him to prison on concocted charges of running prostitution, he knew very well that Dewey was responsible for his freedom too. Meyer and Charlie were certain that Dewey would accept financial support from them—and in return they would be allowed to operate their gambling without much interference."

Lansky traveled all over the United States inviting underworld leaders to travel to Havana in December for a vacation and a meeting with Charlie at which plans for the future would be discussed. Although Lansky gave the impression that he was simply a messenger boy for Charlie Luciano, those in the know were well aware that he was very much in charge of the situation. Lansky had gone along with the idea that at this meeting in Havana, Luciano would be officially elected Capo di Tutti Capi, although the real power, particularly as far as gambling was concerned, lay in his hands. One by one America's chief gangsters—Joe Adonis, Frank Costello, Joe Profaci, Willie Moretti, Mike Miranda, Albert Anastasia, Joe Bonanno, and Vito Genovese—flew into Havana. From New Orleans came Carlos Marcello and the Al Capone heirs, Charlie and Rocco Fischetti. Dandy Phil Kastel was there, and Santos Trafficante came from Florida. Stacher was present as Lansky's right hand in dozens of enterprises. Known as Doc Harris and sometimes merely as Baldy, Stacher, with Barnett Sugarman and Abe Green as his partners, was involved in the juke-box business, running the Runyon Sales Corporation from 123 Runyon Street, in

Newark. He had been in the Brown Vintner Company with Joseph Rheinfield, Lou Holtz, and Abner Zwillman, but sold the assets to Seagram's after repeal. He was connected with Jerry Catena in a business called the Public Service Tobacco Company, and was active in the related slot-machine business for Lansky.

The official reason for the get-together was to celebrate the arrival of Frank Sinatra, who was to sing at the Nacional at Christmas time. As Doc Stacher said, "The Italians among us were very proud of Frank. They always told me they had spent a lot of money helping him in his career, ever since he was with Tommy Dorsey's band. Lucky Luciano was very fond of Sinatra's singing. Frankie flew into Havana with the Fischettis, with whom he was very friendly, but of course our meeting had nothing to do with listening to him croon. The meeting took place in the Hotel Nacional and lasted all week. Everybody brought envelopes of cash for Lucky, and as an exile he was glad to take them. But more important, they came to pay allegiance to him. A number of the younger guys were doubtful about paying allegiance to the old-timer, as they called him, but Meyer backed him a hundred percent and nobody wanted to cross the Little Man. He was handling most of their finances and was the key figure in their gambling income. Meyer kept in the background as always, but nobody at that meeting was in the faintest doubt who held the whip hand."

Luciano again emphasized the philosophy he and Meyer had worked out back in the twenties: avoid bad publicity and dissension in the ranks—no unnecessary wars. Then they discussed detailed plans to turn the Caribbean into the center of the greatest gambling operation the world had ever seen. Land would be bought on the Isle of Pines, just off Cuba and politically part of it, and the whole island would be converted into a kind of international Monte Carlo. It was a bigger plan than Las Vegas, bigger than anything the organization had ever tackled.

Everybody was enthusiastic, and not even Meyer Lansky foresaw that trouble was brewing in Washington as news began to percolate to the United States that Lucky Luciano was living in Cuba. The chief of the Narcotics Bureau, Harry Anslinger, was convinced that Luciano had returned to Cuba to speed up the flow of drugs from Europe to the United States. He was sure this was the main purpose of the meeting in Havana which reunited almost the entire American underworld. Anslinger sent several agents to Havana, and one of them, Ray Olivera, succeeded in tapping

Luciano's telephone. Anslinger then complained to the Cuban ambassador in Washington that Luciano's presence in Cuba was a danger to the United States. He gave details of how both Lansky and Luciano were bribing Cuban officials to enable Luciano not only to live on the island but also to engage in a wide-ranging plan to smuggle narcotics. There was certainly some element of truth in this. Among the gangsters who had flown to Havana to meet Charlie Luciano were several, including Vito Genovese, who were deeply involved in running narcotics to the United States.

For the next two months Lansky was to pull all the strings he could to keep his friend in Cuba. He flew to Havana again and again, reminding Batista of the enormous bribes they had been paying him over the years and demanding his cooperation. Batista did use what influence he could to prevent any interference with the underworld's plans, but Luciano did not make things easier for himself. He had reverted to his basic characteristic of enjoying the high life, going to lush parties in Cuba and being seen in the company of beautiful Cuban and American women who enjoyed the excitement of becoming mistresses of the gangster they had read so much about in the newspapers.

In Washington, Anslinger was exerting very heavy pressure on Cuba, demanding that Luciano be expelled and sent back to Italy. Under counterpressure from Lansky, the Cuban police chief, Benito Herrera, and Interior Minister Alfredo Pequeño resisted Washington's demands. These officials and others, including a Cuban congressman, had all been heavily bribed in the past by the Lower East Siders. Now the debts were called in, and Cuba continued to resist all demands to expel Luciano. Doc Stacher later commented: "Here was Lansky being at his most loyal. There was really no reason for him to protect Lucky so much. He no longer needed Lucky's influence at all—everybody knew he was really the man behind the gambling empire."

Anslinger also went to President Truman and convinced him that the smuggling of drugs from Cuba to the United States was a major threat to the youth of the country. Truman promised all the backing his commissioner needed, and Anslinger declared publicly that until Cuba made up its mind to expel Luciano the United States would embargo the shipment of medical supplies and drugs to Cuba.

In response President Grau San Martín complained bitterly of injustice and bullying, and the Cuban director of public health, Dr.

José Andreu, prompted by Lansky, denied Anslinger's claim that narcotics traffic between the two countries had increased. "We will resist American pressure to cut off Cuban supplies of legitimate drugs," he said passionately.

But the Cubans could not fight back forever against the might of America. Clearly they would have to get rid of Lucky Luciano sooner or later, despite the millions of dollars paid into the pockets of Batista and his puppets. Batista warned Lansky that Charlie would have to go, and Lansky gave the message to Luciano. Lucky himself, however, was so enjoying his life in Cuba that he refused to take Lansky's advice to leave voluntarily, and when American pressure became too much, Luciano was first placed under house arrest, then taken under armed guard to the Tiscoria immigration camp on the island. A request that he be expelled not back to Italy but somewhere in South America met with strong hostility in Washington.

In February 1947, Lucky Luciano was sent back to Italy aboard a Turkish vessel, the S.S. *Bakir*. The only hope Lansky and his other friends had was that he would be able to return to the United States if Dewey beat Harry Truman in the presidential election. The Lower East Side leaders were convinced that if Dewey won, they would be able to influence him by having backed his campaign. Then the man who had imprisoned Lucky Luciano would provide an open door for him to return to the United States.

Besides the grandiose plans for the Isle of Pines and the apparently improved situation of Luciano, another less pleasant matter was discussed at the Nacional Hotel meeting in December 1946. This was the question of Bugsy Siegel and the Flamingo Hotel. Thanks to Lansky's influence, most of the underworld leaders had contributed large sums of cash to build the Flamingo. Bugsy and Virginia and Lansky were commuting from Los Angeles to Las Vegas, trying to get the hotel finished on time. One of the problems was that Bugsy had given Virginia Hill a free hand in decorating and furnishing the hotel. "She did this in a most elegant but extravagant way," Doc Stacher said. "It was costing us a fortune."

At the meeting "Lansky shocked everybody when he explained that the cost would be not one million but six million dollars before the Flamingo was finished. There was a terrible outcry about this and he calmly told them not to get excited, that this was only peanuts compared with the money that was going to be made. He said that Bugsy himself had raised money from a number of film stars, and that two of his financial backers, Samuel and his brother Harry Rothberg—they had put up a quarter of a million dollars between the two of them—were getting impatient.

"But there was something that troubled the other guys even more than the costs and the delays. Some of them knew that Virginia Hill kept flying off to Zurich, and when anybody asked her what she was doing in Switzerland she was pretty vague—looking at furnishings and curtains for the hotel and so on. None of the West Coast people believed a word of it, particularly when news came back that she had stashed something like half a million bucks in a numbered account in a Zurich bank. We all understood that this meant Bugsy was skimming off some of the construction money for his private bank account. He was totally under Virginia's influence and we all knew she had a huge appetite for dollars. He was so much in love with her that he did anything she asked him, no matter how crazy.

"This sort of behavior meant only one thing in the underworld. Bugsy was going to be hit. Meyer knew that too, but he did all he could to save his friend. He begged the men to be patient and let Bugsy open the hotel, 'and then we can settle matters with him if we find out he's been cheating us.' "

Stacher remembered Lansky's plea very painfully. "It was the first time I ever heard Meyer become so emotional, when he appealed to the members not to be too harsh with Bugsy. Meyer couldn't deny that Siegel had betrayed the trust placed in him, but he pleaded with everybody there to remember the great services that Bugsy had performed for all of them. They looked at him stony-faced without saying a word, and Meyer realized that Bugsy's fate was sealed. But because of the great respect they all had for Meyer, they agreed to give him a little time to try to resolve the problems that Bugsy had created for them. Meyer left the conference and made a quick flight to California to see Bugsy. But when he came back he told me, 'I can't do a thing with him. He's so much in that woman's power that he cannot see reason.' "

Siegel did accept Lansky's advice that he had better do something pretty quick to ward off the criticism for taking so long to finish the Flamingo. As a result of Lansky's intervention he decided to have the grand opening the night after Christmas, even if all the facilities weren't complete. Meyer made it brutally clear to Bugsy that his fate would depend on whether the opening night was a success or not.

On Christmas Eve, as the leaders of the American underworld were celebrating at the Nacional Hotel, there was a momentous encounter between Meyer Lansky and Charlie Luciano. It was during an elaborate banquet for Sinatra—unreported in the Havana papers because of Lansky's influence but hugely enjoyed by the underworld figures. Lansky told Stacher later that halfway through the dinner Charlie Luciano took him aside and said, looking him straight in the eyes, "Meyer, I know your feelings for Bugsy. I know you love him as much as you love your own brother, even your sons.

"But, Meyer, this is business and Bugsy has broken our rules. He's taking our money and stashing it away in Switzerland. He is betraying us. He is cheating us. He knows it and you know it."

Stacher believes that Lansky realized, "as we all did," that his friend Bugsy had gone through an astonishing change of personality since he fell in love with Virginia Hill. Even Bugsy's wife could stand it no longer, although up to that time she had forgiven him for his scores of love affairs with actresses and dancers. Virginia Hill was something else again and she was living quite openly with Bugsy Siegel. Esther Siegel had confided in Lansky and appealed to him to do what he could to get Bugsy to break off with Virginia Hill, and Lansky had tried. He had even gone to Chicago to see his old friend Joe Epstein, who felt responsible for Virginia Hill long after she left him. As Stacher reported it, this veteran bookmaker "shrugged and admitted to Meyer that he was still giving her money on a monthly basis."

Lansky was amazed that the hardbitten Joe Epstein could behave this way, even though he had been in love with her. Virginia had left Epstein and lived with Joe Adonis and several other gangsters before Bugsy Siegel fell in love with her, but Epstein continued to support her. There was nothing he could do, he said, to break up the relationship between her and Bugsy. As Epstein said to Lansky with feeling, "Once that girl is under your skin, it's like a cancer. It's incurable."

Lansky went back to Esther and told her that nothing was going to cure Bugsy of his infatuation. According to Stacher, he said to her, "I've seen them together and they're like two teenagers in love. There's nothing you can do about it."

Lansky told her that the only thing that might possibly bring Bugsy to his senses was to sue him for divorce. "She did it—she trusted Meyer's judgment—but Bugsy showed not the slightest remorse. She got a Reno divorce and went back to New York, but Bugsy's feelings for Virginia seemed to get stronger every day they were together."

In Havana two of Lansky's partners, Moe Dalitz and old-timer Longie Zwillman, appealed to Meyer to bring Bugsy under control before it was "too late." Too late meant only one thing, as Lansky the realist was well aware. But it was Charlie Luciano who at the Christmas Eve party warned his old friend that "unless Bugsy makes a great success of that hotel, you know as well as I do that he'll have to be shot. And if you don't have the heart to do it, Meyer, I will have to order the execution myself."

Stacher remembered: "I saw Meyer a few minutes after he had spoken to Charlie. I could hardly believe it. There were tears in his eyes. I started to ask him what was wrong, but then I held my tongue. Meyer went straight up to his room and for two hours we didn't see him. The banquet for Sinatra went on without him. I could tell that Meyer was going through a terrible crisis, but I only realized afterward that he must have been trying to think up some way of saving Bugsy Siegel."

During those two hours Lansky telephoned Lou Rothkopf, who ran the Hollenden Hotel in Cleveland, and ordered Rothkopf to contact Mickey Cohen immediately. Cohen was in Los Angeles as Bugsy Siegel's lieutenant and bodyguard. Lansky warned Rothkopf, "I want you to tell Mickey Cohen to stay close to Bugsy at all times—never let him out of his sight. If anything should happen to Bugsy, Mickey Cohen will answer to me."

The next day the underworld leaders went on with their meeting in Havana, but the thoughts of most of them were in Las Vegas.

The Flamingo was a fabulous place, certainly, worthy of notice whether or not one had investments in it. A million dollars had been invested in giving every bathroom its own separate sewage pipes. The Del E. Webb Construction Company of Phoenix had been given orders to use only the best woods, the best marble, the best equipment. To complete enough of the hotel to have the opening, Siegel had flown in plasterers, carpenters, and other key workers from as far afield as San Francisco, Denver, and Salt Lake City, paying them a bonus of fifty dollars a day for speed. When Bugsy was told that the furnace he wanted could not be altered to fit into the space allowed for it, he simply ordered: "Blow it up and rebuild." There were problems with the air-conditioning system, which was vital for a desert city like Las Vegas, and because of the haste of construction there were other mistakes which had to be rectified. All took time and money, but Bugsy Siegel was desperate.

Finally, on the evening of December 26, as Meyer Lansky sat with his friends in Havana, Siegel opened his Flamingo Hotel with Virginia Hill at his side. His influence in Hollywood was such that Jimmy Durante, Baby Rose Marie, the Tune Toppers, Eddie Jackson, and the full band of Xavier Cugat were there to welcome the expected stream of guests who would be invited to inspect the casino and the guest rooms and services of the hotel, as well as its theater, cocktail lounges, and restaurants. A famous chef had been brought from Paris, and George Jessel was master of ceremonies.

To make absolutely sure the hotel would be full, Siegel had chartered Constellations to fly the guests in from Los Angeles, but the weather in Los Angeles was so bad that the planes could not take off. To make matters worse, Siegel had made a major mistake; the period between Christmas and New Year's is considered dead in the entertainment world, and it is not certain that even if the planes had flown, all those invited to fly free would have made the journey. A few of his friends came, including George Raft, Charles Coburn, George Sanders, and some others, but there were many missing faces—and missing dollars.

The news reached Havana at once. The opening was a flop. A total disaster. For two weeks Siegel struggled on, and the casino alone lost over a hundred thousand dollars before he gave up and ordered that the hotel be closed.

At the Nacional, the day after the disastrous opening, Lansky tried again to save Siegel. He proposed to his fellow guests that the corporation that owned the Flamingo be thrown into receivership to bring the losses to a halt. A syndicate would be set up to buy out the corporation, and under new control and capable accounting it would continue with the project. Some of the leaders were unhappy about the scheme, but Luciano backed Lansky's determined reasoning that money was going to be made in Las Vegas and it was going to be made with the Flamingo, once the difficulties were ironed out.

Stacher said, "I've heard some wild stories about Bugsy Siegel flying down to Havana to plead with Lansky and Luciano to give him a chance. Bugsy knew very well that he was in deep, deep trouble, but he didn't go to Havana. What actually happened was that he left Las Vegas and went to where he was living with Virginia Hill, at 810 North Linden Drive in Beverly Hills. Then Bugsy flew to Mexico with Virginia and married her. I think she tried to persuade him to fly off to Europe with her and use the money they had stashed away in Switzerland. She surely knew from her experience that Bugsy's life was in danger. But I will say this for Benny—even though he was so besotted with his girl, he knew there was no point in running away. He was never a coward. He would stay in the United States and face whatever was coming to him.

"When Bugsy got back from Mexico he flew straight to Las Vegas. Meyer had managed to get an extension of time for him, and he reopened the Flamingo in March. The place still wasn't ready, but in April things slowly started to get better. In May I think he reported a profit of over a quarter of a million dollars." Bugsy was now concentrating all his energies on the hotel. Apparently deciding that Virginia was a distraction, he sent her to Paris for a holiday, promising that he would either join her in France or ask her to fly back to him as soon as he had solved the remaining problems at the Flamingo.

Both Stacher and Lansky were still doing all they could to save Bugsy Siegel. Back in the United States, they spoke to the various gang leaders and assured them that Bugsy would turn the tide, and in the spring they were quick with the news that he had succeeded.

By the middle of June 1947, Siegel had convinced himself that all was going well. He flew to Los Angeles and cabled to Virginia to join him there. In the afternoon he went for his weekly manicure to Harry Drucker's barber shop in Beverly Hills. There he met an old friend who was a film maker. Siegel looked calm and relaxed for the first time in months. That evening he went to the rented house on North Linden Drive with a close friend, Allen Smiley. Mickey Cohen was not in the house, but Virginia's brother, Charles Hill, was upstairs in a bedroom with his girl friend. Siegel was sitting on a sofa, talking to Smiley, when a bullet crashed through the window into his head and knocked out an eye. Four more bullets followed in quick succession. Three of them missed, but the two that struck home were quite sufficient.

Later that evening two men, Maurice Rosen and Gus Green-baum, walked into the Flamingo Hotel, where Moe Sedway was in charge. They told Sedway to take it easy, that there had been a change in ownership. The staff were to continue with their work as though nothing had happened. Because both Rosen and Greenbaum had worked for Lansky in Miami, Havana, and New York, it was immediately assumed that he was behind the killing of Siegel. But

Joe Stacher and Lansky maintained then and later that the killing was done on orders of Luciano alone, orders that were probably conveyed direct to Jack Dragna. Still smarting over Bugsy's usurpation of his territory, Dragna would have been wholeheartedly pleased at the assignment. He had waited a long time.

Officially the name of the killer remained unknown, but Luciano's word was still law, even from Italy. "It was clear to us afterward that he had ordered Bugsy to be shot," Stacher said. "Maybe he did it even before he left Cuba. Only Lucky could have ordered Mickey to make himself scarce."

Despite Lansky's denials, it has been widely asserted that he was responsible for Siegel's death. Certainly Esther Siegel remained loyal to Meyer. In 1959, questioned by the FBI at her home on East End Avenue in New York City, she said, "I first met Meyer Lansky about 1926 and always thought very highly of him. He was best man at my wedding in 1928. He and my husband were closely associated socially and in business."

In Chicago, Joe Epstein, as soon as he heard of Bugsy's death, got in touch with Virginia Hill Siegel in Paris, told her to stay there, and sent her some money to do so. Virginia was deeply depressed and tried to kill herself. She later told investigators that Bugsy Siegel was the one man she had ever really loved. A few weeks later, when Lansky asked her, she gave back the money Bugsy had spirited away to his Swiss bank account. She obeyed orders about how to behave and refused to comment about Siegel's death. Virginia eventually did kill herself with an overdose of drugs in March 1966.

Under Gus Greenbaum's management, backed by Lansky's new syndicate, the Flamingo became a gold mine, as Lansky and Siegel had predicted.

Meyer Lansky in the late 1930s.

OPPOSITE PAGE

ABOVE Meyer Lansky (fourth from left) awaits trial at Ballston Spa, New York, in 1952 on charges of gambling, conspiracy, and forgery.

BELOW LEFT Lansky outside a Manhattan courtroom after his hearing on a charge of vagrancy was postponed. The charges were dropped.

BELOW RIGHT Escorted by detectives, Lansky arrives at the West 54th Street police station in New York for questioning in 1958.

ABOVE Lansky arrives at a Miami jail in 1970 to be booked for possession of Donnatal.

RIGHT Mrs. Meyer Lansky spits in the face of a Miami television reporter during an altercation at Miami International Airport in 1972.

OPPOSITE PAGE

ABOVE A recent photograph showing Lansky being driven in his car in Florida.

BELOW Lansky's walks with his dog are well known to Lansky watchers.

BELOW Uri Dan and Lansky on a
hilltop overlooking Jerusalem.

BOTTOM Dan and Lansky talk as
they climb a hill on the outskirts of
Jerusalem.

STERN MAGAZINE

STERN MAGAZINE

29 The Italian Pensioner

Lansky's oldest close friend was dead, and the man who had been closest of all was back in Italy. Lansky held to the code and did not change toward Luciano after Siegel was killed. He still made sure Lucky got his income—every month at least $25,000 went to Europe by various couriers so that Lucky could have a comfortable exile—and by 1948 Lansky was planning other help for his friend.

Doc Stacher was involved. "Meyer knew that Charlie felt out of things in Italy, and there were some signs that his influence wasn't as strong as it used to be. That was unbearable for a man like Charlie. Meyer decided to demonstrate his friendship for Lucky by planning a trip to Italy, and for once he let it be known that he wouldn't mind if the news got out."

At the same time there was more startling news. Stacher had known for some time that Lansky had been quietly seeing a great deal of a small, fair-haired woman named Thelma Scheer Schwartz, who had been his manicurist in the barber shop of the Embassy Hotel in Miami. "He had introduced her to a few of us as Teddy, this was the only name he ever called her. She was five years younger than Meyer—he was forty-six by then—and taller, but when they were together this didn't bother either of them. Meyer had such an air of authority that you didn't think of him as a small man when you were with him. Teddy knew Meyer was a gambler, and I expect she knew about all the other stuff. She never interfered and never questioned. She simply accepted that this was the way he was. Quite a contrast to poor Anna. Teddy was always totally loyal to him and they were really happy, those two. It was a great romance for them both.

"Teddy was a divorcée when she first met Meyer, and had children from the previous marriage. She had had to be very frugal, and Meyer couldn't change her. On the rare occasions when Meyer visited a casino not as owner or part owner but just for fun, he used to give Teddy money to try her luck on the roulette wheel or at blackjack. No matter how much he gave her she always gave him back three quarters of it, and she'd feel guilty for the rest of the evening if she lost the few dollars she had actually staked. Meyer got so he took her everywhere with him. He could discuss any business in her presence and she never interfered.

"They were married on December 16, 1948, and some of Meyer's friends wanted to turn the wedding into a big glittering affair. But this wasn't his way. Only a few close friends were invited.

"The couple lived in a penthouse apartment at 40 Central Park West. It was pleasantly furnished but without any great ostentation. Teddy took a lot of trouble to make it an agreeable home and Meyer gave her a free hand. The apartment represented her own quiet taste and she was particularly proud of the way she had saved money by buying furniture at sales and scouring the stores for bargains. Meyer was very generous with Teddy. He gave her quantities of jewelry and fur coats, but she always used to protest, saying he spent far too much money on her. Meyer enjoyed spending money on Teddy, and when they went traveling she always looked great, dressed from Fifth Avenue."

Lansky planned to take Teddy with him when he sailed to Italy in the summer of 1949. It would be a delayed honeymoon for them. But before their departure, they got a taste of what was in store now that Lansky had let his plans become public knowledge. Lansky remembers it angrily. "Just before we left, narcotics agents came to my apartment on Central Park West. I invited them in, but the way they behaved I had the impression they were going to smash the place to pieces. They cross-examined me about my trip to Europe. For some reason they had it in their heads that I was involved in narcotics. I told them over and over that I had nothing whatever to do with dope peddling, never had, never would. But there was a campaign against me, and as an FBI agent once told me, 'There's always good publicity in interviewing Lansky.' This makes headlines in the newspapers and the public gets the impression that the agents are doing their job. As soon as the narcotics people left, J. Edgar Hoover sent down his FBI boys. It was as though he didn't want the narcs to feel they had the edge on him. He made a great show of his agents interviewing me and then bugging my room on the ship."

FBI agents had their own version of events. When talking with Lansky at his apartment—where they noted that he had a "colored maid"—they reported that he told them: "I am a common gambler, I guess. . . . If I just met you casually, I would call myself a restaurant operator. If we warmed up to each other I would tell you I was a common gambler." The agents added, "Lansky seemed to resent the bad name which he feels he has been undeservedly given. . . . He stated that he formerly sold the franchise for Wurlitzer juke boxes for New York, New Jersey, and Connecticut but was no longer in that business. He claimed to own stock in the Consolidated Television Company which has previously been reported as racket owned." When Lansky told the agents that his son Buddy was a patient in New York's Bellevue Hospital, where he was "under treatment by Dr. Howard A. Rusk for cerebral palsy," the agents commented: "It would be interesting to determine if Buddy Lansky is a paying patient in this city institution in view of Lansky's close association with certain Tammany figures."

Whether the FBI launched an inquiry into Buddy's sickroom status is not known, but the agents were certainly thorough in keeping an eye on his father. "The sailing of Lansky was covered by the New York press, who reported that Michael Lascari and wife of 1111 Park Avenue were present at the bon voyage party in the regal suite of the *Italia,* which was liberally sprinkled with orchids and hampers of champagne."

"It was a game," Lansky says, "but a nasty one for Teddy and me. It gave the authorities a lot of publicity, but I was outraged. They knew I never touched drugs in my life."

When he and Teddy boarded the *Italia* on June 28, Lansky said again that he had every intention of visiting Lucky Luciano in Italy. Luciano was a boyhood friend. Luciano had been to prison and then released. He had paid whatever debt he owed to society. Surely a man had the right to visit his friends. "I am going openly to Europe and I am going openly to see Luciano."

Lansky's friends sent or brought champagne, food, and flowers to his honeymoon suite on the liner. One of the guests was Vito Genovese, who was unaware that one of the reasons for the visit to

Luciano was to discuss how to handle some startling information that had come to light about this powerful Mafia figure.

Throughout the Lanskys' European journey they were followed by FBI and narcotics agents. "I used to recognize them and invite them to have a drink with me. They weren't even embarrassed—they used to accept my hospitality. They were trying to bug our hotel rooms, but they did it very incompetently, and I kidded them about their lack of professionalism. That was the only time they were at a loss for words throughout our wedding trip."

The Lanskys went to Palermo, Sicily, and then on to Naples, but they did not at that stage go to see Charlie Luciano. Lansky hired a car and drove leisurely up through Italy. He did not telephone Luciano until he reached Rome. Then Lucky explained that it would be difficult for him to travel to the capital because of restrictions placed on him by the authorities there, so Lansky went back to Sicily, to Taormina. It was a happy moment for both men when Meyer introduced Charlie to his bride and in turn Lucky introduced Igea Lissoni, whom he was living with. The two men had a lot to talk about, and after reminiscing a bit they got down to business. Number one on the agenda was Vito Genovese.

This stocky, dark, Naples-born Mafia leader had clashed with Meyer Lansky from the earliest days in the 1920s, when he first joined the Lower East Side outfit. He had objected to working closely with Jews, but Luciano had made it clear that if Genovese was to be part of the group he would have to accept the situation. Genovese had done so reluctantly, and had remained relatively uncontrollable. At the time of Luciano's arrest, information had come to light about his killing of a minor rival known as Ferdinand "the Shadow" Boccia, in October 1934.

Now Lansky said to Luciano, "You remember that when Don Vitone"—his sardonic nickname for Genovese—"wanted to go to Italy back in the 1930s, I was the one who opposed it." Luciano remembered very well. He and Lansky had agreed that Vito Genovese was a danger to all of them and had wondered if the only way to prevent trouble was to let him be arrested and face the chair for the Boccia killing. The Shadow was a small-time crook who had the good fortune to stumble on a businessman from Brooklyn with a weakness for poker. Boccia let him win a few games and then suggested that he knew where much larger stakes could be played for. "With your luck," the Shadow had flattered the rich Brooklyn businessman, "you can win a fortune. I'll set up a game for you." With a man named Mike Miranda, and with Genovese organizing the game, the merchant was taken for $150,000. Genovese had promised the Shadow a third of the earnings, but as Boccia awaited the payoff for the biggest coup of his life, Genovese double-crossed him by hiring two killers, Ernest "The Hawk" Rupolo and Willie Gallo, to shoot Boccia. After they killed the comparatively harmless Shadow, Genovese gave Rupolo $175 more to murder Gallo. The offer was accepted but Rupolo only wounded his companion, and Gallo went to the police. Rupolo ended up with a nine-to-twenty-year sentence for attempted murder.

Lansky and Luciano also knew about another indefensible Genovese killing. In 1932, "Don Vitone" had met Gerarddi Vernotico's wife and fallen in love with her. Genovese ordered Vernotico to be killed by two of his henchmen, Michael Barrese and Peter Mione. They strangled Gerarddi on the roof of a building and an unfortunate witness, Antonio Lonza, who stumbled upon the body as the two men were leaving, was also killed. To cover up the way he had gotten rid of his beloved's husband, Genovese then had both Barrese and Mione killed. He married Anna Vernotico at once, but later she discovered Genovese's role in slaying her first husband and took her revenge by sleeping with Genovese's friends and finally telling the police all she knew about him. Instead of reacting in his characteristic savage way and having Anna bumped off, Genovese revealed that she was his one weakness: he could not bring himself to harm her.

What troubled both Lansky and Luciano even more than his savagery was Genovese's fascination with drugs. Before the Second World War, Luciano, believing that Lansky was swayed by his personal dislike for Genovese, refused to listen to Lansky and let Genovese go to Italy to dodge arrest, carrying with him two million dollars, part of his share of the organization's bootlegging income.

Now in Taormina Lansky reminded Luciano, "I was always unhappy about his going off to Italy. I've found out since the war that he used a big part of his money to support Mussolini's thugs, those gangs that went around beating up political opponents and pouring castor oil into them. Charlie, while you were in jail he helped the Fascists and was a bona fide traitor to America—and you and I were trying to help the United States win the war." Lansky pounded hard: "Besides the drug dealing, I have positive proof that Genovese helped the German and Italian secret service to recruit Sicilians, Italians, and German-speaking Americans during the war.

He gave them names of people that German and Italian intelligence could set up as spies and couriers. He told the Nazis where agents could hide out and personally briefed a lot of them about how to get on in New York. That's the war record of our friend Genovese."

According to Lansky, Luciano simply shrugged his shoulders and said quietly, "I guess I was wrong all along. They've told me about him over here, too. You were so against Vito even in those days that I thought you were being unfair to him. O.K., Little Man, you handle Vito as you think best. I know you'll wait for the right moment."

Just how big a mistake Lucky had made in his early assessment of Genovese was proved later, when Genovese schemed to have Luciano shot even though he was now harmless and out of the way in Italy. Genovese moved against Luciano's empire and tried to murder all his New York allies who remained loyal to Charlie. Joe Adonis fled to Italy because Genovese was clearly gunning for him, but Adonis managed to escape with several million dollars of his own savings, which were a consolation to him in Europe.

Genovese's rampage continued, and he turned his attention to one of the "Jew boys" he had hated for so long, Abner Zwillman, Lansky's mentor, who had made the mistake over the years of poking sarcastic fun at Genovese. After his long romance with Jean Harlow, Zwillman had finally married and settled down in West Orange, New Jersey. Like Lansky he had always abhorred violence, and in the 1950s—although still involved in gambling—he had moved away from the rackets. On February 27, 1955, Zwillman was found dangling from wires in the basement of his home. At first it appeared to be suicide, but Lansky knew better. Said Lansky, "Genovese was behind that killing. He just ordered his killers to make it look like Zwillman had taken his own life. And there was good reason for people to believe this theory at the time, because Longie was in trouble with the tax people. But it was a Genovese murder. I know."

Lansky had believed for a long time that Genovese was aiming for the ultimate revenge, the slaying of both himself and Charlie Luciano, and if Zwillman's murder was not proof enough, the attempted murder of Frank Costello two years later clinched it. On May Day 1957 Genovese sent a gunman known as Vincent "the Chin" Gigante to carry out the assassination. This former prize fighter, who had run to seed and weighed over three hundred pounds, shot Costello as he was about to walk into his residence in the elegant Majestic Apartments, at 115 Central Park West. Gigante fired only once and, believing that his aim had been impeccable, lumbered away, but Costello survived.

To this day Lansky declines to discuss his reprisal, but his close friend Doc Stacher related admiringly how Lansky moved against Don Vitone a few months after Costello was shot.

In November 1957, as a preliminary to establishing himself as king of the entire Mafia in the United States, Genovese called a national meeting of gangster leaders in the Sullivan County community of Apalachin, in Upstate New York. "Meyer and I were invited but he sent word that as it was November he did not want to make the journey north from Miami. He was suffering from flu at the time. In fact, none of Lansky's closest friends went to the meeting."

The local sheriff was tipped off that several interesting gangsters would be found at the home of a Buffalo businessman called Joseph Barbara. The police surrounded the house, and during the raid the hundred or so visiting gangsters fled in all directions. Sixty were arrested, and although none came to any harm as a result of the gathering, Lansky knew he had damaged the reputation of Genovese forever by making him look so totally foolish. "Nobody to this day knows that it was Meyer who arranged for Genovese's humiliation," Doc Stacher said.

"Then Meyer trapped Genovese. The bait was set by one of Meyer's couriers, Nelson Cantellops. Meyer had been angry with Nelson because he got himself mixed up with running drugs at the same time he was working for Meyer. When Nelson was caught, Meyer refused to help him and he went to Sing Sing on a narcotics charge. Then, using his brother Jake, Meyer passed the message to . Nelson that he would forgive him if he would take on a little job. Cantellops was promised a pension for life. So our friend Nelson Cantellops, despite the danger he'd be in, asked for an interview with the Narcotics Bureau in New York and told an agent, George Gaffney, that he could provide information about how Genovese and his partners were smuggling narcotics from Europe to the United States.

"Cantellops was well briefed. He named Vito and twenty-four others. He gave exact details of where and how the drugs were imported, because Meyer had this information from his spies in the Genovese organization. The Narcotics Bureau was delighted with this information and in exchange got Nelson out of Sing Sing. Nelson was the main witness when Genovese and all his partners were convicted on narcotics charges. Genovese died in 1969, still serving his fifteen-year sentence, but even from prison he kept sending out a stream of instructions to kill his enemies, including Meyer Lansky. Meyer kept his word, of course. Nelson got a hundred-thousand-dollar bonus and some kind of minor job that let him collect a monthly pension of several thousand dollars. He died in a fight in a night club in 1965, but as far as I know there wasn't anything sinister about his death."

Luciano and Lansky met several times after Lansky's first visit in 1949. Because there was so much publicity about their meeting at Taormina, they had get-togethers in Paris, London, and frequently in Geneva. Presumably Lansky told his friend how the war with Genovese was progressing, but there were other topics. Lansky sent Luciano a brand-new Buick in 1951, which amused both of them. It reminded them of the days in the 1920s when they spent so much time servicing the big cars they used for bootlegging and other operations.

"What made me especially angry in the 1950s was that the narcotics authorities seemed determined to pin the running of opium and other drugs from Europe to America on Charlie and me," Lansky says. "Every time I visited Charlie things started up again."

The story of how the United States, in cooperation with the Italian authorities, broke an international drug operation has been told in many versions, though never completely. Lansky sees it in unique personal terms. "The man behind this was Charles Siragusa. I think he had been working as a narcotics agent in the United States and in France. He was out to make himself a big hero and the most convenient way to do it was to keep associating Lansky and Luciano with drug running. This got him a lot of publicity and impressed his bosses back in America so much that Anslinger sent him to Italy to get proof that we were involved with narcotics. In 1950 Siragusa bribed one of Tommy Lucchese's couriers to plant some drugs on Charlie on a visit to Naples, where Charlie was living. His name was Eugenio Giannini. I heard about it and sent a message to Charlie to watch out for Giannini."

Although he was far away from New York, for which he was so homesick, Luciano never lost his big-city cunning. He tipped off the Italian police that Giannini was smuggling penicillin. This was a highly charged issue in Italy at the time, because the public resented the way black-marketeers were selling penicillin to people with money when others were dying because they could not get hold of antibiotics.

"I don't know how Charlie did it, but I know poor Giannini had nothing to do with penicillin. While this stupid hoodlum was trying to plant drugs on Charlie, he managed to get in first and plant penicillin on him. Giannini was arrested and under cross-examination admitted that he had been hired by Siragusa to try to set Charlie up. I told Tommy Lucchese about this, and as soon as Giannini got back in the United States he was in serious trouble," said Lansky.

In 1952 the unfortunate Giannini was assassinated by persons unknown in his hideout in East Harlem. Lansky says, "What really made me mad was that after this attempt to get Charlie and me involved with drug running, Siragusa simply reports back to Washington that Luciano has been in touch with the most notorious criminals in the United States, including Meyer Lansky and other chiefs of the underworld who visit Italy—and that he can prove Luciano received big sums of money from these visitors.

"Of course we sent money to Lucky. He was our friend and partner. But no one ever produced any proof that this money had anything to do with drug running. No one has ever come up with the slightest scrap of evidence that I was mixed up with drug running. If it were true, I'd be in prison today."

That first meeting at Taormina, when Lansky introduced his bride to Charlie and the two men sat up all night talking about their past, was also the setting Lansky chose to clue Charlie Luciano on how the gambling business was developing in the United States.

Doc Stacher explained how the system worked from the 1950s on. "It sounds complicated but it wasn't. Meyer had decided long ago that we must reinvest the money that had been coming in ever since we made our fortunes in bootlegging. Arnold Rothstein originally taught all of us the lesson—take the money from these various activities and use it in an intelligent way. Rothstein spent a lot of his on high living, but that wasn't the way Meyer chose. I don't know who it was who first decided to call the system 'laundering,' but that's what it was—to wash clean, by that I mean make legal these vast cash flows, particularly from gambling.

"The money had to find its way into legitimate business without anybody knowing where it came from. Meyer set up a system of couriers and these men, carrying enormous sums of cash in their suitcases, would catch planes to South American cities where Swiss banks held accounts. The best method, however, was to send the money direct to Switzerland, where numbered accounts were opened in Zurich and also later in Geneva.

"Then Meyer worked out a scheme of buying or setting up corporations and businesses in the United States. The directors and owners of these companies might be legitimate businessmen, and Meyer and I and others worked from behind the scenes and controlled the company stock. We would borrow the money from the Swiss banks—which really meant we were borrowing our own money. Interest was paid in the proper way and this interest went straight back to Switzerland. So we were paying interest to ourselves for our own money. There was another advantage to the system, too. This interest was tax deductible in the United States. We were paying taxes and avoiding problems, and of course the interest was helping to cut down our tax burdens. When gambling became legal in more places, Meyer worked out a new method of gearing up our profits. Hotels like the Flamingo in Las Vegas and others where we became involved had to produce books for the income tax authorities, of course. They used to watch us like hawks. We kept clean books and paid our taxes, and we still had enormous profits. But to increase them Meyer worked out something else. Maybe 20 percent of the profits was skimmed off as the money came into the sealed-off and guarded offices of each hotel. This 'cream' was never put on the books and went straight to Switzerland. It was never taxed at all."

It was only by accident that the American authorities became aware of how profits from even legitimate gambling casinos were being skimmed off.

In May 1957, when Frank Costello was shot by Genovese's incompetent gunman, the police who arrived as Costello lay bleeding on the ground made an intriguing find in his pocket. It was not the eight hundred dollars in cash that interested them, but a tiny scrap of paper with the following written on it: "Gross. Casino win as of 4-26-57: $657,284. Casino win less markers [IOUs]: $434,695. Slot wins: $62,844. Marks: $153,745."

Not only did Frank Costello refuse to reveal the name of the man who had tried to kill him, he claimed he knew nothing about the brief note. Federal officials launched a thorough investigation and discovered that the figures in Costello's pocket matched exactly the turnover of the casino in the Tropicana Hotel in Las Vegas, in which Costello had an interest. Costello also had a share in three other Las

Vegas hotels, as well as the Beverly Country Club in New Orleans and the Beverly Hills Club in Los Angeles. He was in partnership at the Tropicana with Meyer, his brother Jake, and Phil Kastel. The paper from his pocket gave the authorities an inkling of the fortunes being spirited away before the casinos' books were made up.

Still refusing to discuss the slip of paper, Costello went to prison briefly for contempt of court and tax evasion. When he was released, he went into semiretirement and died peacefully in 1973.

During the 1950s Lansky and his wife went to Europe often to meet with Luciano. The two men reminisced, joked, and enjoyed each other's company. But Luciano in exile must have had pangs of envy when Lansky talked about his business innovations. In reality Charlie Luciano had been pensioned off, and although it was widely believed in the United States that he played an important role in American crime during the years of his exile, his influence was very limited.

When Luciano died of a heart attack at Capodicino Airport in Naples on January 26, 1962, he was a bitter and broken man. He resented the way his former colleagues were able to live in freedom in the United States. He knew his monthly pension, although generous by normal standards, was a drop in the ocean compared to the income of his friends from the Lower East Side. His last days were especially lonely because the woman he had grown to love, Igea Lissoni, had died of cancer. And although he was living at the time of his death with a young woman known as Adriana, he was lonely and miserable.

The American authorities allowed his body to be brought home, where it was buried in the family plot in St. John's Cathedral Cemetery in Queens. The only genuine mourners present were his two brothers, Joseph and Bartolo. Lansky and Luciano's other friends, expecting the sort of scene that occurred, did their mourning in private. Scores of other people were at the grave side, however—police, FBI men, narcotics agents, and a clutch of newspapermen, curious and unweeping at the burial of Lucky Luciano, one of the most colorful of all American gangsters.

30 The Cuban Connection

In the early 1950s Meyer Lansky was rebuilding on a much larger scale the gambling empire that had flourished in Cuba before the war. He kept in close touch with his friend Batista, still in exile in Florida, and with Carlos Prío Socarrás, who had replaced Ramón Grau San Martín as president in 1948. Prío too was a Batista man and therefore under Lansky's control as well. One clue to how much money was poured into the island in the form of bribery to Prío Socarrás was provided by his extraordinarily extravagant house, which cost $2,000,000 to build at a time when the only income of the Cuban president was supposed to be his $25,000 annual salary. Lansky didn't mind paying, but he believed that Batista should return to the island and reestablish full control. Without his presence Cuba might return to political or economic chaos and imperil the plans for expansion.

Playing the role of a quiet kingmaker, Lansky flew back and forth between Florida and Cuba, paving the way for Batista's return by lavishing more money on the Cuban authorities. At first Prío Socarrás resisted the idea of Batista's comeback, but money sent to his bank account in Switzerland changed his mind. As a result Lansky's friend was allowed to return to Havana in triumph.

American Naval Intelligence men were well aware of Lansky's role in the island's affairs, and according to Stacher some very high government officials had long talks with Lansky, as they had had during the war. Lansky had no illusions about the sort of pressure that could be exerted on him, and he did all he could to persuade

Batista to avoid repeating his mistake of flirting with the Communist Party. In any event, said Stacher, Meyer was fervently anti-Communist and always had been. There was no need for the American government to urge him on.

To this day Lansky declines to discuss the political role he played in Cuba during the 1950s. But it seems clear that Batista wanted to make his move earlier and Lansky advised his friend to be cautious and wait for the 1952 election. In 1952, however, the two other candidates who were running against Batista were well ahead in the polls. Telling his friend Meyer to keep away from the island for a while because there were going to be "problems," Batista struck on March 10, 1952, and with a group of his bodyguards and loyal followers seized control of Havana. The army rallied to his cause—senior officers had not forgotten Batista, who had always treated them well—and President Prío Socarrás made no effectual resistance.

With Batista now firmly in the saddle, Meyer Lansky got to work on the blueprint he had been drawing up for the past four years. Instead of opening more of the small casinos which had flourished in the past and were now flourishing again, he envisioned vast and luxurious superhotel complexes of the sort he and Bugsy Siegel had built in Las Vegas. The hotels would be superbly equipped and would have the very best restaurants and other facilities to match. The highest-paid and most popular entertainers in the world would be on show.

Working on the well-known principle that it's better to use other people's money than your own, Lansky persuaded Batista to have the Cuban government help finance the venture. Batista had every reason to cooperate, since he was promised a generous cut of the profits, and he forced through laws that made it easy for Lansky to create the gambling paradise he had in mind. The government agreed to back every dollar invested on the island by foreigners with a dollar of its own, and to give every hotel that cost more than a million dollars the precious prize of a gambling license. Fees for such licenses were nominal, and the casino hotels would not have to pay Cuban taxes. In addition, licensing duties which the government normally applied to expensive imported building materials were waived. Personnel from the United States—the croupiers and others needed to run the casinos—were given special visas to live on the island and were also exempted from paying taxes. Soon Cuba was undergoing a frantic boom as hotel after hotel rose along the sea front in Havana.

"But there was still unemployment on the island," Lansky said, "and I thought I would do something to help. I got Sammy Bratt, who worked for me in the United States, to open a casino school in our Montmartre Club in Havana. It was a functioning casino, but hundreds of Cuban youngsters were trained there to become efficient operators at blackjack, roulette, and the other games. We also taught them something about running a hotel properly. It was hard work because they were uneducated, and it would have been easier to import Americans. But I ran it as a kind of social experiment."

Those who had worked with Lansky from the early days now reaped more benefits from their loyalty. One after another they were invited to come to Havana and given a stake in one or several of the hotels rising at breakneck speed in Cuba. Moe Dalitz and other former partners who were once members of the famous Cleveland Syndicate during the bootlegging days were given priority, and they eagerly invested. But when outsiders like Santos Trafficante, from Tampa, Florida, tried to muscle in and set up their own casinos on the island, they were cold-shouldered. As Batista told Trafficante bluntly, "You have to get approval from the 'Little Man' before you can get a license on this island." The outraged Trafficante was given only a minor role on the island and never forgave Lansky for it. Meyer's hostility to Trafficante, who ran a numbers racket in Florida, dated from the time he made the mistake of trying to cut into Lansky's own territory in Miami.

Jake Lansky was appointed pit boss at the Hotel Nacional, with the job of keeping an eye on how the hotel was run and seeing that profits were correctly reported. The man put in charge as manager was Sam Tucker, another old friend who had previously looked after the Beverly Hills Club. Lansky and his friends were also involved in the Sevilla Biltmore as well as the Havana Hilton. For himself Lansky had the enormous Riviera Hotel built at a cost of $14,000,000. Much of the money was Lansky's own but his name never appeared on the official list of owners. Doc Stacher said later, "Meyer had a very weird sense of humor. He never laughed very much. But one of the few jokes I ever saw him make was when he called himself the kitchen manager of the Riviera. He put himself down on the payroll and solemnly declared the salary to Internal Revenue as his main source of income. We used to kid Meyer about his abilities as a chef, and he would smile a little when we asked him, 'What's on the menu today, cookie?' "

George Raft, an old friend who had grieved at the death of Bugsy Siegel, was soothed with a job as a kind of superior toastmaster at the Capri Hotel, and Lansky brought in a number of well-trained lieutenants from Las Vegas. These included Eddie Levinson, from Newport, Kentucky, who had worked at the Sands and the Fremont in Las Vegas; Irving "Nig" Devine, who had operated casinos for Lansky at Miami Beach and Las Vegas; and Herman Stark, who had cooperated with Meyer in the early days in New York.

Soon chartered planes were bringing high-stakes gamblers to Havana from all over the United States. Batista still got his cut on all profits, and Batista's brother-in-law, Roberto Fernandez y Miranda, got his payoffs from the slot machine, or one-armed bandit, part of the operation. Some ordinary Cubans benefited too, but the bulk of the population had no share in the money that the foreign high-rollers brought in.

Lansky had been determined that his children should grow up as part of the normal American scene, but Buddy was more than content to work for his father. No illegal activities were involved. Buddy was shifted from one hotel to another in Florida, Nevada, and Cuba, working either in the reception area or as a switchboard operator. Many of Lansky's friends were startled to see his son in such menial jobs, but others realized that the person who mans the switchboard of a major hotel has a position of considerable importance. He can learn an immense amount about the activities of the guests. The story is told that Aristotle Onassis as a young man began his rise to fame and fortune with a job at the switchboard of a Buenos Aires hotel, where he picked up financial tips that started him on the road to becoming a multimillionaire.

The halcyon days in Cuba during the 1950s were not to last, however. The bearded revolutionary Fidel Castro and his band of guerrillas took power at the beginning of 1959. Batista and his closest allies fled, as did the wealthy American gamblers who had for so long enjoyed losing their money on the island. Lansky himself caught one of the last planes leaving Havana for Miami, and he ruefully related later on that he had to leave behind $17,000,000 in cash which just missed being shipped out and distributed to his various partners via Switzerland.

When the Cuban guerrillas came into Havana they smashed up hundreds of slot machines, to them the symbol of "Yankee imperialists" in their country. Doc Stacher, however, was positive that "for a while Castro stopped his revolutionaries from tearing the casinos to pieces. Fidel Castro is tough and realistic. He knew all about the enormous profits of the casinos, and he knew he needed experts like Meyer to run them. Meyer had barely got back to Miami when a message came from Fidel via an intermediary that the revolution was not opposed to the operation of casinos if the government shared in the profits."

Said Stacher: "I've read stories that Meyer or other members of our organization tried to bribe Castro by offering guns and money before he came to power. That's not true at all. None of us would have gained anything from having a Communist regime in Cuba. If anything, we tried to support Batista so that he would be strong enough to resist any revolution. There was never any attempt to support Castro. On the contrary, we all disliked him intensely, and we knew that if he came to power it would be a disaster for us.

"Meyer was astonished to be approached by Castro. He made contact with the CIA agents he knew and they advised him, 'Listen to what he has to say, play along with him. And report everything to us.'

"Meyer did not actually go back to Cuba himself. He wanted to go, but we thought he ought to send some of his lieutenants who ran the casinos instead. So he sent them, but to show good faith Meyer let his brother Jake go along.

"Then Meyer came up with the most astonishing plan I ever heard from him. He indicated to the CIA that some of his people who were still on the island, or those who were just going back, might assassinate Castro. Among the hundreds of young Cubans we had trained to work in the hotels as croupiers and under managers, many certainly realized that their own futures were in jeopardy under the Communist regime. Meyer was convinced that he could pull this off, that his gunmen could kill Castro. Whether that would overturn the revolution was another matter, but Meyer thought that if Castro could be eliminated there was a good chance for Batista to make a comeback. He tried hard to persuade the CIA agents that he could have Fidel removed, and he told them that he was quite prepared to finance the operation himself.

"But Meyer got no encouragement from them, and he was very depressed when they said there was no possibility of anyone giving him the go-ahead for such a plan.

"Meyer called off the negotiations with Castro, and Fidel was so furious that he jailed most of our guys on the island, including Jake, who spent twenty-five days—very uncomfortable ones—in prison in Havana.

"Then Meyer intervened directly with Castro and told him that it was a question of honor for him to release Jake and all the others who had gone there in good faith to make a business deal. The fact that the deal fell through was no reason for them to be put in prison. Castro kept the money we had left behind, but he sent Jake and the others safely back to America."

In the early days of Castro's dictatorship, Meyer Lansky used every political influence he could to try to get rid of Fidel. He made contact with two men he knew very well, one of them a gambler called Dana C. Smith, who had lost thousands of dollars in Havana casinos when Batista was still in power but had not let that dent his friendship with Lansky. Dana had been with a group of men, including Richard Nixon, who flew from Miami to Havana in the early 1950s. Lansky's other contact, who had also been a member of that party, was George Smathers, a U.S. senator from Florida and a close friend of Nixon. Lansky and Nixon had met some years earlier, on one of Nixon's numerous visits to Miami, and in the days when he was practicing law in Whittier, California, Nixon had met Bugsy Siegel. Mickey Cohen, Siegel's right-hand man, boasted that he had raised money for Nixon's early political campaigns.

From one point of view, the three men's visit to Havana was not a success. Smith lost heavily playing at the Sans Souci casino, which was run by Norman Rothman, an ally of Meyer Lansky, and was unable to pay his debts. When Rothman threatened to sue, it was Nixon who came to Smith's rescue by calling on the American Embassy in Havana to use its influence with Rothman to get him to stop his legal action against Smith. Knowing that Smathers shared his views about the menace of Castro, and that he was fighting hard to persuade the Eisenhower Administration to take action against Castro, Lansky now appealed directly to him.

"Whether Smathers went to Nixon is something I do not know," Stacher said. "But certainly Meyer pressed Smathers very hard, urging him to use his influence to persuade the administration to accept his assassination plan."

It was later reported that Smathers used his friendship with John F. Kennedy to help persuade him to try to destroy Castro by an armed invasion of the island. Smathers was in reality doing no more than what Meyer had wanted to do in the early days of Castro's rule.

But by the time of the Bay of Pigs invasion in 1961, there was nothing Lansky could do. His men had left the island.

When the authors asked Lansky pointblank if he had tried to play a role in international politics by getting rid of Castro, his eyes hardened. He looked straight ahead and said, "I'm not going to discuss my relationship with Castro. Now or ever. But you'll appreciate that I was opposed to him both from a personal point of view and also because of the danger to America if his regime got a stranglehold on the island. A number of people came to me with a number of ideas and of course I had my own suggestions to make. It was no secret that I was well known in Havana and did have influence. But I don't think I should go into details of what was said."

Pressed to elaborate, Lansky went on: "Many things have been said about me and Castro. When I was in Havana I did what I could to help the people I employed. For instance, I tripled the salaries of all the staff who were working for me. This angered the Cubans, at least the wealthy ones. They said I was spoiling the local people.

"In 1959 there were all sorts of strange stories about my having to leave Cuba in a hired submarine. That's ridiculous. Not even the CIA believed that one. But they did ask me what I thought of Castro and I wrote out my answer at some length, warning them about trouble in the future. They seemed rather skeptical at the time, but you only need to look at Castro's troops fighting for Communists in other parts of the world, like Africa, to see that I was correct."

In April 1959, when Castro came to the United States to address the United Nations General Assembly, Lansky was in a hospital with his first heart attack. But the news had leaked out about his hostility toward the Cuban dictator. "I was lying in the hospital bed when a reporter phoned and asked, 'Is it true that you've given orders for Castro to be murdered?' I couldn't help laughing. There I was flat on my back, not even sure I'd get out of the hospital alive."

Lansky had cut his losses in Cuba and was concentrating on his old love, Las Vegas, by then, but his suggestion about eliminating Castro, rejected though Stacher said it was, soon found an echo in official thinking in Washington. In December 1959 the CIA Western Hemisphere Division Head wrote to Allen Dulles, head of the CIA, saying that the elimination of Castro "could and should be carried out." He wrote that "many of the informer people believe that the disappearance of Fidel Castro would greatly accelerate the fall of the present Communist government."

Dulles liked the scheme, but on reflection said that the "quick elimination" of Castro was not "in active consideration." Some of his staff disagreed with him, however, and advocated eliminating not only Castro but his brother Raul and their ally Che Guevara. In 1979 it was revealed that the CIA revived Lansky's idea of recruiting Mafia men to assassinate Fidel Castro, and that Castro's elimination was discussed at a State Department meeting in 1963. As far as is known, Lansky was not consulted.

31 Las Vegas

Hour after hour, night and day, the planes bringing passengers from all over the world come wheeling into the airport at Las Vegas. As they cross the Nevada desert they become more than modern jets. They are chariots bringing human sacrifices to the great god of gambling. In them millions of men and women flock to Las Vegas to try their luck. To the moralist Las Vegas is all evil rolled into one. To the gambler it is paradise. To Meyer Lansky and Bugsy Siegel, the pioneers who converted this little desert town into one of the most famous cities in the world, Las Vegas was simply the gateway to riches.

Today, Las Vegas represents something like two billion dollars a year in sheer profit to the businesses and conglomerates that own the hotels and their casinos. A third of the total population of this desert town is involved with gambling. Ten million people make their way to Las Vegas every year, and of these five hundred thousand people pass through the airport every month. They are no sooner on the ground than the slot machines beckon to them as they walk down the corridor from their plane. A welcoming voice from the loud-speakers wishes them "Good luck." And good luck is what every visitor expects. The men and women who come to Las Vegas are absolutely convinced that a fortune can be made at roulette, blackjack, baccarat, the slot machines, or keno.

Meyer Lansky, with his philosophy of gambling as a basic passion, explains the success of Las Vegas: "In that town we give everyone—everyone—the opportunity to gamble."

The largest, plushest hotel there today is owned not by the

Lansky organization but by Metro-Goldwyn-Mayer. The Grand Hotel is the very last word in luxury and high living. The shows in its enormous theater match anything on Broadway. The food it serves at extraordinarily low prices is prepared by the finest chefs. True to Lansky's philosophy, it is comparatively inexpensive to stay at the Grand Hotel, just as it is at any of the other luxurious hotels that line the Strip, the four-and-a-half-mile section of U.S. Highway 91 that passes through central Las Vegas. But to get to a restaurant, a toilet, a bedroom, to the sports facilities, the swimming pool, the gymnasiums, the saunas, the hairdressers, the shops in the lobby, you always have to pass through the casino. The casino is open twenty-four hours a day. There are no clocks on the walls and there is no conception of time; once inside the hotel you can't tell whether it's noon or midnight. Bright lights and strong air-conditioning insulate the visitor from the harsh desert sun and cool dark nights outside.

The hotel lobbies are alive with the most beautiful professional and part-time hookers in the world. With a practiced eye for the men who leave the gambling tables with money in their pockets, the women offer their services at the current rate of a hundred dollars. Sophisticated and charming, they have a sales talk that is hard to resist: "I'll give you the time of your life," one will say. "I'm an expert, and I promise you that once you've been with me you'll be back."

You cannot escape the gambling. As you have your excellent breakfast, the waitress points to the keno cards and places a pencil on your table. As she pours the coffee she's ready to take your marked card with your bet and place it for you.

Strangely, Las Vegas is an honest place for gamblers. No known cheating goes on in the casinos. There doesn't have to be any, because the odds are carefully calculated. The hotel collects a certain percentage of every bet you make, and the inflexible law of averages means that the longer you stay in Las Vegas, and the more often you chase the luck that is just about to turn in your favor, the more absolutely certain you are to lose.

Las Vegas is gambling for the common man. You can play roulette in shorts, open-necked shirt, bare feet, or even your bathing suit in the hotels along the Strip. This is one way in which Las Vegas is totally different from the elegant casinos of France, England, and other European countries. In addition, games such as roulette are played at far greater speed to insure maximum profits.

And you can gamble as little as a quarter, a dime, or a dollar.

There are hundreds of one-armed bandits in every hotel, as well as sawdust joints like the Horseshoe, the Pioneer, the Lucky Strike, or the Golden Gate. Men and women stand before them hour after hour, punching in their quarters or silver dollars, expecting the jackpot. Betting that sort of money in a typical European casino would bring a sneer to the face of the sleek croupiers. In Las Vegas everybody is made to feel welcome. As one hotel manager put it, "We've taken the concept of gambling normally reserved for the moneyed class in Europe and turned it into a mass business. Working-class and middle-class people can come here in total equality. They can gamble one dollar or a million. To us in Las Vegas it's all the same."

You can bring your children to Las Vegas, a thought that would make any European casino operator shudder, and they are taken care of so they won't interfere with your reason for being here. There is even a hotel called the Circus-Circus, where hundreds of pinball-style arcades, Disneyland-style games, and other fairground amusements are available for children. Overhead are first-class circus acts, with men and women walking the tightrope or hurtling through the air on their trapezes. While all this is going on, the parents are hard at it down below in the casino.

There are hundreds of tales of gamblers who hit it lucky in Vegas and of those who shoot themselves in the head. There was the businessman, for instance, who flew in from Toronto. He was a frequent visitor to Caesars Palace, and when he arrived in the winter of 1978 the hotel management was surprised to see his wife with him. The records showed he was a genuine high-roller, and the couple received VIP treatment when they registered. The guest remarked to the desk clerk that his wife was tired of seeing her husband fly off to Las Vegas four or five times a year and had decided to come along to see what it was like.

The journey from Toronto had been a long one and she was tired. "I need a nap," she said.

Her husband suggested that she go up to their room and rest awhile, but he was determined to get down to serious business and start playing his two favorite games, roulette and craps. His wife agreed to meet him for dinner.

Several hours later the woman awoke, put on her best dress, and went downstairs to look for her husband. He couldn't be found in the bar or the dining room. She returned to her room and phoned around the hotel to no avail. Alarmed, she called the manager and asked if he knew where her husband was.

"Yes, madam," he replied apologetically. "Your husband paid for your room and left your plane ticket and some money for you. He said he was going to the airport, but I can't tell you what plane he caught or where he went."

In a rage she packed her bags, took a taxi to the airport, and caught the next plane home. She stormed into the house and found her husband asleep in bed. She woke him, but before she had a chance to give him a piece of her mind, he got up and said, "Don't say a word. Follow me." He led her into his study and there, stacked on his desk, was $220,000 in cash. He explained to his astonished spouse: "While you were asleep I got lucky. When I finally realized I was nearly a quarter of a million dollars up, I went straight to the cashier and changed my chips for money. I knew that if I went to the dining room to wait for you, or tried to go up to our room, I'd have to go back through the casino, and if that happened I would try to win even more. So I took my money, put it in a bag, and sent for the manager to give him your return ticket and some money for you. Then I went out a side entrance, got a taxi, and caught the first plane out heading north. It was the only way I knew to resist the temptation of trying my luck all over again."

If the lucky man from Toronto had let himself count up his winnings and losses on all his trips, he would have been less elated. In reality, very, very few win at Las Vegas. As Lansky says, "The only man who wins in the casino is the guy who owns the place."

Lansky would agree that Las Vegas has to be seen to be believed. Especially at night. Along the famous Strip, near the Grand Hotel, are the other superluxury hotel casinos like the Desert Inn, Caesars Palace, the Tropicana, the Sahara, the Dunes, the Riviera. Downtown on Frémont Street, in Glitter Gulch, are the cheaper hotels and the lesser casinos, thronged at all hours. Millions of lights turn the area into a crazy fairyland. It is vulgar or beautiful, decadent or enchanting, depending on whether you are on a winning or losing streak. And you just have to gamble. There's nothing else to do in Las Vegas.

True, it has more churches per square mile than any other city of its size, and at the wedding shops or boutiques or parlors you can get married or divorced faster than anywhere else in the world at any time of day or night. All activities seem to be speeded up to leave you maximum time for gambling.

Las Vegas, which means "the meadows," was founded by Spain, then taken over by the Mexicans. In 1864 Nevada became part of the United States. Up to the twentieth century, virtually the only people who called it home were a clan of Paiute Indians. In the nineteenth century the Mormons tried to convert them to Christianity, but the Paiutes were too ignorant or too smart and insisted on idling away their time playing a kind of roulette in the sand with bones and colored sticks. In disgust the Mormons went back to Salt Lake City and left the Paiutes to their gambling. Later on, the Union Pacific Railway Company extended its track to Las Vegas, so that the mining companies could gouge out the gold and silver ore which was found in the area.

Except for a period between 1910 and 1930, gambling was always legal in Nevada. It was because of this that Meyer Lansky had his eye on Nevada even during Prohibition. Moving cautiously, the Lower East Side outfit took over the wire service in the area and made some other minor investments. At the end of the Second World War, Bugsy Siegel—working with Moe Sedway, Gus Greenbaum, and Israel "Ice Pick" Alderman—bought a small night club in Las Vegas, which was still nothing more than a dusty stop in the middle of the desert. The group soon sold El Cortez and invested the capital in the Nevada Project Corporation, the vehicle for financing the Flamingo.

Moe Sedway was important because the casinos then depended heavily on bookmaking, which they ran in conjunction with table gambling, and they needed a wire service to obtain racing results. Sedway was an expert at running the wire. Alderman was a friend of Lansky's from bootlegging days. He came from Minneapolis and had been arrested many times for robbery, murder, and a number of other crimes but never convicted. His nickname came from his manner of killing rivals by sticking an ice pick into the victim's ear and thus into the brain, killing him instantly. Greenbaum was in most ways an admirable representative for the Lower East Side outfit and their allies. He had the necessary toughness, as he demonstrated when two gangsters from Kansas City, Tony Broncato and Tony Tombino, carried out the only successful armed robbery in the history of Las Vegas. The two Tonys got away with a mere thirty-five hundred dollars in cash, but Greenbaum was outraged at this personal insult. The two gangsters went into hiding but were found and killed in Los Angeles by the gunman Jimmy Fratianno. That was the last time such a raid took place in Las Vegas.

Other participants in the development of Las Vegas included Dave Berman, once in Sing Sing on a kidnaping conviction; one-time brothel operator Albert C. Abrams; and Morris Rosen, whose son married Siegel's daughter Millicent.

When Greenbaum took over the Flamingo after Siegel's death, within the first year he wiped out Bugsy's losses and reported a satisfactory profit of $4,000,000, a figure which of course did not include the cash skimmed off each day in the heavily guarded cages where the bookkeepers and accountants worked. One after another, new hotels followed the example of the fabulous Flamingo.

The ownership of the Flamingo passed from hand to hand, but it is clear that Lansky had a stake there at least until 1960, when the casino was sold to Morris Lansburg, a businessman from Miami Beach. Even then Lansky got a cut from this deal, receiving a fee of $200,000 for his part in the negotiations. Moe Dalitz and his partners from Cleveland had control of the Desert Inn and the Stardust, and Phil Kastel built the Tropicana. Lansky himself was connected with several hotels, including the Thunderbird, where his friend Clifford Jones represented his and Jake Lansky's interests. As Lansky saw it, "We had the expertise to do it. A lot of people tried to do the same thing and they came unstuck because they didn't know how to run a casino."

A case in point is the story of how two brothers from Miami, Ben and Sam Cohen, opened their own gold mine in Las Vegas. It cost them $10,000,000 to build the Riviera and immediately they found themselves in desperate financial trouble. Gus Greenbaum was recruited to try to turn the tide at the Riviera, and the Cohen brothers were forced out as the Riviera began to prosper. But this time Greenbaum made two mistakes. First he hired a man named Willie Bioff, who had once testified against a number of Chicago underworld figures and caused them to be sent to prison. Willie Bioff was blown up in his truck in Las Vegas and his body scattered all over the road by the force of the blast. Then Greenbaum started cheating and pocketing money from the casino. In December 1958 he and his wife were found dead in their home in Phoenix.

"Meyer and I were shocked at this unnecessary violence," Stacher remembered, "but with some of those groups in Chicago there was no controlling their old-style Mafia tactics."

In general, though, "differences were ironed out peaceably in those early days in Vegas. For instance, when they were building the Stardust Hotel, which was the largest one then, Dalitz complained that it would give too much competition to his Desert Inn. The man behind the Stardust was Antonio Stralla, or as we called him Tony Cornero, an old bootlegging friend. It looked like an old-fashioned war might break out, but Meyer suggested a meeting and we all flew in for it. I was there with Dalitz, and his right-hand man, Kleinman, was there, and Longie Zwillman and so forth. We worked out a deal that gave each group an interlocking interest in each other's hotels, and our lawyers set it up so that nobody could really tell who owned what out there."

Stacher knew what he was talking about. In exile in Israel he told the authors, "I was the man who built the Sands. To make sure we'd get enough top-level investors, we brought George Raft into the deal and sold Frank Sinatra a 9 percent stake in the hotel. Frank was flattered to be invited, but the object was to get him to perform there, because there's no bigger draw in Las Vegas. When Frankie was performing, the hotel really filled up."

The American government has made repeated attempts to bring charges against the men who opened up Las Vegas. In 1968 Moe Dalitz was unsuccessfully charged with income tax evasion. In 1971 Meyer Lansky, together with five other men who had interests in the Flamingo Hotel, were accused of siphoning money from the Flamingo casino into Swiss bank accounts and "crime syndicate coffers." The indictment charged that the skimming totaled more than $30,000,000 from 1960 to 1967. Lansky was accused of having hidden interests in the Flamingo during those years. In 1967 Kirk Kerkorian and his operator company, the Tracy Investment Company, bought the Flamingo for $12,500,000. The point against Lansky was that he had received fees when the hotel was first sold to Lansburg's group in 1960 and again when Lansburg sold it to Kerkorian; it was alleged that Lansky had secret holdings in the hotel during the entire time. The federal grand jury that indicted the Flamingo operators was guided by Justice Department Strike Force attorneys from Washington whose interest was also focused on the Dunes Hotel, owned by the Continental Connector Corporation, an electronics-component firm with headquarters in Woodside, New York. Continental Connector was suspended from trading on the Stock Exchange by the Securities and Exchange Commission on grounds of irregularities. None of these charges resulted in convictions for Lansky.

Lansky's old friend Abner Zwillman, also active in Las Vegas, was the first member of the Lower East Side outfit to become involved with Howard Hughes, who quickly became another Las Vegas legend. Zwillman introduced Jean Harlow to Hughes when he was young, dashing, rich, and handsome. Hughes launched Jean Harlow on her acting career, and also went to bed with her, but apparently Zwillman was ready to give her up. During Prohibition, Zwillman provided Howard Hughes with whiskey, and later on this inveterate gambler was invited to try his luck at the Flamingo. Whether Hughes was ever a guest there is not known, but he did buy twenty-five thousand acres of desert land in Nevada for a mere $25,000. He moved to Las Vegas himself in November 1966 and rented the whole ninth floor at Moe Dalitz's Desert Inn.

Both Lansky and Stacher recalled that Howard Hughes made frequent visits to Las Vegas, sometimes in his own name and sometimes pretending to be someone else. He was always recognized immediately. "Howard was a big gambler," Stacher said, "but he wasn't very lucky. He lost a lot in the casinos and that must have irritated him. When he lost money at Moe Dalitz's place he reacted in a typical Howard Hughes way—offered to buy it for $30,000,000. We sold it to him right there—he was paying in hard cash."

Liking the feel of being a casino owner, Hughes bought up one establishment after another: the New Frontier, the Sands, the Silver Slipper, and other establishments in both Las Vegas and Reno. Within a year or two he had invested something like a hundred million dollars in seventeen casinos, and his establishments were providing 17 percent of Nevada's gambling tax revenue. But Hughes did not have the golden touch that the Lower East Side men had developed in their years of running casinos. Instead of the expected 20 percent legally admitted profit which a Nevada casino generally earns on investment, Hughes at best never made more than 6 percent profit, and by 1970 his holdings showed a loss of several million dollars.

Moe Dalitz told his colleagues a number of anecdotes about this strange man, and Stacher loved to repeat them. For example, "Moe was particularly proud of the Monte Carlo Room at his hotel, where he had a French chef and food every gourmet appreciated. The chef nearly walked out several times because Howard Hughes wanted Campbell's canned chicken soup served to him twice a day. It was bad enough that the chef had to keep sending up those bowls of heated canned soup, but what really infuriated him was when Hughes sent notes down to the kitchen complaining that the soup hadn't been prepared exactly the way he wanted it. It was to be heated to a precise temperature and one or two bits of things added. Moe had to plead with his chef to take no notice—the man upstairs was crazy."

In spite of such problems, Dalitz became friendly with Hughes and was one of the few outsiders he would chat with. During one of their discussions, Hughes, who was obsessed with "the Communist threat to America," spoke heatedly about his hatred of Castro and his regime, "a cancer in the heart of the Americas." Dalitz told Hughes the story of how Lansky had wanted to use members of the underworld to assassinate Castro soon after he took power from Batista. The news galvanized Hughes, who assigned one of his assistants to find suitable "Mafia killers," as he put it, to complete the task Lansky had envisaged. Hughes was later reported to have recruited two underworld figures, Johnny Rosselli and Sam "Momo" Giancana, to assassinate Castro as well as his brother Raul and Che Guevara. This plan, which he apparently discussed with the CIA, was to be carried out at the same time as the officially sanctioned Bay of Pigs invasion of Cuba. So far as is known, the murder attempt never took place, and in the 1970s both gangsters died under mysterious circumstances.

Lansky doesn't have much to say about Howard Hughes, but he will always talk about gambling, past and present. "Today, with the opening of casinos in Atlantic City, I think the American government has realized that you can't stop people from gambling. Now it's all legal and I assume that casinos will be opened in other states. When I read that Japanese businessmen are buying their way into hotels in Atlantic City, and that *Penthouse* magazine has acquired another hotel on the Boardwalk, I can't help smiling at the way people still call me the biggest gambler in the world. It seems a long time ago that Bugsy and I were driving back and forth across the desert trying to get the first casino built."

In the late 1970s the Flamingo is constantly being "improved"— it is newer, bigger, and more luxurious than ever before. In the basement they recently discovered a hole in the ground where Bugsy Siegel used to keep a private safe for the money he skimmed off the daily take. In Las Vegas, if a historical gambling museum should ever be opened, the steel box in which Bugsy kept his illegal profits surely ought to be the number one exhibit.

32 The Synagogue in Geneva

Elegantly dressed, subtly spoken, Dr. Tibor Rosenbaum is also deeply devout. On a summer Saturday in 1965, his son Charles was celebrating his Bar Mitzvah, a holy day in the life of the thirteen-year-old and a proud one for his father. In Geneva, Switzerland, on this special day, Dr. Rosenbaum solemnly shook hands with his guests—friends, relatives, and business associates, as well as leading Israeli politicians and dignitaries come to celebrate with him and his son.

The hundred-year-old Geneva Synagogue stands in the Place de la Synagogue not far from the Rhone River, which flows through the heart of the city. To enter the synagogue you first pass through tall wrought-iron gates discreetly hidden by two trees. The shady little square in front of the house of prayer is dominated by eight trees with branches which intertwine overhead, turning it into a haven of peaceful shadow even on the hottest day. The guests who came to celebrate Tibor Rosenbaum's son's Bar Mitzvah passed by the statue in the square—a little naked boy—and were soon seated in the simple but comfortable interior with light streaming through the stained-glass windows.

In a corner of this synagogue is a small table with casino-style jetons, or discs. It is not that members of the congregation play roulette during the services, but by taking one of the multicolored discs and placing it in a specific numbered slot on the table, they can indicate to the rabbi the size of the contribution they pledge to the synagogue.

As a man who had earned the reputation of being one of the foremost bankers in Switzerland, Dr. Rosenbaum was not surprised to see the two hundred fifty seats in the synagogue filled that Saturday morning. After all, he was the banker for many leading Jews and Israelis and a friend of important personages all over the world. He also had a distinguished lineage. His ancestors had helped start the Chasidic movement and his father and grandfather had been well-known rabbis. A rabbi himself, as well as a Doctor of Philosophy, a collector of Chagall paintings, and a strong believer in astrology, Rosenbaum was honorary treasurer of the World Jewish Congress, the most representative and respected Jewish body in the world; a member of the World Zionist Executive; president of the Mizrachi movement; and a member of the American Society of Heraldry. A firm supporter of Israel, Rosenbaum employed many Israeli citizens, including retired generals, and counted among his friends Amos Ben Gurion, son of the late Israeli Prime Minister; Amos Manor, a former Israeli Secret Service chief who was both friend and employee; and the distinguished president of the World Jewish Congress, Dr. Nahum Goldman.

As Rosenbaum's guests walked down the red carpet to their simple chairs beneath the high, domed roof of the synagogue, the religious hush was marred only slightly by the heavy traffic rumbling along Georges Favon Boulevard. Some of the American guests who had crossed the Atlantic for the service were smiling, and not only at the pleasure of listening to the thirteen-year-old's chanting voice, which reminded them of their own youth. They were also amused at the casino-style jeton table in the corner. Many of these visitors were world authorities on gambling. Although many had not been inside a synagogue lately, the gambling table made them feel at home.

The synagogue was so crowded that a number of the guests didn't go indoors at all but stood in the leafy square chatting quietly among themselves. The shoppers peering at antiques in the nearby stores or sipping coffee in the cafés would have been astonished to know that some of the men standing in the square were not Jews but of Italian descent. They included some of the most powerful members of the underworld in the United States. Not all of their names were known to the public, but together they were a fair representation of what is loosely described as the American Mafia.

Not far from the synagogue in Geneva is the Banque de Crédit International, an institution of more immediate interest to many of the Bar Mitzvah guests than the synagogue. The I.C.B., established by Rosenbaum in 1959, was the culmination of his meteoric rise from poor young refugee to financial leader. Perhaps his charm had something to do with that rise; so did the romantic myth that he had played a heroic role during the war by impersonating a Nazi officer to help a group of fellow Jews escape from a concentration camp. In fact, Dr. Rosenbaum was a wartime refugee from the Budapest Ghetto who had the miraculous good fortune of getting onto a train that brought him to safety in neutral Switzerland.

By 1946, Rosenbaum was the Hungarian delegate to the World Zionist Congress in Basel, where plans were made for resettling refugees and victims of the camps in the homeland of Israel. Working zealously for the Jewish Agency and other bodies that played a part in establishing the State of Israel in 1948, Rosenbaum soon became a well-known figure all over Europe. Jews were also impressed by Rosenbaum's personal piety. He would not work on a Saturday, would not even answer the telephone. He provided a kosher restaurant in his bank for employees, and for the poorer Jews in Geneva he opened another kosher restaurant, the Shalom, where prices were very moderate.

In 1949, Rosenbaum set up the Helvis Management Corporation, whose object was to promote Swiss-Israeli trade. The company did well, but in the 1950s there was a scandal when the Israeli government learned that its Ministry of Health had been accepting payoffs in exchange for approving Helvis contracts. The director general of the Israeli Health Ministry, Yehuda Spiegel, went to prison.

Rosenbaum also had excellent connections with President William Tubman of Liberia. With a Liberian diplomatic passport, which enabled him to travel without customs or currency problems, Rosenbaum was the official Liberian ambassador in Vienna and a member of the Liberian delegation to the United Nations. He worked in partnership with Tubman in setting up rubber plantations and mineral concessions.

Another of his good friends in high places was Prince Bernhard, consort of the Queen of the Netherlands, who invited him to the royal palace in Holland to lecture leading Dutch bankers on good business practices. Here too a scandal ensued, when the Prince sold a castle, the Warmelo, for $400,000 to a Liechtenstein firm, Evlyma, Inc., owned by Rosenbaum's I.C.B. Just why this castle was sold to the Swiss banker for what is described as a ridiculously low price has never been made clear.

Until recently, when further scandals caused the I.C.B. to move its home office, the I.C.B. headquarters with its gold and marble entrance looked like any other solid financial establishment in this solid Swiss city. But the rear entrance, through a neat triangular courtyard on the Rue de la Université, had rather more unusual traffic. Through this entrance came perhaps the most astonishing stream of couriers in the history of Swiss banking. In their elegant suitcases and locked pouches came the millions of dollars in cash which Meyer Lansky and his colleagues had sent to Geneva for safekeeping.

These profits seeking a tax-free home were sent to a number of other banks in Switzerland before the Second World War and again in the late 1940s and early '50s. But by the 1960s the bulk of the money was handled by the I.C.B. In 1967, apparently tipped off by the FBI, *Life* magazine published a series of stories about the I.C.B., and incredulous Americans read that the courier service included a number of known and named men. One was thirty-two-year-old Sylvain Ferdmann, a Swiss citizen with degrees in banking and economics. It was claimed that on March 19, 1965, while Ferdmann was loading suitcases of dollar bills into his car at Miami Airport, a piece of paper fell out of his pocket and was handed over to the authorities. The document read: "This is to acknowledge this 28th day of December 1964 the receipt of $350,000 in American bank notes for deposit to the account of Maral 2812 with the International Credit Bank, Geneva, the said sum turned over to me in the presence of the names signed below." One of the men who signed as a witness was John Pullman, an associate of Meyer Lansky since the 1920s. Convicted of violating U.S. liquor laws, Pullman became a Canadian citizen and later took up residence in Switzerland, where he became a courier for his American friends. Another courier was Benjamin Sigelbaum, a long-time friend of Lansky and once a business partner of Bobby Baker, former Democratic Majority secretary in the U.S. Senate who served a prison term for crimes including grand larceny and tax evasion.

Both Lansky and Stacher had accounts in Rosenbaum's bank, Lansky's having the code name "Bear." The connection between Rosenbaum and Lansky had been brought about by Ferdmann.

Hearing of the vast flow of money which gamblers and other members of the American underworld were shipping to Switzerland, the young Swiss had decided to get the business for his boss. In the 1950s he made contact with Lansky in Miami and the two men became friends as well as business associates. In banking circles in Geneva their link was known as the "kosher connection."

To facilitate their deals, a branch of Rosenbaum's bank was opened in the Bahamas. Ferdmann worked closely with Pullman, who became a very widely traveled man in his service for Lansky. He not only flew from Miami Beach to Switzerland and back but frequently made trips to Las Vegas and to the Bahamas, where gambling was established after the collapse of the Batista regime in Cuba. He also went to Honolulu, where the Lower East Side outfit was hoping to get in on the ground floor if gambling was one day legalized in Hawaii. Pullman had frequent conferences with Lansky, not only in the United States but also on their trips to Europe, including Lansky's wedding trip.

Pullman's stature rose as both he and Lansky prospered. He joined the board and became president of a bank set up in Nassau called the Bank of World Commerce. Others involved in that enterprise were Meyer's friends from the old days who were playing an important part in Las Vegas, men such as Ed Levinson and Irving "Nig" Devine. This bank absorbed some of the skimmed-off profits from gambling. Just as the money from Switzerland was "laundered" back to the United States, funds from the Bank of World Commerce returned to America as loans for members of the underworld to finance legitimate purchases.

One especially interesting bagman, or bagwoman, was Ida Devine, the blond wife of Irving Devine. Nicknamed "the lady in mink" because she liked to dress well for her travels, Ida Devine worked hard. On one trip she flew from Las Vegas to Los Angeles and then went by train via Chicago to Hot Springs to pick up more money there before returning to Chicago. She then flew back to Miami, always holding on closely to her handbag, which contained $100,000 in cash. En route she met several clients and at journey's end the money was handed over to Meyer Lansky.

The smooth-talking Sylvain Ferdmann persuaded Lansky to make him the outfit's main courier by pointing out that as a Swiss citizen he would not have to face the American law courts if he was caught. Ferdmann ranged far and wide in his operations, and FBI agents were convinced he was also involved with Teamsters Union boss Jimmy Hoffa. Ferdmann's duties included transferring funds not only from the United States but also from behind the Iron Curtain. Some was to assist Communist officials who were preparing for their own futures in case they were forced to flee—but money was also being passed through him from Jews who were trying to escape from behind the Iron Curtain.

Not far away from the Geneva Synagogue, at 10 Rue St. Léger, a small street facing the elegant buildings of Geneva University, is the Jewish cultural and social center, where on the evening of his Bar Mitzvah, a party was given in Charles Rosenbaum's honor. The center is a gray-green four-story building with tall wooden doors and long, lace-curtained windows. On the outside is heavy iron grillwork, and handsome balconies hang over the street. The small Jewish population of Geneva—about two thousand people— frequently uses the center for family celebrations such as Bar Mitzvahs and weddings. That evening was one of the most glittering occasions the center has ever witnessed. Behind heavy red draperies women in costly furs and sparkling jewelry greeted old friends and special guests from all over the world. Members of the local community were surprised that so many people with American accents attended the celebration. Meyer Lansky was not there, but many of his friends were.

Some of the arrivals stopped at the entrance to admire the little museum where Jewish relics, ancient Torahs, and religious books from previous centuries were on display. Inside, at one end of the room was a bar where drinks were served throughout the evening, and at the other end the orchestra played as couples danced or talked. Part of the building is used as a cheder, but on this Saturday night the classrooms were closed and the only business at hand was to enjoy the superb food, the excellent drinks, and the good company. Indeed, people who were at the Rosenbaum Bar Mitzvah party still remember it with excitement and pleasure.

During this period Rosenbaum's bank seemed the perfect sanctuary for wealthy people with money they didn't want to declare to tax investigators or other authorities in their own country. It paid one or two percent more interest than any other bank in Geneva, and many Israelis felt that their money was safe because it was run by a pious Jew.

Rosenbaum was certainly a financial genius, but he did not anticipate the crisis precipitated by strains on the whole European banking system in the early 1970s, following the Yom Kippur War and the economic repercussions of the Arab oil boycott and the increase in oil prices. The Geneva banker had invested in what seemed to him at the time highly profitable, or at least potentially profitable, speculative enterprises. He bought land in Brazil and Italy and became a partner in trading companies involving Nigeria as well as Liberia. He also held shares in Israeli textile factories and was concerned in ventures with an investment company set up by the ruling Labor Party of Israel. Since his staff included such respected Israelis as the former commander of the Israeli paratroop corps, Colonel Yehuda Harari, his credentials in Israel were of the very highest caliber.

According to one Israeli intelligence report, Rosenbaum's troubles started when he bought a twelve-hundred-acre tract of land from the Italian royal family for $12,000,000. Not far from Rome, this tract was to be the jewel in the ambitious banker's crown; he wanted to build a complex of houses and hotels on this eminently desirable spot. Unfortunately for his plans, the Italian government declared in 1970 that the area was to be a national park zone; no building of any kind would be considered. Thus the expected $150,000,000 profit for the bank and its favored clients disappeared in a puff of smoke. Heavy pressure was brought to bear on the Italian government but to no avail.

Rosenbaum's troubles multiplied after that, and there was much ducking and weaving as he tried to keep his empire going. Meyer Lansky was one of the few who somehow got an early warning and withdrew his money from the I.C.B. just before the crash—how or why he got the warning is another subject he refuses to discuss. But finally the crash came, and it reverberated around the world. A major scandal erupted in Israel, because millions of dollars contributed from all over the world for the state of Israel had been invested in Rosenbaum's bank by a body called the Israel Corporation. It was no surprise that such large quantities of Israeli money were kept in his vault, because Rosenbaum had always helped Israel. Before 1948, when arms for the country had to be purchased in secret deals, his services were called upon and he was always cooperative. And after Israel became a state, almost 90 percent of its purchases of arms abroad was channeled through Rosenbaum's bank. The financing of many of Israel's most daring secret operations was carried out through the funds in the I.C.B.

The scandal in Israel, however, soon brought out the fact that

Rosenbaum had used Israeli money to shore up his collapsing property deals. Michael Tzur, who controlled most of Israel's foreign exchange, and who was its director general of commerce and industry, was charged on fourteen counts of breach of trust, misuse of funds, and acceptance of bribes to the tune of $1,400,000. Tzur had transferred cash from the Israel Corporation—which had amassed $100,000,000 to be used to build up Israel's economy—to Rosenbaum. Given advance warning about the collapse of Rosenbaum's bank, Tzur rushed to Geneva and managed to rescue most of the $8,500,000 which the corporation had on deposit at the moment, but the damage had been done and the intelligence reports were in.

Tzur pleaded guilty to the charges and was sentenced to fifteen years' imprisonment. At the same time the Swiss authorities charged Rosenbaum with "dishonest management" of the International Credit Bank. One significant discovery was that the banker had been involved with Bernard Cornfeld and his worldwide Investors Overseas Services mutual fund business. The two men had formed a partnership whereby Cornfeld's salesmen and executives were able to transfer to the I.C.B. fortunes belonging to affluent citizens in various countries which had strict export controls over their currency. Cornfeld once came to the rescue of Rosenbaum when he had financial problems, and later, when Cornfeld was arrested after his I.O.S. empire collapsed, it was Rosenbaum who put up his bail money.

Sources available to the authors have also revealed one of the most astonishing deals ever struck between any banker and any government. The information comes from a report made to the Israeli Prime Minister which, because of the heavy damage it would cause, was kept a secret at the time. American authorities had been pressuring Rosenbaum for some time to give them details of Mafia money which had reached his bank. After the Swiss investigation began, a source close to the I.C.B. made unofficial contact with Robert M. Morgenthau, U.S. Attorney for the Southern District of New York, and provided the American authorities with names and details of investments and deposits from the United States.

Israeli intelligence also revealed that Rosenbaum was putting heavy pressure on Israeli government ministers, threatening to expose secret information about how branches of the Israeli defense forces used undercover methods to buy equipment and arms for Israel. Rosenbaum had been entrusted with many secrets involving the bypassing of the damaging De Gaulle embargo of arms to Israel in 1967.

Many Israelis were determined to bring the whole scandal out into the open, no matter what Rosenbaum threatened. So was the philanthropist Baron Edmond de Rothschild, one of Israel's greatest friends. Rothschild was the chairman of the Israel Corporation, and he was enraged to discover that without his knowledge funds had been removed from Israel into Rosenbaum's I.C.B. Rothschild authorized a high-powered firm of U.S. accountants to investigate the full extent of Israel Corporation's losses and the unauthorized movement of funds.

This investigation showed that without any doubt Israel had lost tens of millions of dollars through Rosenbaum's operation. On the other hand, Rosenbaum told the press that he had been responsible for helping Jews trying to escape from South America and eastern Europe to smuggle their funds to Israel via his bank. Rosenbaum claimed that he had not taken a penny from these funds and had provided his services to help oppressed people.

The issue was complicated by Israeli politics. Tzur's trial, over in one day though it involved vast misuse of state funds, was a clear indication that the government had decided it would do more harm than good to drag Rosenbaum's actions into the open and take the chance that he would reveal defense information. The Israeli government brought no charges against Rosenbaum himself.

But Baron de Rothschild continued to delve into the affairs of Rosenbaum, and in 1975 brought charges of mismanagement against him. These charges are still before the Israeli courts, and in January 1977 the Baron declared on the Israeli radio: "Pressure was exerted on me to withdraw the complaints I lodged against Rosenbaum. The pressure was exerted by Israeli personalities as well as members of parliament. This pressure was from the Socialist and religious groups.

"I have refused to bow to this pressure."

Precise details of the information given to Robert Morgenthau from Geneva are a secret between the two men and the U.S. government, but Morgenthau obviously got sufficient ammunition to keep him diligently on the track of the money siphoned from the United States to Swiss banks. Among the men he convicted was Max Orovitz, a friend of Lansky. Morgenthau's blistering attack on the evasion of income tax by men near Meyer Lansky prompted the Internal Revenue Service to launch what they termed a "thorough investigation," which concentrated on Ben Sigelbaum, who had been investing in property in the Cape Kennedy area on Lansky's behalf. Sigelbaum went to trial, but his lawyer, E. David Rosen, defended him successfully.

Morgenthau believed that the Miami National Bank, controlled by Samuel Cohen of Miami, had also been involved in sending millions of dollars to Swiss banks and having the money rerouted back to the United States later. Cohen was a partner of Morris Lansburg, who had bought the Flamingo in Las Vegas and paid Lansky a fee for setting up the deal. With Lansburg, Cohen owned hotels on Grand Bahama Island as well as dozens of apartment buildings in New York City.

Morgenthau's problem was to prove that there were links between Lansky, Cohen, Lansburg, Ben Sigelbaum, Levinson, and others involved in the money traffic. He thought he could show the connection partly through the fact that Lansky's son-in-law was manager of the Eden Roc Hotel in Miami, which was partly owned by Cohen. Morgenthau was convinced that Cohen had skimmed off $2,000,000 from the Flamingo—the money being sent to Switzerland for safekeeping, then returned to the United States for legitimate investments.

As he went on with his investigation, Morgenthau began to press for stricter laws to regulate the flow of funds from the United States to Switzerland. He was not trying to impede legitimate business, but he wanted to put a stop to illegally obtained funds being laundered in Swiss banks and then brought back to America for apparently legitimate investments.

Robert Morgenthau was more and more convinced that real estate enterprises and many other businesses had been financed by money which had been skimmed off from gambling in the United States and passed via the International Credit Bank in Geneva back to the United States where it appeared as legitimate funds. He persuaded Representative Wright Patman of the House Banking and Currency Committee to draft a bill compelling United States citizens to report all investments made through cover operations such as those set up by Bernie Cornfeld, who had created the giant I.O.S. The Nixon Administration clamped down and the bill never became law, but Morgenthau did have the satisfaction of seeing one of Lansky's closest friends, Vincent "Jimmy Blue Eyes" Alo, go to prison in October 1970 for obstructing justice. Before Alo was sentenced, U.S. Attorney Gary Naftalis informed the court, "Alo is one of the most significant organized crime figures in the United States. He is closely associated with Meyer Lansky of Miami, who is at the apex of organized crime."

The Morgenthau investigation showed that over the years Lansky had always guarded the interests of Jimmy Blue Eyes. As he extended his gambling empire in Florida, he gave shares in the Colonial Inn to both his brother Jake and Alo. Naturally, the main attraction of this hotel investment was its highly profitable casino. Although there were competing gambling joints, the cream of high-spending visitors made straight for the Colonial Inn. An intriguing glimpse of the way the underworld operates was provided when a man known as John "Big Jack" Letendre bought some land near the Colonial Inn and set up his own casino hotel, La Bohème. Letendre looked as if he were going to be serious competition, and he resisted attempts by "persons unknown" to buy out his interest in the new casino. Not long after La Bohème opened he was killed in his home, and suspicion naturally centered on the owners of the Colonial Inn. Meyer Lansky, however, protests indignantly. He told the authors, "I've never ordered anyone's killing. I knew nothing at all about the murder of this man. I am and always have been totally opposed to violence." Stacher added that there was some underworld gossip at the time that Letendre had welched on a gambling debt. In any case, La Bohème soon reopened with Jake Lansky in charge.

Morgenthau also found that during this period Meyer Lansky had bought considerable property in the Broward County area known as Gulf Stream Park. Among the local inhabitants there and along Highway A1A, the area became known as "Lansky land." Many hotels were built and the owners included some of Lansky's oldest friends. One was Meyer Wassell, who had gone to school with him on the Lower East Side. Jimmy Blue Eyes and Joe Adonis bought houses in the area, and so did Lansky's bodyguard, Phil "The Stick" Kovolick. Cockeye Dunn, from the New York waterfront, went there when he was on the run from the murder charge and for which he was later executed, and hid out in Lansky's home. It was Morgenthau too, thanks possibly to information received from Geneva, who established a link between Lansky's outfit and Jimmy Hoffa of the Teamsters Union.

The origins of that connection were explained by Doc Stacher: "We knew Jimmy Hoffa right from the early days, because of Moe Dalitz. It's a complicated story, but Jimmy once had a girl friend who married a Detroit man named John Paris. And it was at her house in Detroit that Jimmy Hoffa met Moe when he was just a young man in a group of Jewish boys who worked for Norman Purple in the Purple Gang. There was a war among the Detroit gangs, and when Dalitz's boys got the worst of it Moe left the Purple Gang and set up on his own in Ohio. Our connection with Dalitz started when we established a national network for our bootlegging. Jimmy Hoffa was a friend of Mickey Cohen's, too."

The friendship between Dalitz and Hoffa continued after Dalitz went to Las Vegas for the big money. Hoffa invested money through Lou Poller, who was working for Sam Cohen's bank. These funds, like other money brought into that bank, were sent to Switzerland for laundering by Tibor Rosenbaum's I.C.B. and other banks.

Baron de Rothschild's case in Israel continues. Robert Morgenthau, a Democrat, was fired by the Republican Nixon Administration in 1972 and since then, as New York County District Attorney, he has had no official connection with national and international crime. Rosenbaum's bank is still open in Geneva—at its more modest new address—and the Swiss authorities have not indicted him.

SUMMARY REPORT OF INVESTIGATION

36		

NAMES OF CASE AND ALIASES		RELATING FILES	G-23 LINK
LANSKY, Meyer	SUCHOWLJANSKY, Meyer LIEBERMAN, Morris	C-2 517 814	503
DATE AND PLACE OF BIRTH	DATE, PLACE, AND MANNER OF LAST ENTRY IN U.S	TYPE OF INVESTIGATION
July 4, 1902 Grodno, Russia	July 4, 1911 New York, N.Y., SS "KURSK"	Revocation - Criminal
		NATIONALITY
		USC (Natz.)
OFFICE IN CONTROL OF INVESTIGATION	REPORT MADE AT	PERIOD COVERED BY THIS REPORT
Miami, Florida	Miami, Florida	May 20 to June 22, 195?

SYNOPSIS

Investigation based upon memorandum from the Assistant Regional Commissioner, Investigations, SERO, dated January 21, 1959 requesting that SUBJECT's actual place of residence, for the purpose of bringing new cancellation suit, be fully investigated and present addresses and the availability of all prospective witnesses in the case be furnished.

SUBJECT's place of actual residence found to be 3800 S. Ocean Drive, Hollywood, Florida.

Prospective witnesses interviewed with exception of two, SUBJECT' ex-wife, ANNA LANSKY, and SAMUEL "RED" LEVINE, who could not be located and whose testimony, as indicated by prior interviews, does not appear to be important to the case. Investigation established five arrests which appear to relate to SUBJECT prior to the date of his naturalization and that he stated his occupation was that of machinist, while evidence tends to show that he was engaged in various types of illegal occupations prior to the time of his naturalization.

X PENDING	PENDING INACTIVE	CLOSED	REFERRED TO CONTROL OFFICE

DISTRIBUTION

2 - SERO, Attn: General Attorney
w/1 copy all Exhibits & file.

2 - File

REPORT MADE BY

Joseph A. Thurman

DATE 6-22-59

REVIEWED AND APPROVED

Phillips

DATE 6-23-59

Acting Asst
Investigat...

INVESTIGATIVE REPORT BACK SHEET
Form G-166 D (Rev. 5-1-49)

Top page of a file stamped TOP PRIORITY RACKETEER, recording the investigations made by the Immigration and Naturalization Service to provide evidence for Lansky's denaturalization, on the grounds that he had been engaged in various illegal occupations prior to his naturalization.

FACTS OF THE CASE

Investigation of this case is based upon a memorandum dated September 26, 1952 from the Assistant Commissioner, Investigations Division, Washington, D.C. to the District Director, New York, New York requesting that a complete and thorough investigation be conducted to secure evidence which might be used as a basis for possible revocation of citizenship.

A denaturalization action was instituted in the United States District Court for the Southern District of New York and was dismissed for "Lack of prosecution" on May 18, 1958.

On January 20, 1959 the case was transferred to Miami, Florida with instructions to fully investigate the SUBJECT's place of actual residence for the purpose of bringing a new suit, and that the present addresses and availability of prospective witnesses be ascertained.

The SUBJECT was born July 4, 1902 at Grodno, Russia and entered the United States at New York, N.Y. on April 3, 1911 under the name of MEYER SUCHOWLJANSKY. On August 9, 1921 he filed Declaration of Intention No. 100973 in the   EX."A" U.S. District Court for the Southern District of New York under the name of MEYER LANSKY, the name by which he has been known since childhood. On April 3, 1926 the SUBJECT's preliminary form for petition for naturalization was   EX."B" received by the office of Chief Naturalization Examiner, New York, N.Y. On April 14, 1927 the SUBJECT filed petition for naturalization No. 2271-74174 in the U.S. District Court for the Eastern District of New York. Duplicate copy attached to this report as Exhibit "C". On September 27,   EX."C" 1928 SUBJECT was naturalized as a United States citizen in the U.S. District Court for the Eastern District of New York and certificate No. 2 517 814 was issued to him.

With reference to the SUBJECT's actual place of residence, the writer on January 26, 1959, at the office of JOSEPH P. MANNERS, Special Assistant to the Attorney General,

Miami, Fla. 6/22/59
C-2 517 814   - 2 -

```
TOP PRIORITY
RACKETEER
```

The second page of the same file. Twenty-two exhibits are listed, including the records of five arrests, a statement made by Esther Siegel (Bugsy Siegel's wife), Ahearn's deposition, and reports from narcotics agents.

UNITED STATES DEPARTMENT OF JUSTICE

WASHINGTON, D.C. 20530

Address Reply to the
Division Indicated
and Refer to Initials and Number
RJC:tlu

August 24, 1971

TO ALL TO WHOM THIS MATTER SHALL COME, GREETINGS:

     I certify that the annexed is a true copy of a
Deposition of Daniel Francis Ahearn taken on March 15,
1957, in New York City from the files of the United
States Immigration and Naturalization Service, which
by virtue of my official duties are presently under my
control.

                                  IN WITNESS WHEREOF, I hereto
                                  set my hand on the day and
                                  year first above written.

                            By direction of the Attorney General:

                                  ROBERT J. CAMPBELL
                                  Attorney-in-Charge
                                  Strike Force 18
                                  Organized Crime and Racketeering
                                          Section

Subscribed to and sworn to before me, a Notary Public, for
and within the City of Washington, District of Columbia, on
this 24th day of August 1971.

                                        NOTARY PUBLIC

My commission Expires

Certification of the deposition of Daniel Ahearn by Robert J. Campbell, of
the Organized Crime and Racketeering Section of the Department of
Justice. Ahearn's deposition was part of denaturalization proceedings
against Lansky and cast light on Lansky's early criminal activities on the
Lower East Side.

U.S. Treasury Department
Bureau of Narcotics
Washington, D.C.

July 1961

ME : Meyer LANSKY (Bureau of Narcotics International
List No. 169).

IASES : Born Meyer SUCHOWLANSKY; "Bugs" Meyer; Morris
LIEBERMAN; Meyer "The Bug"; Charlie "The Bug";
Little Meyer; George LIEBERMAN; Meyer LAMANSKY;
Meyer "The Lug".

SCRIPTION : Born July 4, 1902 at Grodno, Poland; Jewish
extraction; 5'5" tall; 145 lbs.; brown eyes,
grey-brown hair; 1" scar on right side of head;
6" operational scar on right shoulder; naturalized in Brooklyn, NYC on 9-27-28.

CALITIES : Resides at 612 Hibiscus Drive, Hallandale,
EQUENTED Florida, formerly resided at 3800 South Ocean
Drive, Hollywood, Florida; frequents Gold
Coast Lounge, Hollywood, Florida; Miami, Florida;
Las Vegas, Nevada; Los Angeles, California;
Havana, Cuba during Batista regime; Italy, France.

MILY : Father: MAX
CKGROUND Mother: YETTA nee GRATCH
1st Wife: Anna CITRON (divorced); children from
this marriage: BERNARD (said to be a
cripple or a paraplegic; used to
operate the Tuscany Motel, Hollywood,
Florida);SANDRA; PAUL (said to be a
West Point graduate, now in the U.S.
Air Force).
2nd Wife: Thelma SCHWARTZ, also known as Teddy.
Brother: Jack LANSKY, notorious racketeer.

RIMINAL : F.B.I. No. 791783; NYC P.D. B# 70258
STORY
10-24-18 - Manhattan - Fel. Asslt. - On 10-28-18
Final Charge - Discharged; Dis. Conduct - Judge
McAdoo

11-14-18 - Manhattan - Dis. Conduct - Fined $2.00
Judge Mancuso

8-16-20 - Manhattan - Dis. Conduct - Fined $2.00
Judge Mancuso

3-6-28 - Queens, NYC - Fel. Asslt. -3-7-28; discharged - Judge Marvin

The first page of a 26-page memorandum, dated July 1961, from
the Bureau of Narcotics.

F B I

Date: 4/23/62

Transmit the following in _____ **PLAIN TEXT**
_____
(Type in plain text or code)

Via **AIRTEL** _____ **REGULAR**
_____
(Priority or Method of Mailing)

TO   :   SAC, NEW YORK

FROM .: ·SAC, NEWARK (92-379)

SUBJECT: ANGELO DE CARLO, aka.
          AR

        IN VIEW OF EXTREME SENSITIVITY AND VALUE OF SOURCE,
CAUTION SHOULD BE USED IF INFORMATION CONTAINED HEREIN IS
INCORPORATED IN REPORTS. PARAPHRASING WHICH WILL INSURE
SOURCE AGAINST COMPROMISE SHOULD BE EMPLOYED.

        NK 2251-C* reported on 4/16/62 that ANTHONY MARRONE
requested JOE POLVERINO to call Windsor 4-4458 and speak
to "CARL or his mother". JOE should explain that MARRONE is
ill and could not make the call himself, but that he wishes
to know where the funeral home is and when the funeral will
be.

        DE CARLO then entered .the room and announced that
PAT BRADEY had died. MARRONE acknowledged that he was aware
of this and was arranging to send flowers.

        Informant reported that DE CARLO, POLVERINO, and
NICKY ALLEN were at The Barn that afternoon.

```
2 - New York
2 - Las Vegas
2 - Chicago
2 - Los Angeles
2 - Miami
14 - Newark
     (1 -  92-379A)   (1 -  92-377)
     (1 -  92-374)    (1 -  92-534)
     (1 -  92-1153)   (1 -  92-752)
     (1 -  92-1203)   (1 -  92-375)
     (1 -  92-747)    (1 -  92-650)
     (1 -  92-740)    (1 -  92-392)
JFB:jfs           ((1 - 137-3514)
(26)
```

Approved: _____ Sent _____ M Per _____
      _____ Special Agent in Charge

Top page of a file from the FBI containing the results of "technical
surveillance" carried out by the Bureau between 1961 and 1965. The
subject was Angelo DiCarlo (De Carlo), a New Jersey racketeer.
Conversations between him and other racketeers in the area were
intercepted by hidden microphones and transmitted by wire to a tape
recorder. Several of the tapes contained significant information about
Lansky's position in the underworld.

DECODED COPY

Radio   □ **Teletype**

URGENT   5-1-63
TO DIRECTOR
FROM SAC NEWARK   011643

ANGELO DE CARLO, AKA. AR; GERARDO CATENA AKA. AR.
    NK 2251 - O* ADVISED YESTERDAY ANGELO DE CARLO STATED
CATENA RECEIVES $150,000 A MONTH FROM HIS LAS VEGAS
INVESTMENTS. DE CARLO SAYS CATENA DOES NOT OWN "PIECES"
OF AS MANY CASINOS AS DOES MEYER LANSKY. STATES CATENA
OWNS LARGE SHARES OF SANDS, FREMONT, HORSESHOE, AND
FLAMINGO. THIS IS FIRST INDICATION THAT CATENA HAS INTEREST
IN FLAMINGO.
    LANSKY, ACCORDING TO DE CARLO, HAS A "PIECE" OF VIRTUALLY
EVERY CASINO IN LAS VEGAS DUE TO HIS EARLY ENTRY AS THE
"PROTECTION" FOR JEWISH ELEMENT WHO ORGANIZED GAMBLING
INDUSTRY THERE. HE LISTED FLAMINGO, DESERT INN, STARDUST,
SANDS, AND FREMONT AS HOTELS IN WHICH LANSKY HAS INTERESTS.
STATES CATENA'S HOLDINGS ALSO STEM FROM HIS EARLY INVOLVEMENT
IN LAS VEGAS THROUGH LANSKY AND LATE ABNER ZWILLMAN. DE CARLO
FEELS ZWILLMAN'S EXTENSIVE INTERESTS SPLIT UP BY CATENA,
LANSKY, AND DOC STACHER ON ZWILLMAN'S DEATH.

RECEIVED: 2:36 PM   FN

EX-120

Decoded copy of an FBI "airtel" giving details of information received
about Meyer Lansky during the DiCarlo technical surveillance.

UNITED STATES DEPARTMENT OF JUSTICE

BUREAU OF NARCOTICS AND DANGEROUS DRUGS
American Embassy, Paris

December 10, 1970

M. Nepote
Secretary General
INTERPOL
26, rue Armengaud
92 - SAINT-CLOUD

51268

Dear M. Nepote:

> IN RE: John BARUCHE
> POB - Idirne, Turkey
> DOB - December 6, 1906
> BNDD File X1-70-0001
> Your File 263/56

Between 1949 and 1955, John BARUCHE was uncovered in our
case NY:S 9673 as the representative in Paris of Saul GELB
Nathan BEHRMAN, and Anthony VELLUCI in an operation
involving the transfer of twenty-five kilograms of heroin
per month to the United States.

BARUCHE was indicted in this case but eluded arrest for
several years. This finally obliged the U.S. Attorney
in the Southern District of New York, after a lengthy
period of time, to dismiss the charges against BARUCHE.

Some time thereafter, the latter reappeared; and, as
reported in my letter 49571 of July 11, 1970, he resumed
what we regard as very suspicious travel to Europe in
1968 and again in 1969. His travel plans were allegedly
to include a one-year trip for pleasure to Spain, Germany,
Italy, and France.

In addition to the suspicious travel of BARUCHE, it has
now been learned that his mentor, the notorious Saul GELB,
has, after serving almost ten years in prison as a result
of his convictions in two narcotic prosecutions in 1955 an
1958, successfully reestablished himself as a major impor
of heroin in New York City.

The first and second pages of a letter to the Secretary General of Interpol
from the Bureau of Narcotics and Dangerous Drugs. The letter claims that
Saul Gelb, a known heroin trafficker, had close links with Meyer Lansky.

In the past, GELB's extensive narcotic trafficking operations have come under the aegis of Meyer LANSKY and Harry STROMBERG. STROMBERG, in fact, was convicted in the same narcotic prosecution during 1958 in Federal Court in New York City with GELB, BEHRMAN, and VELLUCI.

It is noted that a report emanating from New York and transmitted by this office to ICPO-Interpol in Tel Aviv via the General Secretariat alleged that LANSKY and STROMBERG were in Tel Aviv along with Hyman SEIGEL, Didy BLOOM, and Joseph STATURE negotiating a narcotic transaction.

The possibility exists that LANSKY's and STROMBERG's visit to Tel Aviv, if a fact, is related to GELB and BARUCHE's activity.

The Hyman SEIGEL reported is believed identical to a criminal associate of LANSKY named Hyman SIGAL. Didy BLOOM is believed identical to Solomon BLOOM, alias "BLUBBER", born in New York on September 7, 1909, a known associate of GELB and STROMBERG.

The Joseph STATURE reported is apparently identical to Joseph STACHER, alias "DOC", born in Russia on September 6, 1901. Our files reveal that STACHER, a notorious figure in underworld organized gambling activity in the United States, has lived in Tel Aviv since 1966.

The following action is requested:

> The ICPO-Interpol Central National Bureaus in Madrid, Wiesbaden, Rome, and Paris (Central Narcotic Office) are requested to establish frontier alerts and other necessary measures to control John BARUCHE's travel into and within their territory and advise this office of his movements.

> ICPO-Interpol (C.N.B.) Berne may wish to do likewise in view of BARUCHE's history of utilizing Swiss banks to further his illicit narcotic trafficking activity.

OFFICE OF THE

DISTRICT ATTORNEY

OF SARATOGA COUNTY

September 27, 1971

DISTRICT ATTORNEY
LOREN N. BROWN
CORINTH, N. Y.

FIRST ASSISTANT DISTRICT ATTO
DAVID A. WAIT
SARATOGA SPRINGS, N. Y.
ASSISTANT DISTRICT ATTORNE
STEPHEN A. FERRADINO
BALLSTON SPA, N. Y.
DAVID L. RIEBEL
JONESVILLE, N. Y.

United States Department of Justice
Organized Crime & Racketeering Section
26 Federal Plaza
New York, New York   10007

Attention: William I. Aronwald
             Special Attorney

Dear Mr. Aronwald:

Pursuant to your request I am enclosing herewith a certified
copy of the extract of minutes of the sentencing of Meyer
Lansky. I can find no other records relative to this matter.
The prosecution was not handled by the Saratoga County District
Attorney's office but by special appointees of the then Governor.

Very truly yours,

Loren N. Brown

LNB:vlm

Enc.

Letter accompanying a record of the minutes of the sentencing of Meyer
Lansky in 1953, from the office of the District Attorney of Saratoga
County.

United States District Court

FOR THE

Southern District of Florida

MAR 24 1971
U. S. District
Southern Dist.
of Florida

UNITED STATES OF AMERICA

v.

MEYER LANSKY

No. 71-136-JK

To¹ The United States Marshal or any other authorized agent or officer

You are hereby commanded to arrest MEYER LANSKY   and bring him

forthwith before the United States District Court for the Southern   District of **Florida**

in the city of **Miami**   to answer to an   Indictment   charging h im   with

Criminal Contempt, in that he refused to appear before the United States

Grand Jury in the Southern District of Florida on March 10 and 11, 1971,

pursuant to lawful subpoena and court order

in violation of   Title 18, U.S.C. Section 401

Certified to be a true and
correct copy of the original.
Joseph I. Bogart, Clerk
U. S. District Court
Southern Dist. of Fla.

By _____ Deputy Clerk
Date APR 21 1971

Dated at Miami, Florida

on   March 24th   1971

Bail fixed at $200,000 SURETY

By _____
                              Clerk.

_____
                              Deputy Clerk.

RETURN

District of   ss

Received the within warrant the   day of   19   and executed same.

_____

By _____

¹ Insert designation of officer to whom the warrant is issued, e. g., "any United States Marshal or any other authorized officer"; or "United States Marshal for .... District of ...."; or "any United States Marshal"; or "any Special Agent of the Federal Bureau of Investigation"; or "any United States Marshal or any Special Agent of the Federal Bureau of Investigation"; or "any agent of the Alcohol Tax Unit."

A 1971 warrant for Lansky's arrest, made out in Miami.

IN THE CRIMINAL COURT OF RECORD

IN AND FOR DADE COUNTY, FLORIDA

Case No. 70-3318

STATE OF FLORIDA,   *
                                     *
            Plaintiff,   *
                                     *
-vs-   *
                                     *
MEYER LANSKY,   *
                                     *
            Defendant.   *
                                     *
* * * * * * * * * * * * *

            Transcript of proceedings had and

testimony taken in the above-entitled cause, heard

before the Honorable CARLING STEDMAN, Judge of the

Criminal Court of Record, at the Metropolitan Dade

County Justice Building, Miami, Florida on Thursday,

June 18, 1970, commencing at or about 11:00 o'clock

a.m.

            - - - - - - - - - - - - - -

Lawrence S. Friedman, C.S.R.

1150 NORTHWEST 14TH STREET
MIAMI, FLORIDA 33136   TEL. 377-1013

First page of the transcript of *State of Florida* vs. *Meyer Lansky*, 1970.
Lansky was acquitted of the charge of being in unlawful possession of
Donnatal, a barbiturate, on his arrival at Miami International Airport after
a trip to Mexico.

Nov. 7, 1976.

Dear Uri:

It was a pleasure to talk to you. I was glad to hear that that you are proud of your missions around the Country.

If I can be of assistance to make your stay more comfortable don't hesitate to call on me.

Uri, your suggestion to me to write for posterity is worth a serious thought but I don't want to rush any thing. Whether I will ever devote myself to writing a book isn't definite as of now and I doubt if ever while I'm alive. I'm not interested in discussing this writing with anyone else, only Uri Dan will I talk to, and their it dies.

Money doesn't interest me at present. What I'm interested in knowing from you is what the outline would have to be to make my biography saleable.

After I am aware as to what you want to know about me, I will then decide whether I am interested in writing in the future.

Again I want to make it clear I will not discuss this matter with anyone else but Uri Dan at present. Uri, I will call you after a few days after mailing this letter. If you think you should see me before you leave for Israel you be my guest. It is always a pleasure to see and be with you, my friend. All the best.

Sincerely
Meyer

Two of the many letters written by Meyer Lansky to Uri Dan (above and overleaf).

Oct. 28, 1977.

Dear Uri:

Your letter brought a very pleasant greeting.

I well understand the pleasure of seeing your son Bar-Mitzva. I'm sorry to have missed him in N.Y. May he have a long, happy life.

What is really wrong with those cowardly bastard politicians of Israel. I think Burg is not big enough or ashamed to face up to his error.

I don't know if you missed the article by a visiting law professor Milton Klug. I am also enclosing an article on the F.B.I. and Interpol. I have given you an article Interpol before when you were in U.S. Iwish Burg read this article on Interpol. I gave Yoram book on the history of Interpo months ago.

Uri, if you intend to write on my denial of a visit and wish a statement from me I will be happy to assist. I would love to battle this bastard and the rest of them.

Uri, if ever you want me to speak or see a friend of yours please let me know before - it would be my pleasure to meet a friend of yours otherwise I am careful. I never know when it may be a trick.

All the best. Please let me hear from you. My best to Pickel and family also the friend I met with you.
My best to your family and all our friends.

Shalom
Meyer

33 "Top Priority—Racketeer"

For a man who has the reputation of being the brains behind organized crime in the United States, Meyer Lansky lives a surprisingly inconspicuous life. He has a comfortable apartment in a building called Seasons South, at 5001 Collins Avenue in Miami Beach. Still trim and alert-looking, he dresses quietly but well. His apartment is furnished modern style, with blue the predominant color. American landscapes are on the walls, and there are shelves covered with glassware. He enjoys entertaining in the kitchen. Nothing gives the faintest inkling of his wealth. Every evening he likes to take his old dog, a Tibetan Shih Tzu, for a stroll along Collins Avenue. He looks like any other prosperous retired businessman in a city where people seek peace and sunshine in the evening of their lives, and the neighbors have no cause to complain about loud noises, gunshots, or unsavory visitors.

"You're so comfortable here. Why did you suddenly decide to fly off to Israel in 1970?" the authors asked Meyer Lansky.

Lansky replied, "My life was becoming totally impossible. In the few years before I decided to go to Israel I had FBI agents following me night and day.

"They had their cars parked around my home. My telephone was bugged. If I wanted to call a friend I had to do it from a phone booth. Sometimes I would turn around and talk to the men who were following me. Usually they were embarrassed, but occasionally they would tell me frankly that they were acting on orders and that somehow or other they were going to pin me down for something or other.

"Books and articles accuse me of every crime under the sun. Committees like the Kefauver Committee and people like Robert Kennedy, when he was attorney general, pointed the finger at me. Yet why is it that with the great power of the United States behind them, they were never able, or willing, to put me up in a court and accuse me with the proof that I was a so-called 'master criminal'?

"I'm sure you'll think I've got a persecution mania, but I'll give you an example of just how determined the authorities were to prove that I was a criminal. In February of 1970 I decided to take a vacation in Acapulco, in Mexico. I had a heart problem and ulcers besides. I needed the rest badly. My old friend Moses Polakoff came along, and some friends, businessmen, came down from Canada.

"The minute I got to Mexico—a trip I had not tried to hide in any way—there were headlines back in Miami saying that there was a convention of the heads of organized crime in Acapulco.

"Now if I were really the head gangster of all the criminals in the United States, would I go so openly and without trying to put on a beard or disguise myself somehow? And would a respected man of the law like Moses Polakoff participate in such a gathering? But to my amazement I read in the papers that this was 'Operation Underworld.' "

Lansky checked in at the Acapulco Hilton, Room 993. Moses Polakoff was next door. Lansky had several meetings at the Acapulco home of his friend Leo Berkovitch, who had moved down from Canada several years before. The newspaper headlines and Lansky's FBI shadows alerted the United States and Canadian authorities, who sent special agents to Acapulco to find out what was going on in "Operation Underworld." Gambling must have been one of the subjects discussed by Meyer and his Canadian friends, despite his protestations that he was on vacation, but the agents sent to Acapulco discovered nothing very exciting going on, although a very close watch was kept from February 15 to 28. Nevertheless, the Mexican authorities were asked to intervene.

Says Lansky, "The next thing I knew was that three policemen came to my room at the Hilton. They knocked at the door, and when I asked them in they said they'd come to interrogate me about a report from sources unknown that I was involved in a robbery of valuable paintings from a museum in Mexico City. I was a bit surprised and said I wasn't in the business of art theft. Nevertheless, they searched my room thoroughly, took my suitcases apart, and for some reason took a lot of photographs."

The only find the U.S. agents were able to report back to headquarters was that they had come across a man by the name of Frank Pasquale, who was found to be suspect number 574 on the International Narcotics list. An attempt was made to have Pasquale arrested and questioned to find out if he had any connection with Meyer Lansky. The efforts were not successful, as suspect number 574 vanished into thin air before he could be taken into custody by the Mexican authorities.

But "they were determined to get me somehow. On March 5, when I flew back to the United States, a squad of high-powered customs officials stopped me at Miami International Airport and said they were going to search me.

"I didn't protest. This was their right and I didn't have anything to hide. Suddenly one of the men shouted, 'Hey, I've got it.' He was holding up a bottle of pills he'd found in my shaving kit. I told him he could save himself a lot of trouble because the pills were Donnatal, which my doctor had prescribed for my ulcers. They apologized and gave me back my pills and I went home.

"Three weeks later, while I was at home talking to my wife, there was a knock at the door. Like in some bad movie, somebody yelled, 'Open in the name of the law.' I opened the door and they handcuffed me and took me to the police station, where they accused me of illegal transfer of drugs. I asked them what drugs. They said those tablets the customs authorities had found on me. I said again that they were Donnatal tablets for my ulcers, and my lawyer got me out on bail.

"Next day the newspaper headlines said, 'Lansky Charged with Traffic in Drugs.' When the case came to trial, my doctor sent a letter saying he had prescribed the tablets for me, and I was acquitted. But there were no headlines about that, just a little four-line item buried on an inside page.

"After that I was harassed even more. I was followed every time I walked the dog. Then I got a bad shock. One night one of the FBI agents walked up to me and said, 'I have information from Washington that the FBI has heard about someone threatening to kidnap your grandson. Do you know anything about this?'

"I was alarmed. When my son Paul and my daughter-in-law had their first child they insisted on calling him Meyer. I begged them not to do it—I said it's bad enough there's one Meyer Lansky getting bad publicity. You really don't want a newborn infant to have publicity dogging his name all his life. But they insisted on it, and I was very touched.

"I asked the agent to come with me to the nearest phone booth and I telephoned my son in Washington State. Paul said it was mostly just a matter of the school authorities taking precautions to guard my grandson. Newspapers were making a great fuss at the time with some fool story about my being worth hundreds of millions of dollars, and the school people had warned Paul that this might invite the attention of kidnapers. But there was also some indication that strange people were following my grandson. I felt sick at heart. My family was in danger because of all those stories about me.

"I had a long talk with that young FBI agent as we walked home. He was embarrassed but honest, and he told me, 'Mr. Lansky, you're the victim of the political scheming and ambitions of people who are using your name to make themselves famous. If the FBI really had anything against you, we'd never let you walk around the way you do. You'd be under arrest. Your quarrel is with the politicians. They're your enemies, not us.' "

There is no doubt that from the 1950s on the authorities made painstaking efforts to check every facet of Meyer Lansky's career. The major object of these investigations was to either revoke his naturalization or prosecute him for tax evasion.

An official report, stamped "Top Priority—Racketeer" and dated June 22, 1959, stated bluntly: "Investigation of this case is based upon a memorandum dated September 26, 1952, from the Assistant Commissioner, Investigations Division, Washington, D.C., to the District Director, New York, New York, requesting that a complete and thorough investigation be conducted to secure evidence which might be used as a basis for possible revocation of citizenship." Denaturalization action was instituted in the U.S. District Court for the Southern District of New York, but was dismissed for "lack of prosecution" on May 18, 1958, and in January of the following year the case was transferred to Miami.

The core of the case against Lansky was that he had failed to reveal his police record when he applied for naturalization papers. Investigators unearthed five arrests in his early years. Some were minor charges and others more serious. None resulted in Lansky's being sent to prison. For instance, on November 15, 1918, when he was sixteen, Lansky, then living at 482 Grand Street, was arrested by Officer Weiss after a complaint of annoyance by a certain Sarah Ginsburg of 370 Madison Street. He was fined two dollars.

Ten days later the youth was again in trouble, this time arrested by Officer Hughes on a complaint by Lena Freidman, a neighbor of Sarah Ginsburg. This time Lansky was charged with felony, but Magistrate McAdoo dismissed the charge.

Department of Justice investigators went to great lengths to try to interview the police officers involved in all five arrests. As far as Officer Hughes was concerned, "it has been found that there were 21 police officers by the name of Hughes in the New York Police Department at the time of this arrest. Of the 21 officers by the name of Hughes . . . 11 are now deceased. The remaining 10 have been interviewed and it has not been possible to identify the arresting officer among the group."

Doc Stacher had his own version of Lansky's early arrests. "In the first one, Meyer was taken to a cell with Charlie Luciano—he was twenty-one—and Bugsy Siegel, who was only fourteen. The police arrested all three of them when they were found in the apartment of a screaming woman who had been badly beaten up. The boys told the judge that Meyer had been going home minding his own business when he heard calls for help. He went into the building and found Bugsy and Luciano fighting over the woman. Lansky intervened to save young Bugsy from being beaten up by Charlie. Charlie was released, and when Meyer appeared before the judge, Bugsy testified on his behalf. The woman didn't appear, and the story was so confused that the judge just fined Meyer two dollars and told him to behave himself in future.

According to Stacher, the true story was that Siegel, Lansky, and Luciano had gone to the woman's apartment to beat her up because she was trying to blackmail Lansky and Luciano. She suspected that they were responsible for the disappearance of the son of the Irish policeman who had arrested Luciano and had him sent to Hampton Farms Penitentiary. The beating was to impress on her that unless she kept quiet, worse things would happen to her.

Eight years later Siegel came across the woman in a bar. She clearly had not learned her lesson. Although she had kept her mouth shut about the disappearance of the Irish youth, she told Siegel, "I hope you've grown up, sonny boy, since I met you as a kid." She mocked his sexual prowess and said that at the time he beat her up he was still wet behind the ears. "You wouldn't have known what to do with me anyway."

It was the wrong thing to say to Bugsy Siegel. As she left the bar he followed her and raped her in a nearby hallway. He was arrested, but the charges were dropped when his friend Meyer had a few discreet words with her and persuaded her not to give evidence.

The third time Lansky was arrested was on August 15, 1920, when he was nineteen. Officer O'Rourke arrested the youth for breach of the peace but got his name wrong and called him Ray Lansky. Again it was Stacher who filled in the details: "Joe Masseria's men were trying to muscle in on the territory Meyer and Bugsy had marked out as their own. A fight broke out and the Italians got the worst of the affair. The cops came and Meyer was arrested and fined two dollars."

Lansky was arrested again on March 6, 1928, on a complaint by John Barrett, and charged with felonious assault. This was soon after the shooting of Daniel Francis Ahearn, who had been invited to the "party" at which Barrett was "taken for a ride." Lansky says firmly, "Bugsy and I had nothing to do with Ahearn's being shot," but a good friend of Ahearn's, a fellow gunman known as Pete Bender, was sure that Lansky or Siegel had done it, and let it be known that he would settle the score with both of them. Bender disappeared soon afterward.

On March 9, after Bender had vanished, Lansky was charged with homicide. Barrett decided to keep quiet, Bender's body was never found, and all charges against Lansky were dropped.

It was these 1928 arrests that were to haunt Lansky for many years, and to provide law enforcement investigators with hours of interviews and dozens of elusive clues. Tracked down by investigators in the late 1950s, the man whom the Lanskys had known as John Barrett was still extremely reluctant to testify; his interviewer was "unable to predict with any certainty whatever what his testimony might be." It appeared that Daniel Francis Ahearn, who had given his deposition about the Barrett shooting in 1957 and was still in prison, continued to be the only former Lansky-Siegel associate with the retentive memory that the government needed.

Lansky's first arrest after his marriage in 1929 was in April 1932 in Chicago, where he and Luciano were trying to make peace among the warring underworld factions. The police interrogated both men for two days and then reluctantly released the New Yorkers.

After the Second World War, Lansky was indicted for gambling activities in the club La Bohème. The Broward County Grand Jury dropped the charges when it was discovered that the club was run and, on the record, owned by Meyer's brother Jake. Jake was fined a thousand dollars but later this penalty was rescinded.

The only time Meyer Lansky has ever gone to prison was in 1952, when he was arrested as a common gambler. It occurred after the Kefauver investigation revealed that gambling was going on in Saratoga Springs, a resort in Upstate New York. Lansky pleaded guilty and was sentenced to ninety days in prison. "That was the only crime I've ever been convicted of," Lansky told the authors.

The charges in this instance related to the Arrowhead Inn, on the outskirts of Saratoga, and Joe Stacher was charged along with Lansky. Stacher was fined $10,000 and received a suspended sentence of one year in prison. Lansky says, "Yes, I was sent to prison, but it was only a gambling charge. I could gamble legally in Nevada and Florida but not in Saratoga. But everybody knew there was gambling up there. The place was full of casinos. I had investments in the Arrowhead Inn and in the Piping Rock casino too. I'm sure the reason why the cops in Saratoga suddenly took action was that Governor Dewey ordered an investigation because of the Kefauver Report. It was just bad timing.

"I'll tell you a story about those ninety days," Lansky said, smiling. "I asked the guards to bring me a dictionary and a Bible. I thought I might as well use the time to improve my mind and study the holy book. A few days later I was astonished to see in the newspapers that I'd turned religious and was going to become a Christian. This had something to do with the fact that a priest used to come to visit the other prisoners. I had asked for a rabbi but no one had come. So the priest came to visit me, maybe because he thought I was lonely. Finally, on the last day of my imprisonment, a rabbi turned up. I said to him, 'Rabbi, they've tried to make a Christian out of me. By the time you decided to come to my rescue, I could have been thrown to the lions several times over.' "

Lansky was released from prison on July 21, 1953. Shortly afterward he moved his residence to Florida, closing down his New York apartment.

Lansky says, "Over the years they've tried every way they could to find me guilty of all sorts of offenses. The income tax people were on my back all this time, too."

The Internal Revenue Service had apparently decided that Lansky could be nailed. Over the years it had managed to get a number of gangsters behind prison bars for evading income tax when all other methods of pinning down their underworld activities had failed.

The IRS investigation got under way about 1950, and a special agent from Internal Revenue, Joseph D. Delfino, spent three years beavering away. Ultimately Lansky's tax reports for 1944 through 1958 were all combed. Delfino remarked upon the extraordinary number of large cash deposits and withdrawals from Lansky's account at the Manufacturers Trust bank in New York, and other investigators found the same pattern. Delfino recommended prosecution for tax evasion for 1945 and 1947 but could not recommend a "criminal prosecution case" or a "fraud penalty" for 1948-1952. The overall conclusion of the numerous IRS investigators at that time was that Lansky "failed to report . . . substantial amounts of income . . . Such a conclusion is buttressed by the evidence of concealment of assets and sources of funds . . . Lansky [is] accustomed to conducting his business transactions largely in cash . . . [and to reporting] various amounts of income from 'sporting gains' or 'commissions.' "

Painstaking searches for nonexistent business records were described in voluminous reports, and the IRS's stern conclusion was:

> Investigation revealed that Meyer Lansky willfully and deliberately attempted to defeat and evade a large proportion of his income tax liability for the years 1944, 1945 and 1947 by willfully omitting income mainly derived from gambling activities, thereby causing a substantial understatement of his gross and net income and taxes due for those years.
>
> It is therefore recommended that full penalties be asserted on the additional taxes due for the years 1944, 1945 and 1947.
>
> It is further recommended that criminal proceedings be instituted against Meyer Lansky in the Southern Judicial District of New York for the willful attempt to defeat and evade a large portion of his income taxes for the years 1945 and 1947, under Section 145(B) of the Internal Revenue Code.

Lansky paid the additional tax assessments and there was no prosecution. Internal Revenue kept trying, but finally IRS Regional Counsel Arthur B. White wrote that "as there were no possibilities of making out a criminal case against Meyer Lansky the case is accordingly marked 'closed.' "

Lansky says, "They've got some pretty good brains in the Revenue Service. They've jailed people like Moe Annenberg, Frank Costello, Al Capone, Waxey Gordon, Johnny Torrio—hundreds of people. If I was really guilty, surely they would have got me. What can one man do against all their lawyers and other experts? If I finally wasn't even prosecuted, I have to be innocent, right? And the same is true for the Immigration Bureau's charges.

"I became an American citizen in September of 1928. It was a very proud moment for me. The ceremony took place in Brooklyn Federal Courthouse, and all my family and friends came. I remember how wonderful I felt when I left that place with the naturalization papers in my hands. Maybe you can imagine how mad I was when the government tried to denaturalize me in 1952. They raked up all my petty arrests before I applied for citizenship, and the next year they pulled Ahearn out of prison to tell a pack of lies about my alleged misdeeds when I was a young man. But the attempts to deport me failed again."

The proceedings to have Lansky denaturalized and deported were also dismissed "for lack of prosecution."

"It's no joke being arrested," Lansky says, thinking of another narrow escape. "I remember going back to New York on February 11, 1958. The minute I got off the plane I realized I was being tailed. On Broadway, when I got out of the cab, I was arrested. They cross-examined me for several hours asking what I knew about the murder of Anastasia—which is why I remember the date. Of course I knew nothing, so to save face, they booked me on a vagrancy charge. I was freed on a thousand-dollar bond.

"Batista played a little joke on me. He announced publicly that I wouldn't be allowed to return to Havana so long as these 'serious charges' were outstanding against me. Naturally they were dismissed. And when I returned to Cuba, Batista and I had a good laugh over the whole thing."

One thing that angered Lansky far more than any arrest was in a Department of Justice document dated August 24, 1977. Originally drawn up by Agent James J. Kearney on July 26, 1961, it was headed: "Federal Bureau of Investigation Memorandum 'Meyer Lansky.' " The document was witnessed and signed by Robert J. Campbell, Attorney in Charge, Strike Force 18, Organized Crime and Racketeering Section.

In the report (Bureau File No. 92-2831) Kearney details Lansky's career and also discusses his children. He describes Lansky's daughter, Sandra, as "a divorcee of doubtful reputation resident New York City." The father said furiously, "Sure she's divorced, and I was damn sorry about it. But does that make her reputation 'doubtful'? Is it right for them to smear my daughter that way?"

The FBI report also states:

> Subject is not employed at present, but has been in the gambling business, legally and illegally, most of his life. Subject started criminal career in 1920s as a muscle man in alcohol wars; graduated into gambling; and after World War II has dealt exclusively in gambling. Since Castro drove him out of Cuba his gambling has been quiescent. Subject numbers among his associates some of the most notorious gangsters of the past and present era, almost all the members of the gambling crowd, movie stars, hotel men, and reputable businessmen. Investigation fails to disclose any present business or enterprise he is engaged in or any illegal activities he might be engaged in at this time.

The investigators also visited the first Mrs. Lansky at her apartment on West Eighty-sixth Street, New York City. Anna Lansky said she knew her husband had been engaged in illicit gambling activities while they were married but used an auto rental business with Bugsy Siegel as a respectable front. She said her husband was a white-collar worker, always engaged in "clean fingernail occupations."

The FBI then tracked down Jake Harmatz, who had owned Ratner's Restaurant, at 138 Delancey Street. The restaurateur said that the Lansky brothers, Siegel, and others used to meet in the back room of Ratner's. Because "they were good customers, big spenders and treated the waiters good," he had not minded their using the room. He admitted, said the investigator, that he had heard rumors in 1928 that Lansky and Siegel were gangsters and bootleggers, "but stated he had no direct knowledge."

From February 22, 1961, until July 12, 1965, agents of the FBI had a hidden microphone in a clubroom called the Barn on Route 22, Mountainside, New Jersey. The Barn as well as a restaurant in front of it was owned by a man called Angelo "Gyp" DiCarlo, or De Carlo, also known as Ray DiCarlo.

The conversations of DiCarlo and his associates were recorded and transmitted by wire to a tape recorder. From the tapes the FBI prepared transcripts, referred to as logs. They were handed over to the Organized Crime and Racketeering Section of the Department of Justice. When the information seemed particularly hot, summaries of the conversations were sent to Washington immediately.

According to an FBI report, some of the intercepted material revealed "significant information regarding the place of Meyer Lansky in the United States underworld." Explaining that the brothers Jerry and Gene Catena were "top figures in the Vito Genovese family" of the Cosa Nostra, the agents cited a tape made in 1962 in which DiCarlo says that "Jerry Catena's income is greater than anyone else around . . . except Meyer Lansky. . . . Nobody's got Meyer, he's like a horse." This was interpreted by the agents as "indicating that no one in the Cosa Nostra controls Lansky."

They added:

> DiCarlo and Russo discuss an organized crime associate named Jimmy Blue Eyes, a nickname for Vincent Alo, who has acted in the 1960s as a liaison between Meyer Lansky and the Cosa Nostra, a position he inherited from Jerry Catena. . . . DiCarlo mentions Alo's interest in three Broward County (Florida) casinos (Green Acres, La Bohème and Colonial Inn) all owned and operated during the 1940s principally by Meyer Lansky. On September 16, 1950, Meyer Lansky, Alo and six others pleaded guilty to illegally operating these three Broward County casinos. DiCarlo then discusses Lansky's role in Las Vegas and the stealing of money from the Flamingo Hotel and Casino by Lansky, Catena and Alo. Lansky is presently under indictment in connection with his hidden and illegal control over the Flamingo. DiCarlo's conversation indicates that, indeed, there was a conspiracy on the part of Lansky and others to steal or "skim" money from the Flamingo.

The taped conversations revealed that skimmed-off money from the casinos was forwarded to Lansky, Catena, DiCarlo and others, according to the wire-tappers.

> . . . there is a further reference to the Flamingo and Lansky's partnership with Sam Cohen . . . and the receipt of the skim money in a satchel every month or so at the Crown Hotel (in Miami). This is a common method of delivering the stolen money from Las Vegas to Lansky in Miami. . . . One gets a further insight into Lansky's role of importance to the Italian mob by the statement that only one other Jewish hoodlum is

recognized by the Italians, Moe Dalitz (then record owner in the Desert Inn and Stardust in Las Vegas).

Further tapes rushed to Washington

> . . . demonstrate Lansky's involvement in Bahamian casinos along with Vincent Alo and "Trigger" Mike Coppola. DiCarlo states that Lansky has more points (a larger percentage ownership) in Las Vegas casinos than everyone else put together. . . . DiCarlo also states that Lansky is the "key" to the Italian-Jewish syndicate cooperation. . . . [All these ownership "points" are] in violation of Nevada law and under federal law . . . are felonies. DiCarlo's own association with Lansky beginning at least back in the Broward County Inn—and his pre-eminent position in New Jersey–New York organized crime circles as a lieutenant in the DeCavalcante family—demonstrate that indeed he is in a position to know what he is talking about. . . .
>
> Finally . . . DiCarlo once more compares Catena's share of Las Vegas skim, stating it to be $150,000 per month, but even this is not as much as Lansky's. He lists Lansky as having a piece of virtually every Las Vegas casino, and having shared in the extensive interests of the late [Abner] Zwillman along with "Doc" Stacher and Jerry Catena. Zwillman's pre-eminent position in organized crime in New Jersey was extensively set forth in the Kefauver Committee report.

The FBI report ends with the dry statement: "The evidence uncovered by these wire intercepts was all collected without court authorization and thus is inadmissible in American courts." But "despite the fact these logs could not be used in a United States court, it is felt that since this information was obtained from the lips of unsuspecting La Cosa Nostra members it is highly trustworthy and illustrative of the way organized crime actually operates." This document too is signed by Robert J. Campbell, Attorney in Charge, Strike Force 18.

"The FBI was determined to get me," says Lansky. "They had no evidence, so they tried to associate those people with me, claiming that everything they said was true whenever they mentioned my name. They'd made up their minds that I was guilty of just about every crime, and they worked illegally to make what they called 'facts' fit their crazy theories."

It was abundantly clear to Lansky that pressure was on him from every direction. If one charge was dropped, another took its place. When the case against him for illegal possession of barbiturates was dismissed, on June 17, 1970, his buddies Nig Rosen and Phil Kovalick congratulated him as they drove him home, but Lansky was not deluded.

"I decided then that I should leave the United States," he says. "I was still a citizen and there were no charges out against me at the moment, but I felt that somehow or other, just like Dewey framed Charlie Luciano on those prostitution charges, something was in the works. That FBI kid had been pretty blunt, and I wouldn't have been surprised at almost any kind of frame-up."

34 Shalom!

"Before I left the United States, I talked it all over with Teddy and telephoned Joe Stacher in Tel Aviv. Both of them agreed that I should go to Israel and Teddy would follow me."

It was in many ways a natural decision. Like most Jews, Lansky had been elated when Israel became a country in 1948. He remembers that he followed very carefully the bitter battles of the Israeli War of Independence. Then one day in early June "two Israeli representatives came to see me in New York, introduced by a prominent American Jew.

"They asked me to help Israel. 'What's the problem?' I asked. 'I'm at your service.' The Israelis explained that their Provisional Government was worried about arms shipments from the United States to Egypt. The tiny Israeli Army was battling the Egyptians in the Gaza Strip and in Sinai, and while this was going on Egypt was buying arms from American arms dealers and smuggling them to the Port of New York for shipment. There was an embargo here on arms shipments to the Middle East, but the Egyptians were getting a lot of stuff through. The Israelis gave me the name of an American in Pittsburgh who was sending big shipments to the Arabs.

" 'O.K.,' I said, 'I'll handle it,' and I went over to New Jersey and talked to a few people about how to stop the shipments at the docks. Part of the Pittsburgh consignment fell overboard, and most of another cargo was by mistake loaded onto ships bound for Israel."

Theoretically the embargo was supposed to be fair to both sides in the conflict, but it was hitting Israel far harder. The Arab states had already bought more than $14,000,000 worth of surplus American arms, and Arab money was buying arms both in Britain and on the Continent. The British government, hostile to the newborn state, had a lucrative business supplying arms to the Arab states and would not sell to Israel. Arms had to come from the United States. Yehuda Arazi, a top-ranking agent from Tel Aviv, was sent to New York to speed up the process, which now had to be carried out illegally. Forty-year-old Yehuda Arazi had spent a good part of his life buying weapons for the Jewish underground in Palestine when the British ruled that part of the world. Now the tall, graying agent, using the name Albert Miller, made contact with members of the Lower East Side outfit in New York.

The Israeli agent had no scruples at all about dealing with anyone who could help him get the arms he needed, and he was the one who made contact with Meyer Lansky. The "Little Man" was invited to meet "Albert Miller" at the Hotel Fourteen, on the corner of 14 East Sixtieth Street, between Madison and Fifth avenues, where a small group of Israelis had set up their underground purchasing commission.

Meyer Lansky smiled when he realized that in the basement of the hotel was the Copacabana night club, where his friends liked to find "the prettiest girls in New York." Many criminal deals took place in the plush surroundings of this night spot, too, and although Lansky was not much of a man for night life, he had sometimes met Joe Adonis, Charlie Luciano, Frank Costello, Bugsy Siegel, and others there.

Yehuda Arazi said bluntly, "I know that the Mafia, or whatever you want to call it, controls the Port of New York. I have information about your and your associates' activities during the war. Can you do us a favor now? Can you find out exactly what arms are passing through the port destined for Arab countries? And what's more, would it be possible for you to have some of those arms stolen and put on ships bound for Haifa?"

Lansky promised to do what he could, and he managed to do a lot. Through Joe Adonis and Albert Anastasia a steady stream of intelligence information about Arab-bound arms reached the Hotel Fourteen. Some of these shipments vanished; others were landed in Haifa Harbor. The longshoremen also helped Israeli agents conceal the arms they were purchasing in America and smuggling to New York.

Lansky had other, earlier memories that made him devoted to the cause of Israel. "I was on a visit to Cuba back in 1939 when I found out that a shipload of Jewish refugees was in Havana Harbor and not allowed to land. I was told that some of the passengers were so desperate they had jumped overboard and swum ashore. Something had to be done. I called the chief of immigration, Colonel Benitos, and said I thought it was disgusting that he was planning to deport the people who had managed to get into Havana. I told him I would put up a five-hundred-dollar guarantee for each of the people who had swum to freedom, that I would take full responsibility for seeing that none of them would be a burden on his country. He agreed, and at least I was able to save one family.

"I've always tried to help people who were fighting anti-Semitism. Once a Jewish lawyer by the name of Spira had the nerve to sue the Ford Motor Company because he claimed that Ford himself was distributing anti-Semitic propaganda in America. It was a hopeless battle and Spira spent every cent he had. When the trial was over I saw to it that he had enough money to get back on his feet.

"And so, for too many reasons to even talk about," Lansky says, "I went to Tel Aviv—and Doc Stacher was one of the first people to greet me there."

After making a deal with the American authorities about his income tax evasion, Joseph Stacher had been allowed to leave the country in 1964 and had gone to Israel, where he bought a villa in the resort of Caesaria. He also had a suite of rooms in the old Sheraton Hotel in Tel Aviv, which he preferred after his wife died of cancer in 1970. Stacher, well dressed and with a shiny bald head, became a prominent figure in Tel Aviv. Despite his expressed intention to live quietly, not long after he emigrated he became the center of a controversy that vastly entertained the whole country. Worried about whether he would get Israeli citizenship, Stacher sought out Menachem Porush, an Israeli member of parliament from the religious group Agudat Israel. Said this Orthodox M.P., "My contact with Stacher came in 1966, when friends of Frank Sinatra appealed to me to help Joe after he had been virtually deported because of his misdealings with the income tax authorities."

The bearded Menachem Porush owed a debt to Frank Sinatra and his friends, who contributed heavily to the fund raising which he organized every year in the United States for religious educational institutes in Israel. "So when they asked me to help Stacher, I agreed right away," he said. Porush introduced Stacher to a number of Orthodox people and institutions in Jerusalem, including the ultraconservative Jews who live in the Jerusalem suburb of Mea Shearin, and Stacher and his wife spent a lot of time and money helping them, visiting them in their poor wooden houses and buying refrigerators, washing machines, and other things these devout, impoverished people needed.

Stacher's interest in religion at this stage of his life was not totally altruistic. The Ministry of the Interior, which would decide whether or not he could obtain Israeli citizenship, was run mainly by people from the religious parties. Stacher offered to invest $100,000 in Porush's plans to build homes for young, strictly Orthodox Jewish couples, but Porush used the money to build a kosher hotel, the Merkaz, in the Holy City of Jerusalem.

The two men quarreled, and the dispute became so bitter that they took it to court. Israel was convulsed with laughter at the whole case. Stacher claimed that the money had been a loan. Porush retorted, "The minute he got his passport from us he stopped giving money to charity. I didn't see him any more. Now he wants his money back."

The matter became more complex when it developed that the hundred-thousand-dollar deal had been made via Liechtenstein, where Porush had set up a company called Nachalat Israel Trust. Stacher complained indignantly that not only was he unable to get back the loan which was supposed to be used to build charitable institutions, but he had not received any interest on the money. Instead, Rabbi Porush was skimming off the profits from the Merkaz Hotel for himself. Chuckling Israelis wondered how on earth Joseph Stacher, one of the great figures of American crime, had been ripped off by the devout, naïve-looking rabbi.

After that, Stacher became known all over the country as one of the leaders of what Israeli newspapers called "The Kosher Nostra," as distinct from "The Cosa Nostra." And the newspapers had a fine time with the news that the rabbi had been a frequent visitor to Las Vegas as Stacher's guest. There were undignified scenes in the courtroom as Stacher's lawyer called the rabbi a swindler and Porush's man counterattacked, "Stacher is a criminal."

Stacher won the case, and Rabbi Porush had to hand back the loan in its entirety. By the time Lansky joined him in Israel, in 1970, Stacher had also won Israeli citizenship.

Lansky and Stacher spent a great deal of time in each other's company. They were frequently seen walking or sitting on a bench in deep conversation in Tel Aviv's Independence Garden, which is near the Sheraton and overlooks the Mediterranean. The two men also played a lot of poker together, but only in their own homes. They did nothing whatever to cause problems with the Israeli police. True to his cautious nature, Meyer Lansky tried to remain out of the public eye in Israel.

Stacher, however, had very few inhibitions and continued to enjoy the role of philanthropist. The ludicrous episode with Porush did not stop him from contributing to many charities. But later on, perhaps because Lansky was no longer nearby to urge discretion, Stacher once more did something that might well have got him into the headlines. On October 23, 1973, on last day of the traumatic Yom Kippur War, the guns were still roaring along the Suez Canal. Israeli armored columns were deep in Egypt, advancing on the road to Cairo.

A private limousine managed to make its way through the Sinai Desert and military police were somehow persuaded to let it continue across the bridgehead at the canal. From there, dodging shells and bombs, it drove straight to the headquarters of the division commander, General Ariel Sharon. The driver, a former soldier himself and now a fifty-year-old civilian from Tel Aviv, managed to make contact with the general's adjutant, saying that he had a gift from an admirer in Tel Aviv. At this stage of the war Sharon was indeed the hero of all Israel. He had crossed the canal and struck deep into the heart of the Egyptian defenses, thus turning the threatened defeat of the Israeli Army into a victory.

In the heat of battle there was no time to open the huge package and it was put aside. The car returned to Tel Aviv. But the next day, after the cease-fire, somebody suddenly remembered the package and opened it.

General Sharon, his head bandaged from a wound, was astonished when tins of shrimps in tomato sauce, mussels in white wine, and other delicacies from the best Parisian food stores came tumbling out of the box. Alongside the array of food, including caviar and smoked salmon, were half a dozen bottles of Dom Perignon champagne, complete with crystal glasses from Bohemia, as well as a few boxes of Havana cigars.

General Sharon did not hesitate. The food was laid out for his staff and everyone else who happened to be at headquarters. It was the best meal many of them had ever eaten, not just since before the war, but in all their lives.

Sharon was criticized for eating luxury food in the midst of war, but he pointed out that he never bought this sort of food, and as it had been a gift he saw no reason why he should not share it out for everyone to enjoy. As he put it, "The mysterious package seemed to land on our heads in the same way that manna arrived in the midst of the Israelites when they were crossing this very desert in the opposite direction."

Years afterward Stacher told the authors that he had sent the food. "I kept quiet about my gift because people accused me of being involved with criminals and I didn't want to embarrass Sharon. I sent the stuff just to express my admiration for him and his staff. Meyer and I had used the same tactics of striking hard when least expected when we were fighting the Irish in the old days on the Lower East Side. Of course the defeat of the Egyptians was far more important, but I like to see a man go on the attack, and that's what Sharon did."

After his wife's death Stacher was involved in a number of love affairs. One of his girl friends was twenty-two-year-old Helen Cole, who worked as a secretary. She shared Stacher's affections with Dolly Gurevitz, a redheaded law student. Helen tells the story of her romance with Stacher this way: "I was sitting in a coffee house in Tel Aviv when a man in a dark suit, smoking a cigar, came up to me and put down on my table two hundred Israeli pounds. 'It's for you, baby,' he said. I didn't want to take the money. In fact I gave it back to him. Then he invited me to have dinner and after that we met very frequently. I didn't care if he was a gangster and the head of the Jewish Mafia, as he was called. He had immense charm and personality. But I was intrigued by his past and I used to ask him about it. He would just laugh and say, 'Questions are asked only at Passover, and it's not Passover time. No more questions, Helen.' It amused me that a man who was supposed to have been a great bootlegger didn't make use of his own goods. The only thing I ever saw him drink was milk.

"Joe was great fun to be with," Helen Cole went on. "He loved to joke in his juicy American slang, and we went to all the best places. He had his own valet and his own chauffeur. He lived in great luxury and went swimming every day to keep fit.

"When Frank Sinatra came to Israel I went with Joe to see the show in Jerusalem, and afterward we had dinner with Sinatra. They were very good friends, I could see, Joe and Frank. Joe told me he loved Frank like a brother."

Dolly Gurevitz also enjoyed Stacher's attentions. "When he was introduced to me, he said I reminded him of an old friend of his, a film actress known as Jean Harlow. I'd never heard of her, but later I read about her and discovered that she had been the girl friend of Howard Hughes and some gangsters. Joe used to tell me how much he loved gambling and about the times he spent fortunes in his casinos with famous people. The only times he ever sounded homesick were when he talked about Las Vegas."

The publicity Stacher received for his various exploits, especially his financial manipulations, did not help Meyer Lansky. Lansky too applied for citizenship, but found that the Ministry of the Interior, which had been criticized for the way Stacher had gone about getting an Israeli passport, was now far more cautious. If Joseph Stacher was allowed to remain in peace in Israel, the same cannot be said for Meyer Lansky.

In 1971, soon after Lansky went to Israel, he was indicted by a federal grand jury in Nevada for conspiring to defraud the U.S. government of income tax on $36,000,000 in profit from crime syndicate operations in Las Vegas. Lansky, through his lawyers, was already petitioning for Israeli citizenship on the basis of the law of return, part of the legal doctrine of Israel since 1950. When it was established the law said simply that any Jew whose mother was Jewish had the right to go to Israel and become a citizen.

This was the situation until 1962, when Dr. Robert Soblen fled to Israel from the United States after conviction for conspiracy to commit espionage. By law Soblen should have been allowed to stay, but very heavy pressure was exerted on the Israeli government to have him sent back to New York. Robert Kennedy, the American attorney general, cabled Prime Minister David Ben Gurion in protest, and the Israeli ambassador in Washington was told that the United States would be extremely displeased if Soblen was not returned immediately.

Israel's defense depended on American support, and there was no way to resist such high-level pressure. Seventy-two hours after Soblen arrived in Israel he was placed aboard a plane at Lod Airport. Waiting for him was an FBI agent who was supposed to guard him all the way back across the Atlantic. Soblen secreted a knife from his lunch tray, covered himself with a blanket, and cut his wrists. When the plane reached Heathrow Airport, in England, Soblen was taken to a London hospital and died there.

Because of the Soblen scandal, the 1950 law of return was

amended with a clause that permits the denial of Israeli citizenship to a person with a criminal past likely to endanger public welfare.

Lansky's wife joined him in Tel Aviv, but life there was not easy for them. The American authorities exerted immense pressure on the Israelis to have Lansky returned to the United States to face the charges against him.

On May 18, 1971, the American Embassy in Tel Aviv wrote Lansky that his passport had been canceled. Then Minister of Interior Dr. Yosef Burg flew to the United States for discussions with the Justice Department, which provided the Israelis with a number of documents and books reciting Lansky's activities. Included was a report by Professor D. R. Cressey, a member of the President's Commission on Law Enforcement and Administration of Justice, called *Theft of the Nation*, published in 1969. Israelis read a summary of Professor Cressey's report in the *Jerusalem Post:*

> The career of Meyer Lansky, a poor Russian immigrant, who began his work in organized crime as an executioner and boasts that his enterprise is bigger than United States Steel, is not likely to be frequently duplicated in the future. For that matter, even now there are few businessmen, criminal or noncriminal, who possess the untrained organizational genius which enabled Lansky to become the world's most successful money mover and corruptor. Specifically, toleration of Lansky probably rests on Cosa Nostra's need for expert knowledge about gambling, especially casino gambling.

The Justice Department also gave the Israelis a list of Lansky's criminal convictions, which moved the Minister of Interior to say that these seemed remarkably mild for a man who was supposed to be such a notorious criminal. The Justice Department had an answer to this: the insignificance of Lansky's criminal convictions was due to the fact that local sheriffs and other law enforcement officers were in Lansky's pay or otherwise indebted to him. However, they had been forced in 1950 and 1953 to bring at least minor charges against Lansky because of the publicity he was receiving. And the authorities pointed out that there were charges against Lansky, including two outstanding indictments, one by a Florida grand jury on March 25, 1971, and the other by the Nevada grand jury, both connected with illicit gambling activities. It was because of these indictments that Lansky's passport had been canceled.

The Minister of Interior was told further that perhaps the most damning allegations against Lansky were in the report of a special committee headed by Senator Estes Kefauver of Tennessee. During 1950 and 1951 the Kefauver Committee had heard hundreds of witnesses, including Lansky and other top-ranking gangsters, and it had concluded that gambling enterprises in the United States were the bedrock of organized crime in American cities. The men operating these gambling enterprises were "the survivors of the murderous underworld wars of the prohibition era," and crime was now "on a syndicated basis to a substantial extent in many cities." The report added that there were two such major crime syndicates, one of them centered in Chicago and the other the Costello-Adonis-Lansky syndicate based in New York.

The Israelis were told that Lansky had refused to answer the committee's questions about his business activities and his associations with such people as Lucky Luciano, Frank Costello, and Joe Adonis. A witness who had talked was a man called Barney Rudinsky, who claimed he was employed as a debt collector for gambling clubs. He claimed he had never killed anyone without a go-ahead from above, and that until at least 1940, killings had to be cleared with Lansky.

The Kefauver investigations had their origins in two conferences the senator attended in 1950, the American Conference of Mayors and the United States Attorney's Conference. At the first of these gatherings he heard such figures as Fletcher Bowron of Los Angeles and De Lesseps Morrison of New Orleans say that organized crime was out of control in America's cities. These two mayors and others who knew about local conditions claimed that they were totally unable to do anything about this very serious and growing problem.

The U.S. attorneys, however, told Kefauver that this was an exaggeration, that there was no serious organized crime problem in America. According to these specialists, there were hoodlums all over the country but they were no real problem to municipal and local authorities who had the guts to go after them.

Kefauver went back to the Capitol and sponsored a resolution to create a Special Senate Committee to Investigate Organized Crime in Interstate Commerce, and the committee was established in May 1950 under his chairmanship. Although his targets accused him of using his anticrime crusade to further his own political ambitions, there is no doubt that Kefauver during the years 1950-1951 exposed more information about criminal activities in America, and delved into those activities more searchingly than any similar investigation before or since. What increased the impact of his hearings was that they coincided with the time when television was becoming a major news and entertainment medium. Millions watched his "circus" as the committee moved from city to city around the country.

Kefauver began his hearings on May 26, 1950, in Miami. He was helped there by the fact that a great deal of work had already been carried out by the Greater Miami Crime Commission, headed by Dan Sullivan. This was Lansky territory and the names of Meyer and Jake cropped up in the hearings again and again.

In October 1950, Lansky was called to testify in New York City. Disregarding advice, he appeared without counsel and quietly refused to answer a great many questions. Nor would he produce his business records; he explained that the revenue people were investigating them. He acknowledged knowing such gangsters as Charles and Rocco Fischetti, Tony Accordo, Jack Dragna from California, Trigger Mike Coppola, Longie Zwillman, Joseph Stacher, Frank Costello, Joe Adonis, and Frank Erickson. He knew Phil Kastel and had also been a lifelong friend of Charlie Luciano, whom he had recently visited in Italy.

When Lansky was subpoenaed a second time, Moses Polakoff appeared with him. Elderly Senator Charles W. Tobey of New Hampshire, a committee member, startled onlookers by attacking Polakoff because he had defended Luciano: "How did you become counsel for such a dirty rat as that? Aren't there some ethics in the legal profession?"

Polakoff replied indignantly, "Minorities and undesirables and persons with bad reputations are more entitled to the protection of the law than are the so-called honorable people. I don't have to apologize to you."

Senator Tobey retorted, "I look upon you in amazement," and Polakoff said, "I look upon you in amazement, a Senator of the United States, for making such a statement."

After Kefauver intervened to cool the atmosphere—"Mr. Lansky is the witness"—Polakoff described Lansky's and Luciano's cooperation with the Navy during the Second World War. But the committee focused on many areas involving Lansky, including his links with many forms of organized crime, his juke-box industry, and, of course, his gambling investments.

For almost a year and a half the Kefauver Committee listened to more than six hundred witnesses, from criminals to high officials.

Kefauver himself became so well known that he nearly became the Democratic presidential candidate in 1952. After all the hearings were ended, the committee issued a sobering report:

> The structure of organized crime today is far different from what it was many years ago. Its power for evil is infinitely greater. The unit of organized crime used to be an individual gang consisting of a number of hoodlums, whose activities were obviously predatory in character. Individual gangs tended to specialize in specific types of criminal activity such as payroll or bank robbery, loft or safe burglary, pocket picking, etc. . . .
>
> New types of criminal gangs . . . emerged during prohibition. The huge profits earned in that era together with the development of twentieth-century transportation and communication made possible larger and much more powerful gangs, covering much greater territory. Organized crime in the last thirty years has taken on new characteristics. The most dangerous criminal gangs today are not specialists in one type of predatory crime, but engage in many and varied forms of criminality. . . . The more dangerous criminal elements draw most of their revenues from various forms of gambling, the sale and distribution of narcotics, prostitution, various forms of business and labor racketeering, black-market practices, bootlegging into dry areas, etc. . . .
>
> We have seen evidence of the operation of the Costello-Adonis-Lansky crime syndicate, whose headquarters is in New York, in such places as Bergen County, N.J., Saratoga, N.Y., Miami, Fla., New Orleans, Nevada, the West Coast, and Havana, Cuba. . . .
>
> The Mafia is the cement that helps to bind the Costello-Adonis-Lansky syndicate of New York and the Accardo-Guzik-Fischetti syndicate of Chicago as well as smaller criminal gangs and individual criminals throughout the country. These groups have kept in touch with Luciano since his deportation from this country. . . .
>
> The Mafia today acts closely with many persons who are not of Sicilian descent. . . .

Lansky discussed his Kefauver Committee appearances in detail with the authors. "I was called twice to testify," he said. "Kefauver wanted me to tell him all about the connection between gamblers and the politicians, and between the bookmakers in the hotels in Florida and what he called 'organized crime.'

"People don't know this, but I was called to see Kefauver in private between the times I appeared before him in public. I knew he liked to gamble, so I asked him, 'What's so bad about gambling? You like it yourself, I know you've gambled a lot.'

"Kefauver smiled at me and said, 'That's quite right. But I don't want you people to control it.' I was convinced that he meant 'you Jews and you Italians,' and that infuriated me. I said to him, 'I'm not a kneeling Jew coming to sing songs in your ears. I'm not one of those Jewish hotel owners in Miami Beach who tell you all sorts of stories just to please you.' Kefauver saw I was angry. He said, 'Mr. Lansky, you're very famous,' but I didn't swallow that bait. I said to him, 'I will not allow you to persecute me because I'm a Jew.'

"Suddenly Kefauver switched course and said to me, 'What about your son at West Point?' He was implying that I'd managed to get Paul into West Point by using special connections, and that really made me angry. I told him that my son had got to West Point the same as everyone else did, by getting character recommendations and studying hard for the exams.

"Kefauver saw I was ready to get up and walk out. He said, 'No, no, I've nothing against your son. I won't mention him.'

"But he was a hypocrite. In the very next session of the committee there was a question about how my son got into West Point and Kefauver implied again that I'd used connections."

Lansky spoke more strongly about his personal encounters with Kefauver than about the more recent material on him that the U.S. Department of Justice turned over to the Israeli Interior Department. As the bombardment of information continued, Israelis and the press got the report of another Senate committee, this time headed by Senator John McClellan of Arkansas, which in the late 1950s and early 1960s investigated improper activities of labor and management. Its report called Lansky "one of the country's top gangsters" and associated him with the Mafia. And in July 1971 a Senate committee investigating organized crime was told by Vincent Charles Teresa: "Gambling is the single most important activity for organized crime. . . . Meyer Lansky is the biggest man in the casino gambling business. . . . That's the way it has been for many years."

Teresa, a member of the Mafia, went on to explain:

Gambling is far more important than any other business in the mob. Narcotics may be big in New York with the drug store gangsters but in Boston the leaders wouldn't touch it. . . .

Gambling is the standby and the foundation. From it comes the corrupt politicians and policemen, the bribes and the pay-offs and sometimes murder. If you could crush gambling you would put the mob out of business. You'd have them back on the pushcarts as it was in the old days.

All the other rackets, they are secondary to gambling. They run it all from the housewife that puts a nickel on a number all the way to the casinos in Las Vegas, Monte Carlo, London, Portugal, all over the world. . . . The mob has barrels and barrels of money, and it all starts with the man or woman who puts a nickel on the number at the corner store every day. . . . From that nickel number they have built casinos all over the world, they have gone into legitimate businesses, they've gone into politics and they've paid politicians. What they do with that nickel number is fantastic.

As an example of how the mob's control stretched everywhere, I can tell you about George Raft's Colony Sportsmen's Club in London which is owned by Alfie Sulkin. George Raft was a figurehead until the British deported him. Dino Cellini is involved in that club and so is Meyer Lansky. I know because I ran gambling junkets and we couldn't put a junket in there without their O.K. It's the same at Paradise Island in the Bahamas. Cellini has to O.K. you before you can put a junket in there.

When you lose fifty thousand dollars in London on credit, you don't come and send the money to London. You pay Cellini and Meyer Lansky. . . .

Loan sharking is tied to gambling. Gamblers bet and then can't pay when they lose. Say a man loses two hundred dollars on a firm bet, and doesn't have it. You offer it to him, to be repaid at ten dollars a week and five percent juice. That's the interest per week. When he can't make it with you probably because he's still gambling you offer him more with a little less interest. Pretty soon he owes you a thousand dollars.

The juice is what hits the borrower. On four hundred dollars he owes me, he has to pay me twenty dollars a week, that's only the juice. He can pay me twenty dollars a week for five years and he still owes me four hundred dollars. Most of the people who go to loan sharks are gamblers.

Vincent Teresa's testimony was particularly obnoxious to Lansky, who told the authors he had never met the man and called Teresa's seminar on gambling "a pack of filthy lies."

Also sent to Tel Aviv from Washington was a British document, a Royal Commission report on gambling in the Bahamas in 1967. In this report Sir Stafford Sands, governor of the Islands, stated that Lansky had approached him in 1960 offering him a two-million-dollar check in exchange for a permit to operate gambling clubs in the Bahamas.

In addition, the Minister of Interior had on his desk the testimony of Daniel Francis Ahearn; a Bureau of Narcotics document of July 1961 which asserted that Meyer Lansky was "one of the nation's leading mobsters, one of the top Jewish associates in a syndicate composed of high-ranking hoodlums of Italian extraction who controlled the major rackets in the United States and Canada"; and a report from the Internal Revenue Service stating that "Lansky's history shows that he has been a criminal all of his adult life."

Surmising the dimensions of this barrage, and hoping against hope that he could withstand it and stay in Israel, Lansky told anyone in Tel Aviv who would listen, "If I was guilty of all these crimes, surely the mighty forces of law and order in the United States would have brought me to justice long ago."

35 Outgunned by Phantoms

Lansky pulled every string he could to get permission to stay in Israel and become a citizen. Back in the United States there was heavy pressure on Samuel Rothberg, one of the early Flamingo investors, to do what he could to help his old friend Meyer. As a leading figure in the Israel Investors Corporation, Rothberg had played a prominent role in supporting Israel financially, and he was able to ask his close friend Louis H. Boyar for help.

Boyar, a wealthy Los Angeles businessman, was at various times vice president of the American Friends of the Hebrew University and a member of the university board of governors; chairman of the board of governors of the Israel Bond Organization; and chairman of the board of the Israel Investors Corporation. He was involved in philanthropy in the United States and in Israel, and had made a million-dollar donation to start the Los Angeles Chemistry Compound at the Hebrew University. Boyar's wife died in the 1960s and he gave the money for the Mae Boyar High School in Jerusalem as a memorial for her.

This particular American had great influence in Israel, and his influence was not merely a matter of donations. It went straight to the top—to Golda Meir, then the Prime Minister.

Boyar and Golda Meir had been close childhood friends. She had emigrated to Palestine, but Louis had stayed in the United States and built a multimillionaire's fortune with a building and construction business in Los Angeles. On one of his frequent trips to Israel, Lou Boyar renewed his friendship with Mrs. Meir, and after that they got together whenever he was in the country. They were extremely fond of each other. When they met they embraced warmly and they had dinner together whenever the busy Prime Minister could find time. Lou made no secret of his admiration for Golda, and she in turn showed how fond she was of him by giving several garden parties in his honor.

The staff at the Goulash Restaurant, their favorite haunt, always gave the couple a quiet table in the corner, and there in the summer of 1971 Lou reached across the table, took Golda's hand, and proposed marriage. Golda leaned across the table and kissed her old friend, but as she said afterward to her colleagues, making no secret of the proposal, "I was married once when I was nineteen, and once was enough for me." She told Boyar, "I'm very grateful and flattered, but I think it's better if we remain friends."

Not long after the marriage proposal, Sam Rothberg visited Boyar in Israel. Lansky drove to Jerusalem to meet the two men at the Tower Suite of the King David Hotel. At first Lou Boyar was indignant at being asked to intervene in a matter that had nothing to do with him. He told Lansky bluntly, "Let's not mix the old past with the beautiful present of Israel." Then Rothberg intervened, reminded his old friend about their long friendship, and pleaded that surely this was the time to return the favors Lansky had done for Israel. Boyar reluctantly promised to help, and, having promised, he arranged to make his pitch for Lansky under the best possible circumstances.

He invited Golda Meir to have lunch with him at the Goulash Restaurant, and as usual she found time for her old friend. Lou Boyar was the first to arrive. In the Chevrolet car he used in Israel he drove out to the restaurant, which is in the Bet Hakerem (House of the Vineyard) district, in a romantic garden surrounded by olive trees. The restaurant itself is tiny, with only a few tables, and was built out of the ruins of an old Arab home. Minutes later the Prime Minister's limousine, driven at great speed by her chauffeur, swept up to park beside Boyar's gray Chevy. Golda's four-man body-guard team, known locally as the gorillas, were out of the car the second it came to a stop.

One opened the door for her, two searched the garden and prowled among the olive trees, while the fourth went in the restaurant to check out the other patrons. With their walkie-talkies they kept in contact with each other while they patrolled through-out the lunch.

One of the bodyguards was Mordechi Rachamim, who had won fame when serving as a security guard aboard a Zurich-bound El Al plane. As it landed the aircraft was attacked by a squad of Palestinian terrorists. The first one off the plane, Mordechi let fly with his Baretta and killed or wounded every one of the attackers, although they had machine guns and hand grenades. Mrs. Meir was so impressed by his bravery that she appointed him one of her bodyguards.

Seated in the Goulash, Boyar and Mrs. Meir talked quietly, then Boyar switched to Yiddish for his appeal. He urged the Prime Minister not to be too harsh against Lansky, saying to her, "You know what it was like in those days. There were a lot of very poor Jews and they did what they could to survive in the United States. Meyer Lansky's no angel, but I don't think he'll do Israel any disservice." He mentioned Lansky's work for Israel and went on to make what his friends later described as a "big speech" on Lansky's behalf.

At first Mrs. Meir was shocked. She told her friend that this was a matter of high politics and old friendships didn't count. "The State of Israel," she said, "cannot become involved in sentimental issues about old times," and she lectured Boyar very firmly. Israel's first Prime Minister, Ben Gurion, was right when he described her as "the only man in my cabinet."

Yet Boyar's plea did have some result. Golda Meir had been thinking of having Meyer Lansky expelled immediately, and instead, after she had regained her temper, she told Boyar she would leave the matter to the courts.

Boyar then appealed directly to Burg, the Minister of Interior, and asked him to let Lansky stay in Israel, again pointing out the services Lansky had rendered the country. Relations between Boyar and Golda were cool for a while, but their old friendship soon reasserted itself. When Louis Boyar died of a heart attack in 1976, there was a large funeral and tributes from all over the world flowed in, but Boyar might have been most pleased by a note to his family that read simply, "Deepest condolences from an old friend, Golda."

Boyar's intervention may have been responsible for a reprieve for Meyer Lansky, but meantime "Lansky fever" was increasing in the Israeli newspapers and apparently in U.S. officialdom. Via the American Embassy in Paris the Bureau of Narcotics and Dangerous Drugs sent a message to M. Nepote, Secretary General of Interpol, at his headquarters in Paris, that they were on the track of a

John Baruche, who was the representative in Paris of Saul Gelb, Nathan Behrman, and Anthony Velluci in an operation that transferred twenty-five kilograms of heroin per month to the United States.

Baruche's "mentor," the notorious Saul Gelb, after serving almost ten years for narcotics prosecutions in 1955 and 1958, had "reestablished himself as a major importer of heroin in New York City." In the past, Gelb's narcotic trafficking operations had "come under the aegis of Meyer Lansky and Harry Stromberg. Stromberg . . . was convicted in the same narcotic prosecution in Federal Court in New York City with Gelb, Behrman, and Velluci." The letter continued:

> It is noted that a report emanating from New York and transmitted by this office to ICPO-Interpol in Tel Aviv . . . alleged that Lansky and Stromberg were in Tel Aviv along with Hyman Seigel, Didy Bloom, and Joseph Stature negotiating a narcotic transaction.
>
> The possibility exists that Lansky's and Stromberg's visit to Tel Aviv, if a fact, is related to Gelb and Baruche's activity.
>
> The Hyman Seigel reported is believed identical to a criminal associate of Lansky named Hyman Sigal. Didy Bloom is believed identical to Solomon Bloom, alias "Blubber" . . . a known associate of Gelb and Stromberg.
>
> The Joseph Stature reported is apparently identical to Joseph Stacher, alias "Doc," born in Russia on September 6, 1901. Our files reveal that Stacher, a notorious figure in underworld organized gambling activity in the United States, [lives] in Tel Aviv . . .
>
> ICPO-Interpol (C.N.B.) Tel Aviv is kindly requested to advise if any evidence of travel to Tel Aviv by Meyer Lansky, Hyman Sigal, Harry Stromberg, and Solomon Bloom has been uncovered on or about November 21, 1970.

The report was signed by John T. Cusack, regional director of the bureau. Copies were sent to Interpol offices in Madrid, Wiesbaden, Rome, Paris, Berne, Brussels, and Tel Aviv. The Tel Aviv authorities panicked, and at least three North Americans were refused entry. When Ben Sigelbaum, Lansky's friend from Florida, flew to Israel, he was sent back on the next plane out. The same thing happened to businessmen named Bernard Rose and

Jacob Marcus. No evidence was ever publicly produced to justify labeling any of the three men "criminals," as they were called by newspapers like *Maariv* at the time. Sigelbaum protested that he had been to Israel eight times before without any problems—but he would never go there again. Later, when the hysteria died down, Bernard Rose visited Israel again and was allowed to enter without any problems.

The Ministry of Interior denied Lansky's petition for citizenship. The only recourse now was Israel's supreme court, the High Court of Justice. Wearing a light blue blazer and dark blue trousers, Meyer Lansky, looking trim and self-assured, attended the hearing of the High Court of Justice in Jerusalem at which the decision about his application to remain in Israel as an Israeli citizen was handed down. In his petition to the court Lansky had claimed that he was being subjected to a campaign of besmirchment in which he was falsely accused of being a leader of organized crime in the United States. "All I did was run gambling clubs, and I had retired from such activities as early as the 1950s," he asserted.

Lansky also told the court that until 1959 he had been involved in different kinds of businesses such as distribution of juke boxes, ownership of supermarkets, partnerships in race tracks and hotels dealing with gambling. He claimed that in 1959 he retired, withdrawing from all his businesses, and had not returned to any such activities from that date onward. He said that his capital had been invested in oil wells and real estate in the United States, and that for more than a decade he had not been involved with gambling at all. Again Lansky insisted that the material the American government had provided to the Israelis was gossip and ruinous defamation.

The verdict again denied him citizenship. In September 1972, Israel's five-judge supreme court concurred unanimously with the Ministry of Interior's action. "There are grounds to suspect," said the court, "that Lansky has been involved in operations of great violence by organized crime."

Neither Lansky nor the public had any idea at the time that a far stronger persuader than his criminal record had been invoked to insure that the decisions went against him. During this period Israel was counting heavily on the arrival of American-made 114OE Phantom fighter bombers for its defense. Since the Six-Day War of 1967 the Israeli government had become totally reliant on America for arms. President de Gaulle of France had canceled Israel's contract for more of the Mirage jets which had played such an important role in the victory over the Arab countries in that lightning campaign. Jerusalem was deeply concerned about the arrival of Soviet antiaircraft missiles in Egypt manned by Russian crews, and Russian pilots were found to be actually flying the advanced MIGs supplied by Moscow. Israel's aging Mirage fleet was no match for the new Russian planes pouring into Egypt. Golda Meir and her cabinet were well aware of how desperately they needed the modern Phantoms. At the moment when Meyer Lansky was fighting to become an Israeli citizen, the American Phantoms were just beginning to roar across the Mediterranean skies to land at Israeli military bases.

A threat was made, chiefly through Israeli Ambassador Yitzhak Rabin, during the winter of 1970. Beneath Washington's diplomatic language, the essence was: Unless you return Lansky to the United States, there are going to be problems about the delivery of any more Phantoms.

The message was as brutal as that. Any hesitation about expelling Lansky became irrelevant. And yet there may have been some small cracks in bureaucratic unanimity. *Time* magazine complained that although "American officials have made it clear that they would like to get their hands on Lansky, the Israelis seemed curiously uncooperative." And it reported that Interior Minister Burg had stated that Lansky would be "granted special travel documents that would allow him to go to any country that would accept him."

36 "Welcome Back, Mr. Lansky"

Five days before his tourist visa expired, on November 5, 1972, Lansky decided to leave Israel voluntarily. His friends in the country included two Israeli generals who had grown fond of him and who believed his account of being a victim of anti-Semitism. They advised him not to go. "The police won't dare take you by force and stick you on a plane or a ship leaving Israel," they said. But Lansky replied, "If I'm not going to be welcome here, I'd better go."

In the last weeks before his departure he sent urgent requests to Europe and Latin America to try to get visas. He had no intention of returning to the United States, where it looked as if the full force of the government was going to be turned loose on him. Stacher came to Lansky's aid and traveled around the world trying to organize a safe refuge for his friend. As Stacher rightly guessed, the only problem was how much money would be needed to bribe officials.

The first country that agreed to allow Lansky to stay was Paraguay, which consented to grant Lansky a laissez-passer. Bribing Paraguay was an old custom, and the irony of the situation struck Lansky. A number of Nazi criminals had also been granted asylum in that South American republic, including the notorious Dr. Josef Mengele, who had carried out medical experiments on children and adults in concentration camps.

The president of Paraguay, General Stroessner, himself of German origin, was quite happy, however, to welcome anybody who had cash in his pocket. Although he was depressed by the fact that he would not be allowed to remain in Israel, Lansky maintained his sense of humor and said to the authors, "I've always served Israel as best I can. Perhaps in Paraguay I will carry out a last favor for the Jews. I'll go looking for Mengele." He grinned and added, "Should I make the people who protect him an offer they cannot refuse?"

Smoking one of his favorite Silva-Thin American cigarettes, Lansky left his Tel Aviv apartment on the morning of Sunday, November 5, on his way to the airport. His wife's tourist visa was still good. She and their dog would be left behind again, until Lansky found a more or less permanent place. Stacher had obtained travel documents for him, and the Israeli government had helped get permission for him to travel safely to several South American countries, including Venezuela, El Salvador, and Panama.

Lansky had bought a number of different airline tickets, hoping his departure could be secret. Publicity now would be not only an affront to his personal style but a real danger. Wearing a hat and dark glasses, Lansky passed quickly through customs at Tel Aviv's airport. There were no journalists around, and Lansky assumed that all was well.

His only companion was a young, sturdily built Israeli named Joseph "Yoskeh" Shiner. This moustachioed Israeli had worked for his country's security for many years and had been Prime Minister Ben Gurion's personal bodyguard as he traveled around the world. Shiner had left the Secret Service and gone to work for Lansky some months earlier. He had gone ahead of Lansky in the previous weeks and scouted out the places where he thought Lansky might be safe.

But neither Lansky nor Shiner knew that Prime Minister Meir had given strict orders that every movement of Lansky's was to be reported to President Nixon. She was not going to jeopardize the vitally needed Phantoms, no matter whose friend Lansky was.

No sooner had Lansky handed over his passport at the airport than the police stationed there telephoned the Special Affairs Department at Israeli Police Headquarters in Jerusalem. Within seconds Jerusalem was on the line to the FBI station at the American Embassy in Tel Aviv, passing on the exact flight number of the Swissair plane taking Lansky to Europe. This was in turn flashed to American agents in Berne and Geneva.

And so it came about that Lansky's departure from Israel became a forty-hour nightmare. At Geneva, where the plane landed first, Lansky found himself confronting two FBI agents and a posse of Swiss security men. "From that moment on," Lansky says, "I felt like a satellite being traced by stations all over the earth. I hadn't planned to stay in Switzerland anyway, so I took the next flight to Rio de Janeiro, again with Swissair. When I landed there after a long, tiring flight, a Swissair man came up and told me that they no longer wanted me as a customer. He said he had arranged for me to go to Paraguay via Buenos Aires, but not aboard a Swiss plane. He had booked me on an American airline, Braniff."

Said Lansky, "It was obvious that the FBI took advantage of my long flight to Rio to make sure that I'd be put on board an American plane, and one that was scheduled to go on to the United States."

For the four hours he was in Buenos Aires Lansky was kept under guard. Then, when the plane landed in Paraguay, Lansky had a moment when he thought he might be allowed to stay there after all. He was not hindered at passport control when he presented his Paraguayan papers; he even got as far as the cable office at the airport, where he sent a message to his wife in Israel: "Everything is fine."

Then Shiner said, "We're being followed by two FBI agents," and though the Americans kept their distance, immigration officials surrounded Lansky. He protested, pointing out that his papers and visa were valid and had been accepted earlier, but the officials shrugged and forced him to get back on board the Braniff plane. Lansky thought then, and says it was confirmed for him later, that the FBI "put enormous pressure on the Paraguayan authorities not to let me stay there."

At this stage Lansky suggested to his bodyguard, "Look, there's no point in you coming with me. It's clear now that I'm going to be taken back to the United States no matter what." Shiner, however, decided that he would see the mission through.

For the rest of the journey FBI agents stayed close to Lansky and Shiner. When the plane landed at the next stop, La Paz, two Bolivian civilians climbed aboard and told Lansky that he would not even be allowed into the transit area, so all four men remained on board, Shiner next to Lansky and the FBI agents directly behind. In Lima, a platoon of armed policemen surrounded the plane, "as if we had been hijacked. They said, 'You can't come onto our territory.' I said, 'I don't have the plague.' But the official wasn't amused. He was scared and nervous," Lansky remembers.

"My last chance before Miami was Panama City. I had a perfectly good Panamanian visa, but a policeman came up to me as I started to get off the plane and repeated the message I'd heard all over South America: 'You are not permitted to enter our country.'"

Said Lansky, "I was not frightened but I was terribly tired, and I had the feeling of a hunted animal trying to get out of a trap. No matter which way it turns, it's always caught. That was a very disagreeable sensation. When we finally landed at Miami the two agents were highly relieved. They'd been very tense all the way, sitting still and pretending I didn't exist.

"Suddenly, as the plane swooped in over Miami, I stopped being angry. I had changed and shaved and was ready for anything. And 'anything' turned out to be three more FBI men. Before they joined their two friends on the plane, one of them said to me, 'Welcome back, Mr. Lansky.' There was a tone of irony in his voice, but I wasn't being ironic when I told him, 'O.K., O.K., I'm doomed to fight till the end of my days. If you want a fight you'll get it.'"

The agents then arrested Lansky, holding him by both arms as they left the airport. One of them told the assembled crowd of journalists, "With a man of his wealth a very high bond will have to be set to assure his appearance in court." A Justice Department spokesman added that Lansky faced a five-year sentence and a ten-thousand-dollar fine on a racketeering count and a one-to-five-year stretch on tax evasion and gambling debts.

Lansky came back to Miami on November 7, 1972, two and a half years after his arrival in Israel. The fight was on immediately. U.S. Attorney Robert Rust said, "This isn't going to be a case where a man can just flash a roll of money and walk out." David Rosen, representing Lansky, objected to the very high bail asked for his client, and Lansky was finally released on bail of $650,000. As he was being driven back to his apartment on Collins Avenue, he noticed a ticket for illegal parking attached to the windshield of his car.

Meyer Lansky was promptly admitted to a Miami hospital for the treatment of "cardiac insufficiency," as a spokesman at the hospital said, and the case did not come up for trial until the following year.

On February 27, 1973, Lansky went on trial in federal district court in Miami on charges of criminal contempt for failing to obey a subpoena to appear in 1971 before the grand jury investigating his tax affairs. There were other charges against him too, some years later. In February 1977, when Lansky was seventy-five, he was questioned about the murder of Mafia member John Rosselli, whose body was found in an oil drum in Biscayne Bay in August 1976, not long after he had given a Senate intelligence committee some information about his role in the alleged CIA plot to assassinate Fidel Castro. Questioned with Lansky was Anthony Giacalone, who was also being questioned about the disappearance of Jimmy Hoffa, the former head of the Teamsters. At the same time the indictment against Lansky for conspiring to conceal his ownership of the Flamingo Hotel in Las Vegas and evading taxes on $36,000,000 in earnings was still outstanding in federal court in Nevada.

Lansky fought these cases, as he had promised, and as he did so he remained bitter—or perhaps more hurt than bitter—about his eviction from Israel. He told the authors, "I was accused by a few slanderers, writers and reporters who lined their pockets with the money they made by calling me a gangster. In Jerusalem not one person was brought to accuse me personally, nor was I put on the stand to be questioned under oath. I was a Jew among people of my own heritage, who have suffered so much in history by being accused without trial. Now they were wronging me in the same way. When I was flying around South America I could fully understand why I was not allowed to land in any of those countries. Why should any Christian country have a Jew that his own wouldn't accept? I know now that the Israeli authorities themselves worked with Interpol and with the FBI to track me down. This was strictly against the court ruling in Israel, in which it was agreed that I should have a laissez-passer that let me leave Israel freely. I've been told that Interpol agreed to help the FBI because they'd been told from America that I was a drug trafficker. And all those South American countries had been told the same thing.

"That trip could have broken me. My heart nearly went for the second time. I'd had a heart by-pass operation several years before, and the stress of that flight was dangerous. But I survived, and in spite of all I have no quarrel with the Israeli people. I feel I am one of them. I'm angry only with the Israeli government and officials. I've told you about some of the ways I worked for Israel. I also did other things that I took entirely for granted at the time, but maybe they ought to go into the record now. We raised money in our casinos for the United Jewish Appeal, for one thing. The first fund raising in Miami for the State of Israel was organized and initiated in my casino in the Colonial Inn. That was a great evening, with over a thousand people partying and pledging money for Israel.

"The same thing happened in Las Vegas. From time to time big shots would come out and say, 'Meyer, get some of the boys—we need so many millions for Israel.'

"In 1967, during the Six-Day War, I went myself to speak to some of the boys in Miami who were not known as generous when it came to making contributions. I told them this was the time for them to open their pockets, and open them wide. I still keep the letter from my rabbi in Miami Beach, Rabbi Shapiro from the Sinai Synagogue, thanking me for my efforts. So you can understand why I'm angry at the Israeli government—which by the way won't even give me a visitor's visa these days."

As Meyer Lansky fought his court battles in the United States, the controversy over his expulsion rumbled on. Many Israelis continued to protest the decision, and Lansky made several pleas, both directly and through friends in Israel, for the government to change its mind. At the end of 1977 he appealed to the new Israeli Prime Minister, Menachem Begin, asking him to grant him a tourist visa. As Lansky says, "I've traveled all over Europe and now I can even go to Egypt. Why can't I go to Israel?" But apparently the very heavy pressure exerted on Golda Meir still applies to succeeding Israeli governments.

37 Dinner in Miami

In late 1978 Meyer Lansky had dinner with his brother, Jake, and Uri Dan at the Embers, Lansky's favorite restaurant in Miami Beach.

Neat and trim in a gray suit and open-neck shirt, he was recognized by most of the diners. Many who knew him greeted him warmly. Even strangers would come up and say "Hello, how are you, Mr. Lansky?" The patient center of attention would usually stand and swap a few courtesies, then, when he sat down again, sometimes he would whisper, "Who the hell was that? I don't recognize him." He is treated rather like an elderly dignitary and a table is always available for him, no matter how crowded the restaurant.

"Both Teddy and I like living in Miami," he said, "and now that I'm retired we have more time together. But our dearest wish is to be allowed to spend our last days in Israel. To be buried near my grandfather is something I dream about.

"When I was forced to return to the United States in 1971, the reason given was that I was to be tried for my so-called crimes. Well, there've been several court actions, but not a single one of them ended with a guilty verdict. Apparently I'm an innocent man. Surely that's enough proof that the Israelis shouldn't have given in to American pressure.

"Like any family, Teddy and I have had our problems. You've probably heard about the death of Teddy's son Richard."

Yes, Uri Dan knew that in October 1977 Richard Schwartz, one of Lansky's wife's four children from her previous marriage, was shot to death as he sat in a car parked behind his restaurant in Bay Harbor Island, Florida. Schwartz had been scheduled to go on trial on charges of killing Craig Teriaca, son of an alleged underworld figure named Vincent Teriaca. Teriaca had been killed four months before, when he and Schwartz were drinking together and quarreling over paying for a drink. Schwartz pulled out a pistol and shot Teriaca twice in the chest.

It was widely believed in Florida that this was a revenge killing and that Lansky's stepson had been involved with the Mafia. Lansky simply said, "You see, Richard had been drinking too much. He was really an alcoholic—and carrying a gun when you're drinking is crazy, never mind that his was licensed. Several months before he died he had started swinging his gun around a lot. I think it went off accidentally and killed the man he was drinking with. Richard had four children—one of them spent two years in a kibbutz in Israel, by the way. I'm sure his death wasn't vengeance by the Mafia. It was probably suicide, a straightforward family tragedy.

"My own children are all adults now," Lansky went on, "and I love seeing them and spending time with my grandchildren. But they know I want to live in Israel and they've all promised to visit me there if I'm finally allowed to go."

The dinner at the Embers was during the Jewish Chanukah, the festival of lights. In New York, Miami Beach, and other cities, Chanukah signs share pride of place with Christmas trees, since the two holidays are both in December. Banks advertise special Chanukah savings plans along with their Christmas clubs.

Eating his favorite dish, the stone crabs, Lansky said reminiscently, "One of the most impressive things that ever happened to me was to be in Israel at Chanukah time. All over Tel Aviv there were those thousands of children marching through the streets singing, holding their candles and flashlights. When I was their age I was holding the cover of a garbage can, or whatever was handy, to defend myself against rocks and brickbats. Then I would counter-attack with my own bricks."

Jake, Meyer's brother, broad-shouldered, with deep-set eyes and heavy eyebrows, intervened. "Meyer was very brave. He was small but he was afraid of nobody and nothing."

The conversation moves easily from past to present. Lansky is a little sad as he remarks that the dog that was with him and Teddy in

Tel Aviv is blind now. "But he still enjoys his walks and so do I. I spend my evenings watching television or reading," he adds.

He talks a bit about his long war with the press, and it is apparent that he still cares a lot about what is said about him. "Anti-Semites have used my name to attack Jews," he believes. "They've always tried to find reasons to attack me and point out my Jewish background." Yes, he had seen the far-right newspaper *Spotlight*, published in Washington in July 1978, describing him as the reigning chairman of the National Crime Syndicate. Lansky, it said, had even penetrated the Carter Administration, and he was given the title he and Luciano had laughed at so long ago, "Boss of all the Bosses."

The Soviet Union too, in its persistent anti-Israel and anti-Jewish propaganda war, has mentioned Meyer Lansky as a prime example of the "Jewish criminal" who rules the United States. In 1978 the Soviet weekly *Nadliya* said:

> During the 1930s Jewish gangs ruled and controlled the underworld in New York and their leaders were Meyer Lansky and Bugsy Siegel. When the state of Israel was created Meyer Lansky was at the head of the world of crime in the United States. This murderer became the chief bookkeeper of the Mafia and one of the leaders of Murder Incorporated. The American gangster helped Israel to such an extent that Tel Aviv granted him and other generals of the American Mafia without any hesitation citizenship of Israel.
>
> If we remember that Israel has become the new promised land of crime, prostitution and corruption, there is no doubt that in the Israeli army you can find many people like them.

Lansky is asked a question, "If you had your life to live over again, would you lead it any other way?" He thinks for a while and says, "When you ask me that question you send me back to my youth. When I was young I thought Jews should be treated like other people. I remembered that young soldier in Grodno who said Jews should stand up and fight. I guess you could say I've come a long way from Grodno and a long way from the Lower East Side, but I still believe him.

"I wouldn't have lived my life any other way. It was in my blood, my character. Environment certainly had something to do with it, but basically my own personality determined my fate. But I don't mean the personality that the books and magazines give me. People have accused me of all sorts of crimes, but the accusation I still mind the most is that I killed Bugsy Siegel, who was my dear friend always. I kept in touch with his family after he was killed and I saw his granddaughter in the summer of 1971, when she visited Israel. I told her how her grandfather and I had grown up together, and I talked about how it used to be for Jews in this country. Bugsy and I never could stand hypocrisy. People would come to our casinos and gamble and then go back to Washington or New York and make pious speeches about how immoral gambling was. But they didn't make speeches about something I think was a lot worse. When we started out, most of Florida and many resorts in other parts of the country were out of bounds to Jews. Before the Second World War, Jews were forbidden to step inside some hotels and casinos and apartment houses. Our casinos were pleasant places and open to everybody. Jews, Christians, Arabs, anybody could come and gamble.

"And as to bootlegging, I'm not ashamed of that either. A lot of respectable people bought respectability with the money they made."

Lansky was silent for a moment and then changed the subject. He started to talk about Joe Stacher, whom the authors had known well in Israel, and he and Uri Dan exchanged anecdotes about Stacher's last years in Tel Aviv.

"Another guy who wouldn't give up," Lansky said delightedly, and Dan remembered that when Stacher died of cancer in March 1977, Lansky had sent an enormous bunch of red roses, with a white inscription on a black ribbon: "To Doc from Meyer."

Lansky fell silent again, then said very quietly, "To finish answering your question—

"I have nothing on my conscience.

"I would not change anything.

"That is the answer to your question."

Index